Early Childhood
Developmental Education

WHOLE TEACHING
Table of Contents

DEVELOPMENTAL EDUCATION

EDUCATION REFORM

LEARNING STYLES/NEEDS

MULTIAGE

INTEGRATED LANGUAGE ARTS

ASSESSMENT

RESOURCES

This book is printed on recycled paper.

SDE Sourcebook. © Copyright 1993 by The Society For Developmental Education.
All rights reserved. Printed in the United States of America.
Published by The Society For Developmental Education, P.O. Box 577, Peterborough, New Hampshire 03458,
1-800-462-1478.

SIXTH EDITION

Executive Director: Jim Grant
Editor: Deborah Sumner
Cover Design: Susan Dunholter
Cover Photo courtesy of: Marianne DeRise and Mia Marshall
                         Clinton School
                         Poughkeepsie, NY

SDE Design Director: Susan Dunholter
Production Coordinator: Deborah Fredericks
Typographer: Christine Landry

ISBN 09627389-4-8 (paperback)

DEVELOPMENTAL / EARLY CHILDHOOD EDUCATION

Passion - Impaired

by Ginny Stiles

I came across a phrase in an article I was reading the other day. The phrase was "passion-impaired," and the author used it to describe burned-out middle-aged men who prefer boredom because it is safer than passion and intensity.

The phrase has been circling around my brain ever since because it's the perfect adjective for something I've experienced but could never quite describe. It is a state of being I have seen in far too many of the children I deal with. And these are not high school or junior high school kids but 4- and 5-year olds.

Nothing is sadder than 5-year-olds who think they have already seen and done it all: Children who talk of nothing but Nintendo and Teenage Mutant Ninja Turtles but have no idea how a bird intricately builds its nest or where the sun goes when it isn't shining — and who aren't interested in knowing.

Of course, it isn't their fault that they are passion-impaired. Two-thirds of them come from stressed-out families that can barely get them to school in clean clothes. And I live in a nice rural area in Wisconsin, not the inner city. I can only imagine what inner-city teachers must see every day.

It's my job to find the passion, to open eyes and weave a web of intrigue and surprise. This has never taken more skill and energy than today. Indeed, some teachers themselves have be-

> **"It's my job to find the passion, to open eyes and weave a web of intrigue and surprise."**

come passion-impaired due to years of relentless failure to reach many students and the failure of families to support learning and schooling. They become that English teacher who has used the same blue-purple dittos for 30 years or that social studies teacher who assigns pages 415 through 420 the fourth week of every February.

So it is that passion-impaired adults sire passion-impaired offspring taught by passion-impaired teachers. Mediocrity conspires to perpetuate itself.

But the worst thing we can do is admit defeat and give in to the boring, non-creative approach to life. We must surround ourselves with other passionate people because passion is catching. We must keep trying to let students catch it from us. Children bred in front of the television have never felt the warmth of the earth against their backs on a star-lit August night, examined a locust under a magnifying glass, watched blue and red blend together as purple, or seen a kitten born. We mustn't give up. We must insist on a life lived — with passion.

Ginny Stiles teaches kindergarten at Reek Elementary School, Lake Geneva, WI. Reprinted with permission.

Photo by Deborah Sumner

Teachers must share a passion for life with their students.

Kid Stuff

Samuel G. Sava, Executive Director
National Association of Elementary School Principals

As a novice elementary school teacher, I often had parents ask for an evening appointment to discuss their child's "behavior problems." Being green to education and a bachelor to boot, at first I responded only by clucking sympathetically over the ordeal to which each suffering couple was being subjected by their six- or eight- or ten-year-old.

But after overcoming my initial awe at being consulted by parents, I cut back on the sympathy and intensified my listening. It occurred to me that, though a few children did exhibit behavior problems, most of the junior ogres these parents complained about acted pretty much the way their classmates did. Finally I developed a standard response to most of the complaints I was hearing: "As I understand it, your child is acting childishly. Does that sum it up?"

To their credit, most parents caught my point immediately and departed soon after, mumbling that perhaps their "problem child" was not as hopeless as they had feared. But some, unfortunately, missed the irony and applauded my diagnosis: "Exactly! What can we do about it?"

Why, though we never criticize adults for acting adultish, do we so readily fault children for acting childish? The answer, I believe, stems not merely from a quirk of our language (it's hard to construct a sentence in which *childish* is a compliment), but from a defect in our thinking. And that defect is important: it not only helps explain some of the nonsense now being perpetrated as early childhood education, but also threatens the gains we can realize through pre-schooling.

Describe to the average adult a child-centered preschool program based on exploration — in which a skillful teacher exposes children to a wide, rich array of materials and activities to investigate, and takes instructional cues from the interest they display — and the most you can hope for is a glazed smile and a tentative, "That's, uh, nice." But describe a curriculum-centered program based on academic preparation — one in which the children's spontaneous inclinations take second place to the program's efforts to teach them to read, to write, and to recognize numbers — and you're likely to get enthusiastic nods and a comment along the lines of "Now you're talking!" The academic program promotes something recognizable to adults as education, while the child-centered program seems to consist entirely of kid stuff.

Yet kid stuff is precisely what kids need at the preschool stage of development. Just as food has to be minced, creamed, and pureed for infants until they develop teeth, so learning has to be proportioned to young mental digestions. And for preschool children, play — which inevitably appears to adults as aimless, often sloppy puttering about with sand, water, paints, and things that go bong — *is* learning. Far from being pointless, such play helps develop young eyes, tiny muscles, and a child's sense of pleasure in mastering small but progressively more challenging tasks.

Part of our problem in respecting childish behavior, I suspect, derives from the fact that — though we've had children around for three million years or so — childhood is a relatively recent invention. Most youngsters through history have been forced to work as early as possible. Sometimes the work was incredibly grim: The 18th-century British Navy used small boys as "powder monkeys," to retrieve ammunition from nooks and crannies where no adults could crawl; if the ships went down in battle, so did the boys. For the same reason, children as young as five were used as chimney sweeps — and sometimes died in choked-up flues. Our own mines and textile mills employed the equivalent of first graders to sort coal and tend spinning machines into the early 1900s, and not until the 1960s did we start to keep the young children of migrant workers out of the fields.

Hence the notion that childhood is sacred territory, not just a biologically inconvenient stage through which its small citizens must be rushed so they can help the family make ends meet, is a modern idea. Even more recent is the belief that sensitive use of the earliest years can produce happy, self-confident children who also do better in school — not because they were taught to read earlier, but because their first efforts at learning yielded success and pleasure, making them eager for more of both.

Thanks to modern laws and social attitudes, we no longer have to defend children against mine owners and mill operators. Now, paradoxically, we may have to protect them against the impatience of loving, well-meaning parents who, anxious to give their young the best possible start in life, are pressuring them to stop acting childish.

A fulfilling childhood *is* the best possible start in life. If we are to realize the immense potential of early childhood education, we must begin by convincing parents of the social, physical, and intellectual importance of kid stuff.

From *Principal*, Jan. 1988. Reprinted with permission.

When You Care Enough . . .

Samuel G. Sava, Executive Director
National Association of Elementary School Principals

Last Valentine's Day, *The Wall Street Journal* ran a superb article on Hallmark Cards. The company, which reporter Dennis Farney called "the General Motors of emotion," produces eleven million greeting cards daily, and though traditional hearts-and-flowers sentiments remain the staple of its annual $2.5 billion in sales, Hallmark conducts a ferocious amount of research to stay on top of shifting attitudes and cater to them.

The results can be sassy. A Hallmark coffee mug, aimed at the liberated woman market, reads: "Men are only good for one thing — and how important is parallel parking anyhow?"

But others, while less amusing, so illuminate contemporary mores that an archaeologist of the 25th century may find a trove of Hallmark cards more indicative of how we lived and thought, *circa* 1990, than all our excavated cities put together. Among the products the company plans for this year:

- Sympathy messages on the death of a pet; Hallmark figures more U.S. households have dogs, cats, parakeets, and fish than have children.
- Divorce announcements, "because about 50 percent of all marriages end in divorce — and people need a way to communicate about it."
- Cards that "harried parents too busy for heart-to-heart talks can slip behind a child's pillow."

Hallmark didn't create any of the trends that lie behind these "greetings"; it is simply supplying a demand that *we* have created. Yet there seems to me something utterly pathetic about the thought of parents so "harried" that they must have a "heart-to-heart talk" scripted for them by writers in Kansas City and — instead of delivering it verbally — tuck it under the pillow of a sleeping child.

Why are these parents so harried? What possible combination of responsibilities could so overwhelm them that they cannot find time to admonish or comfort a troubled son or daughter?

The answer, I think, is that modern disease known as "having it all." Yes! Yes! a decade of magazine articles has assured young adults, you *can* have a marriage, a career, and children simultaneously! No! No! a smiling new breed of pop psychologists has soothed Yuppiedom, you don't have to sacrifice anything! That's old-fashioned thinking!

Well . . . perhaps this new-fashioned thinking has come home to roost. William J. Banach, director of the National Issues Management Program, claims 90 percent accuracy in predicting major education problems over the past ten years. He believes the top issue for the 1990s will be the low esteem in which children are held. "For many, children have become an economic liability," he reports, ". . . or at least a detriment to the good life." And Karl Zinsmeister of the American Enterprise Institute is working on a book —*The Childproof Society* — whose subtitle implies it all: *Are Americans Losing Interest in the Next Generation?*

Gurus come and go, and these two may be alarmists with no more right to our attention than all the tut-tutters who would tranquilize us with assurances that children, like cocker spaniels, can survive a lot of benign neglect and still greet us at the door each night, tails ecstatically wagging. But in publications ranging from *The Journal of Economic Growth* and *Public Opinion* to *Newsday* and *Reader's Digest*, Zinsmeister has argued that "time spent with a parent is the very clearest correlate of healthy child development. There is nothing better you can do for your children than give them your time." His evidence, on topics ranging from day care to the incidence of family breakdown behind teenage criminals, buttresses all other figures we have on the remarkable coincidence between scholastic decline among American students and the absence of parents from the American home.

Since about 1963, when our divorce rate suddenly began climbing into the stratosphere, we have been in the midst of a Family Revolution as significant for our era as the Industrial Revolution was for the 18th century, or farm-to-city migration was for the 19th. It is not better curricula, teachers, or texts that our children need most; it is better childhoods — and we will not see lasting school reform until we first see parent reform. Considering what we know now about the shaping influences of early childhood, we must convince our young adults that a baby should be neither a biological accident nor a marital accessory, but the fruit of a carefully reasoned moral contract with a human being yet unborn.

Perhaps surprisingly, I believe that couples *can* have it all — solid marriage, happy children, fulfilling careers — *but not simultaneously*; two out of three, TV's Barbara Walters said recently, is the most you can hope for. In view of longer life expectancies, however, the shift of labor demands in this service economy from muscle to mind, and the superior performance of mothers returning to the work force after child raising, there's no reason why future parents can't score three out of three.

As long as they remember that the essence of responsible parenthood is *making* time for kids, and that there's no substitute for Mom's or Dad's personal attention. To borrow a line from Hallmark, when you care enough to send the very best, send yourself.

From *Principal*, May 1990. Reprinted with permission.

Investing in Good Beginnings for Children

National attention is finally being given to what educators have known all along--that it makes a difference when children come to school ready to learn. However, recent research suggests that the traditional preschool experience is not enough to ensure good beginnings for children. We must start earlier.

Born to Learn

In the earliest years, children learn more and at a faster pace than at any other time in their lives. Research attesting to this is rapidly being gathered. Joan Beck writes in the *Chicago Tribune* that "the accumulation of neurological discoveries over the last two decades confirms and explains at the cellular and biochemical level the findings of the psychologists, physicians and educational researchers who have linked early learning opportunities to IQ and to success or failure in school and afterwards."

Researchers have learned that:
- By the age of 4, a child's brain will have grown to nearly three-fourths of its adult size;
- By age 3, a child will absorb and recognize about 1,000 words, which is two-thirds of the adult everyday speaking vocabulary;
- If a child suffers undetected developmental problems, such as a delay in language development or problem-solving skills, by the time he enters kindergarten at age 5, it may be too late to catch up.

In the July issue of *LIFE Magazine,* Lisa Grunwald and Jeff Goldberg report on "The Amazing Minds of Infants". The article, which compiles the latest findings of child development researchers, reveals emerging evidence showing that even very young babies have "wonderfully active minds. Babies are anything but blank slates." Says University of Pittsburgh's Mark Strauss, "You can tell the wheels are turning. They're paying attention to the world in incredibly subtle ways."

We must seize upon these young impressionable years, or lose the opportunity forever. "It's not just that the child will learn more," Beck writes, "it's that his brain will actually have more neurons and interconnections so it will become more intelligent and more capable of learning and thinking for the rest of life. Without ample, appropriate stimulation, unused neurons in a young child's brain atrophy and disappear. Vital connections between brain cells never develop. The brain loses much of its capacity and potential--permanently."

Ready To Learn

A school readiness program that capitalizes on the child's potential from the earliest moments of life is Parents as Teachers (PAT). "Beginning at the beginning" is the hallmark of this innovative parent-child early education program with proven results. Based on the philosophy that parents are their children's first and most influential teachers, PAT is a home-school-community partnership designed to give all children the best possible start in life.

From single, teenage mothers to two-parent, well-educated families, PAT assists parents in acquiring the skills to help make the most of these crucial early learning years. The program covers child development from birth to age three then on to kindergarten entry, and suggests parent-child activities which encourage language and intellectual growth, curiosity, and social skills.

Completely voluntary on the part of families, Parents as Teachers provides the following services:
- Personal visits from a certified parent educator trained in child development.
- Group meetings for parents to come together to share experiences, common concerns, and successes. This also provides families the opportunity to participate in parent-child activities.
- Periodic developmental and sensory screenings to provide early detection of potential problems for preventing difficulties later in school.
- A network of resources to assist families in linking with special services that are beyond the scope of the program.

Parents as Teachers has been proven effective. A 1985 independent evaluation of the PAT pilot project determined that participating children were significantly more advanced than other 3-year-olds in language development, social development, problem solving and other intellectual skills. A 1991 Second Wave study involving a larger and more diverse population confirms these findings. A 1989 follow-up study of the pilot project found that PAT children in first grade were still ahead, as measured by teacher evaluation and standardized measures of reading and math. In addition, parents who participated in Parents as Teachers took a far more active role in their children's schooling than did other parents. These successes have led to the implementation of over 1000 PAT programs in 43 states and 3 foreign countries.

By promoting parent involvement in learning, PAT puts children and their parents on the right track for later achievement in school. Parents as Teachers is the first step in ensuring that children will indeed enter the classroom ready to learn.

For more information on Parents as Teachers, contact:
Parents as Teachers National Center, Inc.
9374 Olive Boulevard
St. Louis, MO 63132
(314) 432-4330

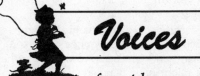 *Voices*

In a hundred years from now it will not matter what my bank account was, the type of house I lived in, or the kinds of clothes I wore, but the world may be much different because I was important in the life of a child.

Author Unknown

IN PRAISE OF PRAISING LESS

Mark Tompkins

Mark Tompkins is an Educational Consultant for High/Scope.

Reprinted with permission from High/Scope Educational Research Fund, November, 1991.

"I like the way Molly is sitting . . . I can tell she is ready for circle time."

"Oh, Joseph, what a beautiful picture you've made today!" "Good job, Darren; you're really getting it!"

Do you frequently make comments to children like "Good job," "Way to go," "Nice work," "Beautiful," or "I like the way Molly is sitting.. . ."? If so, you are like most adults who work with young children. Most of us have probably made statements like these for years. We may have even received training in how to praise.

Many adults praise children liberally because they believe this is an effective way to help children feel good about themselves and their work. Praise is also thought of as a management tool—a way to get children "settled" or ready to start an activity, as in the above example of Molly.

The Drawbacks of Praise

Despite the widespread use and acceptance of praise in early childhood settings, however, researchers and early childhood practitioners have identified many drawbacks to praising children. In her review of the literature on praise, Kamii (1984) concluded that praise leads to dependence on adults because it encourages children to rely on authority figures to solve problems for them and to evaluate what is right, wrong, good, or bad. In another literature review, Chandler (1981) stated that praise can discourage children's efforts, have a negative effect on self-image, and can place students on the defensive. As Hitz and Driscoll (1988) stated in paraphrasing the conclusions of Ginott (1972), "Praise is not conducive to self-reliance, self-direction, or self-control. If the authority figure, in this case the teachers, can judge positively, they can also judge negatively. To judge at all implies superiority and takes away from the children's power to judge their own work" (page 8).

Praise, well-intentioned as it might be, has thus been shown through research and practice to invite comparison and competition and to increase the child's dependence on adults. Too much praise can make children anxious about their abilities, reluctant to take risks and try new things, and unsure of how to evaluate their own efforts.

Alternatives to Praise

All of these drawbacks have led adults working with young children to begin to reconsider their use of praise.

There are three strategies from the High/Scope Curriculum that are alternatives to praise: participating in children's play, encouraging children to describe their efforts and products, and acknowledging children's work or ideas by making specific comments.

When using these strategies, adults working with infants, toddlers, pre-schoolers, elementary-age students, and children with special needs discover that they can rely much less on praise. By creating an environment in which children can make mistakes and learn from them without being evaluated or judged, these adults are helping children learn how to value themselves and their work and to be self-reliant.

Participating in children's play

Making a greater effort to get involved in what children are doing is a good place for adults to start if they want to reduce their use of praise. Consider this recent example from the High/Scope Demonstration Preschool. Becki, one of the achers, noticed that Allison, Graham, and Chelsea were "making pizzas" in the block area. As a way of entering their play, Becki went to the house area and called the pizza store on the telephone, asking if she could have a pizza delivered to her. This led to many other children calling the pizza store and asking for pizza. Becki soon found herself in the pizza store pretending to take orders and help make pizzas while some of the other children delivered them. The next day the teachers built on the children's interest in pizza by having the children make mini-pizzas out of English muffins, cheese, and different toppings at snack time.

Clearly, Becki's actions greatly enhanced the play experiences of Allison, Graham, and Chelsea. However, another adult might have handled the same situation less effectively, by using praise to convey her interest in the children's activities. Upon noticing the pizza-making play, this hypothetical adult might have commented on how "nice" or "terrific" the pizza was.

Compared to Becki's direct involvement in the children's activities, using praise in this way would have been a half-way gesture. Becki told children by her actions that what they were doing was valued and accepted. She was responding to their interests and abilities in the most direct way possible. Her active involvement in the children's play conveyed a more powerful, concrete, and meaningful message to children than any number of praise statements she could have made. In addition, by taking part in their game, Becki not only showed children she valued their activities but also encouraged them to expand on and develop the pizza-making theme. This opened up many possibilities for further learning opportunities to use developing abilities in representation, number, language, and beginning literacy. Becki's involvement in the activity was a catalyst for children as they continued to build on their interests.

Encouraging children to describe their efforts and products

In one of the opening examples, a teacher tells Joseph his painting is "beautiful." There are several potential problems with the teacher's statement. First, what does beautiful mean to Joseph? For many children, similar words like terrific, good job, and super are not specific enough to be meaningful. A second issue is that this statement, however positive, is still an adult judgment that sets the teacher up as an authority. And what about the child on the other side of the easel from Joseph, who is also painting a picture? Praising Joseph could lead the other child to seek the same kind of praise. In this case, the teacher's well-intentioned comment results in children comparing their efforts and competing with one another, and puts the teacher in the position of judging and comparing their efforts.

The alternative is to encourage Joseph himself to describe what he is doing, how he is doing it, and anything else he finds important. A good way to elicit such comments is for the adult to ask an open-ended question: for example, "Would you like to tell me about your painting?" Joseph might then answer, "It's a green bowl with lots of soup in it, and I worked on the painting real hard." Once the child has begun the process of discussing the painting, the adult can extend the conversation in various ways. For example, she might repeat back in general terms what Joseph has said to show him that she is listening carefully: "So you made a green bowl with lots of soup in it . . ."

With these kinds of open-ended questions and comments, the adult initiates a dialogue in which Joseph is the expert on his own work. Encouraging children to describe their activities stimulates the process of reflective thinking that is central to the High/Scope approach. When sensitively used, open-ended questions can help children contemplate and describe what they've made and done. Children recall the high and low points of their experiences and the problems encountered and solved. They become more aware of their own thinking and problem solving and more able to appreciate and evaluate their own experiences and achievements.

Acknowledging children's work or ideas by making specific comments.

The previous section discusses ways to encourage the children themselves to talk about their activities as an alternative to adult praise or evaluation. Often, though, the adult finds it appropriate to make a direct comment on a child's work, either as part of an ongoing conversation or because the child seems to be asking for an acknowledgement of his or her efforts. In these cases, we recommend that instead of subjective comments like "Beautiful," "Nice work," and "Good job," adults make a specific reference to the details of the child's product or the process the child has used. For example, instead of "How pretty," you might say, "On the top of your paper you have blue stripes and on the bottom you have red stripes." Instead of "Good job," you could say, "That is the first time I've seen you put that puzzle together, Donnie. You worked on it for a long time." Such specific comments have the added advantage of being conversation-starters. Praise statements, on the other hand, often dampen conversation. A statement like "Good work, Lisa!" can communicate the message that the conversation is ended and the child is dismissed.

We've tried to make a case that most adults who work with children should use evaluative phrases like "Beautiful," "Good job," and "Nice work" more sparingly. If you decide to join those early childhood staff who are trying to curtail their use of praise, bear in mind that it will take some practice to effectively apply the alternatives to praise. However, you'll soon see the results of your efforts: children who are more independent, self-confident, and cooperative.

Voices

Do You Believe in Miracles?

*When **kids** are trusted, respected, loved and supported —*
MIRACLES HAPPEN!

*When **teachers** are trusted, respected, loved and supported —*
MIRACLES HAPPEN!

*When **principals** are trusted, respected, loved and supported —*
MIRACLES HAPPEN!

Esther Wright
Good Morning Class —
I Love You!

Factors That Influence Developmental Diversity

by James K. Uphoff, Ed.D.

College of Education and Human Services Wright State University

Dayton, OH 45435 • (513) 873-3231

The school bells ring in late summer and thousands of children march through the school house doors without anyone having given any thought as to whether or not these children are ready—physically, socially, emotionally, academically—for the curriculum awaiting them. This document aims to provide you, the parent, with a number of major elements which should be considered as you make this vital decision. These same considerations are also relevant when parents are thinking about giving their child the *gift of time,* another year in the current grade in order to grow and mature, or a year in a readiness, K or a transition K-1 program. Too often parents and school officials alike confuse verbal brightness with readiness for school. *Being bright and being ready for school are not the same thing!* An inappropriate start in school too often "tarnishes" that brightness.

Today's K-3 curriculum has been pushed down by our American "faster is better" culture to the point that what is often found in today's kindergarten was found in late first or early second grade just three decades ago! Many schools are trying to change from the "sit-still, paper-pencil" approach of the present to a more active, involved, manipulative curriculum which enables young children to learn best. However, until this latter learning environment is available for your child, you must consider whether or not the child is ready. The material which follows is presented to help you make this very tough decision!

Each of the following factors indicates a potential for problems. The more of these factors which apply to an individual child, the more likely he/she is to encounter difficulty—academically, socially, emotionally, and/or physically—and each of these areas is crucial to a well-rounded human being. No one factor should be the only basis for making a decision. Look at all of the factors, then decide.

READINESS FACTORS

Chronological Age at School Entrance: My own research and that of many others indicates that children who are less than five and one-half years of age at the time of school entrance into kindergarten are much more likely to encounter problems. This would put the date at about March 25th for many schools. The younger the child is, the more likely the current academic paper/pencil kindergarten curriculum is inappropriate.

Problems at Birth: When labor lasts a long time or is less than four hours; or when a C-section is used regardless of length of labor; or when labor is unusually difficult, the child is more likely to experience problems. Long labor too often results in reduced oxygen and/or nourishment for the child just before birth. Short labor and/or C-section is associated with reduced social skill development. Some studies have found birth trauma to be associated with later emotional problems including, in the extreme, suicidal tendencies.

Early General Health & Nutrition: Poor nutrition in the pre-school years puts the child at greater risk in terms of school success. The child who experiences many serious ear infections during these years has been found to have more difficulty in learning to read. Allergies, asthma, and other similar problems can also inhibit such learning. Any type of illness or problem which results in a passive child—in bed or just "being very quiet" day after day—is more likely to result in a physically delayed development. Lack of body and muscle control can be a major problem for learners.

Family Status: Any act which lessens the stability of the child's family security is a problem and the closer such acts/events occur to the start of school, the more likely that start is to be a negative one. Such destabilizers as the following should be considered.

1. **Death** of anyone close to the child. This includes family, friends, neighbors, pets, etc.
2. **Moves** from one house/apartment to another even though the adults may see it as a positive relocation—more space, own bedroom for child, etc. The child may miss friends, neighbors, the dog next door, etc.
3. **Separation** from parents or close family members whether by jobs, military duty, divorce, prison, remarriage, moves, etc., can create problems for child in early school experiences.
4. **Birth of a Sibling** or the addition of new step-family members can be very upsetting.

Birth Order: If the gap between child #1 and #2 is less than three years, then #2 is more likely to have problems in school. When there are more than 3 children in a family, the baby of the family (last born) often experiences less independence and initiative. There are exceptions to these factors as with the others, but they remain as predictors, never-the-less.

Low Birth Weight: A premature child with low weight often experiences significant delays in many aspects of his/her development.

Sex: Boys are about one month behind girls in physiological development at birth; about 6 months behind at age 5; and about 24 months behind girls at age 11-12. (Some contend that we males never catch up!) Boys need extra time more than girls, but research shows that girls actually benefit from it more. Their eyes, motor skills, etc., etc., are ahead by nature, and when given time become even "aheader"! Boys fail far more often than do girls and have many more school problems than do girls.

Vision: Being able to see clearly does *not* mean that a child's vision is ready for school work. It is not until age 8 that 90% of children have sufficient eye-muscle development to do *with ease* what reading demands of the eyes. The younger the child is, the more likely he/she does *not* have all of the vision development required. For example, many children have problems with focusing. Their eyes work like a zoom lens on a projector zooming in and out until a sharp focus is obtained. Much time can be spent in this process and much is missed while focusing is taking place. Other eye problems include the muscle ability to maintain focus and smooth movement from left to right, lazy eye, and mid-line problems.

Memory Level: If a child has difficulty remembering such common items as prayers, commercials, home address/telephone number, etc., then the child may well experience problems with the typical primary grade curriculum. Many times memory success is associated with one's ability to concentrate—attention span, thus this factor is related to the next one.

Attention Span: Research has clearly shown a strong connection between the amount of time a child spends working on skill content (three Rs) and the achievement level reached. The child who is easily distracted and finds it difficult to focus attention for 10-15 minutes at a time on a single activity is also a child who is probably going to experience much frustration in school. Discipline problems are likely, as are academic ones. Sitting still is very difficult for the typical 5½- to 6½-year-old child and this normal physiological condition is at great odds with the typical sit still/paper-pencil curriculum imposed after Sputnik went up over 30 years ago!

Social Skills: The child with delayed social development is often reluctant to leave the security of a known situation (home/sitter/pre-school/etc.). This child is very hesitant about mixing with other children, is passive, and slow to become involved. Non-involvement is often associated with lower learning levels. Tears, urinary "accidents," morning tummy aches, a return to thumb sucking, etc., are all signals of such a delay. Some research has found correlations between C-section and/or short labor deliveries and problems such as these.

Speaking Skills: The ability of a child to communicate clearly is closely related to maturation. In order to pronounce sounds distinctly and correctly, muscle control is essential. Hearing must also be of good quality and this has often been reduced by early ear infections, allergies, etc. Inappropriate speech patterns (baby talk) and/or incorrect articulation (an "r" sounds like a "w") are major concern signals.

Reading Interest: If a child does not like to be read to, has little desire to watch a TV story all the way through, or rarely picks up a book to read to him/herself, then the odds are high that this child is not ready for the curriculum of the typical kindergarten. Few of us do well those things in which we are not yet interested and our children are no different!

Small Motor Skills: The ability to cut, draw, paste, and manipulate pencils, colors, etc., are very important in today's pushed-down kindergarten. The child who has some difficulty with these, uses an awkward grip on the pencil (ice-pick, one or no fingertips on the pencil, etc.), and/or has trouble holding small cards in the hand during a game is a candidate for frustrations. Eye/hand coordination is vital for a high degree of success.

Large Motor Skills: It is typical for a 5- to 6-year-old child to "trip over a piece of string," yet the typical curriculum assumes major control over one's body movements. Ability to skip, jump on one foot at a time, walk a balance beam, hop, jump from a standing position, etc., is an ability which research has found to be related to overall success with some particular skills tested just before starting school predicting reading success levels in 5th and 8th grades!

> **W**orking together, the home and the school can help each child establish a firm foundation for a lifetime of learning.

SUMMARY

Is my child ready for school? is a major question for parents to answer. This small document merely highlights some of the key factors one should consider when making such a decision. I urge all schools to adopt a thorough assessment procedure which checks all of these factors so as to provide parents with more information upon which to base their decisions.

A child's self-concept needs to be positive. He/she should see school as a good place to be, a place where he/she finds success and support. Giving the child the best start in school demands that the parent and school work together to be sure that the curriculum available will enable this child to find success and positive experiences. Parents can also provide support for the school in its efforts to reduce the amount of paper work in the early grades. Working together, the home and the school can help each child establish a firm foundation for a lifetime of learning.

For more information on transition and readiness programs, see Dr. Uphoff's book Real Facts from Real Schools, *published by Programs for Education, 1990.*

The book provides a historical perspective on the development of readiness and transition programs, presents an in-depth look at the major issues raised by attacks on such programs, and summarizes more than three dozen research studies.

The All Day Kindergarten
Assessing the Need

Nearly 50 percent of all 5-year-olds in this country attend some type of extended or all-day program. Current trends for instruction in an all-day kindergarten urge longer periods of more diverse academic instruction, thus putting today's kindergarteners under pressures that may be too great for their developmental levels. Yet the need for all-day care for children of working parents makes these programs attractive. Experts are proposing a careful look at the all-day kindergarten and some are suggesting a compromise consisting of a half day of a quality kindergarten program followed by a half day of good in-school day care.

In assessing current all-day kindergarten programs, we must ask the following questions and look carefully at the research that provides answers to them.

QUESTION:
Who benefits most from all-day-kindergarten?

RESEARCH FINDINGS:
While a large body of research based on European models of full-day preschool programs is used to support all-day kindergarten, the results are often overstated. The overall effectiveness of pre-school programs is marked especially in children of lower socioeconomic status. There is little or no effect shown on children from the middle class (Adler, 1982; Caruso & Detterman, 1981; Clarke, 1984; Darlington, Royce, Snipper, Murray, & Lazar, 1980).

These positive gains made by some children required support of parents and follow-through programs. The large success of programs such as Head Start was also due to a focus on the whole child — academics, play, and noneducational needs such as health and nutrition.

QUESTION:
Are children today more advanced than those of a decade ago?

RESEARCH FINDINGS:
Those who support all-day kindergarten maintain that various forces influencing today's children — television, pre-school experience, single parent families — make them different from those of a decade ago and therefore in need of a more instructionally challenging curriculum (Helmich, 1985; Herman, 1984; Naron, 1981).

However, there appears to be no empirical data to support the claim that today's children are different from those of 10 years ago. Socioeconomic factors are different, more children have had pre-school experience, and most seem to adapt to the new conditions of early childhood, but there is no proof that their development has been altered or hastened in any significant way (Olsen and Zigler, 1989).

QUESTION:
Does increased time mean increased individualization of instruction?

RESEARCH FINDINGS:
Proponents of all-day kindergarten note that it provides a greater amount of time in which teachers can individualize instruction. In reality, most teachers in all-day programs tend to teach children in groups and not individually (Jarvis & Molnar, 1986, Office of Educational Assessment, N.Y.C.). All-day kindergarten requires special retraining for many teachers that will prove too costly for the majority of small school districts.

QUESTION:
Is more attention paid to nutrition and parent involvement than in half-day kindergarten?

RESEARCH FINDINGS:
Success of the Head Start program clearly points out that good, nutritious snacks and lunch are important to the child's day. Several studies, however, show that there are problems in many programs with establishing a lunch program for all-day kindergarten (Jarvis & Molnar, 1986).

While parent involvement is cited as a crucial factor in the success of all-day kindergarten, in actuality, it is minimal (Alper & Wright, 1979; Winter & Klein, 1970; Bronfenbrenner, 1974; Deutsch et al., 1983; Radin, 1969; Slater, 1971; Sparrow, Blachman, & Chauncey, 1983; Valentine & Stark, 1979; Waksman, 1980). Given the same socioeconomic factors that are cited as cause for the intellectual advancement of children of the 1980s — working parents, etc. — this type of involvement is very difficult to manage.

QUESTION:
Does a longer school day mean increased standardized test scores?

RESEARCH FINDINGS:
There are sufficient research findings to indicate that the longer school day, which allows more time for concentration on math, reading and language, does increase standardized test scores (Olsen and Ziegler, 1989). In considering these results, however, we must consider whether the increased test scores are consistent across all social class groups and whether these gains are maintained over time.

Several studies show that those who show the greatest increase in test scores are those of low socioeconomic status and children who are bilingual and least ready (Jarvis & Molnar, 1985; Lysiak & Evans, 1976; Winter & Klein, 1970). One study involving only white, middle-class children found no positive effect of an all-day program (Evans & Marken, 1984).

QUESTION:

What are the long-term academic effects of all-day kindergarten?

RESEARCH FINDINGS:

Findings on the long-term effects of all-day kindergarten are ambiguous. One study of a group of Title I kindergarteners (followed through eighth grade) found that the gains were maintained throughout grade school (Neiman and Gastright, 1981). Another study showed higher reading test scores, grades, and fewer retentions in upper grades (Humphrey, 1983). Yet another study found no differences between all-day and half-day students on the California Achievement Tests in later grades (Evans & Marken, 1983). Other studies have produced similar statistics.

It appears that achievement gains best maintained long-term are those of lower socioeconomic status children (Neiman & Gastright, 1981; Mueller, 1977).

QUESTION:

What effect does all-day kindergarten have on a child's self-concept, social development and motivation?

RESEARCH FINDINGS:

The philosophy of Frederick Froebel of the whole child approach to education was common in kindergarten programs until about a decade ago. We have seen the shift in concern from the whole child's development to the child's academic achievement. As with findings on the long-term academic effects of all-day kindergarten, findings on self-concept, social development and motivation are also mixed.

Out of eight studies on development of noncognitive skills, three showed no difference between the two groups (Olsen and Ziegler, 1989). Those studies that showed increases in skills of full-day students seem to indicate that the differences were due to teachers' greater familiarity with their students (Gullo and Clements, 1984).

There is evidence that students who attended full-day kindergarten had better self-concept and attitudes toward science and social studies (Humphrey, 1983). Another study shows teachers' ratings of better social skills in all day kindergarteners, but no difference in those students' attitudes toward school in general (Levinson and Lalor, 1986).

One important study by Evans and Marken (1984) suggests that children in half-day kindergarten showed a better attitude toward reading in later grades.

QUESTION:

Is there an alternative to all-day kindergarten that will meet the needs of children and parents?

RESEARCH FINDINGS:

Although the total picture through careful research on the all-day kindergarten issue is not complete, several things are obvious. There is a strong trend toward equating general educational advancement with performance in basic skills, especially standardized test scores. The whole child is being ignored if not forgotten. And there is a trend toward placing on young children the responsibilities that have previously belonged to older children (Elkind, 1981; Cohen, 1975). Common sense tells us that the quality of life, intellectual development and school achievement will not improve simply by being in school for more hours.

What, then, is the alternative given the fact that half of the kindergarteners in America have two working parents?

Experts are proposing the educare alternative — a half day of school combined with quality in-school day care following. This arrangement would meet the needs of children and parents while maintaining developmentally appropriate programs for the kindergarten.

Such a program would allow flexibility for parents and children. Working parents would know their children had quality care between the end of school and the end of work, while children of non-working parents could go home at the end of the half-day.

Educare would be "taught" by certified child development aides who are paid less than teachers. Costs can be reduced, and teachers won't have to take on the additional role of care-taking.

Educare would make use of school resources and space, provide appropriate time for play and unstructured activity vital to the development of young children, and provide a safe, affordable alternative to additional after-school care.

Summary of research compiled by Deborah Olsen and Edward Zigler, (1989). "An Assessment of the All-Day Kindergarten Movement." Early Childhood Research Quarterly (Vol. 4, #2, pp. 167-186). Norwood, NJ: Ablex Publishing.

Note: To request resource list of research articles, contact: The Society For Developmental Education Northgate P.O. Box 577, Peterborough, NH 03458 (603) 924-9621.

Developmental Education

Bibliography
Compiled by SDE presenters

If you would like help locating any of these books, contact Crystal Springs Books, 1-800-321-0401.

Ames, Louise Bates. *Questions Parents Ask.* New York: Crown, 1988.

_____. *What Do They Mean I'm Difficult?* Rosemont, NJ: Programs for Education, 1986.

Ames, Louise Bates, and Ilg, Frances L. *Child Behavior.* New York: Barnes & Noble Books, 1955.

_____. *The Child from Five to Ten.* New York: Harper & Row, 1946.

_____. *Your Two-Year-Old (Terrible or Tender).* New York: Dell, 1980.

_____. *Your Three-Year-Old (Friend or Enemy).* New York: Dell, 1980.

_____. *Your Four-Year-Old (Wild and Wonderful).* New York: Dell, 1980.

_____. *Your Five-Year-Old (Sunny and Serene).* New York: Dell, 1981.

_____. *Your Ten-to Fourteen-Year-Old.* New York: Dell, 1989.

Ames, Louise Bates, and Chase, Joan Ames. *Don't Push Your Pre-Schooler.* New York: Harper & Row, 1980.

Ames, Louise Bates, and Haber, Carol Chase. *He Hit Me First (When Brothers and Sisters Fight).* New York: Dembner Books, 1982.

_____. *Your Seven-Year-Old (Life in a Minor Key).* New York: Delacorte, 1985.

_____. *Your Eight-Year-Old (Lively and Outgoing).*

_____. *Your Nine-Year-Old* (Thoughtful and Mysterious). New York: Delacorte, 1990.

Ames, Louise Bates; Baker, Sidney; and Ilg, Frances L. *Child Behavior (Specific Advice on Problems of Child Behavior).* New York: Barnes & Noble Books, 1981.

Ames, Louise Bates; Ilg, Frances L.; and Haber, Carol Chase. *Your One-Year-Old (The Fun-Loving 12-to 24-month-old).* New York: Delacorte, 1982.

Ames, Louise Bates, et al. *The Gesell Institute's Child from One to Six.* New York: Harper & Row, 1946.

_____. *Your Six-Year-Old (Loving and Defiant).* New York: Delacorte, 1979.

Arent, Ruth P. *Stress and Your Child.* Englewood Cliffs, NJ: Prentice-Hall, 1984.

Barbe, Walter. *Growing Up Learning.* Reston, VA: Acropolis, 1985.

Bettelheim, Bruno. *A Good Enough Parent.* New York: Alfred A. Knopf, 1987.

Bluestein, Jane. *Being a Successful Teacher — A Practical Guide to Instruction and Management.* Belmont, CA: Fearon Teacher Aids, 1988.

Bluestein, Jane and Collins, Lynn. *Parents in a Pressure Cooker.* Rosemont, NJ: Programs for Education, 1990.

Boyer, Ernest. *Ready to Learn: A Mandate for the Nation.* Princeton, NJ: The Foundation for the Advancement of Teaching, 1991.

Brazelton, T. Berry. *Working and Caring.* Reading, MA: Addison-Wesley, 1985.

_____. *To Listen to a Child — Understanding the Normal Problems of Growing Up.* Reading, MA: Addison-Wesley, 1986.

Bredekamp, Sue, ed. *Developmentally Appropriate Practice in Early Childhood Programs Serving Children from Birth through Age 8.* Washington: NAEYC, 1987.

Coletta, Anthony. *What's Best for Kids.* Rosemont, NJ: Modern Learning Press, 1991.

Coplan, Theresa and Frank. *The Early Childhood Years.* New York: Putnam Publishing Group, 1983.

Dodson, Fitzhugh. *Give Your Child a Head Start in Reading.* New York: Simon & Schuster, 1981.

Elovson, Allanna. *The Kindergarten Survival Book.* Santa Monica, CA: Parent Ed Resources, 1991.

Gilmore, June E. *The Rape of Childhood: No Time to Be a Kid.* Middletown, OH: J & J Publishing, 1990.

Grant, Jim. *Childhood Should Be a Precious Time.* (poem anthology) Rosemont, NJ: Programs for Education.

_____. *I Hate School.* Rosemont, NJ: Programs for Education, 1986.

_____. *Jim Grant's Book of Parent Pages.* Rosemont, NJ: Programs for Education, 1988.

_____. *Worth Repeating.* Rosemont, NJ: Programs for Education, 1989.

_____. *Developmental Education in the 1990's.* Rosemont, NJ: Programs for Education, 1991

Grant, Jim, and Azin, Margot. *Every Parent's Owner's Manual.* Mini-booklets. (for 3-to-7-year-olds.)

Hayes, Martha, and Faggella, Kathy. *Think It Through.* Bridgeport, CT: First Teacher Press, 1986.

Hoffman, Carol M. *Curriculum Gone Astray.* Peterborough, NH: Crystal Springs Books, 1993.

Holt, John. *How Children Fail.* New York: Dell Publishing, 1964, 1982.

Horowitz, Janet, and Faggella, Kathy. *Partners for Learning.* Bridgeport, CT: First Teacher Press, 1986.

Labinowitz, Ed. *The Piaget Primer.* Reading, MA: Addison-Wesley, 1980.

LaBritta, Gilbert. *I Can Do It! I Can Do It! — 135 Successful Independent Learning Activities.*

Lamb, Beth, and Logsdon, Phyllis. *Positively Kindergarten.* Rosemont, NJ: Modern Learning Press, 1991.

Lansky, Vicki. *Divorce Book for Parents.* New York: New American Library, 1989.

LeShan, Eda. *When Your Child Drives You Crazy.* New York: St. Martin's Press, 1986.

Linderman, C. Emma. *Teachables from Trashables — Homemade Toys That Teach.*

Miller, Karen. *Ages and Stages.* Marshfield, MA: Telshare Publishing, 1985.

Moore, Dorothy N., and Moore, Raymond. *Home Grown Kids.* Irving, TX: Word Books, 1984.

National Association of Elementary School Principals. *Early Childhood Education and the Elementary School Principal.* Alexandria, VA: NAESP, 1990.

National Association of State Boards of Education. *Right from the Start: The Report of the NASBE Task Force on Early Childhood Education.* Alexandria, VA: NASB, 1988.

Nichols, Elisabeth. *Young Children at Work.* Rosemont, NJ: Programs for Education, 1988.

Northeast Foundation for Children, Inc. *A Notebook for Teachers: Making Changes in the Elementary Curriculum.* Greenfield, MA.

Ohio Department of Education. *The Ohio Early Childhood Curriculum Guide.* Columbus, OH: Ohio Department of Education, 1991.

Reavis, George H. *The Animal School.* Rosemont, NJ: Programs for Education, 1988.

Singer, Dorothy, and Revenson, Tracy. *How a Child Thinks: A Piaget Primer.* Independence, MO: International University Press, 1978.

Uphoff, James K. ed. *Dialogues on Developmental Curriculum: Pre-K-1.* Rosemont, NJ: Programs for Education, 1987.

Vail, Priscilla L. *Clear and Lively Writing.* New York: Walker & Co., 1981.

White, Burton L. *The First Three Years of Life.* New York: Avon Books, 1979.

Wolf, Elizabeth Kjorlaug. *Meanwhile Back to the Child.*

For Children, Too

Cohen, Miriam. *First Grade Takes a Test.* New York: Greenwillow Books, 1980.

_____. *No Good in Art.* New York: Greenwillow Books, 1980.

_____. *See You in Second Grade.* New York: Dell, 1990.

_____. *When Will I Read?* New York: Greenwillow Books, 1977.

_____. *Where's George?*

_____. *Will I Have a Friend?* New York: Collier Books, 1967.

Kraus, Robert. *Leo the Late Bloomer*. New York: Windmill Books, 1971.

_____. *Leo the Late Bloomer Bakes a Cake*. New York: Windmill Books, 1981.

_____. *Leo the Late Bloomer Takes a Bath*. New York: Windmill Books, 1971.

Pass, Linda. *Taking a Test: The Inside Story*. Rosemont, NJ: Programs for Education, 1988.

Trisler, Alana, and Cardiel, Patricia Howe. Words I Use When I Write. Rosemont, NJ: Programs for Education, 1989.

Anti-Hurrying

Elkind, David. *All Grown Up & No Place to Go*. Reading, MA: Addison-Wesley, 1984.

_____. *The Hurried Child*. Reading, MA: Addison-Wesley, 1981.

_____. *Miseducation*. New York: Alfred A. Knopf, 1987.

_____. Grandparenting: *Understanding Today's Children.*

Healy, Jane. *Endangered Minds.*

Packard, Vance. *Our Endangered Children*. Boston: Little, Brown & Co., 1983.

Postman, Neil. *The Disappearance of Childhood*. New York: Dell, 1982.

Winn, Marie. *Children Without Childhood*. New York: Penguin Books, 1984.

Grade Re-Placement

Ames, Louise Bates. *What Am I Doing in This Grade?* Rosemont, NJ: Programs for Education, 1985.

_____. *Is Your Child in the Wrong Grade?* Rosemont, NJ: Modern Learning Press, 1978.

Ames, Louise Bates; Gillespie, Clyde; and Streff, John W. *Stop School Failure*. Rosemont, NJ: Programs for Education, 1972

Grant, Jim. *I Hate School*. Rosemont, NJ: Programs for Education, 1986.

_____. *Worth Repeating*. Rosemont, NJ: Programs for Education, 1989.

Healy, Jane M., Ph.D. *Your Child's Growing Mind*. New York: Doubleday & Co., 1987.

Hobby, Janice Hale. *Staying Back*. Gainesville, FL: Triad, 1950.

Moore, Sheila, and Frost, Roon. *The Little Boy Book*. New York: Clarkson N. Potter, 1986.

Osman, Betty B. *No One to Play With*. New York: Warner Books, 1982.

Sachar, Louis. *Someday Angeline*. New York: Avon Camelot Books, 1983.

Uphoff, James K., and Gilmore, June E. *Summer Children — Ready or Not for School*. Middletown, Ohio: J&J Publishing Co., 1986.

Early Childhood/
Developmental Education Publications

Childhood Education
Journal of the Association for Childhood
    Education International
Suite 315
11501 Georgia Ave.
Wheaton, MD 20902

Early Childhood News
Peter Li, Inc.
2451 E. River Rd.
Dayton, OH 45439

Early Childhood Research Quarterly
Ablex Publishing Corp.
355 Chestnut St.
Norwood, NJ 07648

Pre-K Today
730 Broadway
New York, NY 10003

A Newsletter for Teachers
Northeast Foundation for Children
71 Montague City Rd.
Greenfield, MA 01301

Young Children
National Association for the Education of Young Children
    (NAEYC)
1509 16th St. NW
Washington, DC 20036-1426

Audio / Video Resources

Ames, Louise Bates. *Part I: Ready Or Not: Here I Come!,* video.

_____. *Part II: An Evaluation of the Whole Child,* video. (Available from Programs for Education)

Bluestein, Jane. *"Win-Win" Discipline for Parents (and Teachers) in a Pressure Cooker,* video. (Programs for Education)

Coletta, Anthony. *Developmental Parenting,* audio tape. (Programs for Education)

Gesell Institute of Human Development. *Ready or Not Here I Come!* Video/16mm film, 1984. (Programs for Education)

Grant, Jim. *Jim Grant Live,* audio tape. 1985.

_____. *Grade Replacement,* audio tape.

_____. *Worth Repeating,* video.

_____. *Do You Know Where Your Child Is?,* video, 1985. (All four available from Programs for Education)

Haines, Jackie. *Gesell Seminar,* audio tape. (Programs for Education)

Johnson, Robert. *Implementing a Developmental Program,* audio tape. (Programs for Education)

Page, William. *The Basics: Time, Play and You,* audio tape, 1986. (Programs for Education)

Uphoff, James K. *Readiness for School: Setting the Stage for Success,* audio tape. (Programs for Education)

Vail, Priscilla L. *Raising Smart Kids: Commonsense, Uncommon Needs,* audio tape, 1986. (Programs for Education)

Webb, Gwen. *Is Your Child Ready?,* filmstrip, audio tape, video.

_____. *Questions Parents Ask,* video.

Address of Order Department:
    Programs for Education
    P.O. Box 167
    Rosemont, NJ 08556
    1-800-627-5867

Child Advocacy Organizations

Children's Defense Fund
122 C Street NW, 4th Floor
Washington, DC 20001

Child Trends, Inc.
2100 M Street NW
Washington, DC 20037

Privately supported child advocacy organization.

Research organization that studies social changes affecting children.

EDUCATION REFORM

Resolutions — 1993-94

National Association of Elementary School Principals

1. Student Disabilities

NAESP urges school systems to provide educational programs that will permit all children to develop their abilities and aptitudes to the fullest extent possible.

The Association endorses and supports the concepts embodied in the Individuals with Disabilities Education Act and Section 504 of the Rehabilitation Act of 1973, with emphasis on early identification beginning at birth, guaranteeing that all youngsters, irrespective of handicapping and/or health conditions, are entitled to a free appropriate education in the least restrictive environment.

The Association also recognizes that compliance with these legal mandates presents additional managerial and administrative duties that impede the orderly and efficient delivery of educational services to all students.

NAESP supports continuation and expansion of related services to local districts by appropriate state and community service agencies. Additional state and federal financial support is imperative for local school districts to comply with the provisions of these laws.

2. Compulsory School Attendance

NAESP recognizes that students who do not attend school on a regular basis develop gaps in their learning.

NAESP also recognizes that students who have poor attendance patterns at the elementary level are more likely to drop out before graduation from the secondary level. Attendance patterns set in the early years of school often continue through secondary schooling and the workplace.

NAESP reaffirms the value of regular school attendance and urges local and state associations to support legislation which enforces compulsory school attendance.

3. Drug-Damaged Children

NAESP recognizes the increasing number of children in a school whose diminished abilities to function successfully are the direct result of substance abuse by parents or children themselves.

NAESP strongly urges that school personnel and community agencies be aware of and respond appropriately to the unique needs of these drug-damaged students.

4. Home Schooling

NAESP believes education is the cornerstone of American democracy. In order to guarantee an enlightened electorate capable of governing itself, the American people must ensure quality education for each citizen.

NAESP asserts that this is most effectively done through cohesive organization in formal settings in which resources can most beneficially be brought to bear.

NAESP is concerned with the increasing number of individuals and groups who are avoiding education in the traditional setting in favor of at home schooling.

Home schooling may:

1. deprive the child of important social experiences;
2. isolate students from other social/racial/ethnic groups;
3. deny students the full range of curriculum experiences and materials;
4. be provided by non-certified and unqualified persons;
5. create an additional burden on administrators whose duties include the enforcement of compulsory school attendance laws;
6. not permit effective assessment of academic standards of quality;
7. violate health and safety standards; and
8. not provide the accurate diagnosis of and planning for meeting the needs of children with special talents, learning difficulties, and other conditions requiring atypical educational programs.

When alternative options such as home schooling have been authorized by state legislation, resources and authority should be provided to make certain that those who exercise these options are held strictly accountable for the academic achievement and social/emotional growth of children.

NAESP urges local and state associations to address these issues as important educational issues.

5. Violence to Children from Outside School

NAESP believes that schools and school property must provide safety and security for students and adults who have chosen to work with children. NAESP views with alarm the increase in violent acts toward children including child snatching, hostage taking, kidnapping, stalking, and terrorism.

NAESP urges school personnel to be constantly vigilant in their efforts to prevent harm to children and to avoid disruption of the educational process.

The Association further urges both the judicial and executive branches of government at all levels to deal decisively and firmly with individuals who engage in these heinous acts.

6. Role of the Principal in Teacher Evaluation

NAESP affirms that evaluation of teacher performance is a vital part of instructional improvement in the schools.

NAESP believes that the principal has the major responsibility for continuous teacher evaluation and must be involved in the development of evaluation instruments and systems. These systems must include diagnostic and prescriptive processes directed toward improved professional performance.

NAESP believes principals should have professional growth opportunities enhancing their ability to evaluate personnel.

7. National PTA

NAESP believes the National PTA is a unique and effective feature of American education. It has a long and successful history of working with our Association as an advocate for children.

NAESP commends the National PTA for its continuous efforts and actions as a child advocacy group and is committed to strengthening the relationship with the PTA at the national level.

8. Higher Education

NAESP believes that it is essential for institutions of higher learning to work in collaboration with practitioners at the building level to facilitate mutually beneficial training programs for educators.

NAESP supports a common national system of accreditation to help ensure quality preparation. The Association also encourages higher education personnel to become directly involved in teaching / learning experiences at the local building level.

9. Media

NAESP recognizes that the media, particularly radio and television, are powerful teaching devices and urges educators to develop programs for teaching students to become more discriminating users.

NAESP believes that the character of a child is significantly influenced by the sum total of experiences and that violence conveyed and viewed by means of the public media has a negative influence on the growth and formation of the total person.

NAESP urges the media and the public to accept an obligation to bring about constructive, accurate, non-violent and well-balanced presentations. The media exercise a pervasive influence on children and society and have the potential for being a positive educational force.

Therefore, NAESP recommends that educators, in cooperation with parents and other concerned citizens, agencies, and associations, seek to influence the policies and practices followed by the mass media particularly as they relate to violence, sexually explicit material, use of alcohol and tobacco, and advertising in programs viewed by children.

10. Coordination of the Instructional Program

NAESP believes that each child's education is a planned sequential developmental process. School principals must continue to be actively involved in the curriculum planning, implementation, and evaluation of this process.

Special emphasis should be placed on the development of the necessary skills of cooperation, competence, and confidence in order to prepare today's youth for the 21st century.

The Association urges local districts to recognize and encourage the principal's leadership role in coordinating the elementary with the secondary school curriculum.

11. Early Childhood Education

NAESP applauds the fact that legislation now exists in every state which allows children to receive kindergarten instruction in the public schools. NAESP believes that state principals' associations should make mandatory full-time kindergarten programs a top legislative priority. NAESP urges every elementary school principal to move as quickly as possible to ensure that schools provide a well-designed, developmentally appropriate program which meets the social, physical, emotional, and academic needs of kindergarten children.

NAESP urges principals to review recent research dealing with brain growth and development, along with longitudinal studies on the benefits of Head Start and other early childhood programs. Such research provides educators with additional insight and justification for the establishment of quality educational programs for children prior to the age of kindergarten.

NAESP also believes that state principals' associations should make pre-kindergarten programs an additional legislative priority, and urges local school principals to exert leadership in gaining community understanding and financial support for the implementation of pre-kindergarten programs as part of the elementary school experience. NAESP views quality pre-kindergarten experiences as a priority for all children.

NAESP further believes that pre-kindergarten personnel and programs should meet the certification and license requirements as outlined by individual states.

NAESP urges that professional growth programs for principals include experiences in all areas of early childhood instruction.

12. Instructional Materials

NAESP recognizes the value of the availability of a variety of instructional materials. NAESP believes sufficient funding for all such materials including textbooks should be provided by legislative bodies.

The Association feels that all materials should be selected to match the learning objectives specified in the curriculum.

Publishers need guidance from educators to assure that their products are being developed to address specified educational outcomes. NAESP urges elementary principals to provide leadership in this area and to actively participate in the process used by state and local agencies to select and adopt instructional materials.

13. Physical Wellness

NAESP is vitally concerned about the physical well-being of America's youth. NAESP recognizes the importance of providing programs which emphasize instruction on fitness, nutritional habits, use of leisure time, and coping with day-to-day stress.

NAESP believes that childhood is the time to begin the development of active and healthy lifestyles.

NAESP urges educators to promote physical wellness experiences for elementary and middle school students.

14. Programs of Choice

NAESP believes that programs of choice should not be federally mandated. Choice is only a small piece of a comprehensive total program.

Programs of choice should:
1. be locally developed, locally controlled, carefully constructed;
2. have a clear statement of goals, guidelines, and procedures;
3. include parent involvement in the planning and development of local programs;
4. be an opportunity for local schools, given sufficient and equitable funding, to provide unique programs;
5. take into account "equal access" for all students in a district;
6. not exceed class size limits;
7. not negatively impact racial or socio-economic balance;
8. not divert money from public schools to private schools.

15. Drug and Substance Abuse

NAESP recommends increased efforts be made to improve existing drug and substance abuse prevention programs in schools and to provide and ensure an early understanding of the harmful effects of the use of drugs, all tobacco products, alcohol, and other substances.

NAESP further urges cooperative action be taken by appropriate groups to prevent access to and use of these substances by school-age children. NAESP abhors the glorification of substance abuse by the entertainment media and encourages increased efforts to control the direct and indirect promotion of substance abuse.

In an effort to promote these recommendations, NAESP urges local, state and national education organizations to take a leadership role in establishing a national campaign with the objective of having all alcohol advertising removed from television and radio.

16. Ecology Education / Energy Conservation

NAESP recognizes the importance of developing a future citizenry dedicated to environmental protection and urges all school systems to include fundamental concepts of ecology education and energy conservation in their curriculum.

NAESP urges its members to study the use of energy in their respective buildings and take assertive leadership in minimizing waste. The implementation of energy conservation and recycling programs will require an educated public.

Therefore, the curriculum should include an emphasis upon the global ecological interdependence of humans with their environment and an appreciation of the need to protect and conserve our limited resources.

NAESP urges educators to assume a leadership role in ecology education and energy conservation. NAESP believes in a clean, litter-free environment and strongly encourages reducing, reusing, and recycling materials in schools, homes, and communities.

17. Mathematics Education

NAESP recognizes that great expansion in technology intensifies the vital need for high levels of proficiency in elementary and middle school mathematics instruction, particularly as it builds a foundation for secondary and higher education.

Elementary and middle school principals are, therefore, encouraged to establish and monitor a mathematics program which provides for sequential skills instruction, problem-solving techniques, continuous assessment of individual pupil progress, and evaluation of total program effectiveness. Particular attention should be given to NCTM standards, technology, instructional strategies, and staff development as we prepare today's youth for the 21st century.

NAESP urges principals to take a strong leadership role in mathematics education by providing appropriate materials and learning environments, and planning inservice training to update the mathematics backgrounds of elementary and middle school personnel.

Beyond 'A Nation At Risk': Schools, Communities, and Learning

by Keith Geiger
President, National Education Association

Ten years ago, the National Commission on Excellence in Education warned that America was *A Nation At Risk* — that "a rising tide of mediocrity" threatened "our very future as a nation and a people." We've learned a lot over the last decade about school improvement, and about children.

Today we know with certainty that all children can learn. And we know how to educate them. Across the country, faculties are reshaping the structures and cultures of their schools. They are re-creating schools as places where students and teachers work and learn together. They are reworking curricula, revising instructional methods, and redefining teachers' roles. They are forging stronger links between schools, parents, and communities.

In short, teachers and principals are struggling to redesign their schools to meet the needs of their students and their country in the 21st century. They're coming to grips with the challenge of educating more of America's young people better than ever before. And they are guided by a genuine respect for the different talents of children and adults, a recognition that not all children are — or learn — alike, and the understanding that our diversity is a source of our strength.

Why then, given the great educational strides being made, do so many young people still fail to reach their potential? Why, after a decade of reforms, aren't more American schools excellent? Why do we remain "a nation at risk"?

For one thing, we wasted precious time on top-down, mandated education reforms. It took too many years for policy makers to realize that more-of-the-same wasn't the answer — that the 19th century one-size-fits-all factory model of schooling had outlived its usefulness. It took too long to acknowledge that meaningful school restructuring takes resources — intellectual and financial. And it took too long to recognize that school change must be fundamental, must be systematic, and must come from the bottom up — from school faculties and local communities.

> *Teachers and principals are struggling to redesign their schools to meet the needs of their students and their country in the 21st century. They're coming to grips with the challenge of educating more of America's young people better than ever before.*

The second reason America is still at risk is that few heeded the most important, but most overlooked, message implicit in *A Nation At Risk*: that the educational achievement of our children is a reflection of our society.

In the words of a 1992 Carnegie Foundation special report: "The evidence is overwhelming that the crises in education relate not just to school governance but to pathologies that surround the schools. The harsh truth is that, in many communities, the family is a far more imperiled institution than the school, and teachers are being asked to do what parents have not been able to accomplish."

Not only do we expect America's public schools to educate. We also expect them to halt drug use, reduce teen pregnancy, end gang violence, feed and improve the health of the nation's young people. In many urban communities, schools are the only institutions stable enough to take on these tasks.

We now understand the complexity, and the interrelatedness, of the problems besetting America's children. School improvement is necessary, but it's not sufficient. What's needed is a comprehensive approach that addresses the multitude of crises in young lives — from medical care to violence to dysfunctional families.

As Secretary of Education Terrel H. Bell said at the time of *A Nation At Risk:* "Our schools can rise no higher than the communities that support them." We've still not taken this lesson to heart.

In 1983, America was at risk because too few people understood the magnitude of the problems facing our nation's youth. Today — tens of thousands of studies and reports, pilot projects and conferences later — we're at risk because we've not made the national commitment necessary to rescue our children and our schools.

A Nation At Risk told us that our system of public education is essential to our nation — that we dare not let our schools fail. We know that every child is valuable. We know that every child can learn. Ten years after *A Nation At Risk*, it's time we begin to act on these truths.

Where We Stand

By Albert Shanker, President
American Federation of Teachers

Working Together

The scene is a tenth reunion and three college friends run into each other. They are all teachers, and soon they begin to talk shop. Two of them are fed up. One says she is a stickler for the rules and pushes her students hard. The other admits that she tends to be easy on her kids because "They have enough problems already." But as different as their approaches are, the two agree that most kids nowadays are hopeless; they can't or won't learn. On the other hand, the third teacher, who teaches in a school with the same kinds of students as her friends, says that most of her kids are good workers and achievers. She is now trying some new ways of running her classes. Cooperative learning is one of them, and so far the youngsters are doing well.

How can we account for the friends' different attitudes and experiences with their similar students? It could be differences in talent or temperament, but in a recent study, "Contexts That Matter for Teaching and Learning" (Stanford: Stanford University, Center for Research on the Context of Secondary School Teaching, 1993), Milbrey McLaughlin and Joan Talbert suggest another possibility. McLaughlin and Talbert found that the degree of collegiality in a school, and especially a department within a school, makes an enormous difference in teachers' response to their students and in students' achievement.

The survey involved nearly 900 teachers in 16 California and Michigan high schools. In noncollegial settings, where teachers seldom if ever discuss their teaching with colleagues—and would be uneasy doing so—McLaughlin and Talbert found that teachers tend to stick with the methods they are used to. And they do this even if the methods do not and have never worked very well. As a result, they often get discouraged, and they often conclude that their students are not capable of learning.

But in collegial settings, teachers are accustomed to consulting colleagues and using them as resources. Not only does this provide help with immediate problems; it also leads teachers to continually look at and question their teaching practices and work to make them more effective. McLaughlin and Talbert's data show that teachers in this kind of professional community feel more positive about their teaching and their students and that their students are substantially more successful than youngsters taught by the noncollegial teachers.

We can see the connection between collegiality and good teaching in the successful schools of some other industrial

Teachers in a professional community feel more positive about their teaching, and their students are more successful than youngsters taught by noncollegial teachers.

nations. As Harold Stevenson and James Stigler tell us in *The Learning Gap* (New York: Simon and Schuster, 1992), one reason Asian teachers get excellent results with their students is that teachers in a given grade work together, over time, to plan and then to revise their lessons.

Other professions also understand this connection. Lawyers routinely consult each other about their cases, and education reformer Phillip Schlechty describes how health-care providers in teaching hospitals hold a "mortality and morbidity conference" after a patient dies. Everyone who had anything to do with the patient is involved in reconstructing the record of treatment. What was the diagnosis on admission? What treatments were ordered? What were the results? And what might have been done differently? These conferences are not a way of assigning blame: They are an ongoing education program that helps the health professionals analyze their performance and decide how they might improve it.

McLaughlin and Talbert's findings about good teaching and collegiality have important implications for professional development and for school reform. Most districts think of professional development in terms of courses or workshops that train teachers in what is considered good teaching practice. But what kind of course could possibly compare with a group of teachers acknowledging problems, sharing ideas, trying new ways of doing things and evaluating results on an ongoing basis? And what kind of reform instituted from the outside could possibly be successful without this kind of professional community to support it?

Because the professional community the study talks about involves teachers' working together at a school level, some people will be reminded of shared decision making, a strategy for education reform that has lately swept the schools. The two are not inconsistent with one another, but shared decision making is usually a question of school governance and administration—how will the bell schedule be set up or where will the computers be relocated? In contrast, collegiality has a powerful effect on the quality of teaching—in other words, on the basic mission of the school. If McLaughlin and Talbert are right, the best investment the national or state or local governments could make in education would be to start helping to build this ongoing process in all our schools.

Class size

Giving students a chance to succeed

This is the second in a series of articles focusing on issues covered in the proposed Education Reform Act, S-3125.

Some teachers feel like the old woman in the shoe—they have so many children, they don't know what to do.

Class size: Teachers say it affects everything they do with children; parents petition boards of education to reduce it; opinion polls show the public considers it of major importance to pupil achievement. Yet in 1988 newspaper headlines quoted the U.S. Secretary of Education as saying smaller classes would not appreciably increase student achievement.

How can something we *know* to be true be subject to such attack?

Why is it that some contend that research does not substantiate the value of small class size?

In 1986 the Educational Research Service, an independent nonprofit corporation based in Arlington, Va., published an analysis of class size research. In its review of seemingly contradictory research, ERS found that many studies were flawed. However, the analysis, which still stands as the most definitive work on the subject, does conclude that research verifies some benefits of small class size.

Most effective: 15 pupils or less

And one significant fact, cited even in the negative report by the U.S. Department of Education, stands out: Class size has its most significant effect when the number of pupils is 15 or less.

NJEA has promoted a maximum class size of 15 since 1984.

Some NJEA affiliates have pursued this issue in their local school districts. Working with parents, local associations have lobbied local boards of education to deal with overcrowded classes. What one administrator calls the "mad mom phenomenon" sometimes works.

NJEA's members have decided that this issue needs to be addressed statewide. The proposed Education Reform Act (S-3125) calls for class sizes of no more than 15 "except for those classes which by the nature of the activity conducted therein, require participation of more than 15 pupils."

Move to reduce primary grades first

Current regulations governing special education classes would remain. In prekindergarten classes the limit would be 10 students. The bill calls for a phasing-in of these limitations beginning with primary grades.

Why primary grades? For one thing, gradual implementation would enable districts to plan for the change over a period of years.

For another, the ERS survey identifies the primary grades as most clearly benefitting from smaller class size. Moreover, as the Head Start program has demonstrated, children who get off to a good start do better all the way through school.

Affects skills, behavior

In smaller primary classes, ERS says, students' attitudes and behavior, as well as learning, improve. A positive attitude, appropriate behavior, and a good base in learning give children the opportunity to succeed.

The research also indicates that children master mathematics skills and reading skills more quickly in small classes. Obviously students who master the basics early on have a greater chance for educational success.

But primary grades aren't the only ones that benefit from fewer children per class. Class size is especially critical for economically disadvantaged students, the ERS survey found.

Key element in reaching the needy

Children from homes where concern about basic survival comes first and where resources are limited need even more individual attention from school and from the school staff. That's possible only in small classes.

Students of lesser academic ability also prove to benefit from smaller classes. The opportunity to receive individual attention and the more relaxed atmosphere of small classes apparently allow these students more opportunity to succeed.

In small classes, teaching practices and approaches such as individualization, creativity, small-group activity, and interpersonal regard flourish, ERS says while also contending that more research needs to be done to validate the "presumed superiority" of these activities.

Teachers need to adapt techniques

On the other hand, the report also says that class size does not make a significant difference in student achievement if teachers don't adapt their techniques to small groups. The report calls for "providing teachers with the support and training needed to optimize learning conditions."

Education is more than learning what's going to be on a test. It's learning how to get along with others, feeling a sense of self-worth, finding out what we can contribute to our world. Smaller classes offer better opportunity for these aspects of "affective learning."

Staff members also benefit, says the research. Teachers have more positive attitudes toward their work and better perceptions of their own effectiveness in small classes. That's good for the profession and for children.

A better way to measure class size

One of the frustrations of dealing with the class size issue is quantifying the data.

In New Jersey, for example, the student-teacher ratio for 1987 reported by the state was 14-to-one. Impossible, you say?

No, it's just that the way this figure is calculated is misleading. It's done by dividing the number of students in a district by the number of certificated staff. And when guidance counselors, school nurses, child study team members, librarians, special teachers, resource room teachers, compensatory education teachers, part-time staff, and others are added in, the result is a distorted view of class size.

At the same time, the number of students those members serve shouldn't be ignored either and may warrant other studies.

NEA has published a booklet entitled "At Last—A Better Way To Measure Class Size." It provides a formula for coming up with a more accurate figure for class size in a school district and tips for organizing the study.

Dividing students by teachers to determine class size fails to convey important facts about the condition of education in our schools. Instead of counting numbers of students, we should be counting sizes of groups in which students are instructed. Individual students may be members of more than one group.

NEA suggests finding the "median student" in your school.

Finding the elementary school median

A simple method for elementary schools is:
1. Arrange the classes in your school in order of size from the largest to the smallest. For example: 37, 31, 29, 21, 19, 12, 11.
2. Find the total number of students in all the classes by totaling the numbers in each class.

    For example: $37 + 31 + 29 + 21 + 19 + 12 + 11 = 160$

3. Add 1 to the total number of students and divide by 2 to find the number of the "median student."

    Using the example: $\dfrac{160 + 1}{2} = 80.5$

4. Count down from the largest class until you come to the median student.

In the example above, there are 68 students in the two largest classes. The 80.5th student would be in the next largest class, which contains 29 students. Consequently, the average class has 29 students.

Measuring at the secondary level

Counting numbers of students and teachers in secondary school classes has been difficult because of the huge variety of special arrangements possible, and the fact that all-day intact classes are rare.

Often the issues of class size and teacher workload—which is also an important topic—become confused. But to measure average class size at the secondary level we ignore the number of teachers.

Instead, we list the number of students who meet for each "period" and these are tallied in a frequency distribution similar to that for elementary schools.

Again, you would find the median student, then count down to find the size of that individual's class.

Include regular classes only

In a survey, ask school staff to report the number of students in each class they teach. Ask them to exclude from that report all classes which don't represent regular classroom instruction, such as individual counseling, therapy, small recital or recitation meetings, small group remediation, etc.

For a copy of "At last—A better way to measure class size," contact NEA Communications, 1201 16th St. NW, Washington, D.C. 20036, (202) 822-7200.

Linking class size to success

Too often, decisions in education are based on economics.

How much will it cost? Will we need more space, more equipment, additional staff?

Class size, unfortunately, is no different, points out NJEA Executive Director James Connerton.

"A lot of lobbying usually has to take place by parents, school staff, and others to convince districts to set up manageable class sizes," Connerton states. "In many cases, unless a hue and cry goes up, the financial consideration outweighs educational advantages.

"Rarely will a district reduce class size because that is the educationally sound approach which benefits the students. Instead, it will look at the financial repercussions and the facilities available."

But class size does affect students' education, NJEA members have repeatedly verified in surveys, roundtables, hearings, and other activities.

Students work better, behave better, and learn more in smaller settings, they say. Teachers have a better chance to address individual needs—from those who need more remedial help to the gifted and talented.

The Education Reform Act—S-3125—introduced by Senators Ron Rice (D-Essex) and Matthew Feldman (D-Bergen)—recognizes the need and current stumbling blocks.

If adopted, the bill would limit the number of pupils in nearly all classes, in grades kindergarten through 12, to 15 pupils. The only exception would be "classes which by the nature of the activity conducted ... require participation of more than 15 pupils".

The maximum would include mainstreamed classified students, unless other laws set lower class sizes for those special pupils.

In prekindergarten classes, the maximum would be 10 pupils.

Under the bill, districts would be required to meet the class size requirements under the following timetable:

● Grades pre-K through 2—by Sept. 1, 1990;
● Grades three and four—by Sept. 1, 1992;
● Grades five through eight—by Sept. 1, 1996;
● Grades nine through 12—by Sept. 1, 2000.

The class size restrictions could not be waived by the commissioner of education or other regulations, the bill notes.

The legislative measure also would answer the local financial arguments by requiring state aid to cover the additional costs required by the bill.

"If we're serious about providing our youngsters with the best education possible—a thorough and efficient education—then it's time to take steps to ensure that every child works in a classroom conducive to academic success," Connerton notes. Small class size can pave the way.

PHOTO BY RON WILLIAMS

Small class size benefits students, Pohatcong demonstrates

Last year the Shimer School in Pohatcong had 48 children in kindergarten and two half-time kindergarten teachers. When the district discovered that it would have only 25 or 26 kindergarteners this year, what did the district do?

It kept the two teachers and reduced the class sizes.

What's the impact of having 12 students rather than 24? Denise Moyle, a 15-year veteran of the school district, says she can do an even more effective job of giving students the start in school they need.

Improved classroom climate, self-esteem

Her experience substantiates the research. For one thing, the classroom climate is more positive. "From the beginning, everything was better," relates Moyle. "The children were comfortable. They weren't overwhelmed by being crowded in with so many other children. Just remembering each other's names wasn't a trauma as it often is.

"We try to mold the children into a unit. We've been able to do that much faster and easier this year. The kids have bonded together; they're really friends with their classmates."

As a teacher Moyle finds she can pick up small problems she might otherwise have missed. And the children develop more self-esteem. The child who might otherwise blend in—"fade away"—gets pulled into the discussion, she observes.

Discipline? "I can stop a problem before it begins. Other years I've had to be a drill sergeant. Now I'm more relaxed and so are the children."

Building academic base

Why is kindergarten important? "This is the year we get children ready to be students. We need to give them a solid base, socially and academically."

Moyle's students come to school with varied skills. "Some don't know their letters or numbers. Some have never held scissors, or can't hold a pencil properly, or can't dress themselves, or go up and down stairs properly. These are all things that take individual attention. I can give that to this group of students."

Parental involvement, another plus in education, also improves with smaller classes. Moyle finds she has more frequent and more extensive contact with parents.

During the kindergarten open house the second week of school, she met the parents and now knows them by sight. During the fall conferences she not only had more time to spend with parents but knew more about each child so that the conference was more thorough.

Who benefits most from the smaller class size? Again verifying the research, Moyle says "the child with special needs. By definition that child needs more time with the teacher. I can give it. I don't have to put 23 on hold to work with one."

But all children master skills more quickly in small groups, Moyle finds. She can review on a daily basis with virtually every student.

Provides more instructional time

In kindergarten Moyle says children need to change activities often. She sets up 15-to-20 minute teaching blocks, then changes the activity. That takes less time with a small group. "It used to take as much time to get activities organized as it did to do them. Now we have more time for learning."

The bottom line: "The child's needs are met."

Pam Moschini agrees. The speech specialist at Shimer School, Moschini believes this year's kindergarteners will have a much better foundation for first grade. Because they've each had time to participate, their verbal skills are more highly developed.

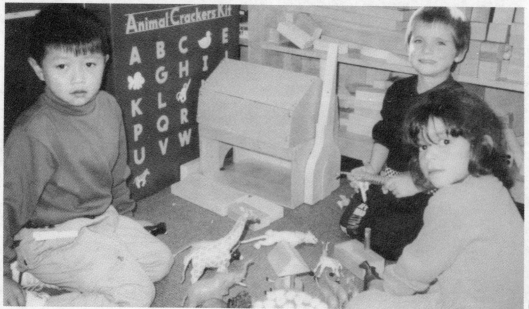

Photo by Linda Blandini

An added benefit—teachers and specialists will be able to cover more material this year than ever before, both Moyle and Moschini point out.

Why did Pohatcong take such an enlightened approach to the declining number of students? Assistant Principal Jerry Clymer credits a "child-oriented" board of education. When the administration recommended maintaining two classes, the board agreed with no objection.

"This is the children's first introduction to public school," says Clymer. "Even those who have been to nursery school need lots of time and care." He says the small class size enhances the work of excellent staff members—"I'd stand them up against anybody"—and offers greater flexibility in the learning process.

Parents, some of whom called last year hoping for the continuation of two classes, are very pleased. Notes Clymer, "It was financially feasible, so we did what was best for the students."

A student gets some individual help from teacher Denise Moyle.

10 steps for a class size campaign

The National Education Association suggests associations take these steps in campaigning for smaller class size.

1. Determine whether or not it's time to take a new look at class size in your district. Talk with your NJEA-NEA UniServ representative about your goals, as well as dealing with project obstacles and pitfalls.

2. Select a small cross-section of members to serve on a "class size calculation team" to obtain the data you need.

- Include representatives of staff from all school levels in the district (elementary, middle/junior high, and high school).
- Include someone who is familiar with assignment patterns of counselors, traveling teachers, and resource specialists.
- Make sure you include individuals who like to work with numbers and accounting.
- Invite three parents who are active in the schools to join the team. Make sure parents represent all school levels.

3. Consider initiating a pilot project in a small number of school buildings prior to implementing a systemwide study. Take into account seasonal problems, such as the start of the school year, holidays, and semester breaks.

4. Alert association leaders in each building that the project is underway and let them know how they can help develop the data base.

5. Examine the findings of the class size calculation team and discuss them with association representatives. Look at such issues as:

- Are the data clear?
- Are there surprises?
- Do the findings confirm long-held beliefs?
- Are there deficiencies in the reporting process which need to be checked?
- What do the team's findings reveal about class size across the district and within buildings?
- What are the possible uses of this information?

6. Have the team summarize its findings in a report that includes background on why you initiated the project.

7. Visit school buildings, distribute the report widely among members, and brief school leaders across the district.

8. Determine how to use the data to accomplish the Association's instructional improvement goals through vehicles such as joint study committees with management, inservice workshop discussions, presentations to the school board.

9. Share the information with your NJEA-NEA UniServ representative and NJEA Research & Economic Services.

10. If your data warrant distribution to broader audiences, develop an external communications plan. Consider scheduling the kick-off of class size information to coincide with events such as American Education Week, open house, staff inservice days, legislative lobbying. Review ways to reach targeted audiences, such as local and state association leaders in your region, parent organizations, news media, and school study groups.

Reprinted with permission from the *NJEA Review*, official journal of the New Jersey Education Association, Vol. 62, No. 7, March 1989, pp. 14-19.

The Case for Untracking

Anne Wheelock

What does it take to replace tracking with heterogeneous grouping? Successful schools identify nine characteristics.

For years, American schools in pursuit of reform have been caught between two competing demands: mandates for excellence and mandates for equity. Yet, quietly, an increasing number of schools are moving to offer both high-quality education and equal access to knowledge. How? By dismantling unproductive grouping practices that have undermined education for all but a few students. We call these schools "untracking schools."

Since 1990, the Massachusetts Advocacy Center, with the support of the Edna McConnell Clark Foundation, has identified untracking middle schools across the country in an effort to document their success in promoting both excellence and equity for all students. Approximately 900 letters to educators around the country produced some 250 nominations of such schools. We asked each of them to complete a detailed questionnaire. Their responses along with site visits and telephone interviews revealed clues to the *process* of untracking and lessons for others considering alternatives to tracking. What we learned is testimony to the resourcefulness, persistence, passion for excellence, and capacity for risk-taking that characterize the best of our educational leaders.

What does it take to replace a comfortable practice like tracking with alternatives? Educators identify nine ingredients.

A Belief That All Students Can Learn

The direction that untracking takes in a given school evolves from a commitment to the learning of all students at high levels. Untracking schools view reform of grouping practices as a means to an end, not an end in itself.

While the *means* of untracking include eliminating separate groups of students categorized by ability and providing equal access to valued knowledge to all students through reshaped curriculum and instruction, the *goal* of untracking is improved learning for all students within democratic school communities.

"Academically, we're working to raise the floor *and* raise the ceiling," notes Karla Deletis, superintendent of schools in Wellesley, Massachusetts. John D'Auria, principal of the Wellesley Middle School, adds:

> If tracking would help us accomplish our goals at this school, then we would use it. But we believe in producing active learners, critical thinkers, and risk-takers, and tracking our students by ability quite simply doesn't allow us to achieve our goals.

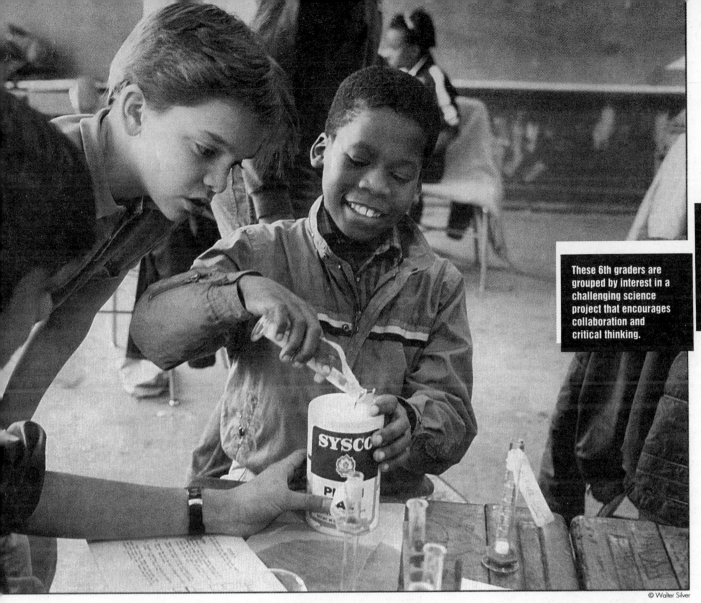

These 6th graders are grouped by interest in a challenging science project that encourages collaboration and critical thinking.

© Walter Silver

This belief in untracking sustains educators throughout the demanding process of organizational change. As Donald LeMay, principal of Valley Junior High in Carlsbad, California, stresses, "Untracking is a challenging proposition. No one is going to do this if they do not believe it is possible and necessary."

A Belief in Change as a Process

A second characteristic of untracking schools is their orientation to institutional change, not as an event but as a comprehensive process that touches every aspect of school life. While at first blush untracking focuses primarily on the regrouping of students, success is unlikely without reforms in curriculum, instruction, assessment, and counseling that complement the new grouping arrangements.

Classroom reforms that support heterogeneous grouping typically reflect a commitment to "leveling up" rather than "watering down" practice. As John Delaney, principal of the Parker Middle School in Reading, Massachusetts, reports, "When we are selecting a new curriculum or introducing a new teaching approach for heterogeneous classrooms, we select the approach we would traditionally choose for our most facile learners." What Delaney and other educators emphasize is that curriculum and instruction suitable for multi-level groups must draw from the conceptual, inquiry-based curriculums and methodologies often reserved only for those students labeled gifted and talented.

Thus, curriculum and instruction in untracking schools often focus on developing thinking skills in content

areas through a variety of interesting learning projects. Sometimes these schools use a curriculum like Philosophy for Children, which might have been reserved for top-track students but that works equally well, perhaps even better, with heterogeneous classes. Sometimes they initiate a curriculum that acknowledges new thinking about multiple intelligences such as *Immigration 1850*, developed at Howard Gardner's Project Zero. Or they might use a curriculum specifically designed for heterogeneous groups, like Foundational Approaches in Science Teaching (FAST), developed at the University of Hawaii. In other cases, teachers design their own curriculum, which is frequently thematically organized, experiential, and oriented to a variety of cultural perspectives.

> Looking back on their untracking experiences, principals observe that parents can make or break school change.

High Expectations for All

Third, untracking schools purposefully weave norms of high expectations and inclusion into the entire fabric of school life. These schools avoid retaining students in grade or segregating them through pull-out approaches. Instead, recognizing that some students need second, maybe even third, chances for success, they offer mastery learning, extra periods for review of particular subjects, and extended days or school years for vulnerable students. Rather than assume that only some students need preparation for post-secondary education, these schools counsel all students for the probability that they will seek higher education at some point in their lives.

In addition, since untracking schools define extracurricular activities as sources of learning in their own right, participation is based on students' interests (sometimes reinforced by a contract stipulating attendance and commitment) rather than on selection or eligibility criteria. At Jericho Middle School in New York, for example, students with physical disabilities may be full members of the cheerleading squad. Further, if the number of students trying out for the class play exceeds the number of speaking parts available, the school puts separate productions into rehearsal and assigns those students

enrolled in onstage parts in one production to backstage roles in the second. Schools like Jericho distribute scarce resources—donated tickets to community sports and cultural events, adult mentors, opportunities for field trips, access to the computer lab, and the like—fairly so that *all* students can expand their horizons.

In untracking schools, all students, not just a few, are acknowledged for their contributions, progress, and achievement through "Good Citizen Honor Rolls" and postcards sent to *every* parent. Similarly, they try to ensure that high-status roles—student government representatives, office helpers, dispute mediators, school tour guides, hall safety guards, and cross-age tutors—are open to all, including special education students. Finally, in schools with culturally diverse populations, opportunities for learning honor nondominant cultures and languages by incorporating aspects of students' home cultures into all domains of school life—including morning announcements, hallway bulletin boards, thematic curriculum, and two-way language learning.

Such changes in routines reflect a deep commitment to core beliefs about the role of schools in developing intelligence and expanding opportunities for student success. As schools untrack, they play out beliefs that school practices should nurture all dimensions of intelligence rather than define and measure fixed ability. Second, they reveal a commitment to developing students' aspirations rather than circumscribing students' dreams. They also treat students as citizens of a learning community rather than products of an assembly line. Finally, educators in untracking schools act on the belief that persistent effort rather than inborn ability is a precursor to success in life and the basis for lifelong learning.

A Partnership of Leaders and Teachers

Fourth, the relationship between the principal and teachers in untracking schools is critical to their success. In these schools, principals involve a variety of constituents in developing the mission of the school, articulate that mission in a variety of arenas, and ensure that the mission is fulfilled. In doing so, they may have to challenge traditional beliefs about child development and intelligence, nurture alternative belief systems, assess the potential leverage for institutional change, negotiate for resources, and open doors to resources so that teachers can strengthen their own learning.

Just as principals in untracking schools are called on to be risk-takers, they must foster conditions for risk-taking among their staff. They do so by encouraging teachers who try innovative ideas to describe their successes and failures to others, while promoting self-assessment among teachers by temporarily suspending teacher evaluations. These principals themselves must have a thorough knowledge about research on tracking, an understanding of instructional alternatives, and some grounding in organizational change. In addition, they must be able to act politically to address the concerns of all constituent groups. In response to skeptics, they must be ready to respond in a compelling way to questions like, "How do you plan to make sure that my advanced child won't be bored in heterogeneous classes?" and "How can you ensure that my child is not going to be overwhelmed when you mix her in with smarter students?"

At the same time, principals in untracking schools must work with teachers to introduce reform where it really counts: in classroom practice. This requires gauging the readiness of staff for change and working with teachers to identify appropriate professional development approaches, including teacher-directed efforts. As teachers from the Graham and Parks School in Cambridge, Massachusetts, emphasize:

> It's what happens with kids *after* mixed-ability grouping occurs that matters. This must be put into teachers' hands—by empowering them, having them *critically* examine the current program, investigate other schools through visits or reading, and then develop their own ways.

The Value of Parent Involvement

Looking back on their untracking experiences, principals observe that parents can make or break school change. They emphasize the importance of involving parents at an early point in planning and implementing heterogeneous groups.

Some schools educate parents about alternatives to tracking by inviting them to attend classes using new teaching approaches or programs introducing new curriculum. By piloting new approaches and publicly reporting the results, other schools persuade parents that untracking strengthens the mainstream of the school so that all students will master complex material. Still other schools take advantage of a phase-in process to allow parents a choice between heterogeneous and homogeneous grouping until all teachers are prepared to teach all children effectively.

Often the most vocal parents in opposition to heterogeneous grouping are those who expect their children to enter gifted and talented programs. These parents may be politically powerful and sophisticated in countering arguments in favor of heterogeneous grouping. However, they may reconsider their position when they understand that inclusive schooling will offer all students

an education that is sometimes reserved only for students labeled gifted.

A Hospitable Policy Context

While some schools are untracking with little encouragement from the formal educational hierarchy, many gain momentum from supportive district- or state-level policies. For example:

■ The Massachusetts Department of Education (1990) has not only issued a policy advisory and sponsored professional development programs to encourage alternatives to ability grouping, but has tied discretionary dropout prevention and remedial grant funding to untracking.

■ California's Middle Level Partnership program and the Department of Education's report *Caught in the Middle* (1987) have encouraged inter-district clusters of middle schools to pool resources to initiate and sustain heterogeneous grouping.

■ New York's "trainer for trainers model" has created a pool of professionals who offer staff development and technical assistance to schools implementing mixed-level classrooms.

■ In Nevada (1990) and in Maryland (1989), policy studies and advisory positions regarding appropriate practices for adolescents suggest that middle-level schools group their students heterogeneously.

■ In districts—including Ann Arbor, Michigan, and San Diego, California—central office and school staff

have worked with school board members to review and publicize research on tracking. They've also initiated studies of local tracking patterns, resulting in a formal policy and timetable to promote alternatives.

In the absence of a favorable public policy context, many schools forge ahead, drawing support from positions taken by the National Council for Teachers of Mathematics, the National Middle School Association, and the research of Jeannie Oakes (1985) and others. Middle schools especially have found that recommendations for heterogeneous grouping by the Carnegie Council on Adolescent Development (1989) can provoke discussion and generate support for untracking. They also report that these sources give proposed reforms credibility and encourage school decision makers to take risks they might not otherwise take.

A Multi-Year Plan

The complexity of change required for successful heterogeneous grouping requires planning, and many schools acknowledge this by adopting timetables that span three to seven years.

A school's plan may reflect the numerous steps necessary to prepare for untracking: disseminating research about tracking and its alternatives, visiting other schools with heterogeneous classrooms, researching curriculum appropriate for diverse classrooms, and identifying resources for staff development. The plan may also outline a specific timetable for implementing heterogeneous grouping in whatever form the school has chosen—whether flexible grouping, "controlled heterogeneity," grouping for multidimensional intelligence, inclusive integration of students with all levels of disabilities into the school mainstream, multi-language or multi-age grouping.

Productive planning assures those most uncomfortable with change that they will not be forced to change overnight. It can also provide a framework for shaping classroom practices to mirror research findings. As Sandra Caldwell, principal of the Middle School of the Kennebunks in Kennebunkport, Maine, reports, "We question practically everything. We ask whether our practices align with research, and when we find gaps, we work team by team to figure out action plans to close them." In short, untracking schools may have not one, but many, plans for change implemented at different times by different actors.

Purposeful Professional Development

Untracking schools agree that reform cannot take place without focused professional development. Some have engaged in activities that seek to strengthen the school as an organization through goal-setting and team-building exercises. Others begin with a review of "high expectations" teaching strategies, sometimes using the Teacher Expectations, Student Achievement (TESA) program to reduce the potential for differentiated instruction within heterogeneous classrooms. Many schools have introduced all their teachers to research and training in cooperative learning and complex instruction. Some, like Milwaukee's Parkman Middle School, have designated one or more teachers as implementers to assist other teachers in incorporating new techniques into their classrooms. Finally, staff development must also accompany the introduction of any new curriculum—whether it is a packaged one or one designed by teachers.

Phase-In Implementation

Finally, untracking schools recognize that reform does not happen overnight. To the contrary, given the deep changes in school culture, curriculum, and instruction that accompany successful untracking, schools often introduce alternatives in stages. Their strategies differ, depending on such factors as teachers' readiness, parents' concerns, and availability of resources for professional development, curriculum change, or instructional innovation. Whatever the beginning point, most schools understand that the end point is a more-inclusive learning community.

Some untracking schools start by merging the bottom tracks in all or most subject areas into the middle tracks, while providing extra support through co-teaching or additional time for tutoring. Other schools phase in heterogeneous grouping beginning at the lowest grade level and add a grade every year. Still other schools introduce changes department by department, as subject-area teachers identify and prepare to implement new curriculum specifically designed for groups of diverse learners. Finally, schools that have already organized into teams or schools-within-a-school may untrack one team at a time—with the ultimate goal of introducing heterogeneous grouping schoolwide.

Is It Worth It?

While untracking demands focused, purposeful attention over a number of years, seasoned educators tell us that it *is* worth the effort. In untracking schools, achievement is up for "low" and "average" students, while undiminished and sometimes improved for "high" students. Untracking schools cite improvements in discipline, school climate, and teacher morale. As Roene Comack, a teacher at Harding Middle School in Cedar Rapids, Iowa, says, "I've never worked so hard being creative, but I'm also convinced that I'm teaching better." And Sue Galletti, former prin-

cipal of Islander Middle School in Mercer Island, Washington, speaks for many educators involved in untracking when she concludes:

> What I've *stopped* seeing is very talented, bright children feeling they're not worth a bit of salt because they haven't made it into an elitist program for students labeled "gifted." I'm seeing all kids realize there are lots of kids who can contribute to learning even when what they contribute is different from them.

This is excellence. This is equity. ∎

References

California Department of Education, Superintendent's Middle Grade Task Force. (1987). *Caught in the Middle: Educational Reform for Young Adolescents in California Public Schools*. Sacramento: California State Department of Education, Bureau of Publications.

Carnegie Council on Adolescent Development. (1989). *Turning Points: Preparing American Youth for the 21st Century*. Washington, D.C.: Carnegie Corporation of New York.

Maryland State Department of Education, Maryland Task Force on the Middle Learning Years. (1989). *What Matters in the Middle Grades: Recommendations for Maryland Middle Grades Education*. Baltimore: Maryland State Department of Education, Bureau of Educational Development, Division of Instruction.

Massachusetts Department of Education. (1990). *Structuring Schools for Student Success: A Focus on Ability Grouping*, Quincy: Massachusetts Department of Education, Bureau of Student Development and Health.

Nevada State Board of Education, Middle School Task Force. (1990). *Right in the Middle: Today's Young Adolescents, Nevada's Future*. Carson City: Nevada Department of Education.

Oakes, J. (1985). *Keeping Track: How Schools Structure Inequality*. New Haven: Yale University Press.

Anne Wheelock is a Policy Consultant for the Massachusetts Advocacy Center, 95 Berkeley St., Suite 302, Boston, MA 02116-6237. She is the author of *Crossing the Tracks: How Untracking Can Save America's Schools* (New York: The New Press, 1992).

Improving Language Instruction in the Primary Grades: Strategies for Teacher-Controlled Change

J. Amos Hatch

All good teachers want to improve the quality of experiences they provide for children. In recent years, much has been learned about alternative ways of organizing and presenting language instruction for primary-age children (e.g., Schickedanz, 1986; Early Childhood and Literacy Committee, 1988; Freeman & Hatch, 1989; Morrow, 1989; Raines & Canady, 1990). Most teachers currently working in primary classrooms were prepared to teach (and were taught themselves) using traditional skill-oriented, phonics-based, basal-centered approaches. Many of these teachers are interested in alternative, more integrated approaches but lack the self-confidence to stop what they have been doing well in order to adopt unfamiliar instructional strategies with which their success is uncertain (Mosenthal, 1989). This article offers teachers, supervisors, in-service specialists, and administrators a guide for improving language instruction using

J. Amos Hatch, Ph.D., was a kindergarten and primary teacher for 12 years and is now associate professor of early childhood education at the University of Tennessee in Knoxville. During 1989 and 1990, he developed a whole language pilot project with the Tennessee State Department of Education.

Wondering how to move slowly toward a whole language educational approach in your kindergarten or primary class? Read on!

a model that values teachers' professional judgment and encourages change in small, comfortable stages.

The movement toward developmentally appropriate practices (Bredekamp, 1987) and what is usually called whole language instruction (Goodman, 1986; Altwerger, Edelsky, & Flores, 1987) is causing thousands of primary teachers to examine and sometimes question the ways they are accustomed to teaching. I had the opportunity, during the 1989–90 school year, to work with 1300 teachers participating in the Tennessee State Department of Education Whole Language Pilot Project. The objectives for that year's experiences were to familiarize teachers with whole language principles and practices and to get them to try small doses of an integrated approach to language arts in their classrooms. Our goal was not to have teachers "doing whole language" by the end of the year, but to have teachers reflecting on their current practices and making their own decisions

about what would work for them given their own abilities and preferences, the needs of the children, and the expectations of the schools and communities in which they work.

Feedback from teachers participating in the pilot project confirmed the efficacy of several strategies for accomplishing gradual, organized, thoughtful change. Central to all of these strategies is the assumption that teachers know best what they and the children can do; therefore, teachers must have ultimate control of the change process. We are confident that an approach that trusts and values teachers works better than what has frequently been done in the past—namely, identifying teachers' current methods as deficient, providing a prepackaged program for teachers to implement, and expecting them to put the new program into effect immediately.

What follows are examples of strategies for improving primary language instruction. It should be noted that teachers in the project did not undertake change without support and a solid information base. Monthly teleconferences were presented on a variety of whole language topics, and teachers were encouraged to try activities in their classrooms after viewing the teleconferences, reading articles and book chapters related to the topics under consideration, recording ideas and reflections in journals, and meeting with other project participants (for a more complete description of the project, see Hatch, 1991).

Make changes in one area at a time

Each teleconference in the project included a live interview and call-in segment featuring teachers who were experienced and comfortable using integrated whole language methods. As these teachers were asked for advice about getting started, they invari-

ably suggested that teachers not try to convert their classrooms into whole language environments overnight, but that they begin by focusing on one area at a time. The rationale for such an approach is that change involves risk and uneasiness for teachers and sometimes creates confusion and uncertainty for primary-age children. By keeping changes within one area, anxiety-producing factors are reduced and made more manageable than when large-scale change is introduced all at once.

Many teachers begin with the area of writing when they move in the direction of a whole language approach. In the project, we presented five generalizations for guiding emergent writing that provide a framework for helping teachers think about altering writing activities in their classrooms (Graves, 1983; Calkins, 1986; Harste, Short, & Burke, 1988; Strickland & Morrow, 1989):

1. every primary classroom should have a writing center;

2. children should write every day;

3. teachers should model effective writing behavior;

4. children's writing should grow out of real experiences; and

5. young writers should be given opportunities to share their work with others.

In beginning to address these generalizations, a kindergarten or first grade teacher may set up a writing center with many different kinds of paper and writing instruments, while at the same time arranging with an upper-grade teacher to have older children volunteer to come to the classroom and write younger children's dictated comments in experience journals. A second grade teacher may supply a writing center with cardboard, staples, contact paper, wallpaper, and other materials for producing and binding books written by children, and establish an author's chair arrangement through which young authors can read and receive feedback on their writing from others. A third grade teacher may help children establish their own classroom publishing companies complete with authors, illustrators, and editors and implement the use of teacher-response journals through which two-way written communication is established between children and teacher.

Writing is only one possible area for making a beginning, and the activities suggested are only examples of many alternatives. Other teachers have started by incorporating more high-quality literature into their programs (Routman, 1988) or organizing more instruction around thematic units or projects (Katz, 1988; Raines & Canady, 1990). The idea is that by limiting alterations to one dimension of language arts instruction, change becomes less threatening and teachers feel more in control.

Establish a manageable change plan

A related strategy for improving language instruction is for teachers to break big changes into a sequence of manageable steps that allow them to move forward at their own pace and stay within a reasonable comfort zone. Such an approach builds positive momentum by giving teachers and children successful experiences along the way to major change. In addition, if small changes do not work out, making modifications and adjustments is relatively easy. Finally, a planned, sequential approach permits teachers to stay on a particular step for as long (or as briefly) as they feel is necessary. Wholesale change that is outside teacher control has none of these advantages.

© 1992 Quiel Begonia

The use of classroom time is an important issue in integrated, developmentally appropriate language instruction. We suggested a sequence of possible steps to encourage more flexible uses of time instead of the traditional structuring of time around subject matter study—for example, reading groups from 9:00 to 10:30; spelling from 10:30 to 11:00; and so forth (Bredekamp, 1987). For a primary teacher who structures a major portion of the morning around reading groups and seatwork, a first step to "opening up" the use of time might be to continue with reading groups while changing the expectations for children not in the reading group that is meeting. Instead of doing workbook pages, ditto sheets, and "boardwork," children could work on group projects, individual research, personal reading and writing, center activities (such as science or math), reading with a partner, or any number of activities that encourage children to spend time in meaningful interaction with text, content, and other learners.

A next step might be to divide the school day into flexible time and scheduled time. The morning could remain structured by subjects (with integrated activities during reading groups), while the afternoon is organized around projects, thematic unit study, or other integrated activities. Future steps could be to try using the valuable morning time more flexibly or to experiment with keeping scheduled time for only three mornings per week. The final step, for those who are comfortable with it, might be to try using flexible time for all or most of each day.

The notion, no matter what the desired change, is to set up a logical sequence of changes and to try these changes deliberately and thoughtfully. Goals and timelines may be helpful, but these must belong to the teachers making the changes and must be open to alteration as teachers discover what works, what does not, what makes sense, and what does not. Some teachers, for instance, may take several years to move completely away from scheduling classroom time around subject areas; some may never reach that point. What matters is that they have looked closely at an important dimension of their work and made active decisions about their classroom practices. We believe that both they and the children will benefit from this kind of professional analysis and decision making.

Young Children •

Using a whole language approach isn't an all-or-nothing proposition. Change your ways and your emphasis gradually, implementing one basic principle at a time, making another change every month or so.

Explore many options: Experiment and adapt

In the pilot project, we encouraged teachers to try at least one new idea each month in their classrooms. Our usual method was to provide some background and videotaped examples organized around a monthly topic (e.g., reading development, integrating the language arts, or evaluation), then to suggest a variety of activities from which teachers were invited to select and adapt as they saw fit. This strategy encourages teachers to look at what theory and research have to say, study what other teachers have done, and make their own decisions about what might be successful in their particular settings.

For example, when discussing ways to use high-quality children's literature as vehicles for integrating language study, we were able to send participants a list of 74 "reading-extension activities." The list was developed by a third grade teacher and included ideas such as having children write a script based on a favorite book, then produce and perform a play; providing materials for children to make banners advertising books that they think others would enjoy reading; and helping children organize a book awards program through which they nominate and vote for favorite books in a variety of categories (for similar activities, see Raines & Canady, 1989).

When evaluation was our topic, we presented a list of 12 assessment strategies, explained their use and appropriateness for whole language classrooms, and emphasized the central role of the teacher's direct contact with children in the evaluation process. The 12 strategies were incidental evaluation, informal observations, anecdotal records, portfolios, folders of various types, self-evaluations, conferencing techniques, scrapbooks, audio/video recordings, concepts about print tests, literacy skills checklists, and miscue analysis (Tucsonans Applying Whole Language, 1984; Teale, Hiebert, & Chittenden, 1987; Harp, 1988; Tierney, 1991).

Other examples of providing teachers with options rather than prescriptions include suggesting a variety of alternatives to traditional ability-grouping (Cullinan, Farr, Hammond, Roser, & Strickland, 1989) and presenting a videotape prepared by the faculty of a successful whole language school showing a wide variety of classroom resources that have proven to be effective in their setting.

Giving teachers information and alternatives means little unless they are also given the power to do their own experimenting and adapting. No matter how many good ideas they hear about, only teachers can process the information in relation to their own teaching styles and perceptions of what is best for the children in their classes. Just as important as giving teachers alternatives is empowering them to take responsibility for studying a variety of choices (including their present practices), selecting some strategies for experimentation with the children, evaluating the effectiveness of the strategies, and making adaptations based on what has been learned. Just as integrated, developmentally appropriate strategies assume that children actively construct their own knowledge, so it is assumed here that teachers construct their own best practices by actively processing information and trying out what makes sense to them.

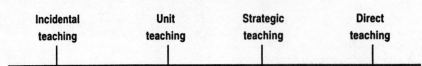

Figure 1. Strategies for Skills Instruction

Incidental teaching	Unit teaching	Strategic teaching	Direct teaching

Use professional judgment

We tried to help teachers accept the reality that classrooms and schools are complex places and that broader perspectives on classroom practices are more helpful than conceptualizing what they do as either "whole or fragmented," "appropriate or inappropriate," "good or bad." One tool for thinking about instruction in more complex ways is to use continuums to represent relationships that go beyond the "either/or" kind of thinking.

Teachers in Tennessee (as in most other states) continue to be held accountable for teaching language "skills" as part of state-mandated instructional management plans. When we discussed skills instruction, we identified a continuum of strategies representing a range of alternatives for teaching skills (see Figure 1). The continuum included incidental teaching (responding to spontaneously occurring "teachable moments"), unit teaching (targeting certain skills imbedded within meaningful units of instruction), strategic teaching (teaching specific skills needed by specific students or groups), and direct teaching (large-group, didactic instruction and practice).

We asked teachers to exercise their professional judgment concerning how to approach skills instruction in their classrooms. We encouraged them to consider and try methods closer to the incidental and unit-teaching side of the continuum, but we openly acknowledged the anxiety that many teachers experience when they know that the children are re-

Figure 2. Uses of Basal Readers in the Classroom

Basals as unnecessary	Basals as limited resources	Basals as curriculum support	Basals as curriculum

quired to take skill-based tests that parents, administrators, and the children themselves use to evaluate success (Mosenthal, 1989). Again, we encouraged teachers to think beyond an "all or nothing" approach to dealing with the dilemma inherent in trying instructional methods that are based on different theoretical assumptions from evaluation instruments that are mandated by law. By stressing the exercise of professional judgment, we wanted to signal teachers that it is just as legitimate for them to decide to carve out 30 minutes per day or one morning per week or the last two weeks before the end-of-year test and use that time exclusively for direct and strategic instruction as it is to decide that skills instruction can be taken care of by applying incidental strategies within the context of meaningful language use.

Another continuum for helping teachers place their instructional decisions within a broadened framework dealt with the use of basal readers in the classroom (Henke, 1988). The continuum (see Figure 2) ranged from "basals as unnecessary" through "basals as limited resources" and "basals as curriculum support" to "basals as curriculum." Here again, we wanted second and third grade teachers to examine the alternatives to marching the children from the beginning of the basal to the back, but not to feel guilty if they made a professional judgment to wait a while before locking their basal materials in the closet. Our notion was to get teachers to examine their current beliefs and practices, to take a careful look at

some sensible choices, to try what feels comfortable, and to make important instructional decisions rationally and professionally. "Either/ or" thinking about basals, skills teaching, or any important instructional area limits opportunities to be either rational or professional.

Implications of teacher-controlled change

In summary, it is important to acknowledge that not every teacher working in primary classrooms has been trained in developmentally appropriate practices or thinks about language teaching in the same ways as whole language advocates. This does not mean that these teachers are automatically "bad" teachers.

Primary teachers involved in change, especially in public school settings, face complex challenges from a variety of sources. They are often overburdened in terms of numbers of children and underequipped with regard to materials, training, and support. Sometimes parents, administrators, and even teaching peers put pressures on teachers that make changing even more stressful and less likely to be successful.

If we are to encourage teachers to improve their language instruction, we must recognize the complex difficulties they face, value their present efforts, and put them in control of their own improvement. As has been demonstrated in the Tennessee project, strategies such as those described in this article can go a long way toward supporting teachers' professional de-

velopment, as well as significantly improving young children's experiences in school.

For further reading

Atkins, C. (1984). Writing: Doing something constructive. *Young Children, 40*(1), 3–7.

Cazden, C. (1981). *Language in early childhood education.* Washington, DC: NAEYC.

Cullinan, B.E. (1987). Inviting readers to literature. In B.E. Cullinan (Ed.), *Children's literature in the reading program* (pp. 2–14). Newark, DE: International Reading Association.

Goodman, Y.M. (1986). Children coming to know literacy. In W.H. Teale & E. Sulzby (Eds.), *Emergent literacy: Writing and reading* (pp. 1–14). Norwood, NJ: Ablex.

Jewell, M.G., & Zintz, M. (1991). *Learning to read and write naturally.* Dubuque, IA: Kendall/Hunt.

Loughlin, C.E., & Martin, M.D. (1987). *Supporting literacy: Developing effective learning environments.* New York: Teachers College Press.

Lynch, P. (1986). *Using big books and predictable books.* New York: Scholastic.

Martinez, M., & Teale, W.H. (1987). The ins and outs of a kindergarten writing program. *The Reading Teacher, 40*(4), 444–451.

Martinez, M., & Teale, W.H. (1988). Reading in a kindergarten classroom library. *The Reading Teacher, 41*(6), 568–572.

Nurss, J.R., & Hough, R.A. (1986). Reading aloud in early childhood classrooms. *Dimensions, 14*(2), 7–9.

Parry, J., & Hornsby, D. (1985). *Write on: A conference approach to writing.* Portsmouth, NH: Heinemann.

Pellegrini, A., & Galda, L. (1985). Social dramatic play and literacy. *Dimensions, 13*(3), 12–14.

Rhodes, L.K. (1981). I can read! Predictable books as resources for reading and writing instruction. *The Reading Teacher, 34*(5), 511–518.

Roskos, K. (1988). Literacy at work in play. *The Reading Teacher, 41*(6), 562–566.

Schickendanz, J.A. (1978). Please read that story again: Exploring relationships between story reading and learning to read. *Young Children, 33*(5), 48–55.

Smith, F. (1985). *Reading without nonsense.* New York: Teachers College Press.

Strickland, D.S., & Morrow, L.M. (Eds.). (1989). *Emerging literacy: Young chil-*

EDUCATION REFORM

dren learn to read and write. Washington, DC: NAEYC.

Temple, C., Nathan, R., Burris, N., & Temple, F. (1988). *The beginnings of writing.* Boston: Allyn & Bacon.

Trelease, J. (1989). *The read-aloud handbook.* New York: Penguin Books.

Vukelich, C., & Golden, J. (1984). Early writing development and teaching strategies. *Young Children, 39*(2), 3–8.

Watson, D.J. (Ed.), (1987). *Ideas and insights: Language arts in the elementary school.* Urbana, IL: National Council of Teachers of English.

References

Altwerger, B., Edelsky, C., & Flores, B.M. (1987). Whole language: What's new? *The Reading Teacher,* 41(2), 145–154.

Bredekamp, S. (Ed.). (1987). *NAEYC position statement on developmentally appropriate practice in programs for 4- and 5-year-olds. Washington, DC: NAEYC.*

Calkins, L. (1986). *The art of writing.* Portsmouth, NH: Heinemann.

Cullinan, B.E., Farr, R.C., Hammond, W.D., Roser, N.L., & Strickland, D.S. (1989). *Teacher's strategies book.* Orlando, FL: Harcourt Brace Jovanovich.

Early Childhood and Literacy Development Committee. (1988). *Literacy development and prefirst grade.* Newark, DE: International Reading Association.

Freeman, E.B., & Hatch, J.A. (1989). Emergent literacy: Reconceptualizing kindergarten practice. *Childhood Education, 66,* 21–24.

Goodman, K.S. (1986). *What's whole in whole language?.* Portsmouth, NH: Heinemann.

Graves, D.H. (1983). *Writing: Teachers and children at work.* Portsmouth, NH: Heinemann.

Harp, B. (1988). When the principal asks: "When you do whole language instruction, how will you keep track of reading and writing skills?" *The Reading Teacher, 41,* 160–161.

Harste, J.C., Short, K., & Burke, C. (1988). *Creating classrooms for authors: The reading-writing connection.* Portsmouth, NH: Heinemann.

Hatch, J.A. (1991, May). Out from between a rock and a hard place: Whole language in Tennessee. Paper presented at the annual meeting of the International Reading Association, Las Vegas, NV.

Henke, L. (1988). Beyond basal reading: A district's commitment to change. *The New Advocate, 1*(1), 42–51.

Katz, L.G. (1988). Engaging children's minds: The implications of research for early childhood education. In C. Warger (Ed.), *Public school early childhood programs* (pp. 32–52). Alexandria, VA: Association for Supervision and Curriculum Development.

Morrow, L.M. (1989). Designing the classroom to promote literacy and development. In D.S. Strickland & L.M. Morrow (Eds.), *Emerging literacy: Young children learn to read and write* (pp. 121–134). Newark, DE: International Reading Association.

Mosenthal, P.B. (1989). The whole language approach: Teachers between a rock and a hard place. *The Reading Teacher, 42,* 628–629.

Raines, S.C., & Canady, R. (1989). *Story s-t-r-e-t-c-h-e-r-s: Activities to expand children's favorite books.* Mt. Rainier, MD: Gryphon House.

Raines, S.C., & Canady, R.J. (1990). *The whole language kindergarten.* New York: Teachers College Press.

Routman, R. (1988). *Transitions: From literature to literacy.* Portsmouth, NH: Heinemann.

Schickendanz, J.A. (1986). *More than the ABCs.* Washington, DC: NAEYC.

Strickland, D., & Morrow, L.M. (1989). Young children's writing development. *The Reading Teacher, 42,* 926–927.

Teale, W.H., Hiebert, E.H., & Chittenden, E.A. (1987). Assessing young children's literacy development. *The Reading Teacher, 40*(8), 772–777.

Tierney, R. (1991). *Portfolio assessment in the reading-writing classroom.* Norwood, MA: Christopher-Gordon.

Tucsonans Applying Whole Language. (1984). *A kid-watching guide: Evaluation for whole language classrooms.* Occasional paper #9, Program in Language and Literacy, University of Arizona, Tucson.

Voices

*T*here is no single recipe for a successful whole language program, but these classrooms seem to share several common characteristics.

Students in whole language classrooms: progress through developmentally appropriate stages; are involved in social interaction throughout the day; share responsibility for their learning; feel comfortable "trying out" and practicing their reading and writing without fear of criticism; evaluate their progress as a natural part of all learning experiences.

Instruction in whole language classrooms: teaches reading and writing through authentic reading and writing experiences; assumes content and process learning are equally important; implements classroom activities which are learner-centered and meaningful; features integration of language processes across the content areas; provides quality literature to support literacy development; has as its goal student empowerment through ownership and choice.

Beverly Eisele
Managing the Whole Language Classroom

Reprinted by permission of the publisher, Creative Teaching Press, Inc.

From "Improving Language Instruction in the Primary Grades" by J.A. Hatch, Sept. 1992, *Young Children,* 47, pp. 54-59. © 1992 by the National Association for the Education of Young Children. Reprinted by permission.

LEARNING STYLES/NEEDS

Teach Me: Don't Label Me

Barbara K. Given, Ph.D

I am not "disabled."
I learn differently.
I am not "handicapped."
I take in and use information
    that is somewhat unique to me.
Others may see me as handicapped
    when they insist on teaching me
    in ways through which I cannot learn
    or when they insist that I demonstrate my abilities
    in ways that are comfortable for them
    but not for me.
It is not I who is out of step, inadequate, handicapped or disabled.
It is the system.
I don't want my teacher to be my pal, but
    I do want a model and a friend.
I don't want my teacher to make life easy for me, but
    I do want a teacher filled with a conviction that what
    he or she teaches is important enough for me to learn
    and
I do want a teacher who has enthusiasm that encourages
    me to keep working until I learn.
I don't want to be the teacher's pet, but
    I do want to be treated as a person worthy of respect
    in spite of my learning style or because of it.
I don't want a teacher who demands praise, but
    I do want a teacher who understands my respect even
    if I show it in an awkward and sometimes hostile way.
I don't want a brain transplant, but
    I do want to learn as much as I am able.
I don't want a label, but
    I do want an appropriate education.
I don't want to be called "learning disabled," but
    I do want to learn.
Teach me.
Don't label me.

Associate Professor Barbara K. Given is coordinator of the Learning Disabilities Teacher Preparation Program and co-director of Southeast Learning Styles Center, George Mason University, Fairfax, VA 22030-4444.

The Power of the Learning Styles Philosophy

by Carol Marshall

In classrooms based on the framework of style, students develop respect for individual differences—their own and those of others—while learning academic skills.

Educational reforms hit the coast of Texas education in 1984 with the force of a hurricane. I was a regional special education consultant serving schools in 11 south Texas counties. I watched with growing apprehension as structures were tightened and standards raised. Along with raised standards and the adoption of a statewide curriculum, there was to be "no more social promotion" in Texas schools. All students would be "challenged" to perform on grade level. It wasn't long before exit level exams stood between students and a high school diploma.

I had been in the classroom long enough to know the kids who would be in trouble under the pressures of reform. I could close my eyes and see the faces in my Title I reading class. These troubled kids were not going to make it without some real help. Motivation was not the problem. "No pass, no play" was "no solution." They needed help, not pressure. Unless educators did something different in the classroom, clearly large numbers of students wouldn't be around for graduation. They were bailing out in record numbers. And when they left school, it wasn't to live happily ever after.

What *could* make a difference was a teacher who cared. Someone who could see symptoms for what they were—a cry for help. It was critical that I find something to bring to both teachers and students that could support learning success. Success in learning is basic to success in life.

1984 was also the first year I heard the term *learning style*. The concept excited me, and it made perfect sense. In the face of the endless variety of human beings who present themselves to the schools each year, it's amazing that educators could ever have believed that everyone learned the same way! In the research on learning style, I could see a framework to explain individual differences, a way to manipulate classroom conditions to support those differences. This was critical information for teachers of students who did not learn easily or typically—but equally important information for supporting the natural differences of all children—including the gifted. What I read, I tried; what I learned, I shared.

Since that time, I have seen dramatic successes in classrooms where teachers use the framework of learning styles to support student learning: in La Porte, Texas, where Baker Junior High School changed its failure rate from 40 percent to 9 percent in two years; at Corsicana High School, where as a result of Principal T. Y. Harp's instructional leadership in learning styles, 27 three-time losers on Texas' exit test all passed and graduated with their peers . . .

Teaching to style represents a philosophical change from tradition to a mutual embrace of accountability: *If students don't learn the way we teach them, then we will teach them the way they learn.* In short, we must teach them how they learn so that they can teach themselves. This philosophy attracts and keeps those educators who realize their students' lives depend on this gift. Such a philosophy also demonstrates a willingness to relinquish "control" for leadership, with the teacher looking, listening, thinking, then planning instruction from the "student up," instead of from the "system down." And everybody wins.

Students learn to understand and value themselves and others. They learn that they have power to contribute to their own learning success. That this wonderful world needs all kinds of people with all kinds of talents and skills.

And teachers win. They preside over classrooms disciplined by mutual respect. Classrooms that are people-shaped and fun! Classrooms in which the most unlikely can offer the most insight. Such classrooms are not permissive, and they are manageable. They are psychologically safe environments that promote active learning, mutual understanding, and respect. Places to develop healthy self-concepts and social relationships along with academic skills. Such classrooms signal the wonder of life-long learning.

Educators must continue to watch the successes of such classrooms. When we look at the growing research on at-risk students to discover that their learning strengths are rarely accommodated in traditional instruction, when we find that those we have labeled "learning disabled" can achieve well when we discover and teach to their strengths, when we find that those who do not share similar learning patterns can be denied their own potential—then it really is time to look to style for the power that it can bring to the re-formation of education. We will continue to be in "system's failure" as long as we resist the concept of the dignity and value of each individual that such a philosophy celebrates.□

Breaking the Cycle of Failure by Building Self-Esteem

by Esther Wright, M.A.

Parents and teachers of children who learn differently must be sensitive to the role that self-concept and self-esteem play in school achievement and behavior. Children who have discipline or learning difficulties frequently exhibit behaviors that reflect a negative self-concept and low self-esteem. Some of the behaviors associated with an esteem problem are:

- shyness and insecurity
- verbally or physically abusive
- low frustration tolerance
- resistant to authority
- self-destructive
- unmotivated
- poor personal hygiene

These behaviors are the product of low self-esteem and keep children trapped in a downward spiral of failure and despair. In order to provide youngsters with an opportunity to break this cycle of failure, it is essential that we become more aware of how self-esteem is formulated and the effect it has on the attitudes and behaviors of young people.

Children are not born with low self-esteem or a negative self-concept. They define themselves ("I am smart/stupid") and determine their worth and value ("I am good/bad") based on their relationships and experiences with significant adults in the early part of their lives . . . primarily their parents and teachers. As they get older, most of the actions they take and the decisions they make regarding choices of friends, schooling and occupation will be greatly influenced by their self-concept and self-esteem.

As teachers and parents, we play a major role in shaping the esteem of our young people. As we interact with them on a day-to-day basis, we must provide them with opportunities to view themselves as capable, responsible and worthy of our caring and support. Our relationships with them and our responses to them, (especially when they are having difficulties) will either contribute to their self-sabotaging self-concept or allow them to see a new possiblity for defining who they are. To be effective with these children, we must remember that they require relationships and experiences that nurture and empower them, in spite of whatever past assessments we have made regarding their behaviors or learning abilities. The investment we make in these children can transform their negative self-concepts of "I can't" or "I won't" into the possibility of "I can" and "I will."

There are many ways that parents and teachers can provide esteeming and nurturing relationships and experiences for children with low self-esteem. Here are the essential ingredients that can make the difference with these youngsters:

- They must know that they are loved, respected and capable.
- They must have frequent opportunities to succeed with challenging activities and projects.
- They should be provided with large doses of encouragement and support when things get tough.
- They must be taught how to communicate their wants and needs and become skilled at problem solving.
- They must understand that failure and hard work are integral to the learning process and an essential part of every worthwhile accomplishment.
- They must learn to acknowledge their strengths and talents and find ways to compensate for their limitations.

> **The greatest gift we can offer children who learn differently is to continue providing them with the experience that they are capable, responsible and valued.**

Teachers like Marva Collins and Jaime Escalante have demonstrated what is possible when adults are willing to work committedly with young people who have little appreciation of their own potential. It requires a determination to intervene in the downward spiral of failure. It also requires our understanding that self-esteem is not developed or altered in a day, but over time. And that children with low self-esteem require more than gold stars and unearned praise to transform their self concepts. They require adults who can see and act on their potential and who will provide whatever it takes for them to be successful.

The greatest gift we can offer children who learn differently is to continue providing them with the experience that they are capable, responsible and valued.

There are a variety of books and programs that focus on the development of self-esteem. Parents and teachers should further investigate this topic and become better aware of how they can turn the downward spiral of failure into an upward spiral of accomplishment and success.

Esther Wright, M.A. is President of the San Francisco/Marin Chapter of LDA. She is an education consultant who specializes in issues related to self-esteem and positive behavior management of at-risk students.

Meeting the Challenge of Educating Children at Risk

Strategies exist that schools can use to ameliorate the effects of the conditions described in this special section, the guest editors point out — strategies that give children at risk real opportunities to be successful learners.

....

BY LINDA J. STEVENS AND MARIANNE PRICE

SOME STARTLING facts have recently come to light concerning the exposure of children to conditions that can negatively affect their learning and put them at risk of school failure. Taken together, these facts suggest that the population of students entering our public schools is changing in ways that educators must address if these children are to reach their full learning potential.

• Some 350,000 newborns each year have been exposed prenatally to drugs, including alcohol.

• More than 300,000 school-age children are homeless each year.

• Some three to four million children have been exposed to damaging levels of lead.

LINDA J. STEVENS is an independent consultant in King of Prussia, Pa., and editor of the Pennsylvania Reporter, *a newsletter published by the Pennsylvania Resource and Information Service for Special Education. MARIANNE PRICE is director of pupil services, Radnor Township School District, Wayne, Pa.*

• The incidence of pediatric infection with HIV (human immunodeficiency virus) has risen dramatically in recent years, affecting some 15,000 to 30,000 children.

• One to two million children are subject to abuse.

• Of the 37,000 babies born each year weighing less than 3½ pounds who live long enough to leave the hospital, many will face substantial learning problems as a result of medical intervention.

The articles in this special section have been assembled to address the implications of these conditions for assessment, instruction, and administrative planning. Three articles describe how exposure to toxic substances affects development and learning. Donna Burgess and Ann Streissguth describe the medical, behavioral, and academic characteristics of fetal alcohol syndrome and fetal alcohol effects and suggest guiding principles for educational programs to meet the needs of affected students. Dan Griffith presents a picture of children prenatally exposed to cocaine that is quite different from that painted by the media in recent years. Based on findings from the longest running longitudinal research program in the country on prenatal exposure to cocaine, he describes the effects on development and discusses interventions for dealing with problem behaviors. Herbert Needleman details the dramatic effects of even low levels of exposure to lead — findings that have been documented in nine countries — and discusses implications for public policy.

John Seidel describes the effects of HIV infection on cognitive, motor, and language performance and discusses the issues associated with serving children with HIV infection in a school setting. Nettie Bartel and Kenneth Thurman discuss the educational difficulties faced by three groups of children whose lives have been saved by modern medical technology but who may face learning problems as a result: children with cancer, low birthweight babies, and medically fragile children.

The effects of societal factors on children are considered in two articles. Michelle Linehan discusses the conditions experienced by children who are homeless, describes their effects on school performance, and recommends intervention strategies, including a statewide training effort. Susan Craig details the effects of abuse on children's cognitive and social functioning and considers implications for instruction.

Finally, Patricia Edwards and Lauren Jones Young challenge us to forge new family/school/community partnerships to meet the needs of children at risk. They underscore the importance of breaking down the barriers between families and schools and capitalizing on family and community strengths.

There are several reasons for presenting information about these diverse conditions in the *Kappan*. First, the substantial population of children at risk means that teachers will face such children in their classrooms in increasing numbers and that administrators must plan to provide appropriate services for them.

Second, it is essential to view these conditions in context and to note their interrelated nature. For example, children who are homeless and living in welfare hotels may be exposed to chipping and peeling paint containing lead in damaging concentrations. Effective planning for

PHI DELTA KAPPAN

appropriate programming must address not only the condition of homelessness but also the possibility that a child should be referred for lead testing. Interventions that do not address both issues will not be effective.

Third, as a result of recent media attention, myths and misconceptions about the effects of these conditions have become widespread. As the findings of systematic and longitudinal research come in, we need to dispel those myths.

Myth: The conditions discussed here are inner-city or minority issues. As Edwards and Jones Young note in their discussion of family/school relationships, children in poverty are at greater risk for some of these conditions. However, while we do not wish to minimize the effects of poverty, there is clear evidence that children from all socioeconomic levels are affected by these conditions. Nor does race determine which children will be affected. Rates of drug use during pregnancy were found to be similar among whites and blacks at 11 hospitals in Florida, regardless of the socioeconomic status of the patients.[1] Fetal alcohol syndrome or fetal alcohol effects can occur in the offspring of any woman who drinks heavily during pregnancy — a behavior not confined to the poor. Moreover, children from affluent families are not impervious to the effects of leaded paint in older homes, in the pipes of a city water system, or in school water coolers. A study in Massachusetts found that 30% of children identified as lead poisoned in early 1988 lived in rural or suburban communities.[2] Abuse and childhood cancer strike all social classes.

Myth: The effects of these conditions on learning, behavior, and projected development are uniform. In fact, there is a considerable range in the effects experienced by children as a result of these conditions. When people hear about "crack babies," they may conjure up an image of screaming, hyperactive, destructive, unresponsive children for whom there is no hope of successful adjustment. These children have been described as a biological underclass, a lost generation. Yet many children exposed prenatally to cocaine who receive appropriate interventions can score as well on measures of global development as their nonexposed peers. Similarly, some children with fetal alcohol syndrome or fetal alcohol ef-

fects may have a measured I.Q. in the normal range, while others may register a score as low as 30.

The ways in which a child manifests the effects of a given condition are related to several factors: 1) *degree* of exposure (e.g., varying amounts of cocaine

> Recent media attention has made myths and misconceptions about the effects of certain conditions widespread.

or lead); 2) *timing* of exposure and treatment (e.g., cocaine or alcohol exposure at different stages of pregnancy or the onset of childhood cancer and treatment at different ages); 3) *duration* of exposure (e.g., amount of time exposed to lead or to being without a home); and 4) *other influences* (e.g., poor nutrition or poor prenatal care).

Just as an assortment of factors, such as nutrition, can negatively affect outcomes, so too can these factors play a positive role in development. When children exposed prenatally to cocaine are provided a supportive environment, decreased head circumference (a marker of biological insult) shows a decreasing correlation with cocaine exposure as children become older.[3] In this special section Seidel notes that, after one year of intervention in a model program for children with HIV infection, there were significant improvements by 42% of children in cognitive skills, by 32% in motor skills, and by 21% in communication skills.

While the conditions described in this special section are distinct, some startling similarities exist in the effects on the cognitive and social performance of children. For example, prenatal drug and alcohol exposure, lead poisoning, homelessness,

and HIV infection appear related to problems with self-regulation — that is, the ability of children to attend to the task at hand. Noncompliance, difficulties in language and communication, problems with social relationships, and difficulties in exercising judgment and making decisions are also behaviors that appear to be associated with several of these conditions.

Noncompliance. Noncompliant behavior may include aggressiveness, failure to comply with teacher directives, or loss of control. Elevated levels of lead have been associated with aggressive and antisocial behaviors. Children who are homeless may demonstrate aggressive behavior as they try to stake a claim to something of their own or as they fight for control at school to counter feelings of lack of control in the rest of their lives. Children with fetal alcohol exposure may demonstrate inappropriate or challenging behaviors in part as a function of their poor communication skills.

Self-regulation difficulties. Self-regulation refers to the ability to attend to, take in, and use information; to organize a calm, regulated state; and to adapt to the needs of a situation.[4] Problems with self-regulation may result in physical or emotional withdrawal from a situation or in loss of control. A high level of activity and distractibility is the most frequent reason that a child with fetal alcohol exposure is referred for diagnosis. Children who are being treated for childhood cancers may also experience difficulties with attention, concentration, and self-organization, while children with HIV infection may display behavior ranging from hyperactivity to autistic-like withdrawal. Lead exposure has been negatively related to children's ability to pay attention, to avoid distraction, and to resist impulses. A child who has been exposed prenatally to cocaine may be unable to attend to a task for more than a few minutes at a time. Children who are homeless may demonstrate poor attention spans, hyperactivity, and difficulty making transitions between activities. A description of effective strategies for teaching self-regulation skills can be found in a recent issue of *Focus on Exceptional Children.*[5]

Language and communication difficulties. Children with acute lymphocytic leukemia are often less expressive than their peers and may have difficulty following multiple commands. Needleman found poorer language development among children exposed to higher levels of lead. Receptive and expressive language delays are often typical of children with HIV infection or of those who have been abused. Griffith observed delays in language development by age 3 in about one-third of the children in his study who were exposed prenatally to cocaine.

Difficulties with social relationships. The impulsivity, poor communication skills, and inability to predict consequences of behavior that are typical of many children with fetal alcohol exposure often contribute to problems with social relationships. Children who have been abused may have problems distancing themselves from their feelings, identifying others as sources of support, and taking the perspectives of others. They tend to reflect the desires of their caretakers and may demonstrate timidity, a fear of strange places, and a reluctance to take risks. Children who are homeless often hesitate to risk forming close friendships, may use withdrawal and introversion as defenses, or may exhibit depression over leaving friends and familiar places.

Difficulties in judgment and decision making. Children affected by fetal alcohol exposure frequently have difficulty predicting the consequences of their behavior. Craig suggests that the failure of abused children to establish themselves as a locus of control may be related to their difficulty in understanding cause/effect relationships.

INSTRUCTIONAL AND CURRICULAR IMPLICATIONS

It is not the label describing a condition that should determine a placement or intervention. Instead, each child's academic, behavioral, and emotional needs ought to be the determining factors. However, we do not think it either advisable or feasible to develop separate sets of interventions for each child or for each condition. A number of factors need to be considered in selecting and developing appropriate instructional interventions.

• *Identify the behavioral trigger for a problem behavior and develop ways to avoid that trigger.* Griffith describes a 2½-year-old who exceeds his threshold for overstimulation as a result of his older

brothers' boisterous behavior. Circumstances can be altered to reduce the incidence of such triggers, perhaps by separating the toddler from his brothers for a time after the brothers arrive home from school.

• *Consider the context of the problem behavior.* A homeless child who arrives at school late could be viewed as noncompliant; yet the lateness could be a result of using public transportation or of not having access to an alarm clock. An appropriate school intervention might be to avoid scheduling an academic subject during first period.

• *Examine the function served by the problem behavior and identify an appropriate alternative behavior.* Take the case of a young child exposed prenatally to drugs who cannot sit still long enough to complete seatwork without pacing around his desk. An observation may reveal that the pacing is a coping strategy that helps the child calm himself to focus on that seatwork. Then consider how the function served by pacing can be accommodated in a way that does not disturb others, perhaps by moving the child's desk or by helping him learn a less disruptive coping strategy.

• *Consider how the nature of the instructional process meets the needs of these children.* For example, Craig notes that children who have been abused need the consistency and predictability of a highly structured teaching method that provides advance organizers, modeling, opportunities for guided practice, and so on.

• *Determine the degree of external structure needed to reduce the likelihood of problem behaviors.* Children with difficulty in self-monitoring often require interventions that impose the structure that they are unable to provide for themselves.

• *Provide interventions across levels.* Many interventions can be used with individual students, in small groups, classwide, or schoolwide. Many students, not just those considered at risk, could benefit from strategies to improve self-regulation skills. For example, having students note on a checklist at regular intervals whether they are paying attention can dramatically increase time-on-task.

School personnel also need to examine the procedures used for making transitions between activities (e.g., assem-

blies, field trips) and locations (e.g., lunch, playground) to determine whether those procedures foster independence and provide the tools to achieve that independence. There should also be consistency in the way such procedures are applied.

Just as there is no single set of interventions for each condition, there is no single most appropriate curriculum for each condition. As the children described here vary in needs and abilities, so curricular options should range from regular education to the functional approach espoused by Burgess and Streissguth for children with fetal alcohol syndrome.

There also are curricular implications if society is to protect future generations of children from exposure to these conditions. For example, dramatic increases in teenage pregnancy, combined with drug use and high levels of alcohol consumption, suggest that instruction on the effects of prenatal exposure to drugs and alcohol should be included in existing drug and alcohol curricula and in sex education and family life education.

FAMILY/SCHOOL/COMMUNITY CONNECTIONS

As Edwards and Jones Young point out in this section, the priorities and values of individual families vary and may differ from those of teachers and schools. Schools must acknowledge and respect a range of family goals, backgrounds, and strengths.

To help bridge the gap between home and school, services should be viewed from the perspective of the family to see what might be considered obstacles or hindrances to access. Teachers often complain that parents do not help children practice literacy skills. Yet school libraries typically are open only to school-age children and only during the day. If school libraries were made accessible to family literacy programs during extended hours, resources on child care could be available, volunteers could perform a range of functions connected with maintaining the library, and family members could share special skills, talents, or interests through a library forum.

Another approach to bringing together schools and families might involve portfolio assessment. Typically, a portfolio consists of a selection of products that are representative of a student's work at school.[6] A modification might involve asking the family and the child to bring in examples of the child's activities at home, such as a picture drawn by the child or a favorite story. This approach demonstrates to children that the skills they have mastered at home are relevant to the tasks that they will be completing at school. In addition, the family is acknowledged as a resource, not merely an audience.

Rather than have schools help parents make instruction at home more school-like, schools should try to incorporate the authentic literacy tasks of the home into their curricula. For example, students could practice their written language skills by writing letters to request repairs to a community playground — an authentic activity that has meaning in the context of their community.

And just as it is important to show the relevance of home activities to school success, it is also essential to communicate to children the relevance of school activities to their lives at home and in the community. For example, in Philadelphia, where the Pennsylvania Horticultural Society's outreach program has worked with neighborhood groups to turn 1,700 vacant lots into neighborhood gardens, the schools have a unique opportunity to build bridges with families that grow produce in the gardens. By teaching vocabulary, science concepts related to the growth and care of plants, and such environmental ideas as the nature of acid rain and the importance of recycling, the schools can help establish the relevance of school activities to family goals and can help create a common ground for communication between school and home and between parent and child.

As Edwards and Jones Young point out, it is essential to go beyond the school and the home to include the resources of the community in meeting the needs of these children. In the case of lead poisoning, for example, the school or the family may refer a child to a physician for testing; the family may then be referred to one agency for lead abatement and to another agency for temporary housing while the lead is being removed from their home.

Ideally, there would be a mechanism for bringing together schools, health care agencies, community resources, and so-cial services to develop prevention, treatment, and support services to meet the needs of children and families. However, even within the constraints imposed by categorical funding and limited resources, there are some strategies that schools can use to facilitate the sharing of resources. For example, to ensure that

> Effective systems should be established for screening children in order to identify those who are at risk.

children of kindergarten age who are homeless are registered for school, a registration desk could be set up in a shelter.[7] School personnel could inform shelter personnel of procedures to refer children for early intervention services. Providers of family literacy services could be invited to school inservice training sessions on reading instruction. What is needed, as Edwards and Jones Young suggest, is an ecological approach to marshaling the resources of the home, school, and community to meet the needs of children at risk.

POLICY IMPLICATIONS

It is essential to examine the legal foundations for action concerning children at risk before considering policy with regard to student assessment, early intervention, and personnel training.

Legal issues. Seeing to it that children at risk are provided an appropriate educational program is not just a choice to be made by enlightened administrators; in many instances, it is a legal requirement. There are several federal laws that affect the actions of schools with regard to these children. Two affect the education of children who are disabled or who have a life-affecting impairment. The Individuals with Disabilities Education Act (IDEA, P.L. 101-476), amended in 1991 (P.L. 102-119), entitles students identified as disabled to "a free and appropriate public education" and guarantees services to preschool children who are disabled and to their families. Some of the conditions described in this issue are included in some states' definitions of developmental delay under this law, which may include those children whose diagnosed condition has a "high probability" of resulting in developmental delays if services are not provided. In addition, Section 504 of the Rehabilitation Act of 1973 requires public schools to address the educational needs of children who have physical or mental impairments that substantially limit a major life activity, such as learning. In 1990 the U.S. Office for Civil Rights established as a priority the identification of special populations of children, such as "crack babies" and children who are homeless, for special education and related services.

Another federal law specifically addresses the education of children who are homeless. The Stewart B. McKinney Homeless Assistance Act, passed in 1987 and reauthorized and amended in 1990 (P.L. 101-645), directs that any "laws, regulations, practices, or policies that may act as a barrier to the enrollment, attendance, or success in school of homeless children and homeless youth" must be reviewed and revised.[8] The National Law Center on Homelessness and Poverty recently filed a federal lawsuit against the District of Columbia public schools, charging that the school system had failed to ensure access to educational services for homeless children under the McKinney Act.

Assessment. Effective systems should be established for screening children in order to identify those at risk for learning and behavioral problems. Currently, only about one in every three to 10 children is tested for lead exposure, although a 1989 amendment to the federal Medicaid law requires all states to test poor children's blood for lead. However, there are some promising developments at the state and national levels. Massachusetts requires parents of children entering kindergarten to show that their children's blood has been tested for lead poisoning at least once, and in October 1991 the

Centers for Disease Control recommended that all children be tested by their first birthday for the presence of lead in their blood.

Recently, many states have implemented pre-referral intervention processes, which can mean a delay of some months before a child can be referred for evaluation. This extended period has serious implications for a homeless child, who may well have moved to a new jurisdiction before the process has been completed. Under the McKinney Act, this and other such policies that can act as barriers to providing service to students who are homeless must be revised.

Early intervention. Griffith makes a compelling case for the efficacy of early intervention in reducing the negative effects of prenatal drug exposure on the intellectual, social, emotional, and behavioral development of young children. The results of another recent study underscore that position.[9] When children born prematurely to low-income families were provided comprehensive early intervention services with high levels of parent involvement, they scored an average of 15 I.Q. points higher at age 4 than children in a control group. Only 2% of the experimental group scored in the mentally retarded range, while almost nine times as many children in the control group did so.

The costs of failing to provide early intervention are enormous. According to projections by the Children's Defense Fund,[10] a dollar spent to improve preschool education could save $4.75 in special education, crime, and welfare costs. Yet half of the states spent less than $25 per child in 1990 on early childhood care and education.[11]

Training. Typically, when we think of training in education, we think of training teachers. But it is essential to include other school personnel, members of families, and members of the community.

Schools must provide training for professional staff members (e.g., nurses, social workers, psychologists), for paraprofessional staff members, and for other adults who play an important role in the lives of children (e.g., bus drivers and secretaries). For example, the school secretary often has the first contact with a child's family and so needs to be familiar with procedures related to the McKinney Act to ease entry into school for children who are homeless.

As Craig notes, many schools are developing "teacher assistance teams" to help teachers deal with students who have learning and behavioral problems. Because of their role in helping to coordinate services, members of teacher assistance teams should be informed of the effects of the conditions described in this special section.

As Edwards and Jones Young suggest, schools need to broaden their conception of families to include grandparents, aunts and uncles, siblings, foster parents, neighbors, and so on. And these individuals need training in strategies for handling the types of problems discussed in this section — noncompliance, language difficulties, and problems with self-regulation, judgment and decision making, and social relationships. Because many agencies in a community may deal with the same families, every effort should be made to share resources. Staff members of recreation centers, mental health workers, police officers, and fire fighters all have roles to play in training — both as resources for training others and as recipients of training themselves.

The number of children at risk appears both significant and alarming. However, school personnel should be particularly cautious about media accounts that sensationalize the dim prospects for these children. It is critical that assumptions about the potential of these children be examined carefully and thoroughly. It is unjust to write off as unteachable "crack kids," children who are homeless, children who are abused, or children who suffer from other conditions described in this special section. Strategies exist that schools can use to ameliorate the effects of the conditions described here and to give these children real opportunities to be successful learners.

But schools cannot do the job alone. Traditional school/home/community relationships must be reconfigured; schools cannot be effective when they work in isolation from the familial, cultural, and community context of the children they serve. However, in collaboration with families and communities, schools are in a unique position to provide the help that can make the difference to the future of these children.

> Schools cannot be effective when they work in isolation from the familial, cultural, and community context.

1. Ira J. Chasnoff, Harvey J. Landress, and Mark E. Barrett, "The Prevalence of Illicit-Drug or Alcohol Use During Pregnancy and Discrepancies in Mandatory Reporting in Pinellas County, Florida," *New England Journal of Medicine*, 26 April 1990, pp. 1202-06.
2. Mary Jean Brown et al., "Lead Poisoning in Children of Different Ages," *New England Journal of Medicine*, 12 July 1990, pp. 135-36.
3. Barry Zuckerman and Deborah A. Frank, " 'Crack Kids': Not Broken," *Pediatrics*, February 1992, pp. 337-39.
4. Stanley I. Greenspan, "Regulatory Disorders I: Clinical Perspectives," in M. Marlyne Kilbey and Khursheed Asghar, eds., *Methodological Issues in Controlled Studies on Effects of Prenatal Exposure to Drug Abuse* (Rockville, Md.: National Institute on Drug Abuse, Research Monograph 114, 1991), pp. 165-72.
5. Steven Graham, Karen R. Harris, and Robert Reid, "Developing Self-Regulated Learners," *Focus on Exceptional Children*, February 1992, pp. 1-16.
6. Robert J. Tierney, Mark A. Carter, and Laura E. Desai, *Portfolio Assessment in the Reading-Writing Classroom* (Norwood, Mass.: Christopher Gordon Publishers, 1990).
7. Yvonne Rafferty, *And Miles to Go . . . Barriers to Academic Achievement and Innovative Strategies for the Delivery of Educational Services to Homeless Children* (New York: Advocates for Children of New York, 1991).
8. Stewart B. McKinney Homeless Assistance Act, Subtitle VII-B, Sect. 721, amended 29 November 1990.
9. Craig T. Ramey et al., "Infant Health and Development Program for Low Birth Weight, Premature Infants: Program Elements, Family Participation, and Child Intelligence," *Pediatrics*, March 1992, pp. 454-65.
10. William Raspberry, "Again, the Alarm Sounds on Poverty and Children: How Few Will Be Wakened?," *Philadelphia Inquirer*, 28 September 1991, p. 8-A.
11. Deborah L. Cohen, " 'Inadequate' State Funding Seen Impeding School Readiness," *Education Week*, 11 March 1992, p. 13.

Ⓚ

Helping the Child Who Doesn't Fit In

Those oddball kids may be suffering from a nonverbal communication disorder.

Stephen Nowicki, Jr. and Marshall P. Duke

W e call them "problem children." They're the ones who:

• Stand too close or touch others in annoying ways,

• Laugh too loudly or at inappropriate times,

• Make silly, out-of-place, and often embarrassing remarks,

• Don't pick up subtle hints regarding the impact of their behavior,

• Mistake friendly actions by others for hostile ones (while believing other children are their friends, when they are not),

• Move too fast or too slow,

• Misunderstand the rules of simple playground games,

• Seem to be "out of sync" with their peers.

While some of these youngsters fall into such well-established categories as behavior disordered or emotionally disturbed, qualifying them for special education placement and remediation, there are many others whose interpersonal and academic problems seem to resist categorization. We believe that many of these troubled youngsters actually suffer from a specific, diagnosable, and correctable disability that we have named *dyssemia,* a term which, like dyslexia (dys=difficulty; lexia=reading), describes a difficulty ("dys") in the use of signs ("semia").

A Communication Deficit

Based on more than two decades of re-

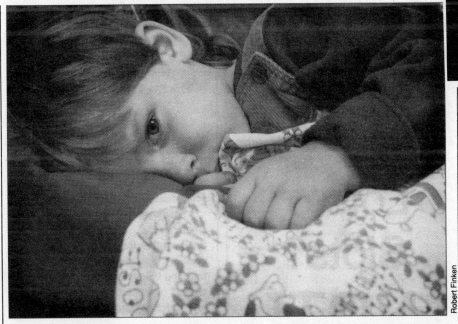

Robert Finken

search with several thousand children, we have concluded that many of these puzzling children actually have a special kind of communication deficit, a sort of body-language version of dyslexia. We believe that they suffer from some form or combination of expressive and/or receptive *nonverbal language deficits*; that they either cannot transmit or "read" the customary nonverbal signals necessary for successful interpersonal relationships. Most dyssemic children have normal to above-average intelligence, and their deficits are more often caused by a lack of comprehension than by an inherent biological defect.

While most adults who work with children try to be sensitive to their feelings, and can tolerate and understand wide ranges of acceptable behavior, the dys-

semic child is often a challenge. In our recent book[*] we have attempted to describe for parents and teachers some simple and practical methods for informally assessing and remediating dyssemia in young children.

We delineate what many consider to be the "parts of speech" in nonverbal language. Among these are rhythm, use of space, facial expressions. postures, gestures, style of dress, and paralanguage (which includes tone of voice, loudness or softness of speech, rate of speech, and the use of meaningful nonverbal sounds such as "mmm").

* Helping the Child Who Doesn't Fit In, by Stephen Nowicki, Jr. and Marshall P. Duke. Atlanta: Peachtree Publishers, 1992. $14.95.

Stephen Nowicki, Jr., and Marshall P. Duke are clinical psychologists on the faculty of Emory University in Atlanta, Georgia.

There are a number of ways that children's nonverbal strengths and weaknesses can be identified (*see box*). One technique might be to have them interpret the actions of television performers (especially on soap operas) with sound and picture alternately turned off. Or you might engage them in informal but focused discussions about the nonverbal behaviors of people observed in shopping malls and other public places, or of children interacting with others in such settings as playgrounds, lunchrooms, and birthday parties.

We do not consider dyssemia to be a disorder or illness, but rather a correctable difficulty. While we are still learning about the role of nonverbal language in the social and personal adjustment of young children, we are confident that there is great promise in remedial efforts based on helping dyssemic children learn to "speak" in a language they have not fully mastered.

We believe that such remediation is possible if parents and teachers become involved in efforts to help children to perceive, correctly interpret, and use important nonverbal cues. Based on our knowledge of these troubled youngsters, we cannot overemphasize the importance of alerting parents and educators to the problems that can result when children do not use nonverbal language properly. It is these adults, who play such significant and influential roles in the lives of young children, who are the most effective resources in helping dyssemic children truly "belong." □

The Six Types of Dyssemia

• *Inappropriate rhythms and sense of time.* These children seem "out of sync" with the pace of others around them. They are either unaware of the need for different rates of speed, or seem unable to alter their pace.

• *Inappropriate use of interpersonal space.* These children seem unaware that they alienate others by standing too close, spreading their toys and belongings into other's "territory," or touching people.

• *Inappropriate gestures and posture.* Children don't realize that pointing at someone, or standing with their arms folded, can be annoying.

• *Inappropriate facial expressions.* Failing to make eye contact, smiling or frowning at the wrong times, and displaying a seemingly grim "school face" can be interpreted as odd or unfriendly actions.

• *Inappropriate paralinguistics (vocal quality).* A shrill laugh, speech that is too loud or too soft, or unusual accenting may be signs of this type of dyssemia.

• *Inappropriate appearance.* Some children may face rejection because of their unconventional dress, poor personal hygiene, or unacceptable personal habits.

Some Facts about Nonverbal Communication

• Nonverbal language is usually seen by others as a truer reflection of how we feel. When words are pitted against nonverbal language, we almost always believe what is being transmitted nonverbally.

• Unlike verbal communication, nonverbal communication is continuous. The average person spends less than 40 minutes a day in verbal communication with others. But we are constantly communicating nonverbally — whether we want to or not.

• Some nonverbal patterns may begin at birth. For example, blind and deaf children appear to show the same facial expressions reflecting their emotional states as their sighted and hearing peers.

• During a typical conversation, we spend from 30 to 60 percent of the time looking at the other person's face.

• While it is possible to avoid making gestures and touching people, we cannot avoid revealing something about our attitudes and feelings in our body posture.

• The foundations of nonverbal social communication are developed within families.

Attention Deficit Hyperactivity Disorder

by Karen Durbin

Attention Deficit Hyperactivity Disorder (ADHD) has been defined as a collection of symptoms, all of which lead to disruptive behavior and are therefore expected to be seen in various combinations in most ADHD children.

The characteristic symptoms of ADHD are not abnormal in themselves. In fact, they are present in all children at one time or another, and only when excessive do they become disruptive behavioral problems. Three distinctions to keep in mind when examining the eight principal ADHD characteristics discussed here are their intensity, persistence, and patterning (Wender 1987). But also note that not all of these characteristics are present in every ADHD child.

1. Inattentiveness and Distractibility

ADHD children are nearly always easily distracted and have short attention spans. At home, these children don't listen to what their parents say to them; they don't mind; and they forget things. Their homework is never finished. When getting dressed, they may leave buttons unbuttoned and zippers unzipped, and even put shoes on the wrong feet. At school, their teachers notice that they have difficulty listening to and following directions, have trouble completing assignments, and often are off-task and out of their seats.

It is important to remember that inattentiveness and distractibility need not be present at all times. Many teachers report that these children do well when given one-to-one attention, and physicians and psychiatrists note good attention spans during brief office visits.

The paradox of ADHD children being attentive under specialized conditions, but unable to pay attention and complete tasks under normal conditions, is confusing to parents and teachers, especially when they see that these children are able to sit and watch television for long periods of time. But, as Pugliese (1992) has observed, television programming *reinforces* the way ADHD children think by switching rapidly from idea to idea and scene to scene, with numerous commercial interruptions. There is constant movement both on the screen and in the minds of the affected children.

2. Impulsiveness

ADHD children tend to speak and act first, and think later (Garber *et al.* 1990). They talk out in class and interrupt others. They rush across streets, oblivious to traffic, and have more than their share of accidents.

These children are often unable to tolerate delays, and become upset when people or things fail to respond as they wish. This may result in broken toys, as well as attacks on siblings and classmates (Wender 1987).

3. Hyperactivity

Hyperactivity, which involves such attributes as restlessness, excessive talking, difficulty awaiting turns in games, and shifting from one uncompleted activity to another (Garber *et al.* 1990), is not always exhibited by ADHD children. They may appear to be normally, or even less than normally, active until they have an important task to complete. It is then that these children, distracted by things that would barely be noticed by anyone else, display the classic symptoms of hyperactivity — constant motion, fidgeting, drumming fingers, and shuffling feet. In the classroom, hyperactive children talk constantly, jostle and annoy others, do a lot of clowning, and are generally disruptive.

4. Attention-Demanding Behavior

All children want and need adult attention, and ADHD children are no exception. The difference is in their insatiable desire for such attention. They have to have center stage, be the clown, monopolize the conversation, and show off. Wender (1987) explains the adult reaction to such behavior:

The demand for attention can be distressing, confusing, and irritating to parents. Since the child demands so much, they feel they have not given him what he needs. Since they cannot understand how to satisfy him, they feel deficient. Finally, because the child may cling and poke simultaneously and endlessly, they feel angry.

5. Learning Difficulties

While ADHD is in no way related to mental retardation, some ADHD children do have similar problems. Their intellectual development may be uneven — advanced in some areas and behind in others. For example, a child may be able to do fifth-grade mathematics, but only second-grade reading.

Problems in perception are more difficult to define and are more complex than simple vision or hearing limitations. ADHD children may be unable to distinguish between similar sights or sounds, or to connect sensations in a meaningful way.

Such difficulties in children of normal intelligence are called specific developmental disorders

LEARNING STYLES/NEEDS

(SDDs), a term that is replacing "learning disabilities." While the most common SDDs are in reading and arithmetic, not all ADHD children have these disorders. Nevertheless, because most ADHD children have learning difficulties, they are often viewed as underachievers.

6. Coordination Difficulties

About half of all ADHD children have problems with various types of coordination. For example, trouble with fine muscle control may result in difficulties in coloring, writing, tying shoelaces, and buttoning. For many of these children, handwriting is perceived as an awesome chore, and the results are often illegible. They may also have difficulty learning to ride a bike and throwing and catching a ball. Such difficulties are especially detrimental for boys because these abilities help win social acceptance, and their importance as building blocks for self-esteem should not be taken lightly.

7. Unacceptable Social Behavior

Probably the most disturbing feature of ADHD, and the one most likely to be the initial cause of referral, is the difficulty that ADHD children have in complying with adult requests and prohibitions. While some may appear to forget what they are told, others may obstinately refuse to comply. Parents often describe their ADHD children as obstinate, disobedient, stubborn, bossy, sassy, and uncaring (Wender 1987).

While these children are often very adept at making initial friendships, they are unable to maintain them because they have to be the leaders, the first ones in line, the ones that make the rules. Unable to see the connection between how they treat others and the way others respond to them, they wonder why they have no friends.

8. Immaturity

It is important to remember that while all of these characteristics can be seen in all children from time to time, in ADHD children they appear to reflect the behavior of children four or five years younger. It may be helpful to consider the actions of a ten-year-old ADHD child as being much like those of a normal five-year-old (Wender 1987).

Diagnosis and Implications

The first step parents should take for a child suspected of having ADHD is a medical examination to rule out physical problems that may show similar symptoms. The second step is for a qualified physician or psychologist to diagnose the child's condition, based in part on a parent questionnaire and teacher assessments.

What are the implications of an ADHD diagnosis on a child's relationships with family and peers? This is an important area, minimized in the past, that may continue to hinder the development of self-esteem even after most or all ADHD symptoms have disappeared.

Because managing these children requires such energy, parents are likely to give more direct orders, feel they need to supervise more, and not allow the kind of freedoms that other children of the same age would be able to handle. Parents may also demonstrate unresolved anger toward their ADHD children. If self-esteem is formed on the basis of how others respond to us, it is easy to see why ADHD children often form low opinions of themselves (Wender 1987).

Peer Relationships

This attack on self-esteem occurs not only within the family, but in the ADHD child's relationships with peers. Because these children lack social skills, they often find themselves without friends. They are not invited to parties; in choosing up sides for games, they are chosen last — or not at all; and they are often teased because they react highly to teasing (Wender 1987). The area of peer relationships is one that continues to be troubling for ADHD children even when most or all of their symptoms respond to treatment. While the attitudes and reactions of adults may improve, studies have shown that peers continued to reject ADHD children even after they had successfully learned social skills.

Treating ADHD: Medication

The most common treatment for ADHD children is stimulant medication, and the three most widely used stimulants are Dexedrine, Ritalin, and Cylert. All have been highly effective in improving attention span, impulse control, restlessness, and compliance with requests from parents and teachers (Anastopoulos and Barkley 1990). Also, by being less bossy, more obedient, and better students, these children are more readily accepted by the people around them at home and in school. They feel better about themselves and about their lives in general.

While treatment with stimulant medication alone makes ADHD children more manageable and attentive in the short term, it is not clear if it will have a long-term beneficial effect on learning. Studies have shown that this type of treatment is not always a panacea (Klein and Abikoff 1989).

Treating ADHD: Therapy

Other treatments that have shown some effectiveness in reducing ADHD symptoms are behavior therapy, cognitive therapy, and combinations of these, with and without medication.

At the Attention-Deficit Hyperactivity Disorder Clinic of the University of Massachusetts Medical Center, two of the most commonly recommended treatment services are parent training and parent counseling (Anastopoulos and Barkley 1990). Even when medication is used, parents must possess the knowledge and skills to manage their ADHD children on evenings and weekends, when medication is usually not taken, and medication-improved behavior may not be maintained.

Parents must also be aware that ADHD children often exhibit forms of psychosocial behavior that cannot be helped through medication, such as aggression, diminished self-esteem, depression, and lack of appropriate social skills (Anastopoulos and Barkley 1990).

Behavior Management

The use of behavior management principles is one way parents can minimize ADHD symptoms and establish positive new behaviors. Behavior therapy is based on the assumption that ADHD children need clear, consistent, and immediate consequences for their behavior (Gordon et al. 1991).

One approach for parents is the use of negative consequences. For example, simply ignoring an attention-seeking behavior is one effective way to eliminate it, particularly with younger children. There are a number of other effective behavior modification techniques, but of paramount importance is the coordination of such efforts between parents and educators.

How Educators Can Help

Because the problems of ADHD children spill over into school, effective classroom intervention is needed. Teachers should know and be able to use the same behavior modification principles used by parents. In addition, however, teachers can benefit from classroom management suggestions like these:
- Maintain a structured program for ADHD children.
- Have them practice positive behaviors repeatedly until they internalize them.
- Give them work paced to fit their capabilities.
- Keep a daily checklist to help them stay focused on their behavior. (Pugliese 1992).

The success of school interventions is dependent not only on the range of cognitive strategies used,

but on a high level of communication and cooperation between parents and educators. The main goal is to instill self-control and reflective problem-solving skills in ADHD children.

However, behavior and cognitive therapies also have some limitations. Research has found, for example, that treatment focused on one academic or social skill does not tend to transfer to another area. It appears that behavior therapy needs to be instituted in each specific setting, and that the success of cognitive therapy is highly dependent on the ability of an adult to provide the needed learning cues and encouragement.

Because successful treatment of ADHD by medication and/or therapy has thus far been elusive, we are left with the realization that affected children need individualized, broadly based, and long-term intervention, and that those who help these children must sustain a high level of optimism, enthusiasm, and energy throughout their involvement (Pfiffner and Barkley 1990).

Is ADHD Curable?

There is no one-shot cure for ADHD. One theory is that treatment intervention is required until the brain matures and is able to produce adequate amounts of required chemicals (Wender 1987). Another theory is that ADHD is a lifestyle rather than an acute disorder and therefore cannot be completely eliminated (Whalen and Henker 1991).

Even though symptoms may diminish or disappear in over half of all ADHD children as they move into adolescence and adulthood, many of them will continue to have symptoms well into their adult years. Psychiatrists recognize an adult form of ADHD as Attention Deficit Disorder, Residual Type (ADD/RT).

For the present, research indicates that ADHD children will derive the greatest benefit from multimodal treatment strategies that combine various therapeutic approaches. But

such treatment requires a long-term, consistent effort by both parents and educators.

Karen Durbin, a teacher at Southwest Elementary School in Belton, Texas, is working toward a master's degree in educational counseling at the University of Mary Hardin Baylor in Belton.

References

Anastopoulos, A. D., and Barkley, R. A. "Counseling and Training Parents." in R. A. Barkley (ed.), *Attention-Deficit Hyperactivity Disorder: A Handbook for Diagnosis and Treatment.* New York: Guilford Press, 1990.

Garber, S. W.; Garber, M. D.; and Spizman, R. F. *If Your Child Is Hyperactive, Inattentive, Impulsive, Distractible: Helping the ADD (Attention Deficit Disorder) / Hyperactive Child.* New York: Villard Books, 1990.

Gordon, M.; Thomason, D.; Cooper, S.; and Ivers, C. L. "Nonmedical Treatment of ADHD/Hyperactivity: The Attention Training System." *Journal of School Psychology* 29 (Summer 1991): 151-152.

Klein, R. G.; and Abikoff, H. "The Role of Psychostimulants and Psychosocial Treatments in Hyperkinesis." In T. Sagvolden and T. Archer (eds.), *Attention Deficit Disorder: Clinical and Basic Research.* New York: Lawrence Erlbaum Associates, 1989.

Pfiffner, L. J.; and Barkley, R. A. "Educational Placement and Classroom Management. In R. A. Barkley (ed.), *Attention-Deficit Hyperactivity Disorder: A Handbook for Diagnosis and Treatment.* New York: Guilford Press, 1990.

Pugliese, Frank. Lecture notes by author, March 10, 1992.

Wender, P. H. *The Hyperactive Child, Adolescent, and Adult: Attention Deficit Disorder through the Lifespan.* New York: Oxford University Press, 1987.

Whalen, C. K.; and Henker, B. "Therapies for Hyperactive Children: Comparisons, Combinations, and Compromises." *Journal of Consulting and Clinical Psychology* 59:1 (February 1991): 126-135.

Whalen, C. K.; and Henker, B. "Social Impact of Stimulant Treatment for Hyperactive Children." *Journal of Learning Disabilities* 24:4 (April 1991): 231.

LEARNING STYLES/NEEDS

Attention Deficit Disorders: A Guide for Teachers

Prepared by the Education Committee of CH.A.D.D. (Children With Attention Deficit Disorders)

Recommendations for Giving Instructions to Students:

1. Maintain eye contact with the ADD student during verbal instruction.
2. Make directions clear and concise. Be consistent with daily instructions.
3. Simplify complex directions. Avoid multiple commands.
4. Make sure ADD student comprehends before beginning the task.
5. Repeat in a calm, positive manner, if needed.
6. Help ADD child to feel comfortable with seeking assistance (most ADD children won't ask).
7. These children need more help for a longer period of time than the average child. Gradually reduce assistance.
8. Require a daily assignment notebook if necessary.
   a. Make sure student correctly writes down all assignments each day. If the student is not capable of this then the teacher should help the student.
   b. Parents and teachers sign notebook daily to signify completion of homework assignments.
   c. Parents and teachers may use notebook for daily communication with each other.

Recommendations for Students Performing Assignments:

1. Give out only one task at a time.
2. Monitor frequently. Use a supportive attitude.
3. Modify assignments as needed. Consult with special education personnel to determine specific strengths and weaknesses of the student. Develop an individualized educational program.
4. Make sure you are testing knowledge and not attention span.
5. Give extra time for certain tasks. The ADD student may work more slowly. Don't penalize for needed extra time.
6. Keep in mind that ADD children are easily frustrated. Stress, pressure and fatigue can break down the ADD child's self-control and lead to poor behavior.

Recommendations for Behavior Modification and Self-Esteem Enhancement
Providing Supervision and Discipline

a. Remain calm, state infraction of rule, and don't debate or argue with student.
b. Have pre-established consequences for misbehavior.
c. Administer consequences immediately and monitor proper behavior frequently.
d. Enforce rules of the classroom consistently.
e. Discipline should be appropriate to "fit the crime," without harshness.
f. Avoid ridicule and criticism. Remember, ADD children have difficulty staying in control.
g. Avoid *publicly* reminding students on medication to "take their medicine."

Recommendations for the Proper Learning Environment:

1. Seat ADD student near teacher's desk, but include as part of regular class seating.
2. Place ADD student up front with his back to the rest of the class to keep other students out of view.
3. Surround ADD student with "good role models," preferably students that the ADD child views as "significant others." Encourage peer tutoring and cooperative collaborative learning.
4. Avoid distracting stimuli. Try not to place the ADD student near:
   air conditioner
   heater
   high traffic areas
   doors or windows
5. ADD children do not handle change well so avoid:
   transitions
   changes in schedule
   disruptions
   physical relocations (monitor closely on field trips)
6. Be creative! Produce a "stimuli-reduced study area." Let all students have access to this area so the ADD child will not feel different.
7. Encourage parents to set up appropriate study space at home with routines established as far as set times for study, parental review of completed homework, and periodic notebook and/or book bag organized.

Using Medication in the Treatment of Attention Deficit Disorders

The use of medication alone in the treatment of ADD is *not* recommended. As indicated earlier, a multimodal treatment plan is usually followed for successful treatment of the ADD child or adolescent. While not all children having ADD are prescribed medication, in certain cases the proper use of medication can play an important and necessary part in the child's overall treatment.

**Excerpt from prepared material. For more information on ADD, contact
CH.A.D.D., 499 NW 70th Ave., Suite 308, Plantation, FL 33317, 1-305-587-3700.**

Carol Zucker

Using whole language with students who have language and learning disabilities

LEARNING STYLES/NEEDS

Zucker is a learning disabilities resource teacher in the Ardsley School District, Ardsley, New York. She has worked to incorporate the whole language philosophy with students representing a wide range of abilities.

The benefits of employing instructional techniques based on a whole language philosophy to enhance literacy learning in a regular classroom are well documented (Butler & Turbill, 1984; Cambourne, 1988; Goodman, 1986; Holdaway, 1979; Weaver, 1990). Support is mounting for the value of this philosophy for students with special needs as well (Hollingsworth & Reutzel, 1988; Poplin; 1988b; Rhodes & Dudley-Maring, 1988).

Instruction for students with learning disabilities often focuses on remediating underlying ability deficits through drill and practice before academic learning can proceed (Rhodes & Dudley-Maring, 1988). In contrast to this, advocates of the whole language philosophy shift the emphasis from a deficit approach to one capitalizing on students' strengths and abilities. In such a climate "students are treated as competent rather than as deficient, as readers and writers rather than as children who have not yet learned prerequisite skills" (Weaver, 1990).

According to whole language philosophy, the fundamental basis for literacy learning emphasizes, among other things, the integration of content curriculum areas and the four related language processes of reading, writing, listening, and speaking in authentic settings. It is based on the premise that students can gain competence in these areas if they are immersed in a literate environment, given opportunities to communicate through print, and provided with supportive feedback (Sawyer, 1991).

Benefits of applying the whole language philosophy with special needs students

Employing whole language methods with special needs students facilitates the learning process by addressing their weaknesses more effectively than traditional models. First, whole language focuses on language processes and thus directly targets the basis for many of these students' learning difficulties. Because it recognizes the integrity of all learners, none is viewed as disabled or deficient (Smith-Burke, Deegan, & Jagger, 1991).

Second, the whole language philosophy emphasizes a developmental approach that enables a more individualized format and increases the likelihood that the students will meet with success. This individualization is particularly well suited to students with learning disabilities who have difficulty keeping up with the typical scope and sequence of lessons.

Third, a whole language teaching philosophy moves away from the reductionist principles that emphasize fragmented skills toward a more meaningful, integrated approach to learning subject material. Hence, the development of skills takes place within the broader context of literacy development (Weaver, 1990). This is especially helpful to students who have sequencing and organization weaknesses.

Fourth, a day in a classroom built around the whole language philosophy permits multisensory language learning experiences that are meaningful, varied, and fun. Learning is greatly enhanced for children with processing difficulties when it involves more than one modality.

Finally, adherence to a whole language philosophy enables coordination of various remedial support services in a way that replaces the fragmentation of different delivery systems of the past. Thus, instruction by the special and regular education teachers, as well as the related support personnel such as the speech and language teachers, is all organized under one thematic umbrella; each professional complementing the other's skills.

The PASS program

The following is a description of a special education class that incorporated the whole language philosophy into teaching techniques that were specially designed to enhance the literacy development of children with language-learning disabilities. This class was the youngest age group at the Concord Road Elementary School in the Ardsley School District's Program of Assisted Studies and Support (PASS), in suburban Westchester County, New York.

The PASS children were referred by the district Committee on Special Education following evaluations and recommendations by professional staff. They were identified as being language impaired and/or having learning disabilities, and in need of special class placement and additional speech and language services. Three kindergartners and two first graders started at the beginning of the year, and three more first graders entered as the year progressed. Some of the children had been in special preschool language enrichment programs, and others came directly from a regular public school setting.

The distinguishing feature of the PASS program was that it did not have self-contained special education classes. Rather, the children were assigned to a regular mainstream homeroom class and began each day there. During the remainder of the day, they divided their time about equally between their regular and special education programs. The PASS program followed the integrative-collaborative model. Thus, the children received daily instruction in many academic and nonacademic subjects in their mainstream class with the assistance of a special education teacher going into that class. Consequently, the children were pulled out of the mainstream class only when they required direct instruction by a special education teacher who employed novel teaching methods in a separate environment. Because of their language disabilities, this setting typically focused on the language arts curriculum, which was compatible with the use of whole language techniques that could be modified to creatively teach the subject material.

My class was such a setting. My main goal for these children was that they attain higher levels of literacy and improve their communication skills. My principal objective was to ensure that my students developed a perception of themselves as competent language learners who would become successful readers and writers (Smith-Burke et al., 1991). To accomplish this goal, I tried to provide them with daily multiple exposures to various kinds of oral and written language and to have them engage in interesting activities that allowed for practice and the development of fluency.

Philosophical framework

I designed my whole language classroom around Cambourne's (1988) seven conditions for successful literary acquisition. Following are some ways in which I created a learning environment compatible with Cambourne's conditions.

Immersion. The classroom environment was print-rich and filled with meaningful literary experiences that were adapted to accommodate the children's special needs. The walls were covered with environmental print (labels, signs, posters) and the children's work (including writing samples, annotated drawings, projects, charts, and small, self-made books). Author studies, both completed and in progress, were mounted for the children to track what they were reading. Everything was appropriate display material and usually coincided with the theme currently being followed.

Demonstration. My students learned through modeling, both by their fellow classmates and me. We took turns leading the class in shared readings from a big book or large print poem written on a chart. Sing-along books were especially popular, and the rhythm and beat in many of them were helpful in sustaining the students' short attention spans and in enabling them to learn new or difficult literary concepts.

Expectation. The high standards I established for the children were the key to the success of the program. I instilled in them the conviction that they would learn to read and write, although it was difficult for them. Focusing on what the children could do, rather than on what they could not, motivated them to build on that base.

Responsibility. I trusted the students to act responsibly to complete the tasks that they often chose. They were active rather than passive learners primarily because *they* directed what they were to learn. I took my cues from their interests and needs and planned a menu of activities from which they could decide what they wanted to do. This self-selection gave them a sense of ownership of their learning.

Employment. The classroom was an exciting, supportive place where children were engaged in meaningful literary processes. They had many opportunities to practice and use the skills they had acquired within this setting. Everyone had a sense of purpose and persistently pursued it, whether in a large group, a small collaborative group, in partnership with another child, or independently at one of the learning stations.

Approximation. From the very beginning, the children knew that my classroom was a safe, risk-free place to learn. Their successes were continuously rewarded, no matter how small. Because they were all at different stages of linguistic competence in their reading and writing, together we contracted individual acceptable standards of performance that were constantly modified as the students got closer to achieving their goals.

Response. Reading and writing conferences, both with classmates and with me, provided the children with opportunities to exchange ideas and receive reactions from others. We practiced how to respond to another's shared work in the author's chair by giving thoughtful comments or constructive critiques. For many of the children, being asked to express their opinions was a novel experience, and they gradually learned to trust their own judgments.

Activities based on the four integrated language processes

The classroom activities were designed to immerse the children in reading, writing, listening, and speaking on a daily basis around a central theme. Through this immersion I hoped they would become more comfortable with and engage more willingly and competently in these processes.

The daily schedule. A typical day in the PASS class consisted of a whole group time, know as "combo" time, first thing in the morning. Combo time lasted for about an hour, with all the PASS students from both kindergarten and first grade together. The focus of combo time was usually on listening and speaking activities related to a shared reading.

During the next hour and again in the afternoon, the children were divided into two smaller groups by grade level. In this "breakdown" time, the emphasis was on teaching specific reading and writing skills within a literary context appropriate to the developmental level of the children. Kindergarten children remained in the PASS class, while the first-grade children returned to their mainstream class. Then the two groups would switch; the first grade would return to the PASS class, while kindergarten rejoined the mainstream. At the end of the day, everyone would reconvene for another Combo time in the PASS room. Figure 1 visually represents the daily schedule, the process it focuses on, and the related activities.

Listening and speaking activities. Morning combo time provided a forum for discussion when the children could talk freely about anything that was on their minds. It enabled a camaraderie to grow among the children and fostered mutual respect and the ability to listen and respond to one another easily.

Following this open forum, the children formed a semicircle on the rug in front of the easel and began the morning's background building discussion for the current theme. Tapping prior knowledge was an integral part of helping children who have difficulty with temporal concepts to feel an initial connectedness to the theme; it also helped them make sense of what they would subsequently be reading by being able to relate it to their personal experiences.

Reading activities. I included several types of reading activities in both large and small group and individualized configurations. These activities, which are described below, were designed to enhance the children's facility with print, promote their use of effective comprehension strategies, and boost their confidence.

• *Large group shared reading activities.* Combo time flowed naturally into the shared reading, using either a big book or an enlarged print poem copied on a chart. Before

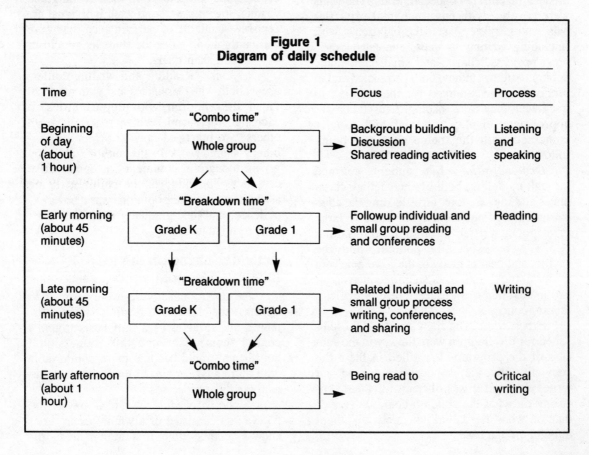

**Figure 1
Diagram of daily schedule**

Time	Focus	Process
	"Combo time"	
Beginning of day (about 1 hour) — Whole group	Background building Discussion Shared reading activities	Listening and speaking
	"Breakdown time"	
Early morning (about 45 minutes) — Grade K / Grade 1	Followup individual and small group reading and conferences	Reading
	"Breakdown time"	
Late morning (about 45 minutes) — Grade K / Grade 1	Related Individual and small group process writing, conferences, and sharing	Writing
	"Combo time"	
Early afternoon (about 1 hour) — Whole group	Being read to	Critical writing

They loved hearing selections repeatedly, so I would allow extra time to give each child a turn to recite the selection in front of the class using a pointer. This made them feel important and served to reinforce the vocabulary and strengthen their fluency. Now that they were all partners in the teaching process they became more attentive and involved.

the first read-through the children would discuss and predict what they thought would happen in the story and why. On the second reading, I would demonstrate relevant phrasing and expression, and emphasize the pronunciation of new vocabulary. I used shared reading time for teaching language skills, reading strategies, story structure, and print conventions through think-alouds. I would also target certain unique features of the story, such as dialogue, rhyming words, or repetitive parts. The children responded eagerly, and I was able to keep their attention for relatively long periods of time.

They loved hearing selections repeatedly, so I would allow extra time to give each child a turn to recite the selection in front of the class using a pointer. This made them feel important and served to reinforce the vocabulary and strengthen their fluency. Now that they were all partners in the teaching process, they became more attentive and involved!

A poignant example of the self-assurance they came to feel was when John came up to me one day brandishing a miniature copy of *The Very Hungry Caterpillar* (Carle, 1979). "I want to read this to the class," he announced, "the way you do. I know how. I practiced at home with my Mom!" "OK," I replied, delighted, "but perhaps it would be easier for the class to see the pictures if you use this larger copy," I said as I withdrew the regular size version from our class library and showed it to him. "No," he stated emphatically. "I want to use my copy. While I read, *you* can point to the pictures in that book," he directed. And that was how we did it. John had gained enough confidence in his ability to read that he was prepared to do so in front of everyone, as he had seen me do every day.

• *Small group follow-up reading activities.* I tried to incorporate additional types of daily follow-up reading experiences that were related to the previous shared reading. Three or four children would engage in a guided reading activity if small books were available to accompany the big book we had read that day. During this time the children would discuss the story in more detail, and/or retell it to the group with each child picking up the story line from where the last person left off. Sometimes we would record this new version on tape. At other times we would invent new characters or make up a new ending for the story.

Several children might also listen independently to the book on a tape while following along with the text and then try to read sections that they were able to. They particularly enjoyed reading with a partner or a student from another class who would often help them over the tough spots.

Frequently, I would be just an outside observer as the children gathered around in a circle and had their own informal book talk.

• *Individualized reading activities.* Daily the children took home a little book from the Wright Group's Sunshine or Story Box reading collection. These little books were placed in manila envelopes that were signed on the front by a parent when the reading was completed. This home reading was preceded by an individual conference in class with me. During the conference we would predict the book's content by its cover and title page and read through it together; we would then discuss the text briefly, giving particular attention to any unique literary features of the book, like unusual pictures or rhyming words. I would also use this opportunity to address whatever specific strategy instruction students required. The following day when students brought the little book back to class, each of them would buddy up with a reading partner and read the book to the partner as I listened from nearby. When they were through, either I or the partner would initial the sheet on the front of their envelope. In this way, a record was maintained of what the children had read which served as a visual reinforcement of their progress. Because the children had read a new book almost every night, they accumulated an impressive list of books, which did wonders for improving their self-esteem and motivation.

Each little book was reread several times at home and at school in order to develop students' reading fluency. Repetition and practice were necessary for achieving fluency; the ability to read fluently was pivotal to changing the children's perception of themselves as able readers.

Because we focused on meaning, the emphasis during the reading process was shifted away from reading with perfect pronunciation or phrasing, to developing strategies that utilized contextual, semantic, and graphophonic clues to improve comprehension.

The children also kept a reading-response log in which they made entries after they completed their books. They could write or draw anything about the book that they wished, as long as they varied the format from day to day. One day Frank wrote the following about the book *Ratty-Tatty* (Cowley, 1987):

> Ratty-tatty is to clever. He stol the wumen egg. The man and the wumen and the cat put the snape trap. I like the part of the book wen the cat stol the catfish.

They now saw themselves as capable readers who could read independently for a variety of purposes; they were willing to read to others, able to think and write about what they read, and comfortable picking up a book to read for their own enjoyment during independent reading time. The real evidence of their empowerment was seeing the children so excited about doing something that had always been very hard for them in light of their language difficulties.

Writing activities. As with reading, I tried to include different types of writing experiences with each thematic lesson. I included both group and individual activities that were either teacher-directed and skills based or student-generated and creative. These activities were designed to develop strategies that fostered written communication for various purposes. We used a process approach, and all children's writing was always shared and celebrated. Below, I explain four types of writing included in the program.

• *Individual writing.* Almost daily, the children wrote in their learning logs about anything that they wanted to, as long as it was related in some general way to the theme. This writing encouraged the children to think about the theme and to express it in written form. For example, when we were working on an author study about Eric Carle, Julie decided to react to the book *The Very Hungry Caterpillar,* which John and I had read together the previous day. We had followed the reading with a discussion and mini science lesson about the process the caterpillar goes through before it turns into a butterfly. She drew several diagrams depicting her interpretation of the changes and wrote:

> The hug caterpillar is a butterfly becase he eat a late. I likke the part wen he get fat and he ture to a cunne. Thn he put a hol in the cuut and cum ot.

When we were studying about seeds and how plants grew, Emily was thinking about planting tomatoes in her garden when she wrote:

> I gow tlmdos becus I like tlmdos. It giv me enjnne. The tlmdos R Ymme.

She accompanied that with very elaborate pictures to illustrate what she meant.

• *Group writing.* Frequently the writing activity involved a group effort. Following a discussion related to the theme we were studying, I organized the children's comments by generating a prewriting web. Then they practiced "writing" the story orally by using the words and phrases from the web as cues and expanding on it. After several repetitions I took down exactly what they dictated onto a language experience chart. This dictation was cut up into sentence strips and placed on the bottom of a large oaktag page. Thus, children had their own pages in their own words, which they then illustrated. When the big book was complete, the children took turns reading it to the class.

Sometimes a wordless book provided the basis for the writing of a sequential story for which the children added their own words.

First, I wrote what they said on sentence strips and put the strips under the pictures to be read as a shared reading. Then these sentences were copied by the children into little books of their own, illustrated, and added to the class library.

• *Individual directed writing.* Directed writing activities were those that emphasized proper sentence form and dictionary spelling and were intended to serve as models of conventional writing or to teach a skill appropriate to the children's developmental level.

In one of their more formal practice writing activities, the children were seated in front of a pocket chart in which there were cards with their current vocabulary words. After selecting the words they wanted to use, they took the cards out of the pocket chart and arranged them on their desks in proper sentence order. Then they copied them into their writing books, adding whatever punctuation was necessary. This allowed for practice in writing conventions while they used their own ideas.

• *Individual creative writing.* As a balance to the directed approach, an unstructured

time was devoted to spontaneous, creative writing. This time was usually tied to the shared reading experience. At these times, in contrast to the directed writing, the children were encouraged to use invented spelling and any format they were comfortable with, as long as they could make their ideas understood.

When we were studying about spring, for example, we brainstormed ideas related to the season by classifying its attributes under different categories (e.g., weather, clothing, foods, likes, dislikes). The children chose to write about those qualities of spring that they especially liked and generated a list of descriptive phrases that we displayed on a wall chart. Next, the children picked out those attributes that pertained to them and made up their own complete expanded sentences. Then they wrote them in little accordion books, illustrated the books, and brought them home, each one being a unique reflection of themselves. One of the pages of Steven's book read,

> I lik wen the rain stps bekz the rainbo cms ot.

Paul wrote,

> It is wrm and You can pla awtsod.

Keith wrote,

> Levs trn green and flawrs gro.

Following a writing process approach helped these students overcome their fears of completing a task with which they had multiple difficulties. Despite perceptual-motor, language, organization, or sequencing problems, the children knew that they had ample time and successive stages of rewrites to go through before the final product was complete. Thus, they became less inhibited about writing and very proud to become authors. It was especially rewarding when their work was published.

• *Culminating activity.* As a final activity at the end of each day, the whole group would come together again for another shared discussion time and a chance to hear their teacher read to them from a book related to the current theme or author study. The primary emphasis at this time was on strengthening listening and critical thinking skills through higher level questioning techniques. Final discussion time also served to reinforce the pleasure of reading so that the children would develop an appreciation for books and become lifelong readers.

Integrated speech and language through storytelling

IEP-designated speech and language services were incorporated during language arts instruction while the children were in the PASS room. The speech and language teacher and I team-taught and planned our lessons around a mutually derived theme. Thus, the speech and language work was integrated into what the children learned in the related language areas. Furthermore, our collaboration eliminated additional fragmentation of the children's day because they didn't have to be pulled out separately to receive this service. Also, as teachers we maximized our instructional potential by complementing each other's areas of expertise and learning from each other.

We decided to involve our students in a storytelling activity because it afforded the children an opportunity to use the language processes of listening, speaking, reading, and writing in an integrated, purposeful way. In addition to language growth, it provided a setting where the children could develop more poise and voice clarity, strengthen memory, and stimulate imagery (Hamilton & Weiss, 1990).

It was springtime, and we were in the middle of a thematic unit on seeds and plants. Because it tied into our theme, we decided to use *Jack and the Beanstalk* as the basis for our storytelling vehicle. We planned activities that required the children to use all their modalities to facilitate their remembering the story.

First, we read the children various versions of the story and had them choose which one they wanted to use. Next, we reread the one they picked several times and reviewed the sequence and the story structure. Third, we had the children retell the story and used flannelboard pictures of different parts of the story to cue their recall. In addition, using special stenciled copies of these pictures, children colored and cut out their own set of storyboard pictures and took them home each night to practice again in front of their families. Fourth, we had them practice retelling the story into a tape recorder so that they could hear the tempo and clarity of their presentation and improve their performance. Fifth, we

Using whole language

60

showed them a filmstrip of the story to help them visualize it through another medium. Then they made their own copies of the book and illustrated them. We thought that experiencing the story might also help the children to remember it better, so we had them act it out, with each child bringing in props from home, making a playbill, and taking turns playing different roles. Finally, after they had rehearsed many times using the flannelboard pieces to trigger their memory, children who wanted to became storytellers in their mainstream classes. Scotty, a child who had been reticent and unsure of himself throughout the year, exclaimed, "Wow! I never thought I could do this. I didn't think I'd ever be able to remember all the parts of the story when I saw everyone looking at me!" It was gratifying for us to see how far he had come.

Author studies

Team teaching was integral to coordinating whole language themes between the student's regular and special education classrooms. To ensure greater consonance between the two settings, the students' mainstream teacher, Mrs. Leo, and I collaborated a great deal. One way in which we did this was when we were conducting an in-depth study of an author.

We would use two basic approaches. The first was for each of us to conduct the same author study but at different times. If the children had already heard one of the author's books in one class (for example, the PASS class), then we appointed those students the resident experts in their other class (for example, their mainstream class). Each expert was given the responsibility of leading the discussion about the author and the book and even asking the class some questions. The children often announced how privileged they were to be able to do this.

In the second approach, both of us conducted the same author study simultaneously. In this case, Mrs. Leo and I had our students read a similar core of books by a selected author, and then extended our readings to include additional books by that author, which we chose separately. This permitted both some overlap and some differentiation. We similarly divided up our follow-up activities. We did one project that was the same and several that were different from each other. They included

dramatizing a story or writing in the same genre, style, or format as the author. We usually allowed the children to choose which project they wanted to do, and whether they wanted to do it in the mainstream or PASS class. This choice afforded them the opportunity to decide where they were most comfortable, thus increasing their likelihood of success. Oftentimes they chose to do both sets of activities.

One positive outgrowth of these author studies was the children's increased familiarity with authors and their works. After a visit to the school book fair one morning Peter excitedly exclaimed, "Look, Mrs. Zucker, look what I bought at the book fair." When I looked down, there was a copy of one of the Eric Carle books that we had recently read during our author study of Carle. "Now I will have a copy of my very own to read," he said proudly. He then marched over to the Eric Carle display poster we had mounted on the wall and emphatically pointed to the name of the book that he had just bought, which was on the list. "See, here's *Swimmy*," he said, and then went on to read all the other titles on the list. "The next time I go, I'm going to get *The Mixed-Up Chameleon* too!" I could not have wished for a better carry-over from our lesson. Peter had become knowledgeable about an author and his books and was excited about literature. He had the makings of a lifelong reader!

The value of whole language techniques

Providing an educational environment that is influenced by a whole language teaching/learning philosophy is very beneficial to children who are language impaired and learning disabled. Instruction based on whole language tenets creates a climate for improvement because it compensates for those factors that often cause students with language and learning disabilities the most trouble.

Learning was facilitated through the use of a multimodality approach in which reading, writing, listening, and speaking were frequently presented throughout the day using the visual, auditory, and kinesthetic channels. Further, each of these language areas was reinforced by varying interrelated methods of presentation and use. Thus, reading was taught through shared reading, guided reading, independent reading, choral reading, sustained silent reading, paired partner reading with a classmate or parent, or listening to a book on tape. Writing was similarly strengthened through observation and modeling from language experience charts, dictation, response journals, creative stories, expository writing, wordless books with provided captions, learning logs, and published students' work from both group and individual efforts.

Speaking and listening skills were developed collaboratively by both the speech and language teacher and me through strategy building activities that correlated with the theme and supported the literature-based reading and writing lessons. These activities focused on improving the children's communication ability and social skills by teaching them to better attend and respond to oral information from both adults and peers. This was accomplished through role-playing, drama, storytelling, sing-alongs, audiotapes, games, flannelboard stories, and formal and informal discussion groups.

The strong social orientation was another benefit of a whole language classroom. The interaction, fostered throughout the collaborative environment, was especially valuable in helping the children learn how to work cooperatively with peers. Partner and small group work helped the students sustain their attention and become more actively involved in what they were doing.

Another positive consequence of a whole language learning environment was that its similarity to the mainstream enabled students to move easily between both settings and feel connected to both settings. Additionally, team teaching prompted greater curriculum alignment between the regular and special education classrooms and furthered the feeling of ownership by the homeroom teachers for their special needs students. Moreover, the students were more frequently included in important aspects of the mainstream experience. Where there was overlap between the programs, the children were often able to take on leadership roles.

The improvement in the students' self-esteem was typified by a comment made by Mrs. Golden as two of them returned to her mainstream kindergarten class. "Mrs. Zucker," she remarked with a grin, "you'd better do something about your children's behavior. They are feeling too full of themselves today!" For students who had started the year with a defeatist attitude, these words were like music to my ears!

When they entered the PASS program, all except one child were achieving at a basic readiness level in both reading and writing according to informal preassessment measures. They had literacy skills that were only sporadically applied in the reading/writing process and were linguistically weak in both the receptive and expressive language areas.

Positive gains were made by the children in all the language areas according to several assessment measures. Portfolios of the children's progress, including quarterly samples of the children's multipurpose writing products, running records, skills checklists, anecdotal records, journals, tape recordings of their reading and speaking, and informal evaluations, displayed growth in linguistic competence across the four language areas of reading, writing, listening, and speaking. Posttesting in June, via the Peabody Individual Achievement Test-R, revealed that almost all of the children gained at least a year or more from the program and were now achieving at beginning- to mid-first-grade level. Children who began the program earlier in the school year evidenced more growth than those who entered later in the year. Some of the children, though still experiencing language difficulties at the end of the year, were outperforming many of their grade-level peers in the mainstream population in both reading and writing ability. In their final reports, some of the mainstream teachers described the children's growth: "Peter has gained self-confidence and is proud of his performance." "Julie has shown improvement in her ability to think critically." "Emily has started to use some original thoughts in her work."

The lasting impact of incorporating a literature-based whole language teaching/learning philosophy in the education of students with language and learning disabilities was that it changed their attitudes and literacy enactments so that they came to see themselves as readers and writers, rather than as failures. They evolved into successful students who were able to employ alternative strategies for achieving independent learning. They were more sociable and communicative because of their experiences in a supportive environment that fostered their development.

Using whole language

References

Butler, A., & Turbill, J. (1984) *Towards a reading-writing classroom.* Rosebery, NSW, Australia: Bridge Printery.

Cambourne, B. (1988). *The whole story: Natural learning and the acquisition of literacy in the classroom.* Auckland, New Zealand: Scholastic.

Goodman, K. (1986). *What's whole in whole language?* New York: Heinemann.

Hamilton, M., & Weiss, M. (1990). *Children tell stories.* Katonah, NY: Richard C. Owen.

Holdaway, D. (1979). *The foundations of literacy.* Sydney, Australia: Ashton Scholastic.

Hollingsworth, P., & Reutzel, D. (1988). Whole language with LD children. *Academic Therapy, 23*, 477-481.

Poplin, M.S. (1988a) The reductionist fallacy in learning disabilities: Replicating the past by reducing the present. *Journal of Learning Disabilities, 21*, 389-400.

Poplin, M.S. (1988b) Holistic/constructionist principles of the teaching/learning process: Implications for the field of learning disabilities. *Journal of Learning Disabilities, 21*, 401-416.

Rhodes, L., & Dudley-Marling, C. (1988). *Readers and writers with a difference: A holistic approach to teaching learning disabled and remedial students.* Portsmouth, NH: Heinemann.

Sawyer, D.J. (1991). Whole language in context: Insights into the current debate. *Topics in Language Disorders, 11*, 1-13.

Smith-Burke, T., Deegan, D., & Jagger, A. (1991). Whole language: A viable alternative for special and remedial education? *Topics in Language Disorders, 11*, 58-68.

Weaver, C. (1990). *Understanding whole language: From principles to practice.* Portsmouth, NH: Heinemann.

Trade books cited

Carle, E. (1979). *The very hungry caterpillar.* New York: Putnam Publishing Group.

Carle, E. (1991). *The mixed-up chameleon.* New York: HarperCollins.

Cowley, J. (1987). *Ratty-tatty.* Bothell, WA: The Wright Group Sunshine Series.

Reprinted with permission of Carol Zucker and the International Reading Association.

Voices

It seems that any learning associated with creating meaning through any medium typically involves some kind of struggle before the full potential of that medium is under control — art, music and mime, as well as print. Furthermore, there appears to be something genuinely pleasurable derived from the struggle which is experienced in these situations. Remove the struggle and you remove the pleasure.

Brian Cambourne
The Whole Story: Natural Learning and the Acquisition of Literacy in the Classroom.

Published by Scholastic Professional Books.

Slow Learners: Students at Risk

by Kaye Johns, Founder and President
The Center for Success in Learning

The following is an address by Kaye Johns, founder and president of The Texas Center for Success in Learning before the Texas Commissioner of Education's Advisory Committee on the 1990-94 Long-Range Plan for Public Education. Johns, a well-known author and topic presenter on the subject of slower learners, has served on three TEA Advisory Committees during the development of rules for Alternatives to Social Promotion and frequently testifies before the State Board of Education.

We believe it is important for the State Board of Education, its Long-Range Plan, and individual school districts to clearly delineate slower learners as part of the at-risk student population.

When slower learners are not mentioned specifically, it is presumed that they should be able to do grade level work, to keep up academically with their peers — and when they don't, it is their fault because they are not motivated, or not trying hard enough. They are blamed because they don't learn as quickly as other children. They are set up to fail.

If they are not identified as a group with significant learning problems, there is no call to action, no reason to do anything differently in the classroom. The assumption is that all children with learning problems are served by special education, and all other students should be able to master nine months of information in nine months' time in a traditional classroom setting.

The basic presumption of "Alternatives to Social Promotion" is that being "at risk" is a temporary condition for students, who should be "remediated" or caught up, when placed in alternative programs or given modifications in classrooms. Slower learners have problems that are not temporary and that are not resolved in one year's time in the classroom. These students are likely to remain academically at risk from kindergarten through grade 12.

And yet, without an acknowledgment of the severity of their problems, slower learners are expected to maintain passing grades of 70, stay on grade level with their peers, earn 21 Carnegie Credits to graduate, and pass the TEAMS Exit Exam just like the other students. Is this realistic?

It didn't used to be. That's why slower learners were so often socially promoted before educational reform. They couldn't keep up and stay on grade level with their peers. If they were unable to keep up *before* educational reform raised the standards, *how will they keep up now?*

Slower learners have not changed. The world has changed. Education has changed, standards have risen — but these students, with their limited capacity to learn, are still the same.

Are we saying these students cannot learn? Cannot one day graduate?

Absolutely not! But we are saying that unless we change the way most of them are being taught, particularly in secondary schools, many of them may not have a chance.

Who is the Slower Learning Student?

We acknowledge that there is no agreed-upon definition of the slower learner. But in general, educators agree that these students are caught in that grey area between average and retarded, generally IQ 70-89.

We are talking about 22% of the population who fall within this IQ range, one in five.

We are the first to acknowledge that IQ scores are imperfect and can be biased. But IQ scores are used to qualify students for special education as well as gifted/talented programs, so they are respected in the educational community.

IQ does not measure a student's grit, drive, determination, ambition, tenacity or perseverance. It doesn't tell us whether the student is lazy or motivated, an under-achiever or an over-achiever — because slower learners are as individual as the rest of us. Nor does it tell us what kind of home students come from, what kind of love and support they receive.

IQ tests do not guarantee a student's success in life — *but they are one of the best predictors we have to indicate a student's likely difficulty in learning, in doing grade level work in school.*

Students Learn at Different Rates

Although the following chart illustrates how far behind slower learners typically are by the time they enter the ninth grade, we know this doesn't just happen in the 8th grade. These students are usually not fully on grade level at the end of their first or second grade, and they fall gradually further behind every year.

This chart is surely our challenge. What would happen if slower learners were picked up in kindergarten and given individualized instruction according to what we know works with these students? Examples are: multi-sensory teaching, peer tutoring, small group techniques, accommodations for learning styles and perceptual strengths, modifications to supplement textbooks with study guides and other materials on an appropriate reading level, tests adapted for clarity, and appropriate study

	9th Grade	12th Grade
IQ 75	5th grade, 5 months	7th grade, 7 months
IQ 80	6th grade, 2 months	8th grade, 6 months
IQ 85	6th grade, 9 months	9th grade, 5 months

skills. If so, might these students do much better than this chart predicts?

Still, this chart stands on historical data as an illustration of the frustration and sense of failure that is constantly reinforced as we expect these students to do grade level work — and their teachers to be able to "catch them up."

Here are educators' comments:

"Students whose mental ability places them in the slow learner range (IQ 70-90) are — because of their limited ability — low achievers. Yet the general public (including the press, state legislators, and members of boards of education) in the current push for minimum competency testing for high school graduation seems largely unaware that no amount of testing, no setting of competencies, and no establishment of standards and remedial programs can cause these students to achieve beyond the limits of their intellectual capacity.

"The public expects that students not in special education should achieve at grade level or at the national average. They do not realize that, by definition of the word 'average,' as many students must be below this mark as above it."

Howard G. Dunlap, "Minimum Competency Testing and the Slow Learner," *Educational Leadership*, Vol. 367, pp. 327-328.

Slower Learners — More Than Half of the Dropouts

If we accept that most slower learning students will be 2-4 years below grade level in their basic skills when they *enter* high school, it is easy to see how they fit into the at-risk population.

"The single best predictor of whether or not a student will drop out of school is his or her level of academic achievement. The typical at-risk student has mathematics or reading skills two or more years below grade level and is not maintaining a scholastic average of 70%."

"Characteristics of At-Risk Youth," *TEA Practitioner's Guide*, Series No. One, p. 26.

"The most common reason for leaving school is poor academic performance . . . . A majority of all dropouts in the National Longitudinal Survey had basic skills in the bottom 20% of the score distribution."

Andrew Hahn, "Reaching Out to America's Dropouts: What to Do?" *Phi Delta Kappan*, Dec. 1987, pp. 256-263.

"It has been estimated that as many as one-third of all students attending school today will drop out before graduation. Of these, more than half could be described as slow learners."

H. Hodgkinson, "Today's Numbers, Tomorrow's Nation." *Education Week*, May 14, 1986, pp. 14-15.

Many Other At-Risk Programs

As at-risk students and their problems are studied, programs are springing up everywhere to help with identified problems — drug and alcohol abuse, teenage pregnancy, counseling for students who are abused, depressed, suicidal. We see a renewed emphasis on helping students with self-esteem; we are working with cultural issues; we are addressing students' needs when they have English as a second language.

When a problem is identified, we develop programs, policies, and strategies to deal with it. Every-one — from the Legislature to the local school board to the district administrative staff, local campus administrators, teachers, parents — even the public — is aware of the need to do something to solve the problem.

When the problem is not identified, it is overlooked at best, or considered not to exist at worst.

This is the primary reason we feel it is imperative that we let parents, teachers and the public know that some children who are not served by special education still have significant problems learning.

We must do something to help teachers learn what works with these children — because research is showing us many things do.

What Works with Slower Learners, Works with Many Other At-Risk Students

Slower learners and other at-risk students do not do well in traditional classroom settings (straight rows, no moving, not talking) with a standard textbook/lecture format. They need multi-sensory teaching through high school.

It is clear from both research and classroom application that the following strategies work for slower learners and other at-risk students, and most students in general:
• Multi-sensory teaching
• Peer and cross-age tutoring
• Small group techniques
• Mixed ability classes, heterogeneous groupings
• Increasing the time spent on a single subject
• Teaching to students' perceptual strengths
• Informal classroom design
• Changing the time of day for testing
• Matching student's strongest period of day with testing time and major academic subjects
• Smaller student/teacher ratio
• Technology/media-assisted instruction
• Extending the classroom to the community

But Aren't Those Simply Good Teaching Principles, Period?

Of course they are. And based on the feedback received from teacher workshops, these techniques are much more likely to be utilized by elementary teachers, although by no means are all elementary teachers taking advantage of these strategies. Why not? Why do many classes still fall into the traditional textbook/lecture pattern at the fourth grade level, or sooner? Why are 95% of academic high school classes still taught in the traditional classroom setting with a textbook/lecture format?

> **We must have high expectations for all children, just as we must believe that all children can learn. But all children cannot learn in the same way, or at the same rate, or even with the same amount of information . . . . We must recognize, respect and support the learning differences in children.**

One reason is that even though most students will do better with the above techniques, they will not be hurt if these techniques are not used. Students with average, or above average intelligence have been making it through school academically for a long time. Some of them may not be excelling as they could and should and probably would if these strategies were used, but they haven't been pushed out of school because they weren't.

Slower learners, on the other hand, are students living on the edge. For them, the difference between a teacher who utilizes the previously mentioned techniques and one who doesn't can make the difference between passing and failing, graduating or not.

Let's identify slower learners specifically as students who have needs to be addressed. Otherwise, where will the impetus, the urgency, for changing what happens in the classroom come from?

But wait! We shouldn't label students!

And yet, we do. We have "labeled" students gifted and talented, honors, learning disabled, emotionally disturbed, visually, auditorily or physically impaired, mentally retarded, minority, transient, economically disadvantaged, non-English speaking, home ec, vocational, and so on.

Why do we have these labels? Because they provide access into services in the school. They describe the program that the student has which has been identified, or they describe the program where the student is placed.

Who says we haven't already labeled slower learners?
• Ask anyone who the "students who fall through the cracks" are.
• Or ask about "shadow children," slower learners in the shadow of the system.
• Or the students in the grey area.
• Or the "dull."
• Or the "borderline."
• Or the "marginal."

We prefer *slower learner* because it emphasizes a positive — these students learn, but they learn slowly.

Think of the cost to the students when we don't identify their problem. Parents often punish them for not trying. Teachers crack down because the children aren't paying attention. Other kids think they're dumb because they don't have any apparent problem. The students feel it's all their fault. If they were better, tried harder, worked longer, then they could learn.

Learning disabled and mentally retarded students don't have to face that. They know they have a problem that isn't their fault, that it is something they have to come to terms with.

All Children Can Learn

We must have high expectations for all children, just as we must believe that all children can learn. But all children cannot learn in the same way, or at the same rate, or even with the same amount of information. More time will not make a slower learner a brain surgeon. We must recognize, respect and support the learning differences in children.

And we must have high but realistic expectations. We do not expect our "C" students to win scholarships to Harvard or Yale, and we do not hold average students to the same goals and expectations as our gifted/talented students. Why then, must we insist that students with below average intelligence meet the same expectations as students with average and above average intelligence? Why do we set them up to fail over and over again? It doesn't take long until they don't even try.

As long as we don't use the term "slower learner" — or some other legitimate, identifying term — to describe these children, we leave them and their parents and their teachers shadow boxing. They can't attack the problem because they don't even know what it is.

When we don't say "slower learner," we're saying it isn't okay to be a slower learner. And it must be. It has to be, because all children are not alike. They cannot be the same.

This article appeared in Instructional Leader, *a publication of the Texas Elementary Principals and Supervisors Association, February 1990. For further information, contact The Center for Success in Learning, 17000 Preston Rd. #400, Dallas, TX 75248, 1-800-488-9435.*

INTEGRATING

INTEGRATING
INTEGRATING

Elementary Students with Multiple Disabilities into Supported Regular Classes

Challenges and Solutions

Susan Hamre-Nietupski   Jennifer McDonald   John Nietupski

Integrated placement of students with multiple disabilities in regular classes (Strully & Strully, 1989) is being advocated by professionals and parents alike. With this model, assistance is provided in the areas of curriculum modification, participation, and social integration by special education/support teachers, paraprofessionals, integration facilitators (Ruttiman & Forest, 1987), and/or nondisabled peers (Forest & Lusthaus, 1990). Students with disabilities are offered increased opportunities for interactions with nondisabled peers as well as meaningful curricular content (Ford & Davern, 1989; Sailor et al., 1989; York, Vandercook, Caughey, & Heise-Neff, 1990).

> *Students with disabilities are offered increased opportunities for interactions with nondisabled peers as well as meaningful curricular content.*

The professional literature has described strategies for preparing regular educators and students for positive integration experiences (Certo, Haring, & York, 1984; Gaylord-Ross, 1989; Stainback & Stainback, 1985) and for teaming special educators with regular educators to promote regular class integration (Vandercook, York, & Forest, 1989; York & Vandercook, 1991). One practical concern for teachers is how they can promote both skill gains and social acceptance while involving students in regular class activities.

This article describes four potential challenges to supported education along with solutions that have been effective in meeting those challenges in an elementary school setting. Our observations are based on 4 years of experience in integrating students with multiple disabilities, including students with moderate and severe mental disabilities or autism with accompanying physical, visual, and/or behavior challenges. Our efforts focused on integrating elementary-age students into kindergarten through sixth-grade classes.

Background

The case of Stephanie, a first-grader, illustrates points in each challenge and solution. Stephanie was a student with multiple disabilities, including mental retardation in the moderate to severe range with accompanying physical disabilities and a vision impairment. She attended a 350-student elementary school in a midwestern community of 35,000 people. When Stephanie was kindergarten age, she spent half her day in a regular kindergarten class. The following year, she spent the entire school day in a regular first-grade class.

Challenges and Solutions

Challenge 1: Providing Functional Curriculum in a Regular Class

Instruction on the functional skills necessary to live, work, and participate in recreation activities in integrated community environments is a critical component of an appropriate education for students with multiple disabilities (Falvey, 1989). Since functional skills such as grooming and dressing rarely are taught in regular education, a challenge to supported education is how to teach these skills in the primarily academic environment of a regular class.

Five possible solutions might be considered to address this challenge. First, partial assistance might be provided by a peer in the context of class activities. For example, when Stephanie arrived at school in the winter, she could remove her boots easily. However, putting on her shoes was time-consuming, and she often missed out on much of the opening routine. One solution was to have Stephanie remove her boots upon arrival and take her shoes to the opening-group area. There she was taught to ask a nondisabled peer for assistance in putting on and tying her shoes. The peer was shown how to assist Stephanie with the difficult steps while encouraging her independence on the easier steps. This solution resulted in positive interactions between Stephanie and her peers, enabled her to take part in the opening routine, and allowed her to progress in this self-care skill.

A second strategy is to identify the "down times" during the school day in which functional skill instruction could be provided without disrupting the class routine. For example, Stephanie often had a runny nose and had not yet learned to blow her nose independently. The support teacher took her aside at such times as arrival, between academic activities, and prior to and after recess and lunch for brief, unobtrusive instruction. As a result, she missed very little regular class activity and she showed increased independence by the end of the school year.

A third potential solution is to provide parallel instruction on functional skills in the regular classroom while peers participate in their academic work. For example, when the nondisabled students were working on place value in mathematics, part or all of that period could be spent teaching Stephanie functional mathematics skills such as matching coins or other skills. One regular teacher reduced the possible stigma associated with parallel programming by identifying nondisabled students who needed similar instruction and rotating them through the self-care lessons with Stephanie. Since the teacher referred to this as a "health" or "hygiene" unit and involved nondisabled students, Stephanie was not singled out as different from her peers. Nondisabled children can benefit from this functional life skills instruction as well as their peers who have disabilities.

When none of the previously mentioned strategies seems feasible, brief removal of the student from the regular class for specialized instruction might be considered. For example, when nondisabled students receive instruction on academic activities clearly beyond the student's present skill level, instruction on functional skills such as bathroom use, snack preparation, and street-crossing outside the classroom may be more appropriate.

Finally, to guarantee that instructional time is not sacrificed, districts should ensure that individualized education program (IEP) goals are drawn from an approved curriculum guide (e.g., Falvey, 1989; Ford et al., 1989). Such a guide can provide assurances that important instructional goals will not be overlooked.

Challenge 2: Providing Community-Based Instruction

Another challenge to regular class integration is including community-based instruction within the educational program. Community-based instruction is needed because of the generalization difficulties experienced by students with multiple disabilities. However, little opportunity for such instruction currently is provided to students in regular elementary education.

In addition to following an approved curriculum guide that includes community-based instruction, two strategies might be employed to address this challenge. The first is to bring the community into the classroom. An example of this strategy was implemented in conjunction with a creative writing unit in which students were required to write about turtles. In order to make this unit more meaningful to Stephanie, who had limited exposure to turtles, arrangements were made to borrow a turtle from a local pet store. After the morning visit by the turtle, Stephanie, three of her nondisabled peers, and the support teacher returned the turtle to the pet store. All four students were able to see, touch, and learn about a variety of exotic birds and animals. As Stephanie and two other students looked at the animals, another wrote down the group's favorite pets and their cost. Upon returning to school, the four wrote and shared a story about their trip and sent a thank-you note to the pet store. Thus, all four students had a community experience that was integrally related to the creative writing unit and allowed the nondisabled students to apply their skills to a meaningful situation. While use of community resources may be difficult to achieve on all units, careful consideration of such opportunities can both enhance the regular curriculum and provide opportunities for community-based instruction.

Another possible strategy involves providing community-based instruction to the student with disabilities in an integrated manner (Ford & Davern, 1989). Small groups of nondisabled students could accompany a peer with disabilities on a rotating basis. The community experiences would allow all students to apply skills being taught in the classroom to real-world settings. For example, integrated instruction in a supermarket could be structured so that a student with multiple disabilities locates various grocery items while peers practice adding costs and comparing prices.

While use of community resources may be difficult to achieve on all units, careful consideration of such opportunities can both enhance the regular curriculum and provide opportunities for community-based instruction.

Challenge 3: Scheduling Staff Coverage

Special education staff can support integrated students in many ways, including (a) making adaptations when needed; (b) assisting the classroom teacher in working with a student; (c) coaching nondisabled peers; (d) providing direct instruction; and (e) facilitating positive interactions among students. The scheduling challenge lies in providing this support when it is needed for the student to participate in classroom activities.

One solution in Stephanie's situation was for the regular education and support teachers to determine cooperatively when support was most needed. The support teacher developed a flexible schedule so she could assist Stephanie during activities that were the most challenging for her and/or were most difficult to individualize.

While scheduling support during critical periods is helpful, teachers occasionally need to support several students in several classes simultaneously. In those situations, university students or parent volunteers might provide additional support. With training, these volunteers could assist in regular classrooms when the support teacher is unable to do so.

Another strategy is to empower regular teachers to assume greater instructional responsibility for students with multiple disabilities. Our experience has been that regular teachers can be as effective as special education teachers in meeting the needs of students with disabilities. Encouraging them to do so, involving them in solving instructional problems, demonstrating particular techniques, and reinforcing accomplishments are all strategies for increasing the competence and confidence of regular class teachers.

Another strategy for dealing with the coverage challenge is to work closely with the classroom teacher to identify when and how nondisabled peers might serve in a support role. For example, activities might be designed on the basis of cooperative learning (Johnson & Johnson, 1989), whereby students become responsible for working together and assisting each other.

One additional solution to providing adequate staff coverage is to reduce class size when integrating a student with multiple disabilities. Sailor and colleagues (1989) suggested that this strategy can make support from the regular classroom teacher a more realistic option.

> *O*ur experience has been that regular teachers can be as effective as special education teachers in meeting the needs of students with disabilities.

Challenge 4: Promoting Social Integration

The final challenge addressed here is that of promoting social integration and friendships between students with and without disabilities. Strully and Strully (1989) argued that supported education is important because it facilitates the formation of friendships and long-lasting, supportive, personal relationships. Research by Guralnick (1980) has suggested that these relationships do not occur simply through integrated physical placement but must be facilitated.

Administrator Support. Administrators can facilitate friendships in several ways. First, students with multiple disabilities can be assigned to the regular school they would attend if they were not disabled, along with children from their neighborhood, making participation in after-school activities such as parties and school functions more feasible (Brown et al., 1989; Sailor et al., 1989).

Second, administrators can set the tone for integration in a school. In Stephanie's school, the principal strongly believed that all children belonged in regular classes and that promoting pos-

itive, cooperative social interactions was an important goal in each classroom. Thus, teachers had a heightened awareness of the social aspects of education and focused on promoting positive relationships among students.

Third, administrators can arrange for after-school social opportunities. Stephanie's principal was instrumental in developing monthly recreational drop-in programs and summer recreation offerings that allowed all students to socialize.

Teacher Support. Regular class teachers, too, can address the challenge of promoting social interactions and friendships. One well-documented strategy is cooperative learning (Johnson & Johnson, 1989), in which rewards and evaluations are based on the quality of the work and student collaboration.

Regular class teachers also can promote a positive social atmosphere by treating students with multiple disabilities as normally as possible. Stephanie's teacher, for example, placed Stephanie's name on the class roster and assigned her a desk, coathook, and materials space amidst those of the other students. She expected, encouraged, and reinforced adherence to classroom rules for all students, including Stephanie. These actions communicated to all students that Stephanie was as much a member of the class as anyone else.

Finally, regular class teachers can actively promote social relationships (Stainback & Stainback, 1987). Stephanie's teacher did so by pairing children for many activities, modeling and encouraging social interactions, and reinforcing students when positive interactions occurred.

Special educators, support teachers, and integration facilitators can address the challenges of promoting social interaction in several ways. They can model and encourage social interactions. Early in the school year, nondisabled students often would ask the support teacher whether or not Stephanie would like to play and whether or not she enjoyed certain activities. The support teacher would encourage the children to ask

Stephanie themselves or show them how to do so. By the end of the year, nondisabled students initiated conversation directly with Stephanie, not through her support teacher.

A second strategy is to develop sensitization sessions that focus on recognizing similarities and differences and getting along with people who are different in some way (Hamre-Nietupski & Nietupski, 1985). In Stephanie's class, her support teacher and the guidance counselor developed a six-session unit on how children are similar and different, how to be friends with those around you, and how to communicate in different ways. Activities included having all children identify their strengths and weaknesses and likes and dislikes, generate specific ways to be friends with people in the class, and learn how to initiate and respond to social interactions. These activities were carried out in a large group that included Stephanie but did not single her out.

Support teachers can develop circles of friends to promote social interactions (Forest & Lusthaus, 1990). In Stephanie's school, a student with autism was integrated into a regular fifth-grade class. The support teacher, concerned about the lack of social interaction, organized a circle of friends with nondisabled volunteer companions. This group identified in- and out-of-school interaction opportunities such as going to the library together and attending the drop-in recreation program, and they socialized with her.

Finally, support teachers can keep parents informed about interaction opportunities and encourage parental support. Stephanie's support teacher regularly kept Stephanie's parents informed about the students she interacted with and upcoming after-school events. On occasion, she even made transportation arrangements so Stephanie could participate with her peers.

Parental Support. Parental support is also necessary to promote social relationships and friendships. Parents can become active in the parent-teacher organization and in school-wide activities. They might encourage their child's participation in extracurricular activities such as Cub Scouts, Brownies, and 4-H or help in initiating play opportunities by having their child invite a nondisabled friend to spend the night or hosting or having their child attend birthday parties. Such activities are extremely im-

portant in making and maintaining friendships.

Parents also can promote social relationships through sensitivity to clothing selection and hairstyle. Nondisabled students, even in elementary schools, are keenly aware of "in" clothing. Since this a sensitive and value-laden issue, interventions may need to be quite subtle. For example, when asked, teachers might suggest holiday or birthday gift ideas for students (e.g., "I've noticed that Stephanie really likes Tracy's [name brand] sweatshirts") as a way to assist parents in facilitating social acceptance.

Conclusion

While we are encouraged by the outcomes of the strategies described here, two limitations should be noted. First, the strategies were developed for elementary-age students. Additional research and demonstration are needed to guide teachers serving older students. Second, questions have been raised about how and the degree to which students with profound, multiple disabilities might be integrated into regular classes. At this point, perhaps those questions should remain open—with practitioners and researchers encouraged to examine them through empirical demonstration activities.

Supported regular education for students with multiple disabilities is not without challenges, but potential solutions are beginning to emerge. It is our hope that, through examples such as these, increasing numbers of school systems will be encouraged to integrate elementary-age students with multiple disabilities more fully into regular education classes.

References

Brown, L., Long, E., Udarvi-Solner, A., Davis, L., VanDeventer, P., Algren, C., Johnson, F., Gruenewald, L., & Jorgensen, J. (1989). The home school: Why students with severe intellectual disabilities must attend the schools of their brothers, sisters, friends, and neighbors. *Journal of the Association for Persons with Severe Handicaps, 14,* 1-7.

Certo, N., Haring, N., & York, R. (1984). *Public school integration of severely handicapped students.* Baltimore: Paul H. Brookes.

Falvey, M. (1989). *Community-based curriculum: Instructional strategies for students with severe handicaps.* Baltimore: Paul H. Brookes.

Ford, A., & Davern, L. (1989). Moving forward with school integration: Strategies for involving students with severe handicaps in the life of the

school. In R. Gaylord-Ross (Ed.), *Integration strategies for students with severe handicaps* (pp. 11-32). Baltimore: Paul H. Brookes.

Ford, A., Schnorr, R., Meyer, L., Davern, L., Black, J., & Dempsey, P. (1989). *The Syracuse community-referenced curriculum guide for students with moderate and severe disabilities.* Baltimore: Paul H. Brookes.

Forest, M., & Lusthaus, E. (1990). Everyone belongs with the MAPS Action Planning System. *TEACHING Exceptional Children, 22,* 32-35.

Gaylord-Ross, R. (Ed.). (1989). *Integration strategies for students with severe handicaps.* Baltimore: Paul H. Brookes.

Guralnick, M. (1980). Social interactions among preschool children. *Exceptional Children, 46,* 248-253.

Hamre-Nietupski, S., & Nietupski, J. (1985). Taking full advantage of interaction opportunities. In S. Stainback & W. Stainback (Eds.), *Integration of students with severe handicaps into regular schools* (pp. 98-112). Reston, VA: The Council for Exceptional Children.

Johnson, D., & Johnson, R. (1989). Cooperative learning and mainstreaming. In R. Gaylord-Ross (Ed.), *Integration strategies for students with handicaps* (pp. 233-248). Baltimore: Paul H. Brookes.

Ruttiman, A., & Forest, M. (1987). With a little help from my friends: The integration facilitator at work. In M. Forest (Ed.), *More education/integration* (pp. 131-142). Downsview, Ontario: Roeher Institute.

Sailor, W., Anderson, J., Halvorsen, A., Doering, K., Filler, J., & Goetz, L. (1989). *The comprehensive local school: Regular education for all students with disabilities.* Baltimore: Paul H. Brookes.

Stainback, S., & Stainback, W. (Eds.). (1985). *Integration of students with severe handicaps into regular schools.* Reston, VA: The Council for Exceptional Children.

Stainback, W., & Stainback, S. (1987). Facilitating friendships. *Education and Training in Mental Retardation, 22,* 10-25.

Strully, J., & Strully, C. (1989). Friendships as an educational goal. In S. Stainback, W. Stainback, & M. Forest (Eds.), *Educating all students in the mainstream of regular education* (pp. 59-68). Baltimore: Paul H. Brookes.

Vandercook, T., York, J., & Forest, M. (1989). The McGill Action Planning System (MAPS): A strategy for building the vision. *Journal of The Association for Persons with Severe Handicaps, 14,* 205-215.

York, J., & Vandercook, T. (1991). Designing an integrated program for learners with severe disabilities. *TEACHING Exceptional Children, 23*(1), 22-28.

York, J., Vandercook, T., Caughey, E., & Heise-Neff, C. (1990, May). Regular class integration: Beyond socialization. *The Association for Persons with Severe Handicaps Newsletter, 16,* p. 3.

Susan Hamre-Nietupski *(CEC Chapter #88) is an Associate Professor, Division of Curriculum and Instruction/Special Education, The University of Iowa, Iowa City,* **Jennifer McDonald** *is a Special Educator, Adams Elementary School, Des Moines, Iowa.* **John Nietupski** *(CEC Chapter #88) is an Adjunct Associate Professor, Division of Developmental Disabilities and Division of Curriculum and Instruction, The University of Iowa, Iowa City.*

Learning Styles / Needs

Bibliography
Compiled by SDE Presenters

If you would like help locating any of these books, contact Crystal Springs Books, 1-800-321-0401.

Differently Abled

Bain, Lisa J. *A Parent's Guide to Attention Deficit Disorders*. New York: Delta, 1991.

Copeland, Edna D., and Love, Valerie L. *Attention Without Tension: A Teacher's Handbook on Attention Disorders (ADHD and ADD)*. Atlanta, GA: 3 C's of Childhood, 1990.

Fagan, S.A.; Graves, D.L. and Tressier-Switlick, D. *Promoting Successful Mainstreaming: Reasonable Classroom Accommodations for Learning Disabled Students*. Rockville, MD: Montgomery County Public Schools, 1984.

Greene, Lawrence J. *Kids Who Underachieve*. New York: Simon & Schuster, 1986.

Harwell, Joan. *Complete Learning Disabilities Handbook*. New York: Simon & Schuster, 1989.

Hunsucker, Glenn. *Attention Deficit Disorder*. Abilene, TX: Forrest Publishing, 1988.

Lerner, Janet. *Learning Disabilities*. Boston: Houghton Mifflin, 1981.

Lipsky, D.K.,& Gartner, A. *Beyond Separate Education — Quality Education For All*. Baltimore: Paul H. Brookes, 1989.

McGuinness, Diane. *When Children Don't Learn*. New York: Basic Books, 1985.

Moss, Robert A., and Dunlap, Helen Huff. *Why Johnny Can't Concentrate: Coping with Attention Deficit Problems*. NewYork: Bantam Books, 1990.

National Association of State Boards of Education. *Issues in Brief*. Vol.11, # 16. Alexandria, VA: NASBE.

Perske, R. & Perske, M. *Circle of Friends*. Nashville, TN: Abingdon Press, 1988.

Phinney, Margaret. *Reading with the Troubled Reader*. Portsmouth, NH: Heinemann, 1989.

Rhodes, Lynn, and Dudley-Marling, Curt. *Readers and Writers with a Difference: A Holistic Approach to Teaching Learning Disabled and Remedial Students*. Portsmouth, NH: Heinemann, 1988.

Rosner, Jerome. *Helping Children Overcome Learning Difficulties*. New York: Walker & Co, 1979.

_____. Visual Motor Program, Auditory Motor Program. New York: Walker & Co., 1979.

Stainback, S. and Stainback, W. *Curriculum Considerations in Inclusive Classrooms: Facilitating Learning for All Students*. Baltimore, Paul H. Brookes, 1992.

_____.*Support Networks for Inclusive Schooling*. Baltimore: Paul H. Brookes, 1990.

Stainback, S.; Stainback, W., & Forest, M., eds. "Classroom Organization for Diversity Among Students," *from Educating All Students in the Mainstream*. Baltimore: Paul H. Brookes, 1989.

Thousand, J., & Villa, R. "Strategies for Educating Learners with Severe Handicaps Within Their Local Home, Schools and Communities." *Focus on Exceptional Children*, 23 (3), 1-25, 1990.

Vail, Priscilla. *The World of the Gifted Child*. New York: Walker & Co., 1979.

_____. *Gifted, Precocious, or Just Plain Smart*. Rosemont, NJ: Programs for Education, 1987.

_____. *Smart Kids with School Problems*. New York: E.P. Dutton, 1987.

_____. *About Dyslexia*. Rosemont, NJ: Programs for Education, 1990.

_____. *Learning Styles*. Rosemont, NJ: Programs for Education, 1992.

Villa, R. et al. *Restructuring for Caring and Effective Education: Adminstrative Strategies for Creating Heterogeneous Schools.* Baltimore: Paul H. Brookes, 1992.

Dealing with Difficult and Unusual Children

Albert, Linda. *Cooperative Discipline — How to Manage Your Classroom and Promote Self-Esteem.* Circle Pines, MN: American Guidance Service, 1989.

Bluestein, Jane. *21st Century Discipline — Teaching Students Responsibility and Self Control.* New York: Scholastic, 1988.

Canfield, Jack, and Siccone, Frank. *101 Ways to Develop Student Self-Esteem and Responsibility.* Needham Heights: MA: Allyn & Bacon, 1993.

Carducci, Dewey, and Carducci, Judith. *The Caring Classroom — A Guide for Teachers Troubled by the Difficult Student and Classroom Disruption.* Menlo Park, CA: Bull Publishing, 1984.

Charles, C.M. *Building Classroom Discipline.* New York: Longman, 1992.

Curwin, Richard, and Mendler, Allen. *Discipline with Dignity.* Alexandria, VA: ASCD, 1988.

_____. *Am I in Trouble? Using Discipline to Teach Young Children Responsibility.* Santa Cruz, CA: Network Publications, 1990.

Dreikurs, Rudolf, and Goldman, Margaret. *The ABC's of Guiding the Child.* Chicago: The Alfred Adler Institute, 1990.

Glasser, William. *Control Theory in the Classroom.* New York: Harper & Row, 1986.

Knight, Michael et al. *Teaching Children to Love Themselves.* Hillside, NJ: Vision Press, 1982.

Kreidler, William. *Creative Conflict Resolution (K-6 Activities for Keeping Peace in the Classroom).* Glenview, IL: Scott, Foresman & Co., 1984.

Kuykendall, Crystal. *From Rage to Hope: Strategies for Reclaiming Black & Hispanic Students.* Bloomington, IL: National Educational Service, 1992.

Mendler, Allen. *Smiling at Yourself — Educating Young Children about Stress and Self-Esteem.* Santa Cruz: CA: Network Publications, 1990.

_____. *What Do I Do When? How to Achieve Discipline with Dignity in the Classroom.* Bloomington, IL: National Educational Service, 1992.

Nelson, Jane. *Positive Discipline.* New York: Ballantine Books, 1987.

Redenbach, Sandi. *Self-Esteem: The Necessary Ingredient for Success.* Esteem Seminar Publications, 1991.

Reider, Barbara. *A Hooray Kind of Kid.* Folsom, CA: Sierra House Publishing, 1988.

Wright, Esther. *Good Morning Class — I Love You!.* Rolling Hills, CA: Jalmar Press, 1989.

Voices

Could It Be This Simple?

When students feel supported and successful in the classroom, they rarely act out.

When teachers feel supported and successful in their school, they rarely burn out.

Esther Wright
Good Morning Class — I Love You!

Inclusive Education Resources

Paul H. Brookes Publishing Co.
(catalog available)
P.O. Box 10624
Baltimore, MD 21285-0624
!-800-638-3775

Center for Success in Learning
17000 Preston Rd., #400
Dallas, TX 75248
1-800-488-9435

The Council for Exceptional Children
1920 Association Drive
Reston, VA 22091-1589
703-620-3660
(publishes *Teacher Education and Special Education* and *Teaching Exceptional Children*)

Exchange
The Learning Disabilities Network
72 Sharp St.
Hingham, MA 02043
(617) 340-5605

Impact
Institute on Community Integration
University of Minnesota
6 Patte Hall
150 Pillsbury Dr. SE
Minneapolis, MN 55455
(612) 624-4848

Learning Disabilities Association (LDA)
4156 Library Rd.
Pittsburgh, PA 15234
(412) 341-1515

National Center for Learning Disabilities
(NCLD)
99 Park Ave.
New York, NY 10016
(212) 687-7211

PEAK (Parent Education and Assistance
Program)
6055 Lehman Dr., Suite 101
Colorado Springs, CO 80918

The Orton Dyslexia Society
Chester Building, Suite 382
8600 LaSalle Rd.
Baltimore, MD 21286-0024
1-410-296-0232

Voices

The integration of children with disabilities is not an issue of "mainstreaming": it is an issue of inclusion. It is very simple. If we want it to happen, it will. It takes time and hard work; the re-education of the adults in any system is a big job. The children are easier for they are less afraid of the unknown. Full inclusion can work. If we involve the children and ask them to help us, it will work beyond our wildest dreams. If we listen to the children and follow their lead, we will see a new system emerge in which all learn and each belongs.

The inclusion of those we have labelled and excluded will liberate our hearts and souls. We will all not only read and write better, but we will be part of creating a more loving and caring world.

Marsha Forest

Reprinted with permission from IMPACT, Vol. 1 (2), Winter 1988 published by the Institute on Community Integration (UAP), University of Minnesota.

Inclusion Education
Bill of Rights

EVERY CHILD HAS THE RIGHT TO:

1. Attend the neighborhood school to which he/she would have been assigned if not for a handicap label.

2. Be assigned to an age-appropriate, typical classroom.

3. Have educational needs met in an integrated, typical, classroom setting.

4. Have available peer tutors and cross-age tutors to assist with a variety of learning tasks.

5. Be a participatory member in cooperative learning groups, not only for positive social interactions, but also for the achievement of group learning tasks.

6. Develop a variety of life-long friendships within and outside of the school setting while participating in school and after-school activities.

7. Have instruction presented using a variety of adapted approaches.

8. Become an independent, individual learner; recognize a comfortable learning style, and learn skills necessary to perform a task and self-evaluation techniques.

9. Develop skills necessary for successful community living and life-long independence.

10. Receive necessary educational supports provided through a variety of qualified personnel within a typical, age-appropriate setting.

Gretchen Goodman

Achieving Inclusion

• **Integrate Students**

• **Adapt Curriculum**

• **Remain Flexible**

• **Use Support Facilitators**

• **Develop School Philosophy**

• **Principles of Natural Proportion**

• **Include All**

• **Develop Networks (TEAM)**

• **Teachers Team**

• **Students in Mainstream**

• **Challenging Yet Assistive**

• **Supportive Community**

• **Respect Selves**

• **Accept Responsibilities**

• **Success Breeds Success**

Gretchen Goodman

Creating Friendly Classrooms

- **Eliminate Competitive Symbols**

- **Use Inclusive Language**

- **Build Community**

- **Use One Another as Resources**

- **Applaud Accomplishments**

- **Employ Children's Literature**

- **Encourage cooperative learning**

- **Develop Peer Partners**

Self-Esteem Strategies

- **Pupil Conferences**

- **Punch Cards**

- **Responsible Time Out**

- **Parents as Resources**

- **Amnesia**

- **Multiple Response**

- **Yarn Ball Activities**

Organizing

- H.O.W.

- Calendars

- Chunking

Classroom Rescripting

- Tape Recorders

- Chunking

- Block Outs

- Highlight

- Cut Corners

- Sequence Steps

- Signal Responses

- Homework Options

- Card Games

- Group Games

- Focus Techniques   1.   2.

                      3.   4.

Hershey Primary School — IST Progress Report

Name _____   **Grade** _____   **Teacher** _____   School Year 19 ___ - 19 ___

Accommodations Checklist

Type of Support

1. Test read orally for students
2. Test explained to student in detail
3. Material taped for the student
4. Instructional material altered or changed to meet student's needs
5. Content material retaught
6. Some individual instruction needed at times
7. Other

LS - Accommodations for learning support student
CS - Accommodations initiated by classroom teacher
IS - Accommodations planned by instructional support team
RS - Accommodations planned by remedial teacher

	1st Period		2nd Period		3rd Period		4th Period	
	Type Support Code	Accommodations	Type Support Code	Accommodations	Type Support Code	Accommodations	Type Support Code	Accommodations
Reading								
Process Writing								
Math								
Spelling								
Science								
Health								
Social Studies								

On Line Outline

WHO: Used by students who are unable to organize, outline, study or write successfully. Also for those who have difficulty focusing or staying on task.

WHAT: An adaptable outline used to record vital information and assist student with locating major points of interest.

WHERE: Incomplete or pictorial outlines are presented on an overhead or directly in front of the student for reference.

WHEN: Used to review learned material or rehearse new topics for discussion.

HOW: Major topics may be presented or sub-topics presented using Cloze or first letter clues.

WHY: Records highlighted information or used to review for a test. Lessens the amount of written work needed and any note taking.

" ON LINE OUTLINE "
SCIENCE

Listen to the tape talk about fall. Write the 4 important words from the lesson.

CHANGES IN THE FALL

1. A_nimals_

2. L_____

3. S_____

4. C_____

Picture This

WHO: Used by students who have trouble listening to stories or lectures, organizing information, comprehending written words, or locating information.

WHAT: Information is presented in charts, graphs, or pictures.

WHERE: Charts, wordbanks, visual clues,and page numbers are pictured on sheets to assist with large blocks of learned materials.

WHEN: Used to help students draw conclusions, relate cause and effect, sequence events, demonstrate relationships, and organize material.

How: Charts, graphs, timelines, calendars, or wordbanks are used to tie visual clues to auditory presentations.

WHY: Simplifies studying, eases reviews, aids in comprehension, relationships, sequencing, and locating information.

Gretchen Goodman

"Picture This"

Whole Language/Timeline

Read the story, If Once You Have Slept on an Island and fill in the time line.

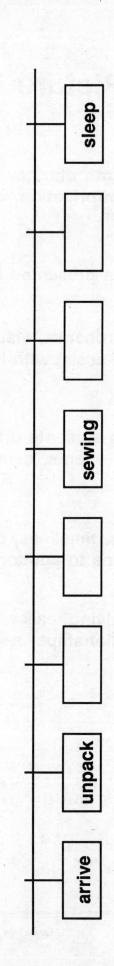

| arrive | unpack | | | sewing | | | sleep |

by Iris Rynbach, Caroline House, Boyds Mills Press

Location Stations

WHO: Used by students who are unable to organize information, those who have difficulty remembering what was read, or those with handwriting deficits.

WHAT: A structured format to aid in reading for meaning and locating pertinent information.

WHERE: Subheadings or text page clues help students to find key topics or vocabulary in written materials.

WHEN: Used as a chapter review, a rehearsal prior to a lesson, as a study aid, a lesson summary, or an as independent assignment.

HOW: Open ended statements are used with pertinent information deleted. Cloze procedures, lists, or definitions are also employed.

WHY: Simplifies recollecting information, locating information, and reading grade level texts.

Gretchen Goodman

"Location Stations"

Reading/Trade Books

Word Bank		
shabby	Mudge	dirty
happy	TV	excited
		washed

1. One night Henry and his father were watching _____.

2. The cat Henry found was very _____.
   This word means very _____.

3. Mudge was very _____ and _____
   to have a cat.

4. The cat loved _____.

5. The cat _____ the dog.

<u>Henry and Mudge and the Happy Cat,</u> by Cynthia Rylant. Bradbury Press

From Abstract To Concrete

WHO: **Used by students who need assistance with comprehension and relating abstract facts to visual, concrete images.**

WHAT: **A visual aid or organizer used to illustrate an abstract thought or concept.**

WHERE: **An abstract idea which is read or discussed is brought to a concrete level using pictorial clues, symbols, or a framework on paper.**

WHEN: **Used to review old information, rehearse new information, and bring learned material to a concrete focus.**

HOW: **Pictures, graphs, symbols, and organizational tool focus on concrete thinking.**

WHY: **Motivates students to relate new information to a personal level, enhances abstract vocabulary, and provides visual assistance for memory.**

Gretchen Goodman

"From Abstract to Concrete"

Title of my story _____

Where it happened _____

In the beginning, the main person was feeling.

In the middle of the story, this person was feeling

because _____

In the end of the story, this person was feeling

because _____

Gretchen Goodman

Putting It To Work

WHO: **Used by students who learn through the tactile, kinesthetic approach of hands-on learning.**

WHAT: **Posters, collages, pictures, letters, interviews, projects, or models are used to put presented, learned knowledge to work.**

WHERE: **Freedom to move throughout the room in small groups and pairs enhances the application of knowledge.**

WHEN: **Used in place of tests, term papers, writing assignments, and to develop cooperative groups.**

HOW: **Provides hands-on higher level application of learned information.**

WHY: **Encourages peer support and group interactions to facilitate putting facts to work in real life situations.**

Gretchen Goodman

Putting It To Work

Social Living

Step by Step Planner

1. Make a family album, a group picture, a clay model, or hand prints from your family.

2. Write one sentence about each member.

3. Draw what your final display will look like.

Be ready to share your final project on _____.

Find It, Define It

WHO: **Used by students who are unable to find necessary words and definitions, or those with weak memory or handwriting skills.**

WHAT: **A structured set up of words and descriptions from stories or chapters to aid in categorizations and explanations.**

WHERE: **Headings and bold face clues are taken from chapters or readings which are necessary for understanding new concepts and categorizing facts.**

WHEN: **Used to improve memory and lessen handwriting while locating information in a chart form.**

HOW: **Terms are arranged by topics and listed on specific charts by categories. Page clues are used for individual or group clues.**

WHY: **Simplifies definitions, categories, and finding key words.**

Gretchen Goodman

Find It, Define It

Page	New Word	What it means	Use it.

Games / Manipulatives

WHO: Used by students for variety, repetition, hands-on reinforcement, and guided practice.

WHAT: A modified card game, board game, whole group game, pocket chart, or study card.

WHERE: Precise directions are given for games and charts. Students engage in classroom activities or tutorial settings.

WHEN: Used for motivation, fun-filled review, increased retention, or an alternative to pencil / paper tasks.

HOW: Redesign favorite card games, board games, folder activities, and pocket charts.

WHY: Encourages social interactions while increasing motivation for those unsuccessful with paper / pencil tasks.

FISHING GAME
VOCABULARY

Cut out small, medium, and large fish. Attach paper clips to their tails. Attach a magnet to a wooden dowel by a string. Place single vocabulary words on the small fish, phrases on the medium fish, and sentences on large fish. All fish go into a wading pool. Children fish for words, phrases, or sentences and may keep those they are able to read.

Domino Game
Vocabulary / Reading

**Use index cards or wipe on / off playing cards. Divide the cards in half.
Children build by matching pictures to vocabulary.**

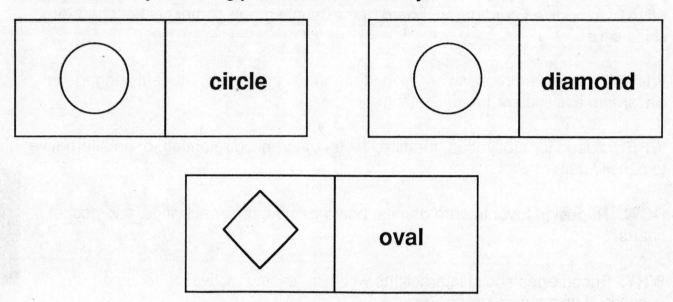

Manipulative Test
Science

Use a magazine. Cut out pictures of living, non-living objects. Place in correct box.

Living	Non-Living

Gretchen Goodman

Manipulative Test
Math

Give each student a large zip-lock bag with a variety of coins in the bag. Place masking tape one half across the bag. Hold up a money sign. Allow children to move the money from the bottom of the bag, across the line to represent correct amounts.

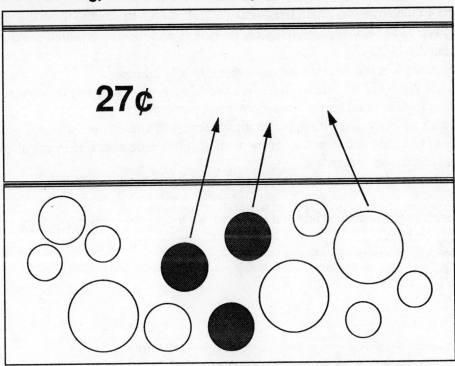

Inclusive Education Checklist

All across the nation, classroom teachers and specialists are being asked to meet the daily challenge of educating all children within the "regular" classroom setting. In order to be truly inclusive, children need to be included in all activities of the classroom and their home school setting. Neighborhood schools will now welcome back a variety of children who previously had been excluded. The following checklist will provide an expedient avenue for the initial inclusive project.

School Community

_____ 1. The school is physically able to include all (ramps, elevators, wheel chair access, lavatories, desks, etc.).

_____ 2. All staff members have received adequate inservice (teachers, teacher-assistants, nurses, janitors, secretaries, administrators, cafeteria workers, bus drivers).

_____ 3. The school's mission statement is in line with the inclusive philosophy.

_____ 4. Support teams have been initiated to ease staff, parents, and community into a "we" philosophy as opposed to an "I" philosophy.

_____ 6. The needs and I.E.P.'s of included children have been described in simplified terms.

_____ 7. The staff is able to positively model the inclusive, accept-all philosophy.

_____ 8. Parents and community task-force members have been inserviced.

_____ 9. The special education and regular education teacher have been provided with time to plan and implement.

_____ 10. Art, music, library, and physical education teachers have become part of the teaming process.

_____ 11. The school is able to grasp the concept of "all education is special" and all teachers are special teachers and begin to dissolve staff and student labels.

Classroom Environment

_____ 1. The children have been prepared for the inclusive project.

_____ 2. A variety of literature has been used to enable the children to see and discuss acceptance of all.

_____ 3. The children have been exposed to speakers, videos, and movies in which people share information about disabilities.

_____ 4. The classroom is set up to facilitate movement for all children.

_____ 5. There are a variety of activities and centers available to meet a variety of learning styles.

_____ 6. Friendship is an integral part of the school-wide curriculum.

_____ 7. All students are provided with opportunities to socialize and interact with one another.

_____ 8. Classroom rules and consequences are written in simple language. They are displayed for all to see and are frequently reviewed.

_____ 9. Children and teachers are able to communicate with each other and employ assisting devices as needed.

_____ 10. The classroom philosophy is one that encourages cooperative learning, peer partners and cross-age study buddies.

_____ 11. There are positive peer role models for all children.

Students

_____ 1. Children enter the classroom at approximately the same time.

_____ 2. Students are situated in the classroom to facilitate their individual learning styles.

_____ 3. Children engage in similar activities at the same time.

_____ 4. Children, regardless of their label, receive the aid of a teacher assistant or specialist as needed within the regular classroom setting.

_____ 5. Children are made to feel welcome and are seen as participating members of a classroom society.

_____ 6. Children are involved actively in classroom routines.

_____ 7. Members of the class assist each other only when needed, yet allow for individual independence as needed.

_____ 8. All students are taught at a developmentally appropriate level.

_____ 9. Student successes are celebrated equally.

_____ 10. Adequate time is provided for peer interactions. Positive interactions are fostered.

_____ 11. Students are able to accomplish individual goals in regular classroom settings.

_____ 12. Children are set up to succeed in the regular classroom setting.

_____ 13. Parents and support staff are available to help children rehearse for expected educational outcomes.

_____ 14. Children are provided with immediate, positive feedback.

_____ 15. There has been documented evidence of a variety of children being included in after school socializing activities.

Developed by Gretchen Goodman

Gretchen Goodman

Children Don't Need Better Teachers . . . They Need Better Childhoods

The State of America's Children

Family/Societal Factors Affecting Today's Children:

- Divorce
- Developmentally delayed children
- Dysfunctional families
- Lack of community connectedness
- Violence — home/school/community
- Lack of manners, respect, sense of propriety
- Lack of social services
- Homeless children
- Lack of health services
- Latch key children
- Mobile population
- Poor quality day care
- Harried, hurried children
- Abused/neglected children
- Discrimination
- Blended families
- Lack of spiritual guidance
- Alcohol/drug related issues
- Children's stress — fear — anxiety
- Television
- Poverty
- Hungry children

LEARNING STYLES/NEEDS

The Discipline/Self-Esteem Connection

Jim Grant

Points to Discuss:

- Discipline Philosophy

- Punishment

- Consequences

- Corporal Punishment

- School Rules

- The Difficult Child

- Self-Esteem

- Teacher stress . . . the high cost of caring

-

-

-

The Discipline/Self-Esteem Connection

Jim Grant

Avoiding Practices That Cause Discipline Problems in the Classroom

"We have met the enemy and he is us."
Pogo

- Discipline programs that are suppressive in nature
- Unfair competition
- A-B-C report cards
- Test-driven curriculum
- Escalated curriculum
- Untrained teachers
- Rigid classroom structure
- Teachers who don't like children
- Inconsistency in the classroom
- Humorless classroom — no fun
- Hostile classroom environment
- Inactivity . . . no movement
- Lack of classroom management skills
- Discriminatory practices
- Boring instruction
- Meaningless irrelevant curriculum
- Large class size
- Lack of aide support in classes with high number of "at risk" children
- Lack of support staff: social worker, counselor and special education services
- Inflexible teachers
- Fixed point curriculum in a fixed amount of time
- Wide developmental range
- School rules that make no sense
- Group standardized achievement tests

The Discipline/Self-Esteem Connection

Jim Grant

Discipline/Self-Esteem Building Techniques That Work

- Chimes/lights/musical notes
- Humor as a tool
- Time-out — classroom, office, home
- "Car Wash" to promote self-esteem
- Rewards — stickers, stars, tickets, etc.
- Moving the student
- The thinking chair
- Lower your voice
- Cease teaching
- Talk to a puppet
- Send a note/letter/card/"happy gram"
- Peer modeling
- Bibliotherapy
- "Crumb of the week"
- In-house field trips
- Positive time-out
- Reading children's names into a children's story
- The forgiveness I.O.U.
- Telephone I.O.U.
- Gift certificates, e.g., extra gym, music, recess and art
- Proximity posture
- Memorizing phone numbers
- Teacher-to-student phone visit
-
-
-

The Discipline/Self-Esteem Connection

Jim Grant

DISCIPLINE:
PUNISHMENT OR TEACHING?

PUNISHMENT = **Anger**

Resentment

Revenge

Sadness

Negativity

TEACHING = **Responsibility**

Alternative Behaviors

Actions/Consequences

Good Judgment

Values

Esther Wright

BEHAVIORS AND CHARACTERISTICS OF STUDENTS WITH LOW AND HIGH SELF-ESTEEM

LOW SELF-ESTEEM	HIGH SELF-ESTEEM
Withdrawn	Participatory
Fearful/Insecure	Self-Confident/Takes Risks
Verbally/Physically Abusive	Friendly
Low Frustration Tolerance	Patient/Persistent
Resistance to Authority	Cooperative
Disrespectful	Respectful
Negative Attitude	Optimistic
Unmotivated	Motivated
Intolerant	Tolerant
Irresponsible	Responsible
Poor Personal Hygiene	Well-Groomed

Esther Wright

A Difficult and Disruptive Child Is a "Needy" Child

What Do Children Need?

Three Perspectives to Consider

William Glasser:

Survival: (food, shelter, freedom from harm)

Belonging: (security, connectedness)

Power: (sense of importance, of being considered by others)

Fun: (enjoyment, having a good time)

Freedom: (choice, self-direction, responsibility)

Richard Curwin / Allen Mendler:

To feel and believe they are capable and successful

To know they are cared about by others

To realize they are able to influence people and events

To practice helping others through their own generosity

Fun and stimulation

Esther Wright:

To be loved unconditionally

To be heard without judgment

To be respected for their unique gifts and talents

To be supported when they are faced with challenge

To be acknowledged authentically

To be successful in areas that are important to them

Children whose needs are not being met become sad, angry, scared children. Determine which of these needs are not being met for your students. Work with the home, school, and community to ensure that your students are getting their needs met.

WHY DO STUDENTS MISBEHAVE?*

1. **ALL STUDENTS HAVE THE NEED TO BELONG, TO FEEL CONNECTED, AND TO EXPERIENCE THEY ARE SIGNIFICANT.**

2. **STUDENTS ULTIMATELY CHOOSE THEIR BEHAVIOR.**

3. **A MISBEHAVING STUDENT IS A NEEDY AND DISCOURAGED STUDENT.**

4. **WHEN THEY MISBEHAVE, STUDENTS ARE TRYING TO ACHIEVE ONE OR MORE OF THE FOLLOWING GOALS:**

   - **ATTENTION**
   - **POWER**
   - **REVENGE**
   - **AVOIDANCE OF FAILURE****

*Based on the work of Rudolf Dreikurs
**Adaptation of Linda Albert, *Cooperative Discipline*

Esther Wright

Who We Say They Are Is Who They Become

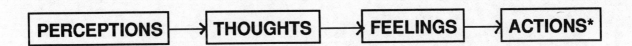

Teacher

Perception: "John is a bad boy"

↓

Thought: "He drives me crazy"

↓

Feelings: Anger, impatience, frustration

↓

Actions: Punitive, negative

Child

Perception: "I am a bad boy"

↓

Thought: "I am not loved or valued"

↓

Feelings: Sadness, fear, anger

↓

Actions: Disruptive, defensive, disrespectful

(*Adapted from *Mastering School Reform*, Goens & Clover)

LEARNING STYLES/NEEDS

Ten Principles of Esteeming Discipline

by Esther Wright, M.A.

1. Always remember that your mission is to serve and support your students.

2. Always speak and act from a place of respect and dignity.

3. Develop relationships with your students that nurture and esteem them.

4. *Respond* rather than react when dealing with discipline.

5. Model the behaviors and attitudes that you expect from your students.

6. Be open to learning from your students.

7. Speak and listen from your heart when communicating with students.

8. Seek support and coaching when you find yourself overwhelmed.

9. Be calm, fair, and firm when dealing with discipline.

10. Remember that students are human and make mistatkes; ditto for teachers!

Setting Up An Esteeming Discipline System

Be willing to take as much time as necessary to set up your discipline program. An effective set-up will prevent many future problems. Repeat the steps as necessary based on student behavior. These steps are best implemented at the beginning of the school year (the earlier the better), but can be implemented any time.

1. Reflect on the purpose, goals, expectations, needs, standards, and values of your classroom.

2. Develop a list of rules/agreements* to discuss with your students
   — should be specific but comprehensive
   — no more than four or five

3. Discuss the classroom purpose, goals, expectations, needs, standards, and values with your students.

4. Answer any questions they may have.

5. Role play the do's and dont's of appropriate behavior.

6. Discuss four to five rules or agreements that will allow the classroom to work effectively.

7. Have students draw, write stories, or demonstrate in other ways their appreciation and understanding of the classroom rules/agreements.

8. Ask students if they foresee any difficulty in following the rules or honoring their agreements.

9. Determine with those students what support they will need to follow rules or honor agreements.

10. Discuss consequences with students.** Identify what responses students can expect if they forget rules or choose to not keep their agreements. (reminders, time-out, call to parents, etc.)

11. Teach children some basic communication and conflict resolution skills.
    (I feel . . . I want . . . I need . . .)

*Agreements allow students to experience ownership and responsibility for the "rules." Some teachers allow students to assist with developing classroom rules or agreements. This also allows for more ownership and responsibility.

**Some children will test the rules to determine if the teacher is really committed to them. It is important to be consistent in dealing with misbehavior early, before it becomes habitual. Remember to remain calm, respectful, and fair when dealing with misbehavior.

© 1993 E. Wright

Pro-Active and Responsive Discipline Interventions

Set up a classroom environment and instructional program designed to meet the needs of your students. If a child is exhibiting disruptive behaviors, implement one or more of the following interventions. Experiment until you find the ones that are effective. Remember that some behaviors are "habits" that may take time to change.

Physical Environment Interventions:

1. Seat the child in close proximity to the teacher.
2. Place the child away from other children who exhibit disruptive behaviors.
3. Place the child away from distractions (traffic areas, windows).
4. Provide the child with a study carrel to cut down on visual distractions.
5. Place masking tape around the floor near the child's desk to clearly indicate the child's boundaries during individual seatwork activities.
6. Play low volume classical music to set a relaxed tone in the classroom.
7. Make buttons and/or signs that say: "I am a good listener," or "I am a good friend." Have the student wear the button or tape the sign to his/her desk. Use illustrations for children who do not yet read.
8. Designate a small bulletin board section to display the child's work and encourage completion of assignments.
9. Try setting up room in a circle or semi-circle arrangement, or with all rows facing the center of the room. These arrangements sometimes result in improved student behavior.

Psychological Interventions:

1. Establish a friendly and positive relationship with each child.
2. Provide children with opportunities to make choices.
3. Provide opportunities for children to be responsible and self-sufficient.
4. Identify children's special interests and talents. Allow children to share these during class time.
5. Be respectful, calm, and confident when disciplining a child.
6. Teach children to be aware of their feelings and their needs.
7. Teach children how to express their feelings and needs appropriately.
8. Acknowledge effort and improvement.
9. Encourage children to support each other; establish a sense of community in the classroom.
10. Bring humor and fun into your classroom whenever possible.

Instructional Interventions:

1. Plan classroom activities that are developmentally appropriate.
2. Provide whatever support is needed to ensure that children experience success at least 80% of the time.
3. Use a multi-sensory approach. Offer opportunities for tactile-kinesthetic learning, especially for active boys.
4. Alternate activities frequently, including opportunities for students to change work/play locations.
5. Assign a "study-buddy" so that each student has a support system.
6. As much as possible, monitor the work of students by walking around the room. Provide support as necessary. Stay in proximity to students who have difficulty attending to their assignment.
7. Provide students with adequate time to complete assigned activities.
8. Give students choices regarding working independently, with a partner, or with a group.
9. Modify assignments for students who demonstrate attention deficits or have perceptual disabilities or fine motor delays.
10. Have mistakes (wrong answers) be OK.
11. Acknowledge effort and improvement.

Do You React or Respond to Discipline Problems?

How we deal with discipline problems dramatically affects our relationship with students as well as the climate of our classroom. When a student is being disruptive, it is sometimes difficult to remain calm; however, we will be much more effective with discipline if we learn how to *respond* rather than *react* to difficult children.

Reaction comes from our emotions:

- ☹ Anger
- ☹ Frustration
- ☹ Disappointment
- ☹ Fear
- ☹ Resentment
- ☹ Sadness

Responding comes from our commitment:

- ☺ To teach by modeling appropriate behaviors
- ☺ To support our students
- ☺ To help our students learn and grow

REACTION:
- Not effective
- Creates tension for teacher and students
- Students become reactive

RESPONDING:
- More effective
- Teacher remains calm, but confident
- Teacher asks question or makes request of student

TIPS FOR BECOMING A MORE RESPONSIVE DISCIPLINARIAN:

- Be aware of what specific classroom behaviors and situations "plug you in"
- Try not to take student behaviors personally
- Take a deep breath
- Count to five
- Ask a question: "What do you need?", or "What is our rule/agreement about . . . ?"
- Make a request or provide a choice: "Please get what you need and then get back to your seat." or "You can choose to honor our rules and agreements or go to time out. Please choose now."

Esther Wright

Building Partnerships with Parents

Teachers and parents want the same thing for children. We want children to be:

- Physically and emotionally healthy
- Able to get along with others
- Successful in school and life

Parents of children who have difficulty in school receive many reports regarding how "bad" their children are. These parents begin to feel frustrated and resentful about their interactions with school personnel. Often these parents are having difficulty with the child at home and are hoping that the teacher can change the child's behavior. In some cases, the child's family may be in crisis (divorce, illness, loss of employment). We must be careful not to alienate the child's parents by assuming that they have the ability to solve the child's school problems.

In order to best serve the disruptive child, we must establish (or re-establish) effective partnerships with his or her parents.

Tips for Establishing an Effective Home / School Partnership

- Communicate your commitment to the success of this student in your classroom.

- Let the parent know that their child's success is dependent on an effective parent / teacher partnership.

- Acknowledge the positive aspects of the child — his/her strengths and talents.

- Identify one or two specific behaviors that need to be improved.

- Work out a plan of support (using the Home / School Partnership Behavior Plan form).

- Decide on the method and frequency of communication between you and the parents.

- Request that the parents practice the new behavior at home as much as possible.

- Jointly determine what additional support is needed (counseling, tutoring).

Home / School Partnership
Behavior Plan

HOME
STRENGTHENING
THE CONNECTION
SCHOOL

Teacher _____

Student _____

Parent _____

Describe behavior that needs to change: _____
_____

Describe desired behavior: _____
_____

Describe benefits of new behavior: _____
_____

Teacher support: _____
_____

Parent support: _____
_____

Other support: _____
_____

Communication plan _____
(phone calls, notes, meetings, how often?)

Date plan to be implemented: _____

Date plan to be reviewed: _____

Teacher signature: _____

Student signature: _____

Parent signature: _____

Esther Wright

Call in the Troops

Some of your students will require one-to-one instructional or behavioral support. If paraprofessionals are not available, call upon community resources when you need additional adult support in your classroom. Some of these people are eager to volunteer an hour or more a week. In some cases, they may be able to support your classroom an hour or more a day.

- Parents (current or past)

- Local business people

- Graduate students from local universities (especially those majoring in psychology, counseling, or education)

- Retired teachers

- Special education resource staff

- ESL resource staff

- High school students (some schools give credit for community service)

- Social service personnel

- Off duty nurses or flight attendants

- Service club members (Lions/Kiwanis/Association of University Women, sororities, fraternities)

Local businesses and service clubs have been known to "adopt" a classroom or a school. They can sometimes contribute funding for special projects and materials, as well as provide volunteer tutors for needy students.

Although inviting members of the community to volunteer in your classroom does not require additional funding from your school district, it does take time to locate people who are available, set up schedules, and provide whatever training will be necessary. Once you have a routine established, however, it will be well worth the time invested.

Programs for Pre-Natally Drug-Exposed Children*

According to the National Association on Drug Abuse, the number of drug-exposed children born each year ranges from 375,000 to 739,000, possibly 18% of all newborns in the United States.

- 5% cocaine
- 17% marijuana
- 73% alcohol

The March of Dimes predicts that by the year 2000, as many as *four million* drug-exposed children will be attending school.

These children exhibit the following behaviors:

- Unable to concentrate
- Overwhelmed by slightest stimulation
- Delayed speech and language development

School officials in Los Angeles recommend that programs for these children include eight elements:

Curriculum: The curriculum should promote active learning through interaction, exploration, and play, as well as concrete experiences, decision making, and problem solving.

Play: These children require a setting that allows for extended periods of play.

Adults: Children need contact with enough adults to promote attachment, predictability, nurturing, and ongoing assistance in learning appropriate coping styles.

Flexible Rooms: Rooms need to be flexible enough that materials and equipment can be removed to reduce stimuli or added to provide enrichment.

Transition Time: These children require a setting in which transition time is seen as an activity in and of itself, with a beginning, middle, and end. This teaches the child how to prepare for and cope with change.

Routines and Rituals: The environment should give children "continuity and reliability through routines and rituals." Scheduling activities in a predictable order over time strengthens a child's self-control and sense of mastery over the environment.

CLASSROOM RULES: Limit the number of explicit rules so that children can explore and actively engage in their social and physical environment. Too many classroom rules can hinder this development.

*Adapted from a Kappan Special Report: "Crack — Healing the Children" by Craig Sautter, November, 1992.

I can only be good to my students if I am good to myself — therefore, I will love, appreciate and nurture myself!

I promise to seek the support of friends, family and fellow teachers when I find myself unable to take the necessary action to have my work be joyful and satisfying.

I will remember that my teaching is a life-altering gift to my students and that the lessons I learn about myself from them are a life-altering gift to me.

Taken from *"GOOD MORNING CLASS — I LOVE YOU"*
by Esther Wright

Tape to Your Desk

"I've come to a frightening conclusion that I am the decisive element in the classroom. It's my personal approach that creates the climate. It's my daily mood that makes the weather. As a teacher, I possess a tremendous power to make a child's life miserable or joyous. I can be a tool of torture or an instrument of inspiration. I can humiliate or humor, hurt or heal. In all situations, it is my response that decides whether a crisis will be escalated or de-escalated and a child humanized or de-humanized."

Haim Ginott

Esther Wright

THE WHYS AND HOWS OF THE MULTI-AGE PRIMARY CLASSROOM

By KATHLEEN CUSHMAN

YOU WOULD never know, talking to the teachers who do it, that running an elementary school classroom of mixed-age children is such a big deal. From the outside, to be sure, it seems a radical concept, ambitious and fraught with difficulties of every kind. Why else would the open-classroom mixed-age experiments of the sixties and seventies have dwindled so sharply in the past decade and a half? Why else are so few public schools now trying it, so few researchers studying it, and so many filled with mistrust at the whole idea of "family groupings" in a primary classroom?

Yet in Norma Leutzinger's combined first- and second-grade classroom at New York City's Central Park East II Elementary School, the concept fits as comfortably as a favorite suit of clothes. Around the room at groups of tables, twenty-eight children work quietly, reading books they have chosen or writing in their journals. They group and regroup frequently, at Norma's prompting: now into a fifteen-minute discussion with the whole class in a circle; now dispersing to chat while they choose materials to work with in groups of two and

Kathleen Cushman writes and edits Horace, _the journal of the Coalition of Essential Schools, a high school reform movement based at Brown University._

three; now intent again at their tables as the teacher and her aide move from child to child to speak with them in lowered voices.

Leutzinger's class, which includes twenty-eight children ranging in age from six to nine by the end of the school year, is one of a small but increasing number of classes in this country where early grades are combined in different ways. We tracked down three of them to see what is going on, both in theory and in practice, when a school chooses a mixed-age alternative to the conventional single-grade system. What we discovered was a range of techniques loosely linked by a developmental, child-centered philosophy of learning but otherwise as idiosyncratic as American education itself. If this is a trend, it is one with room for individual variation; and the schools here represent not only different approaches but different stages of those approaches.

One way to structure classes is that of Central Park East, where teachers like Norma Leutzinger have a combined class of first- and second-graders or third- and fourth-graders, and children stay with the same teacher for two years. Aside from her students' forays outside the classroom for music and the arts, Norma is responsible for teaching all subjects herself, and she organizes

the class differently for instruction depending on her goals. In social studies and science, the group often meets as a whole; but when it comes to math, she will teach two separate lessons at first- and second-grade levels. Language arts is so integral a part of classroom life that it cannot be categorized: sometimes the class meets together, sometimes in small groups, and sometimes on an individual basis.

Across the river in the Brownsville section of Brooklyn, children in a P.S. 41 class of seven- and eight-year-olds are working on simple addition, while in the classroom next door a class of eight- and nine-year-olds does higher-level math problems. But since the classrooms open onto a common hall—along with another room of special needs students ages six to ten—any student can easily move into another class for work in this subject. It takes joint planning to carry this off; the teachers in P.S. 41's "core teams" of three or four teachers share the same free period and lunch period, allowing them time to talk things through. They know all the children in their cluster of classrooms and work with them all at some point, possibly in a project that involves several classes together, or because children cross class lines for special instruction, say, in reading. And though children will not necessarily stay with the same teacher for two

years, the cluster technique de-emphasizes their grade level in favor of an identification with the core team as a whole.

AT P.S. 41, teachers work together to determine how best to share instruction of their different-aged children. But at Sands Montessori elementary school in Cincinnati, teacher Mary Motz knows beforehand exactly what the Montessori system expects in her classroom of six- to nine-year-olds. Montessori schooling is notable in the United States for the extent to which it puts into practice a comprehensive theory, complete with training and materials. Working on the floor around her classroom, some of Motz's students are absorbed in private tasks; others work in mixed-age groups of two or three, helping each other with different activities. All will work their way eventually through a series of learning tasks that make up the Montessori curriculum; and even though one younger child appears to be doing nothing at all with his materials, Motz is happy. "He's watching the children on the next mat," she whispers. "He'll be asking me if he can learn that next."

That expectation of continuous progress through a series of skills marks a few other well-organized educational systems here and abroad. Individually Guided Education (IGE), developed by the Wisconsin Research and Development Center for Cognitive Learning, provides guidance to participating schools that want a "continuous progress" method of learning in a nongraded class. And in Great Britain, where primary schools have been organized since the 1960s into mixed-age groupings, the system expects every seven-year-old, for example, to be able to demonstrate mastery of certain math skills before moving into the next level of mixed-age learning.

All these models depend, at their core, on a philosophy of learning based on the developmental theories of Jean Piaget, Jerome Bruner, and others. Children in the early years of school do not learn at the same pace, such educators agree. In fact, they enter school with a "mental age" that varies by as much as four years, and they progress at their own rate from a largely concrete way of learning and thinking to the more abstract one reached in later stages. Because the pace of this development is so varied, mixed-age advocates say, it makes little sense to sort and label children into fixed grade levels from an early age—especially if the result is retention and an early sense of failure for the child. Better to extend the age range of a primary class and thus provide a nurturing, success-oriented environment for children at widely different developmental levels.

By creating a model that expects diversity rather than uniformity among kids, many of the "problems" in a single-grade class lose their destructive grip over teachers and students both. More advanced students can learn together in mixed-age groups, and slow ones can be given the time they need to master skills at their own pace. At other times, children of different levels can be put in groups where they can learn from each other; the effectiveness of this strategy has been widely recognized in the trend toward cooperative learning and peer tutoring. Social skills grow in a mixed-age group, as children develop attitudes of responsibility and tolerance for those of different capacities. And in classes that stay with the same teacher for more than one year, proponents say, the teacher-student relationship can become so personal that both academic and discipline problems diminish.

The Open Classroom Reborn?

To many teachers who were around in the 1960s and early 1970s, mixed-age groupings sound suspiciously like the "open classrooms" of that era. And, in fact, such groupings only work if certain aspects of the open classroom are incorporated: a flexible use of space that uses "learning stations"; a wide variety of concrete materials available to children as they need them; a teacher's willingness to let children work in small groups rather than lecturing to them en masse; evaluations that record each child's progress through a continuum of skills. But the bugaboos that led many teachers to reject the early open classrooms are by no means ever present in the new mixed-age groupings. Most classrooms have walls, though some open the doors between them. Many teachers work in teams, but just as many classes are self-contained. Some mixed-age groupings take place for as little as an hour of shared time a day; others keep the mixed group together only for certain subjects; and

some keep them together all day. The classrooms visited here represent only a few of the ways teachers interested in a developmental, child-centered approach are moving toward mixed-age groups.

Central Park East is one of the few schools whose open classrooms survived the conservative reform wave of the late 1970s and 1980s, and its director, Esther Rosenthal, points to very practical reasons why the earlier trend toward mixed-age groupings failed. Unlike Great Britain's, most American teacher training programs did not teach developmental theories or provide model classrooms to practice them in, she says. By 1975, when a recession began to spark teacher cutbacks in districts across the nation, the newer teachers were the first to go, and many innovative programs died with their departure. The lack of bureaucratic support also made new ways hard for teachers: Everything from required testing to mandatory grade-level textbooks was organized to counter mixed-age principles. Little wonder, she says, that excitement about the idea among educators and researchers dropped dramatically by the mid-1970s. Still, education runs in cycles, she points out. "We are entering a new cycle with a more humanistic style. Pockets remained here and there, and now that movement is a-borning again."

IN MANY elementary schools, for instance, teachers excited by new pedagogies such as the whole-language approach to reading have begun turning to each other for new classroom structures in which these ideas can be carried out. This could mean teaming with another teacher to share ideas and resources—and even if that teacher is at another grade level, it could mean sharing students as well. The whole-language reading approach provides the flexibility to group children at different ability levels together, encouraging them to work with and learn from each other. Whether teaming is part of the picture or not, whole-language instruction can result, then, in a new openness toward mixed-age grouping.

In some schools, the push comes from another direction. At P.S. 41, the change to multi-age groups was regarded as a first step to getting teachers to try out new pedagogies. Once core teams of mixed-age groups were established, says Assistant Principal Gary Wexler, teachers found it both useful and necessary to personalize their classroom instruction. "Nongrading is the only way to *get* teachers to personalize, sometimes," he argues. "Because the only way nongrading can possibly work is to use cooperative learning, peer tutoring, learning centers." For P.S. 41, multi-age grouping is only one method of generating a spirit of enthusiasm and ownership among its teachers; and though the school's program incorporates only some aspects of the multi-age theory, it clearly has succeeded on one level. The school is alive with cooperation and pride; around the lunch tables and in their common planning period, teachers talk continually about new ways to work with their students together.

Which Ages Go Together?

All these models rest on the principle that children do better when they work in small groups with flexible age boundaries—so that their success is measured not against others of the same age, but by their mastery of new skills as they become ready. How best to mix the ages to achieve this goal is another question. Most educators agree that between the ages of five and eight (grades K-3) children proceed through certain key developmental stages—and during this period they learn best by contact with as many sensory, concrete experiences as possible. But should the five-year-olds be put with the older children?

Few of the teachers combining grades 1 and 2 or grades 3 and 4 think so. "For the most part, the five-year-olds still belong in kindergarten with the babies," says Norma Leutzinger. "There's a big difference in what a five-year-old is ready for."

As she approaches six, a child makes a key transition, these teachers agree—not from a concrete mode of learning to a more abstract one (which happens later), but from a more individual way of learning to a group-centered one. Some schools acknowledge this by creating K-1 (or "transition") combinations where a child can comfortably work in both modes. As a child matures socially, he can work together with the class's older children.

Teachers and researchers also disagree about where the third-grader belongs. At the schools described here, most teachers felt strongly that by third grade a child has moved into a new mode of learning that calls for grouping with fourth-graders. Only in the Montessori elementary school was there a commitment to grouping six- to nine-year-olds (first- to third-graders) together in the same class. At Sands Montessori, for funding reasons, kindergarten makes a class of its own with five- and six-year-olds, though Montessori schools normally group three- to six-year-olds together.

"Montessori classes are divided into overlapping age groups [3-6, 6-9, and 9-12 years old]," says Sands principal Sandra Sommer, "to acknowledge the developmental passages that a child goes through around six years old and nine years old." By including six-year-olds both with younger and older children, Montessori acknowledges the "bubble" that includes some sixes with the fives and some with the older children. A similar process occurs at nine, Sommer says, and so narrow grade groupings of grades 1-2 and 3-4 are inappropriate.

"When you take an eight-year-old away from the sixes and sevens, you miss the beauty of the mixed-age experience," agrees Mary Motz. "By the third year in my class, the older child is very sensitive to the younger ones' progress. He can help check their work, for example, and by teaching a younger child he really shows mastery of the material." Children gain socially from the broader three-grade grouping too, she says, and self-esteem goes up. "A bright child in the middle year can go as fast as he wants, but a slow child in the middle isn't isolated as different."

Still, Motz says, teaching three grades in one classroom is unquestionably harder in some ways. She works all day on Saturday, she says, planning the week ahead: what to present to the whole group, which children need attention in which areas. And like all of the mixed-group teachers described here, she keeps meticulous progress records on each child through a combination of methods. Children keep journals that can be used to track their reading, writing, and language skills; and she records their mastery of specific skills in another log.

Discipline, a potential problem that scares off many teachers from combining age groups, seems less of a problem to Motz. In some ways, this is because she knows her students so well; when only a fraction of the class is new to the teacher each year, she has an automatic advantage. In fact, the theory is that mixed-age grouping fosters good discipline because older children take responsibility as leaders and models for the younger ones. Still, this does make work on the teacher's part; all the classrooms described here give a great deal of attention to routines that foster mutual respect and conflict resolution.

SUGGESTIONS FOR SUCCESSFUL MULTI-AGE CLASSROOMS

• Provide plenty of flexible space and divide it into functional areas or "learning centers."

• Supply a selection of concrete materials to foster math concepts and language play. You won't need twenty-five of everything, since most activities will only involve a few children at a time.

• Provide a wide variety of "real books" at every reading level. If you do use reading textbooks, do so only as a check.

• Structure into the day opportunities for older children to tutor younger ones. Pair a youngster at the early edge of acquiring a skill with one who is more confident but still needs practice. Or allow an older student to check a younger one's work.

• Involve students in making work plans or "contracts" on a daily, weekly, or monthly basis.

• Allow children to freely explore the room and to choose their activities individually or in groups.

• Structure the curriculum around themes that can integrate learning across content areas.

• Use plenty of support staff—in art, music, physical education, special needs. Be sure to include them in planning of curriculum themes.

• Don't sort, track, label, or retain kids. Break down the idea that June is "promotion" time. A child can remain in the group until his mastery of appropriate skills shows he is ready to move on.

• Try sharing responsibilities with another teacher if your subject matter expertise lies in different areas.

• Switch teaching assignments frequently in graded schools. This increases empathy and cooperation among teachers, familiarizes them with students of different ages, and helps them think of themselves as learners.

• Train student teachers in many grades, not just one. Include courses in early childhood development in their requirements for certification.   □

K.C.

What To Do in Class

In a Montessori classroom, children of different ages learn together for both social and academic reasons. But how do they do it? How does a six-year-old work alongside a nine-year-old without one of them being bewildered and the other bored stiff?

The answer, say Motz and Sommer both, lies in the nature of the Montessori curriculum. It covers math, language, and cultural subjects in a series of concrete tasks—bead games, map puzzles, and the like—that can be taught to a larger group and then practiced again and again, with the teacher in smaller clusters and on one's own, until they are mastered. Motz and her students track their progress using monthly or weekly work plans, lists of activities from which the children can make their own choices. Through this tracking, teachers can help assure that each child is always working at the level he or she is comfortable with, prompted to try new things by curiosity about what is going on around him, and taught the necessary skills as the occasion arises. For a class of twenty-four six- to nine-year-olds, Motz makes up half a dozen such work plans or "contracts" monthly, some of which overlap in the academic areas they address.

Motz argues that the contract approach motivates children to acquire skills on their own, like math facts, that might otherwise be punishing rote routines. "The contract is actually unnecessary for most of the class, except as an aid to me," she confesses. "The children know that if they want to use a certain activity they need to take certain steps before they'll be able to. They have freedom; they're not told what day they have to do anything."

Contracts are also a key part of the IGE system, which organizes learning around a four-step cycle of assessment, selecting objectives, following a learning program, and then re-assessment. Using 9 x 12-inch "task cards" the teacher can record each child's progress in six or seven broadly defined areas (such as "letters"). Teachers use formal assessment methods to place children at the start and then move them ahead based on continuous, informal assessments of their mastery.

The Integrated Curriculum

Whatever their formal construct or rationale for teaching mixed-age groups, most teachers use another powerful classroom technique to pull together their learning objectives. Each year they select a theme—whales, for example, or "workers in the neighborhood," or "families from long ago"—and organize every aspect of the curriculum around it. Children practice language skills as they read about the theme and write about it; they measure and graph its component parts using math and science skills. Social studies material like history and geography is all tied in; and the whole class takes field trips together around the theme, practicing social skills along the way. In a class that stays with the same teacher from year to year, the theme shifts yearly; so teachers must plan on at least a two-year cycle.

Integrating a curriculum around a theme allows children of different ages and stages to work together in a group as well as to practice skills at different levels. "I might read an oversized picture book to the whole class," says Norma Leutzinger. "The older kids and early readers will be following the text, and the younger ones will get something from the pictures and the discussion, as well as from being read to aloud." Working together on a theme-related project, an eight-year-old may write down a story dictated by a six-year-old, type it, and bind it into a book illustrated by the nonreader, then give it back to the nonreader, who can use it to practice reading his own work.

The challenge of moving toward a mixed-age grouping can seem formidable when all the standard classroom materials are geared toward single-grade content areas. But in practice, say the teachers who do it, having to come up with theme-related activities and materials is a powerful spur to trying new ways of teaching. Because the children are still at a developmental age at which learning must be largely organized around concrete objects, useful learning materials can be as ordinary as bottle caps, bread tags, and popsicle sticks; and their collection can involve parents in the life of the classroom, too. And teachers learn from each other, sharing ideas as well as materials, planning together, and scheduling joint class activities. P.S. 41 encourages its teachers to visit other schools committed to mixed-age classes, like the model school at Bank Street College of Education.

Another good source of support, ironically, is the guidebook published by the Canadian province of Manitoba for teachers in small rural schools where mixed-age grouping is more necessity than choice. A down-to-earth manual crammed with ideas for themes, schedules, record-keeping and assessment, and dozens of other subjects, it is useful for long-range and short-term planning both. (For ordering information, call EDRS at 800-227-3742 and ask for ED300814.)

DIFFERENT WAYS TO GROUP CHILDREN OF DIFFERENT AGES

One key to the success of a multi-age classroom is a variety of groupings that afford students the opportunity to advance at their own pace, tutor others, and mix with different children. Some types of grouping are:

- **Problem-solving grouping,** in which learners are grouped around a common unsolved topic or problem; for example, a group discussion related to the main idea of a story.
- **Needs-requirement grouping,** in which students are instructed in a concept, skill, or value; for example, extra instruction in consonant blends.
- **Reinforcement grouping,** for learners who need more work in a specific area or task.
- **Interest grouping,** for learners who want, say, to read poetry out loud.
- **Learning-style grouping,** for those with a common pattern of learning, such as through manipulation of objects.

Adapted from Language Arts Handbook for Primary-Grade Teachers in Multi-Graded Classrooms, *Winnipeg: Manitoba, Department of Education, Canada, 1988.*

MULTIAGE

Who Most Benefits?

Do children in mixed-age groupings do better in the long run than those in single-age classes? Some categories of students do, some don't; but none seem to fare worse in mixed-age classes. The research on this question is somewhat inconclusive, partly because just what defines a "nongraded primary classroom" is often not clearly spelled out. Still, study results generally show a pattern of improved language skills among mixed-group students; in other academic areas, tests either favor mixed-age or show no difference. Nobody falls behind, these measures show; although those students on developmental and academic extremes benefit most—boys, blacks, the slow and the gifted, and children with low self-esteem. Some researchers report that such grouping is particularly effective for bright but immature children, who need both academic stimulation and a social environment more suited to a younger child. Others have shown that the longer children stay in nongraded classes the more their achievement scores rise in relation to their ability.

Most of the available research measuring these results is fairly old; but more recent research on how children learn tends to support the mixed-age structure as well. For example, children have been shown to adjust their language from an early age depending on who their audience is—so in a mixed-age class, a younger child could be stimulated to rise to the older children's level. Researchers have shown that in social situations, children spontaneously tend to choose mixed-age situations over same-age ones, lending weight to the argument that such arrangements foster social development. And peer tutoring has been shown to be a particularly effective learning technique between students of different ages—especially if the "novice" is already within a certain key range of the "expert" in her grasp of the topic. Finally, mixed-age groupings make it virtually impossible for a teacher to lecture on the same material to a large group, and research clearly shows that the more personal and individual the lesson, the more effective it is.

So Why Not?

Given all these advantages to mixed-age grouping, why are more schools not doing it? The most conservative answer is that such classes are not necessarily best for every student. Even the National Association for the Education of Young Children (NAEYC), whose 1988 position statement strongly advocates "developmentally appropriate" child-centered practice in the primary grades, recommends family groupings as only one of the desirable ways to achieve this. Classroom groups should vary in composition, the NAEYC says, depending on children's needs, and children should be placed where it is expected they will do best— "which may be in a family grouping and which is more likely to be determined by developmental than chronological age."

Some teachers shy away from mixed-age grouping at first, for understandable reasons. For one thing, over the last twenty years teachers have often been assigned to such classrooms simply to accommodate population overflows, not for pedagogical reasons—and so this has become the least-desirable assignment in the school, involving as it does two entirely separate preparations every day. The solution, say advocates, is to combine the class for many subjects and to adapt one's teaching style to a more individualized approach, rather than lecturing to two "classes" who vary considerably within themselves in any case.

The team teaching that often inspires mixed-age grouping can be difficult for some teachers. "You have to be realistic about the interpersonal stuff," says CPE director Esther Rosenthal. "With collaborative work, you have to be constantly talking about what you're doing, and it gets to be a strain." Other teachers who have teamed up agree that the right match of chemistry and teaching styles can make all the difference in how it works.

Teachers who are not trained to work with different ages at once may object to the idea. Few education schools offer courses that directly support this, and few open classrooms exist for practice teachers to learn in. As an interim step, therefore, some principals re-assign teachers annually to different grades until they are comfortable enough with several levels to combine them easily.

Until elementary teachers must study early childhood education before they work with the early grades—something that is required in Great Britain, and that NAEYC recommends—the skills to run a developmentally based mixed-age program may be lacking. So far, the U.S. educational establishment has simply not supported the development of mixed-age elementary teaching.

The bureaucracy of a central testing system also gets in the way of teachers trying out new ways. "To do this, you've got to trust yourself to introduce skills in your own way," says Norma Leutzinger. Though test results eventually prove that it works, she says, it takes a lot of confidence to change a traditional system.

Finally, a powerful system of textbook publishing that serves mainly single-grade classes impedes progress toward a more developmental approach. In the "scope and sequence" curriculum models of the last decade, children at every grade level were trained in carefully delineated subject areas before they moved on to the next grade. Mixing classes together, even if only for selected subjects, messes up that system. If it is to work, publishers will have to adapt—as they are beginning to already, prodded by the whole-language movement.

In the end, change may come bit by bit, as teachers find ways to team with each other comfortably, to give up absolute control at the head of the class, and to support new teachers on unfamiliar ground. The rewards are many, according to those who do it. "It's a whole different dimension," says Norma Leutzinger, "and it changes you. It's wonderful, but draining—just as intense as having a family. But then you see kids leave you, at the end of your two years together, with the confidence to stand up in front of the class and speak about something. And you see them come back, year after year, they visit your class, you read to them, and you play with them on the playground. I wouldn't do it any other way for the world." □

The Return of the Nongraded Classroom

Major changes in school structure have created a promising new climate for an old approach to education.

Robert H. Anderson

Laima Druskis

MULTIAGE

Has the time for nongradedness in elementary schools finally come? My answer is *yes*! There are powerful forces for educational change in this country that are calling for structural as well as instructional improvements that are wholly consistent with nongraded concepts and approaches. The educational environment has rarely been as favorable as it is today.

Nearly every other dimension of restructuring, including teacher empowerment, teamwork, site-based decision making, and providing more flexible alternatives for students, changes the dynamics of school practice in ways that make a nongraded approach not only more meaningful, but also more attainable.

In virtually every argument for restructuring American schools, there are either explicit references to the rigidity and inappropriateness of the conventional graded structure, or implicit recommendations for continuous progress and changes in present promotion/retention practices. Never before in its checkered history has the graded school, with its lockstep curriculum and competitive-comparative pupil evaluation system, come under such attack not only by thoughtful educators, but also by politicians and business people. No less a figure than W. Edwards Deming, the guru of total quality management, has become a vocal critic of school retention,

Robert H. Anderson is president of Pedamorphosis, Inc., in Tampa, Florida, and coauthor of *The Nongraded Elementary School* and *Nongradedness: Helping It to Happen*.

grouping, and competitive grading practices.

The Trouble with Graded Schools

It is strange that the graded school, with its overloaded, textbook-dominated curriculum, and its relatively primitive assumptions about human development and learning, has held its ground this long. To my knowledge there has never been a respectable body of research or scholarly reflection on the academic and social legitimacy of segregating students by age and providing them with a standard curriculum.

The graded school concept, born of administrative practicality and puritanical traditions, was first introduced by Horace Mann to Massachusetts from Prussia in the mid-nineteenth century. It is unfortunate that these justifications for graded schools persist in the 1990s.

Equally persistent is the historic isolation of predominantly female teachers from each other, often combined with supervisory practices that could be labeled as sexist in today's society, as well as punishment practices that could be labeled as child abuse. Add to this the tendency of many educators and business leaders to continue viewing the tax-supported public school system largely as a funnel for producing unskilled workers at a time when there are no longer an abundance of jobs available to them.

Regrettably, John Dewey's visionary concepts of "educating the whole child" and of appealing to children's multi-dimensional interests and talents failed to gain much momentum until well after World War II. And even today, the use of terms such as "critical thinking," "humane educational practices," or "child-centered classrooms" produce sharply negative reaction in some communities.

Déjà Vu All Over Again?

It is difficult to write an accurate history of nongradedness, partly because there have been so many instances over the years of varied efforts, each with its own label and ground rules, and partly because the extent or success of such efforts were rarely recorded. In the post-Sputnik climate of educational reform, labels such as "nongraded education," "open education," "team teaching," and "individu-

(Photo courtesy of Teaching/K-8, John Flavell (photographer) and Pikeville Elementary School, Pikeville, Kentucky.)

alized instruction" were often used more as expressions of intent than as titles of accomplishment.

However, in many schools and districts across the country, there emerged the forerunners of what is now being defined as nongraded education. The movement began after World War II, when an expanding pupil population produced a corresponding surge of interest in how better to fit schooling practices to emerging understanding of child growth and development. In a climate favorable for "modernizing" schools, a "first wave" of nongradedness began in the 1950s and continued through the early 1970s. In retrospect, however, those early efforts touched only a small fraction of American schoolchildren, and only a few of them led to the establishment of authentic nongraded models.

Therefore, it is inaccurate for any educator to shout "déjà vu!" and to say that nongradedness has already been tried and found wanting. Some fairly good nongraded programs did emerge and thrive over time, notably within the team-taught, multi-aged grouping framework of Individually Guided Education, as developed by the Kettering Foundation and the University of Wisconsin. We are not starting from scratch in the 1990s.

Barbara Pavan, who first surveyed the research literature on nongradedness about 20 years ago, recently completed an update of that research with 64 added studies (Anderson and Pavan 1993). Her findings showed that, in terms of academic achievement and mental health, results favoring graded groups are very rare. Most of the studies show neutral or inconclusive outcomes when graded and nongraded groups are compared, but results favoring the nongraded approach are growing in both quantity and quality.

In a climate favorable for "modernizing" schools, a "first wave" of nongradedness began in the 1950s and continued through the early 1970s.

"There is now," Pavan reports, "definitive research evidence to confirm the theories underlying nongradedness." It appears a nongraded environment especially benefits boys, blacks, underachievers, and students from lower socioeconomic groups, with the benefits increasing the longer that children remain in that environment. Pavan's work also confirms the conclusion that nongradedness is most likely to thrive when teachers work in teams with multi-aged aggregations of children.

What's Holding Us Back?

As seems to be true for all efforts at educational reform, the obstacles to nongradedness are mostly matters of habit and attitude. Some of the more constraining *habits* of teachers include:

• Over-reliance on graded instructional materials and tests;
• Voluntary seclusion in self-contained classrooms;
• Reluctance to take risks or rock the boat;
• Familiarity with graded classes from their own childhoods; and
• Disinclination to pursue new skills through staff development.

Some of the most constraining *attitudes*, closely linked with the foregoing habits, are:

• Resentment (often justified) of administrators' tendencies to embrace every innovation that comes along;
• Skepticism about theoretical, as opposed to practical, ideas;
• Limited acceptance of the slogan, proclaimed by Jerome Bruner, Benjamin Bloom, and others, that "all children can learn"; and
• Conviction that some children can only be motivated extrinsically (*e.g.*, by graded report cards and fear of retention).

On the positive side, the great majority of teachers now in service are better educated, particularly with respect to how children develop and learn, than were their predecessors a generation ago. They are more accepting of individual differences and more aware of the vast array of pedagogical options available to them, including whole language, cooperative learning, and heterogeneous grouping.

Similarly, today's principals are better prepared to assume the role of facilitator, and more willing to share decision-making power with their staffs. Both teachers and principals also understand the great need we have in our schools for professional communication and collaboration.

One of the reasons that nongradedness seems more achievable in the 1990s is that there are now good models available for pupil-peer tutoring and cooperative learning programs, as well as a wider variety of technological aids and instructional materials. Authentic nongraded programs can make good use of these models and materials.

Most advocates of nongradedness believe it is essential for students to belong to a basic aggregation of children that embraces at least two (preferably three) age

Today's principals are better prepared to assume the role of facilitator, and more willing to share decision-making power with their staffs. Both teachers and principals also understand the great need we have in our schools for professional communication and collaboration.

MULTIAGE

groups. Thus, a nongraded primary group might include five-, six-, and seven-year-olds, or six-, seven-, and eight-year-olds. We now know that the most natural learning environment for children calls for heterogeneous multi-age groupings, within which all sorts of homogeneous *and* heterogeneous subgroupings can be created as needed.

I believe that an ideal nongraded grouping should number from 70 to 120 children, in the charge of a team of three to six teachers. It has been demonstrated that a truly nongraded environment is much

---

What Is Authentic Nongradedness?

Authentic nongraded schools should meet, or come close to meeting, the following criteria:

• Replacement of labels associated with gradedness, like first grade and fifth grade, with group titles like "primary unit" that are more appropriate to the concept of continuous progress;

• Replacement of competitive-comparative evaluation systems (and the report cards associated with them) with assessment and reporting mechanisms that respect continuous individual progress and avoid competitive comparisons;

• All groupings to include at least two heterogeneous age cohorts;

• Groups assembled for instructional purposes to be non-permanent, being dissolved and reconstituted as needed;

• Organization of the teaching staff into teams, with teachers having maximum opportunities to interact and collaborate;

• Development of a flexible, interdisciplinary, whole-child-oriented curriculum, with grade-normed books and tests used only as resources (if used at all);

• Adoption of official policies consistent with nongradedness in the school and at the school board level, even where waivers of policy may be required (*e.g.*, reporting enrollments by grades).

"Simply launching a nongraded program is at least a two-year process... To develop a mature and smooth-running operation... may require an additional five years."

---

easier to produce when the philosophy and practices of nongradedness are combined with multi-age approaches and some form of team teaching. In fact, it is almost impossible to find examples of authentic nongradedness within single-age groups of children taught by lone teachers in self-contained classrooms.

Where do you find authentic nongradedness? This is a tough question to answer, for two reasons. First, schools offering programs that can be considered "authentic" (*see box*) are not abundant; and second, there are few accurate listings of these schools should you wish to visit one. The Canadian province of British Columbia probably has the most such schools at the moment, although states like Kentucky and Oregon may soon provide good models. At present, several organizations are cooperating on a project to establish an international registry of such schools, which would serve as models for nongraded education.

How Do You Go Nongraded?

In our 1993 book, Pavan and I propose that one of the first steps should be to take an inventory of your staff's basic beliefs and intuitions. If too many teachers are uncomfortable with the philosophy and prac-

---

tices associated with nongradedness, there is little point in taking the plunge. Conversely, if many on your staff are true believers, mountains can be moved!

The next step is for your teachers to immerse themselves in the literature in order to acquire a sound knowledge base about authentic nongradedness. Such immersion should include the resolution of questions about such matters as pupil grouping, teacher teaming, evaluating pupil progress, dealing with the public, and adopting necessary policies.

You should be forewarned that simply *launching* a nongraded program is at least a two-year process. It takes a lot of time to work out policies and procedures, to make curriculum changes, to prepare the community, and to provide appropriate staff development and training. To develop a mature and smooth-running operation, with an integrated, interdisciplinary, and multi-dimensional curriculum may require an additional five years.

But when it comes to developing an exciting and successful nongraded program, it is well to remember that trite but useful motto: "Rome wasn't built in a day!"□

REFERENCES

American Association of School Administrators. *The Nongraded Primary: Making Schools Fit Children.* Arlington, Va.: The Association, 1992.

Anderson, Robert H., and Pavan, Barbara N. *Nongradedness: Helping It to Happen.* Lancaster, Pa.: Technomic Publishing, 1993.

Bloom, Benjamin S. *Human Characteristics and School Learning.* New York: McGraw-Hill, 1976.

Bruner, Jerome S. *The Process of Education.* Cambridge, Mass.: Harvard University Press, 1960.

Gardner, Howard. *Frames of Mind: The Theory of Multiple Intelligences.* New York: Basic Books, 1983.

Gayfer, Margaret. *The Multi-Grade Classroom: Myth and Reality.* Toronto: Canadian Education Association, 1991.

Gaustad, Joan. "Nongraded Education: Mixed-Age, Integrated, and Developmentally Appropriate Education for Primary Children." *OSSC Bulletin* (Oregon School Study Council), March 1992.

Gaustad, Joan. "Making the Transition from Graded to Nongraded Primary Education." *OSSC Bulletin* (Oregon School Study Council), April 1992.

Goodlad, John I., and Anderson, Robert H. *The Nongraded Elementary School*, 3rd edition. New York: Teachers College Press, 1987.

The Gift of Time

In this novel approach to teaching, primary graders move ahead by staying right where they are

BY DIANA MAZZUCHI AND
NANCY BROOKS

Have you ever said to yourself, "If I could just have that child for two or three more months . . . he (or she) is just beginning to get it."

As first grade teachers, we said that to ourselves every June. One year, we decided to do something about it. We approached our principal and got permission to try something new: We would keep our first grade students for a second year as second graders.

Here's how it works: When Nancy finishes in June with her first graders, she takes her class on to second grade in September, while Diana begins with a new class of first graders. The following year, Diana takes her first graders on to second grade, while Nancy begins with a new group of first graders.

Actually, it's a lot simpler than it sounds. And it has been successful. In fact, it's been so successful that we've now completed three two-year cycles, and we wouldn't want it any other way.

Other benefits. Keeping children for two years in the same classroom is very different from a multi-age classroom. In Vermont, groups of two or more grades in one classroom have long been a fact of life for many schools. We've both taught mixtures of grade levels in one classroom, and although there are advantages to such an arrangement, the two-year span offers other benefits. For one thing, a child's development is seen in a less fragmented way and in a more natural setting when it occurs over time.

Also, a two-year span provides a child

Diana Mazzuchi and Nancy Brooks teach at Academy School, Brattleboro, VT.

> **"Two years in the same class works wonders with children who are shy."**

with greater continuity in experience, both socially and academically. The opportunities to make personal connections with others and with ideas over time are especially valuable for emotional and intellectual growth.

Many children find the consistency that comes with two years with the same teacher and students extremely valuable. For example, by the time Genny was six and a half, she had lived in two states, one foreign country and had attended a total of seven day care facilities. She had never been to kindergarten, nor to an American classroom before. It took the first year for Genny to adjust and begin to read in English. Socially, the other children went from seeing Genny as almost an "alien" to accepting her and liking her and recognizing her strengths. In the second year, she blossomed because all those involved—the teacher, the children, the parents and Genny herself— had time.

Working wonders. Two years in the same class also works wonders with children who are shy. We've had numerous students come out of their shell in the second year because they felt confident about themselves and secure within the group. Holly is a good example. A bright but extremely quiet child, Holly would participate in oral activities within a group, but rarely shared personal opinions of a risk-taking nature. In the second year, however, she was leading many groups in story theater activities and sharing aloud her opinions about books she had read.

Jolie was another two-year student. She was so shy that she rarely spoke, except in a whisper and then usually just to her teacher. An eighth grader now, she is frequently teased about the "good old days" when she didn't talk. It's hard to get her to be quiet now.

Working closely with the same classmates for two years gives children a sense of security.

Visitors to this Academy School classroom are amazed at the level of intensity shown by the children.

Another shining example is Anna. Within the whole group, she would never volunteer anything unless called on, and then only in a very quiet voice. Changes were first noticed in small group project time, when the group would choose activities to do in the listening, game, art and writing areas. In the beginning, Anna went along with whatever the group decided. She was encouraged to speak up and slowly she spoke more and more.

Her mom shared a story of Anna's visit to the doctor. The doctor kept talking over her head to her mom. Anna interrupted, "Hey! Aren't we talking about *my* ears?" At that point, the doctor apologized and included Anna in the conversation. Obviously, Anna felt empowered to speak up for herself.

Support from parents. A two-year teaching span has still other advantages. The teacher definitely gets to know her or his students and their parents. The children and parents, for their part, get to know the teacher. We have much greater support from parents whose children are in the second year. The parents are more comfortable with us. They know our philosophy of education and how it applies to teaching their children.

During the first year, we work hard to

Many children in the two-year program become close friends, even to the point of regarding the class as a family unit.

communicate with the parents. We invite them to share in the learning experiences of their children. We send them newsletters which explain various aspects of the curriculum. The result is that in the second year, we have parents participate in events for the first time. We have greater support for fund-raising, and we have more volunteers in the classroom.

As any teacher knows, it takes time to find out the interests, learning style and abilities of each student in the classroom. All aspects of classroom planning are affected by this knowledge. As a result of having the same child for the second year, the teacher already has this information in depth and can build on it. At the beginning of the second year, the children and teacher immediately get into where they left off last spring.

As far as the curriculum is concerned, we're able to spread certain themes over a longer period of time, allowing each child opportunities to build conceptual knowledge and develop attitudes and behavior for maximum learning. For example, if we study "The Family and Its Needs" in first grade, then in second grade we might study how the neighborhood contributes to the needs of the family.

Frequently, children bring up activities and experiences from the previous year that relate to present activities. We're able to help children carry over information and make connections because we know what concepts and skills our children have to build on.

Familiar figure. For many children, the end of the first grade can be very scary. They're leaving a familiar figure and are not sure until sometime in August (when a letter informs parents and children) just who their teacher will be for the following year. Our children, however, know who they're going to have. They leave the classroom on the last day of school, waving happily and yelling, "See you next September!" To make the bond just a little firmer, we correspond with each child over the summer.

Each teacher has her or his own style, and for many children, making the transition from one teaching style to another can be difficult—especially during the primary years. In addition to a new teacher, there are new routines, new expectations and often new classmates to adjust to. The two-year span, however, enables the child to establish more firmly an identity in what is often a large, institutional setting.

Visitors to our classroom on the first week of second grade are amazed at the level of intensity and focus of our second graders. Relationships have deepened and matured. Kyla remarked to her father how much

another child's reading had improved. "He can really read some things he couldn't read before," she said. She took pleasure in the other child's growth. This kind of group support contributes to problem-solving in the classroom and carries over onto the playground. There's a great deal of evaluation, in the most positive sense, that goes on in the second year.

One mother told us that for her second-year child, the class had become a family unit. When her son had been ill for several days, almost everyone in the class sent him a get-well card. Because her child was diabetic, a sense of security was necessary for him to be able to feel comfortable dealing with his diabetes in the classroom. As a result of the security he felt in the classroom, the mother said, her son had become very independent and competent.

Another child in the same class had to deal with the death of his father. The whole class shared in his sense of sadness and tried to help him through it.

"Gift of time". The most important benefit of the two-year span is the "gift of time" it gives to many children. All children do not learn in the same way or at the same pace, of course. However, that's sometimes forgotten when children do not learn at the pace expected of them. As a result, the children are penalized in some way.

In our two-year span, if a child needs more time to gain understanding, we can build in helpful activities over a longer period of time. There are many cases where a child is reading six months below grade level at the end of first grade. Because he or she is going on with the same teacher, retention is not an alternative. Then, a "miracle" happens! By giving the child the security and comfort of the same group, as well as "the gift of time," the child is able to read at grade level with true comprehension by the end of the second year.

Our approach has been so successful that it's being given serious consideration by other primary teachers in our school. In fact, two teachers are thinking about trying it out with third and fourth graders. We feel that keeping a class for two years would work at all grade levels. The children become such a strong, established group that they deal with any issues that come up in a loving, supportive way. ↓

"We have much greater support from parents whose children are in the second year."

MULTIAGE

Reprinted with permission of the publisher, Early Years, Inc., Norwalk, CT 06834.
From the Feb. 1992 issue of *Teaching / K-8.*

The Multiage, Nongraded Continuous Progress Classroom

Bibliography

Compiled by SDE Presenters

If you would like help locating any of these books, contact Crystal Springs Books, 1-800-321-0401.

American Association of School Administrators. *The Nongraded Primary: Making Schools Fit Children.* Arlington, VA: Author, 1992.

Anderson, Robert H., and Pavan, Barbara N. *Nongradedness: Helping it to Happen.* Lancaster, PA: Technomic Press, 1992.

Ellis, Susan, & Whalen, Susan F. *Cooperative Learning: Getting Started.* New York: Scholastic Professional Books, 1990.

Fogarty, Robin. *The Mindful School: How to Integrate the Curricula.* Palatine, IL: Skylight Publishing, Inc, 1991.

Gardner, Howard. *Frames of Mind: The Theory of Multiple Intelligences.* New York: Basic Books, Inc., 1983.

Gayfer, Margaret, ed. *The Multi-Grade Classroom Myth and Reality: A Canadian Study.* Toronto: Canadian Education Association, 1991.

Gaustad, Joan. *Making the Transition from Graded to Nongraded Primary Education.* Oregon School Study Council Bulletin, Vol. 35, Issue (8). Eugene, OR: Oregon School Study Council, 1992.

_____. *Nongraded Education: Mixed-Age, Integrated and Developmentally Appropriate Education for Primary Children.* Oregon School Study Council Bulletin, Vol. 35, Issue 7. Eugene, OR: Oregon School Study Council, 1992.

George, Paul. *How to Untrack Your School.* Alexandria, VA: Association for Supervision and Curriculum Development, 1992.

Goodlad, John I., and Anderson, Robert H. *The Nongraded Elementary School.* New York: Teachers College Press, rev. 1987.

Grant, Jim. *Developmental Education in the 1990's.* Rosemont, NJ: Modern Learning Press, 1991.

Grant, Jim, and Johnson, Bob. *The Multiage Handbook.* Peterborough, NH: Crystal Springs Books, 1993.

Gutierrez, Roberto, and Slavin, Robert E. *Achievement Effects of the Nongraded Elementary School: A Retrospective Review.* Baltimore, MD: Center for Research on Effective Schooling for Disadvantaged Students, 1992.

Hunter, Madeline. *How to Change to a Nongraded School.* Alexandria, VA: Association for Supervision and Curriculum Development, 1992.

Kasten, Wendy, and Clarke, Barbara. *The Multi-Age Classroom.* Katonah, NY: Richard Owen, 1993.

Katz, Lilian G.; Evangelou, Demetra; and Hartman, Jeanette Allison. *The Case for Mixed-age Grouping in Early Education.* Washington DC: NAEYC, 1990.

Kentucky Department of Education. *Kentucky's Primary School: The Wonder Years.* Frankfort, KY: Author.

Kentucky Education Association and Appalachia Educational Laboratory. *Ungraded Primary Programs: Steps Toward Developmentally Appropriate Instruction.* Frankfort, KY: KEA, 1990.

Kohn, Alfie. *No Contest: The Case Against Competition.* Boston: Houghton Mifflin Company, 1986.

Manitoba Department of Education. *Language Arts Handbook for Primary Teachers in Multigrade Classrooms.* Winnipeg, Man.: Author, 1988.

Miller, Bruce A. *The Multigrade Classroom: A Resource Handbook for Small, Rural Schools.* Portland, OR: Northwest Regional Educational Laboratory, 1989.

_____. *Training Guide for the Multigrade Classroom: A Resource Handbook for Small, Rural Schools.* Portland, OR: Northwest Regional Educational Laboratory, 1990.

National Association of Elementary School Principals. *Standards for Quality Elementary and Middle Schools: Kindergarten through Eighth Grade.* Alexandria, VA: Author, rev. 1990.

_____. *Early Childhood Education and the Elementary School Principal*. Alexandria, VA: Author, 1990.

Oakes, Jeannie. *Keeping Track: How Schools Structure Equality*. New Haven: Yale University Press, 1985.

Province of British Columbia Ministry of Education. *Foundation*. Victoria, BC: Author, 1990.

_____. *Our Primary Program: Taking the Pulse*. Victoria, BC: Author, 1990.

_____. *Primary Program Foundation Document*. Victoria, BC: Author, 1990.

_____. *Primary Program Resource*. Victoria, BC: Author, 1990.

_____. *Resource*. Victoria, BC: Author, 1990.

Rathbone, Charles et al. *Teaching and Learning in the Multiage Classroom*. Peterborough, NH: Crystal Springs Books, 1993.

Society For Developmental Education. *The Multiage, Ungraded Continuous Progress School: The Lake George Model*. Peterborough, NH: Author, 1992.

_____. *Multiage Classrooms: The Ungrading of America's Schools*. Peterborough, NH: Author, 1993.

Virginia Education Association and Appalachia Educational Laboratory. *Teaching Combined Grade Classes: Real Problems and Promising Practices*. Charleston, WY: AEL, 1990.

Wheelock, Anne. *Crossing the Tracks: How 'Untracking' Can Save America's Schools*. New York: New Press, 1992.

Audio/Video Resources

Anderson, Robert H., and Pavan, Barbara N. *The Nongraded School*. Videocassette. Bloomington, IN: Phi Delta Kappa.

Association of Supervision and Curriculum Development. *Tracking: Road to Success or Dead End?* Audiocassette. Alexandria, VA: Association for Supervision and Curriculum Development.

Grant, Jim. *Accommodating Developmentally Different Children in the Multiage Classroom*. 1993 NAESP Annual Convention – San Francisco. Audiocassette. Product #180, available from Chesapeake Audio / Video Communications, Inc., 6330 Howard Lane, Elkridge, MD 21227.

Katz, Lilian. *Multiage Groupings: A Key to Elementary Reform*. Audiocassette. Association for Supervision and Curriculum Development, 1250 North Pitt St., Alexandria, VA 22314, 1993.

Oakes, Jeannie, and Lipton, Martin. *On Tracking and Ability Grouping*. Videocassette. Bloomington, IN: Phi Delta Kappa.

Province of British Columbia Ministry of Education. *A Time of Wonder: Children in the Primary Years*. Videocassette. Victoria, BC: Crown Publications.

MULTIAGE

Voices

*A paradox: education (and society) is in trouble now; at the same time it has a chance to be the best it has ever been. For some, this chance in education is already being realized. These people know that, for them, a small revolution has taken place. Others could take the same challenging, empowering road. All it takes is vision, understanding, knowledge, hard work, and commitment — qualities good teachers have always had. The destination this time, however, is not arrived at through just **any** vision, **any** knowledge, **any** commitment. Where we're going is toward a principled practice, continually examined against a whole language set of beliefs about language and language learning — all in the service of a literate, educated, just society. We hope you will join us in taking that road. It makes a difference!*

Carole Edelsky, Bess Altwerger and Barbara Flores
Whole Language: What's the Difference?

Published by Heinemann, Portsmouth, NH.

Multiage Resources

National Alliance of Multiage Educators (N.A.M.E.)
The Society For Developmental Education
PO Box 577
Peterborough, NH 03458
1-603-924-9256

An Interview with Jim Grant, SDE's Executive Director

What is N.A.M.E.?

N.A.M.E. is the National Alliance of Multiage Educators. This network was created to answer the growing need of educators who are interested in continuous progress practices. N.A.M.E. will give them an opportunity to share ideas, information, and experiences with others who have similar interests.

When did it begin?

The idea for N.A.M.E. was born of a tremendous response to a multiage article that appeared in the fall 1992 issue of *The SDE News.* The network began taking shape in the beginning of 1993, with the official announcement made during SDE's 19th Annual Whole Language •Developmental Education Conference for Elementary School Educators in April 1993.

What is its purpose?

The network's most important function will be to provide a help line service that we call "teachers helping teachers." N.A.M.E. will serve as a clearing house for contacts in different geographical areas and will help people with particular interests and questions find each other.

Teachers and administrators are very excited about having a central network where, through one phone call, they can find people to talk with about common interests such as assessment, gaining parent support, discipline, cooperative learning, and curriculum.

The network will also keep multiage continuous progress educators informed about professional books, materials, resources, "best practices," research, and professional development opportunities.

Special interest groups may form around particular topics, and the network may generate a newsletter of its own. We'll have to wait and see what other possibilities arise. The network's success will depend on the active participation of its members.

How does it work?·

Members can contact the network by mail, fax (1-603-924-6688), or phone (1-603-924-9256). N.A.M.E. coordinators Marguerite Bellringer and Elizabeth Sharkey will field questions, provide names, addresses, and phone numbers of contact people, and refer them to additional sources of information. N.A.M.E. members should anticipate receiving phone calls and letters from other educators. And they shouldn't be shy about contacting others. The ultimate success of the network hinges on the willingness of members to share their experiences and knowledge.

Who can join?

Educators need not be currently teaching multiage classes in order to join N.A.M.E. Anyone with a genuine interest in multiage continuous progress practices is welcome. Individuals can join for a nominal fee of $9 a year. A school, with up to three individuals actively participating in the network, can join for $19 a year.

How does one join?

Fill out the application and send it with your membership fee to: N.A.M.E., PO Box 577, Peterborough, NH 03458. As soon as Marguerite or Elizabeth receive an application, they'll follow-up with a more detailed questionnaire to determine particular areas of interest and level of multiage experience.

The National Alliance of Multiage Educators is a registered service mark of The Society For Developmental Education.

---

n.a.m.e.
NATIONAL ALLIANCE OF MULTIAGE EDUCATORS sm

Membership Application

SB 6
1993-94

PO Box 577
Peterborough, NH 03458

Name:_____

Position:_____

Grade/age levels taught:_____

Home Address:_____

Town/City:_____ State:___ Zip_____

Home phone:_____

School phone:_____

Name of School:_____

School Address:_____

Town/City:_____ State:___ Zip:_____

N.A.M.E. membership will be under (circle one)

    individual   school

___I want to join N.A.M.E. My membership fee is enclosed.($9 individual, $19 school)

For school membership, photocopy and complete this form for each of the 3 members.

The American Lock-Step Graded School Organization

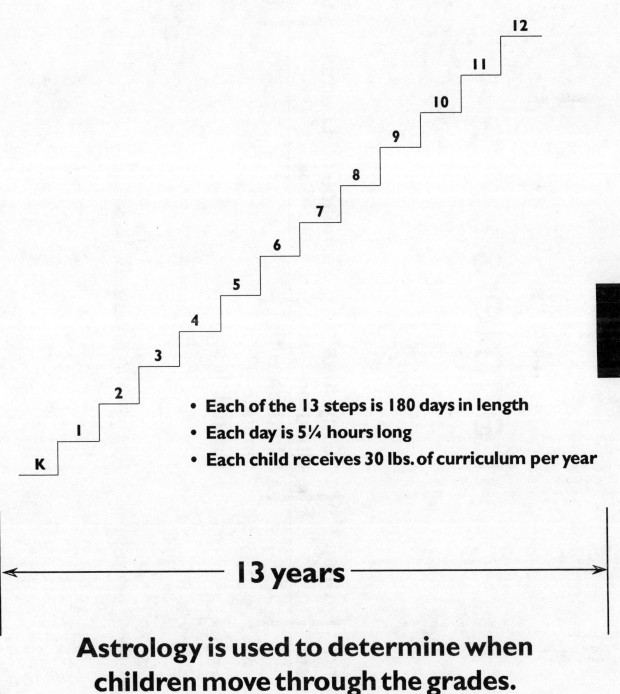

- Each of the 13 steps is 180 days in length
- Each day is 5¼ hours long
- Each child receives 30 lbs. of curriculum per year

← 13 years →

Astrology is used to determine when children move through the grades.

Jim Grant/Bob Johnson

Learners

Learning Disabled | Chap I | "Gray-Area" Children

Children with "Invisible" Disabilities

Non-labeled Learners | Gifted & Talented

The Primary Multiage Classroom

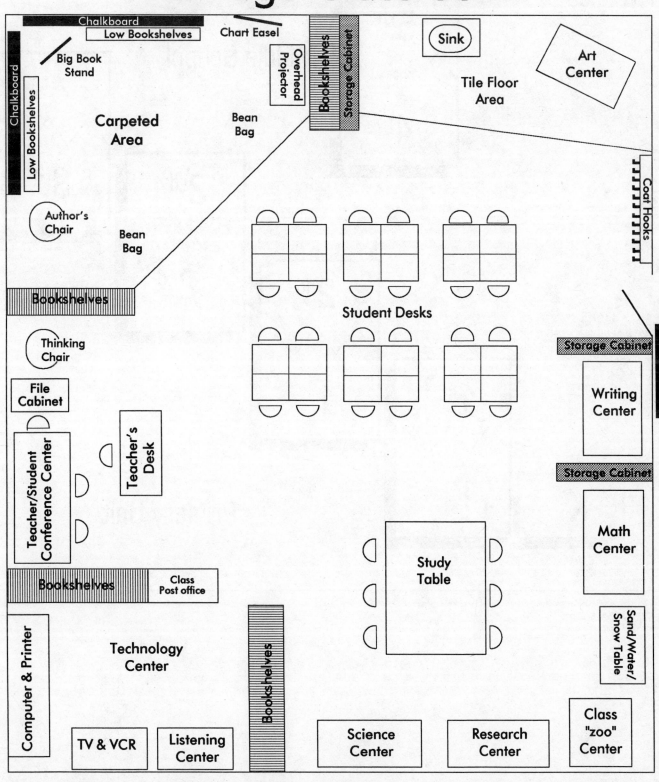

Jim Grant/Bob Johnson

Looping Configuration

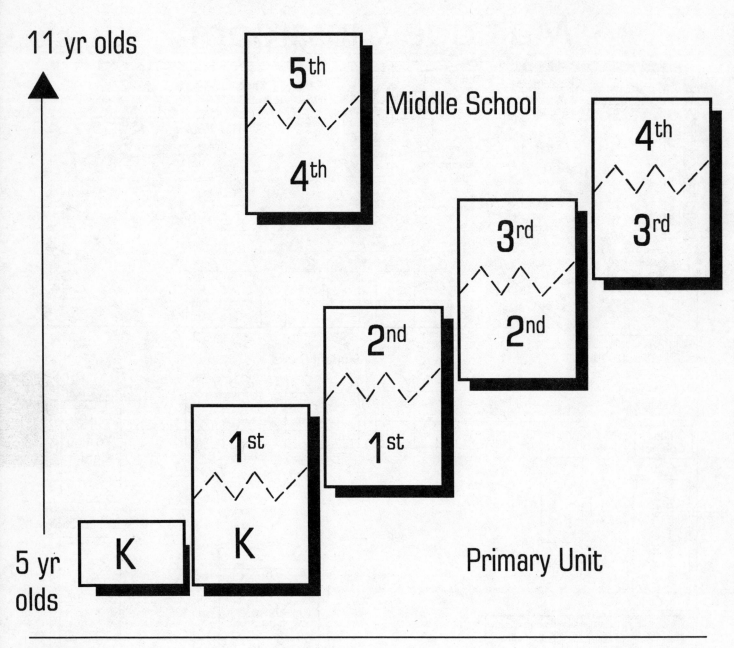

11 yr olds

5 yr olds

5th
4th

Middle School

4th
3rd

3rd
2nd

2nd
1st

1st
K

K

Primary Unit

Notes:

Jim Grant/Bob Johnson

Multigrade Configuration

8 yr olds

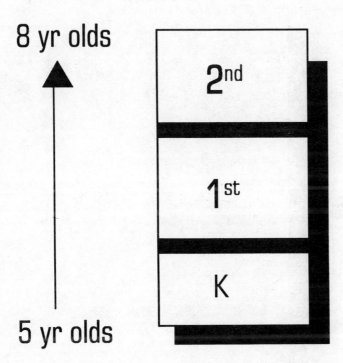

5 yr olds

Usually two or three consecutive grades 5 to 8 yr-olds

Kindergarten may or may not be included in this organization

MULTIAGE

Notes:

Traditional Graded Primary Configuration

9 yr olds

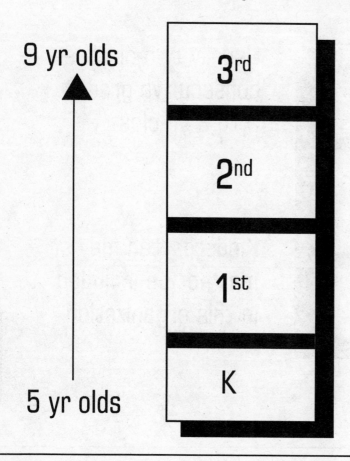

5 yr olds

Notes:

Jim Grant/Bob Johnson

Multiage Grouping Configuration

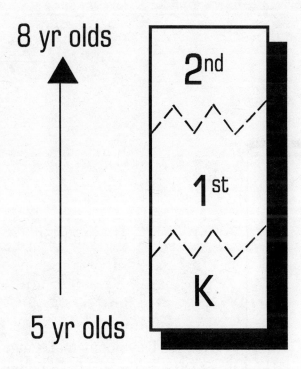

8 yr olds

2nd

1st

K

5 yr olds

Usually two or three consecutive grade levels with 3 to 4 age levels

Kindergarten may or may not be included in this organization

Notes:

Children Enter School on a Broken Front

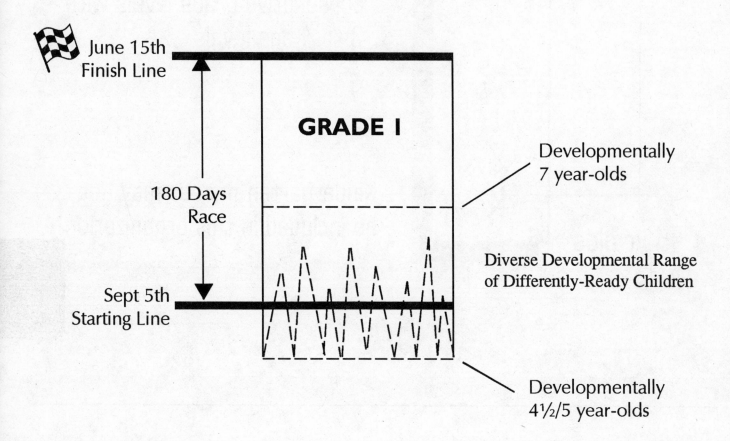

June 15th
Finish Line

GRADE I

Developmentally
7 year-olds

180 Days
Race

Diverse Developmental Range
of Differently-Ready Children

Sept 5th
Starting Line

Developmentally
4½/5 year-olds

Notes:

Jim Grant/Bob Johnson

Inclusion Education in the Multiage Classroom

GRADE ONE	6•7•8 YEAR-OLDS

One-year Placement

Two/three year-Multiage Placement

Differently-abled Children are more readily accommodated in a Mixed-age Setting

Notes:

Age/Grade Configuration

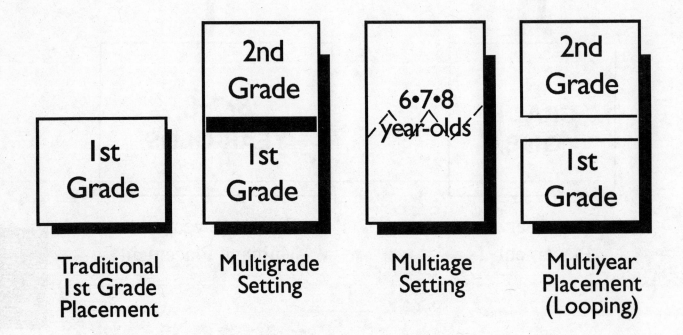

Traditional
1st Grade
Placement

Multigrade
Setting

Multiage
Setting

Multiyear
Placement
(Looping)

NOTES:

Looping Requires a Two-Teacher Partnership

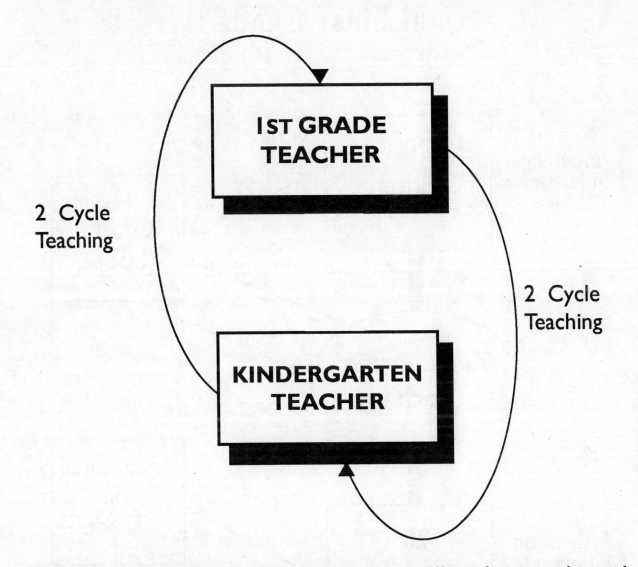

2 Cycle Teaching

2 Cycle Teaching

1ST GRADE TEACHER

KINDERGARTEN TEACHER

MULTIAGE

The kindergarten teacher is "promoted" to first grade with the class and keeps students for a second year.

The 1st grade teacher returns to kindergarten to pick up a new class and begins another two-year cycle.

Notes:

Looping With Kindergarten (½ day) and First Grade

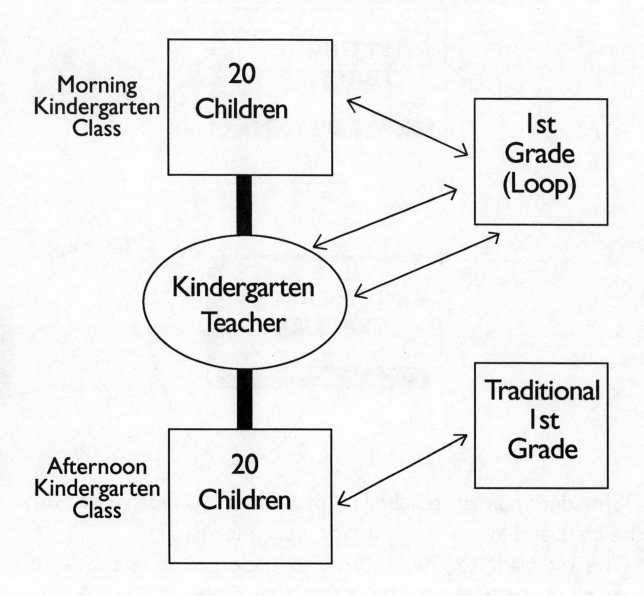

Morning Kindergarten Class

20 Children

1st Grade (Loop)

Kindergarten Teacher

Afternoon Kindergarten Class

20 Children

Traditional 1st Grade

Notes:

Jim Grant/Bob Johnson

Avoiding The Pitfalls: Making The Transition From Graded to Multi-age, Continuous Progress Grouping

- Review the recent research and literature regarding DAP and Multi-age.

- Develop a statement of the program's philosophy.

- Avoid change created by legislative mandate.

- Provide awareness / information workshops.

- Invite teacher initiated change.

- Provide in-service training – developmentally appropriate practices.
  - ✔ Learning styles / modalities, multiple intelligences.
  - ✔ Whole language strategies.
  - ✔ Manipulative mathematics.
  - ✔ Learning centers/themes.
  - ✔ Cooperative learning.

MULTIAGE

Avoiding The Pitfalls: Making The Transition From Graded to Multi-age, Continuous Progress Grouping

- Offer on-going professional development.

- Arrange for on-site visitations.

- Inform and educate teachers and parents.

- Create rather than replicate another program.

- Consider pilot programs.

- Phase-in : Transitioning.
  - ✔ Looping configurations.
  - ✔ Multi-grades.
  - ✔ Team theme teaching.
  - ✔ Team teaching.

Avoiding The Pitfalls: Making The Transition From Graded to Multi-age, Continuous Progress Grouping

- Provide release time for peer coaching.

- Provide regular planning time - during the school day.

- Initially, offer BOTH graded and non-graded classrooms.

- Employ **D**evelopmentally **A**ppropriate **P**ractices.

- Seek out funding sources.

MULTIAGE

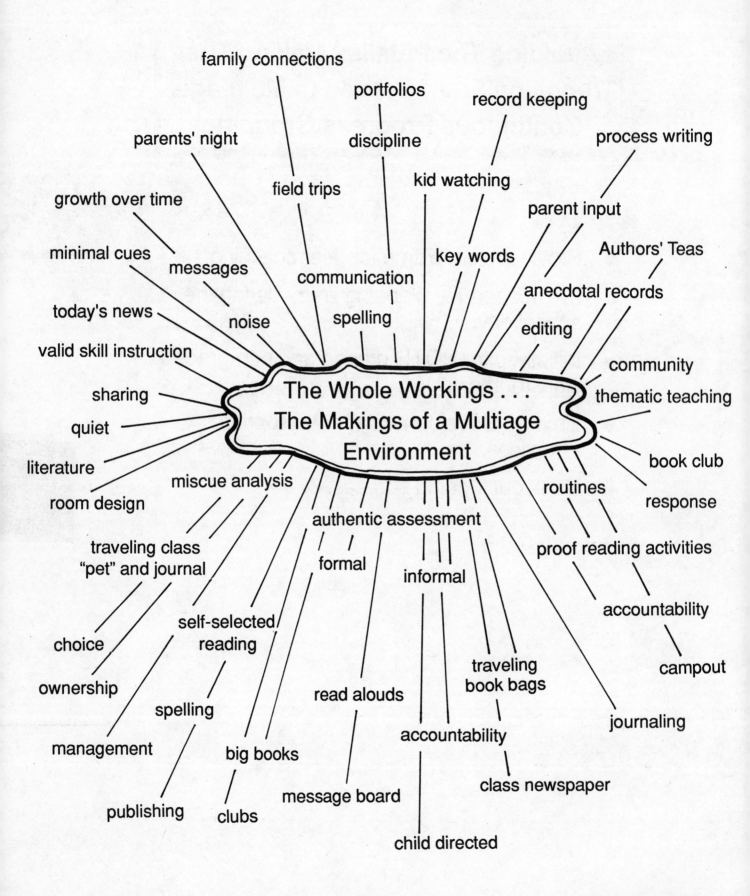

family connections

portfolios

record keeping

process writing

parents' night

discipline

growth over time

field trips

kid watching

parent input

minimal cues

messages

Authors' Teas

today's news

noise

communication

spelling

key words

anecdotal records

valid skill instruction

editing

community

sharing

**The Whole Workings . . .
The Makings of a Multiage
Environment**

thematic teaching

quiet

book club

literature

miscue analysis

routines

response

room design

authentic assessment

proof reading activities

traveling class
"pet" and journal

formal

informal

accountability

choice

self-selected
reading

traveling
book bags

campout

ownership

read alouds

journaling

spelling

accountability

management

big books

class newspaper

publishing

clubs

message board

child directed

Year-Long Theme for a Multiage Primary

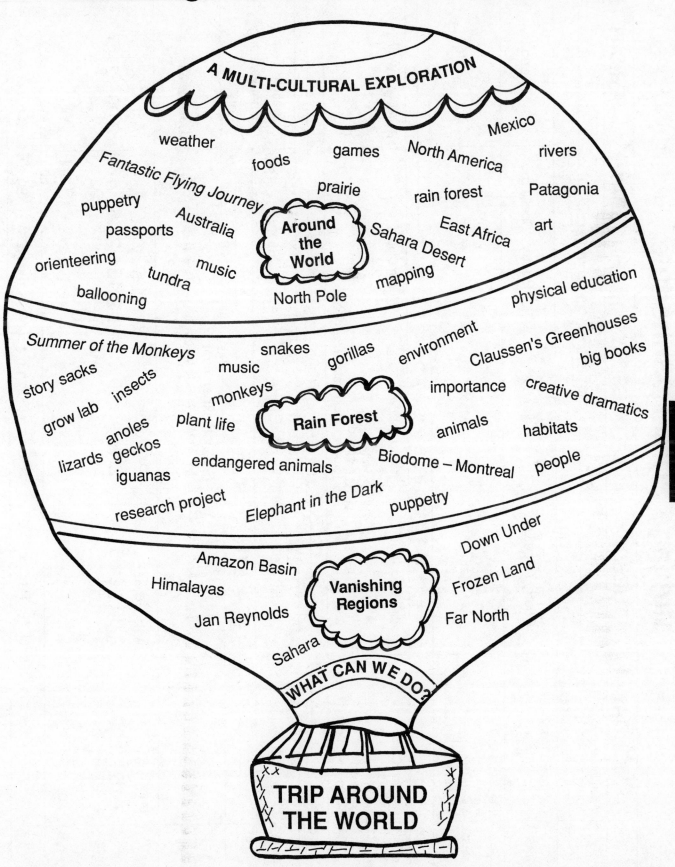

A MULTI-CULTURAL EXPLORATION

weather
foods
games
North America
Mexico
rivers

Fantastic Flying Journey
prairie
rain forest
Patagonia

puppetry
Australia
Around the World
Sahara Desert
East Africa
art

passports

orienteering
music
mapping
physical education

tundra
North Pole

ballooning

Summer of the Monkeys
snakes
gorillas
environment
Claussen's Greenhouses
big books

story sacks
music
importance
creative dramatics

grow lab   insects
monkeys
Rain Forest

anoles
plant life
animals
habitats

lizards geckos
endangered animals
Biodome – Montreal
people

iguanas

research project
Elephant in the Dark
puppetry

Down Under

Amazon Basin
Vanishing Regions
Frozen Land

Himalayas

Jan Reynolds
Far North

Sahara

WHAT CAN WE DO?

TRIP AROUND THE WORLD

Ellen Thompson

MULTIAGE

Multiage Primary Schedule

	MONDAY	TUESDAY	WEDNESDAY	THURSDAY	FRIDAY
8:45 – 9:15	Attendance Lunch money: HL - 1.25 milk - .25 juice - .35	———————— FREE CHOICE TIME ————————			
9:15 – 9:45	Calendar - Today's News Secret Message Proof Reading	Poetry / Spelling	Calendar	Poetry / Spelling	Calendar
9:45 – 10:30	Key Word Day • get new words • write - illustrate • Word analysis activities	Math	Math	Math	Math
10:30 – 11:00	———————— BOOK CLUB / SNACK / RECESS ————————				
11:00 – 11:55	Reading Club • select • read • respond writing group Ms. T	Reading Club	Writing Club • select • write • respond group whole class Ms. T	Writing Club	Reading or Writing Club
12:00 – 12:40	———————— LUNCH / RECESS ————————				
12:40 – 1:10	Story	Story	Story	Story	Spelling Test Silent Reading Story
1:10 – 1:30	———————— Silent Reading ————————				
1:30 –	Math		Science experiment Spelling		
2:15 – 3:00	PE 2:15 - 3:00	Music 2:00 - 2:45	PE 2:15 - 3:00	Library 2:15 - 2:45	Art 2:00 - 2:45
3:00 – 3:10	Dismissal – Pass out papers – Announcements – Stack Chairs				

Ellen Thompson

Lifeline of School-based Activities

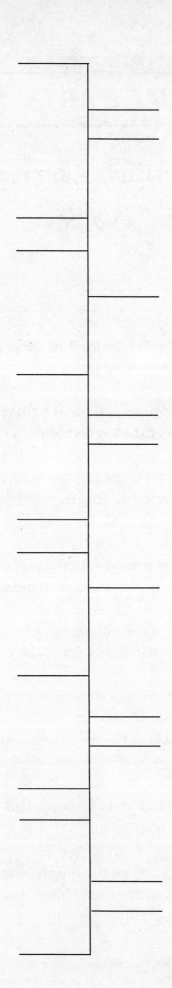

Plot your school "memories."

INTEGRATED LANGUAGE ARTS

Children's Whole Language Bill of Rights

EVERY CHILD HAS THE RIGHT TO:

1. Be literate.

2. A child-centered classroom where the development of language and literacy results from integrated reading, writing, listening and speaking.

3. Teachers who understand the whole language approach; who actively involve parents, and who are empowered by their administrators to be key decision makers.

4. A curriculum that meets the individual's needs and that is organized around broad themes integrating language arts with mathematics, science, social studies, music, art and physical education.

5. High interest, language rich, meaningful reading material such as trade books, which take the place of workbooks and worksheets in the practice of reading skills.

6. Write about subjects that interest him or her without fear of criticism, and to scribble, reverse letters, and to invent spelling and punctuation as a part of his or her growth in literacy.

7. Speak and be heard in the classroom as an important step toward reading, writing and thinking.

8. Active involvement in learning through interaction with other children, manipulatives, toys and appropriate materials.

9. Abundantly supplied libraries, both school and classroom, that include predictable, printless, and pop-up books, poetry, fiction and non-fiction.

10. Progress assessment based on appropriate measurements such as writing portfolios, miscue analysis, book lists, peer reports and student-teacher interviews rather than norm-referenced, standardized tests.

Robert L. Johnson

Whole Language: In the Middle and Across the Curriculum

Some ideas on implementing the whole language philosophy in middle school

BY MARYANN AND GARY MANNING

Many middle school teachers interrelate subject areas by using a common theme. Here, Patti York, a sixth grade science teacher at H. W. Gwinn School, Hoover, AL, reads a map with students as part of a geography theme.

We recently met a longtime friend at a social studies conference. Although we've known her for years, we hadn't seen her for a while. When we worked as consultants in her school, we found her to be one of the best student-centered teachers we knew. Her middle school classroom was alive with the real world of social studies.

As we were catching up on one another's lives and discussing professional ideas, she said, "I know you've been doing whole language workshops lately. I just love whole language teachers. They're all so cute, young and energetic. If I taught primary grades, I'd be one, too."

We were surprised by her comment because we view her as a student-centered social studies teacher. Although the term "whole language" wasn't used when we first knew her, her beliefs and practices were very much like those we now refer to as "whole language." For example, she incorporated fiction and nonfiction literature on a regular basis. Through trade books, she brought the world to her students and instilled in them a lifelong love of learning. She not only read aloud to her students on a regular basis, but also gave them time to read independently.

"Cooperative learning" is another term that wasn't in vogue back then, but her students worked in small groups, sharing their knowledge and inspiring one another. Moreover, she empowered her students as writers. Unlike many middle school content teachers, both then and now, she didn't just assign and grade research reports. She guided students' research, helping them find topics that mattered and resources that were accurate and well-written.

Her student-centered views and practices put her squarely in our movement. Perhaps, after reading this article, she (and you) will declare, "I didn't know it, but I'm a whole language teacher."

Primary-grade turf. Why do so many teachers of grades 4 through 8 view whole language as primary-grade turf? Many, like our friend,

PHOTOS BY MADGE SIDWELL

Maryann and Gary Manning are on the faculty of the School of Education, The University of Alabama at Birmingham and are Teaching Editors of *Teaching K-8*.

INTEGRATED LANGUAGE ARTS

seem to think that whole language teachers are all young and cute, and teach in the primary grades. There are, of course, teachers who fit that description. However, whole language teachers come in many different sizes, ages and grade levels.

In contrast to the view of some, we see whole language as a philosophy that encompasses more than literacy learning. It's a belief system that transcends all content areas and grade levels.

Whole language teachers aren't necessarily alike in their practices, but they do share similar views about teaching and learning. For example:

- Students construct their own knowledge from within, using their prior knowledge.
- Learning is a social process and the exchange of points of view contributes significantly to students' learning.
- Risk-taking and making mistakes are crital in learning, and emphasisis placed on the process, not the product.
- Knowledge is interrelated; thus, the artificial barriers that separate content areas are reduced.
- Classroom learning activities are authentic and resemble the real world as much as possible.
- Students have time to read self-selected books and write on topics they choose.

As you read the above beliefs, you may think, "Those aren't such heretical notions." You may even agree that whole language is appropriate for the content area teacher.

Education in the United States is now recovering from a long depression in which we were dominated by behaviorists. Following the principles of behaviorism, each subject area was broken into separate entities. Learning was often viewed as memorizing isolated bits of information. Since whole language teachers value the holistic nature of knowledge, they think about how they can help students make natural relationships.

It's often easier to implement practices compatible with whole language if teachers have students for long blocks of time. However, teachers in departmentalized situations are successfully using such practices. Let's explore several ideas within the framework of the beliefs listed earlier.

Helping students learn. In whole language classrooms, students select many of the books

> *Since whole language teachers value the holistic nature of knowledge, they think about how they can help students make natural relationships.*

they read and the projects they pursue. In this way, they select texts and activities that are interesting and understandable.

We also encourage students to share what they've learned through a variety of expressive modes such as dramatizing or making journal entries, which helps them to further clarify and extend their thinking.

Peer interaction. Learning is a cooperative affair with students and teachers learning from one another, so it's important that we create a sense of community in the classroom. When students interact with one another, classrooms come alive with a learning "hum" during much of the day.

This learning "hum" arises from several sources as students work with one another in pairs and small groups. We recently observed a middle grade teacher using an effective small group reading strategy as her students studied four pages on a science text. In a group of four, each student read only one of the four pages. The student then shared with the other three students what he or she had learned from reading the page. The teacher encouraged the students to ask questions and discuss information as they shared with one another.

Listening to the learning "hum" during this activity revealed excitement for the content. It was one of those situations when you know you've chosen the right profession.

Taking risks. A 1990's view of learning helps us to realize that students learn through making errors. We now view errors as milestones of growth. We know that errors occur as students try to go beyond their current understandings and achievements. We must,

> *" Why do so many teachers of grades 4 through 8 view whole language as primary grade turf?"*

Geography is still the theme as these sixth graders read their original poems about Canada.

An alternative we often see is one in which a teacher has a group of students for a long block of time for language arts and social studies, and another teacher is responsible for mathematics and science. Another alternative used by some middle school teachers involves the use of a common theme for a designated period of time. Teachers, in collaboration with their students, select a theme such as homelessness and build all of their content learning activities around that topic. Excited students and teachers enjoy the benefits of sharing a theme.

Relevant activities. In whole language classrooms, activities are relevant to students' lives. Students who are interested in a topic and who have a voice in what they do are more interested in learning. As a result, they learn more.

As much as possible, the activities in school resemble activities outside of school. When a student writes a letter in a whole language classroom, for instance, there's a reason for writing it because there's someone who will receive it. After all, that's the way letter writing works in the real world.

Reading and writing. Whole language teachers give students time to read and write during the school day. They guide their students' reading beyond textbook material. One of our middle grade teacher friends, for example, has a reading area in her room in which are science-related paperbacks. Over the years, she keeps enlarging the collection.

In addition to reading, writing is a powerful tool and an integral part of every subject. Unlike the way we used to fill in blanks and answer questions at the ends of chapters when we were in school, students in whole language classrooms engage in a variety of types of writing, ranging from content journals to letters to research reports. Students' writing and thinking improve as they write throughout the day.

therefore, encourage students to take risks and not be afraid of making mistakes.

Last fall, we were working in a middle school when by chance we caught a class in one of those "teachable moments." It was a language arts class where the students write every day on self-selected topics. The teacher knew that if writing were to improve, the students must feel safe and free from ridicule.

During this particular teachable moment, the teacher led a discussion on risk taking in which the class talked about what it meant to take risks and then related the discussion specifically to taking risks when writing. They eventually discussed risk taking when writing and the difficulty they experienced when sharing their writing with other students.

As the discussion continued, the students filled the chalkboard with ways to help each other take risks in class. They even included the idea that they as students have a responsibility to help each other feel safe and secure.

Interrelated subjects. We all understand that subjects are interrelated, and that the division between science and social studies, for instance, is often artificial. A departmentalized situation, where the day is broken up into multiple periods, makes it difficult for teachers to develop stable relationships with their students and do interdisciplinary teaching.

We see teachers interrelating subject areas in a departmentalized setting, but it isn't easy. Numerous organizational patterns have been developed in exemplary middle schools, which involve creating schedules that allow for larger blocks of time and for fewer teachers to work with one group of students.

> **❝** *When students interact with one another, classrooms come alive with a learning 'hum' during much of the day.* **❞**

Final remarks. We all want our teaching to provide an enjoyable and enriching experience for our students. As teachers, we create the curriculum in our classroom based on our own good intuition about teaching and learning, along with our understanding of theory and research. As we engage our students in real, meaningful and whole learning experiences, our goals are further realized. We trust that you—like our friend—feel supported as you read this article, and realize that having a whole language philosophy is consistent with a student-centered view of learning. ↓

Reprinted with permission of the publishers, Early Years, Inc., Norwalk, CT 06854. From the May 1992 issue of Teaching/K-8.

INTEGRATED LANGUAGE ARTS

INSIDE the Whole Language Classroom

Students Delight in Taking Charge of Their Learning

BY KATHRYN F. WHITMORE AND YETTA M. GOODMAN
College of Education, University of Arizona

It's Tuesday morning, and you're the superintendent on a visit to Roosevelt Elementary School to meet with the principal to plan an agenda for the district curriculum committee.

Once you've finished, the principal invites you to stroll with her into the classroom of Chris Brand, who she says, has an exciting year under way with the pre-kindergarten, kindergarten, and first-grade children in a combination class. Always anxious to visit with teachers and children, you enthusiastically agree.

As you and the principal stroll down the hallway to the early childhood wing of the school, you hear young children's voices and quiet background music punctuated by occasional laughter. Some children are sprawled out on the floor of the hallway, creating a story map for Red Riding Hood, the fairy tale they've just listened to on a tape recorder.

The group draws Red Riding Hood's house, details the path through the woods to Grandmother's house, and labels essential areas and characters.

They tell you, "We're making a map about the plot of the story," as you peer over their shoulders. One child proudly points out her personal contribution to the map.

A teacher-made sign on the door says: "Welcome! This is a children's workshop. The chil-

*All photos courtesy of Elizabeth Borton Elementary
School and Butterfield Elementary Sc...*

dren in this classroom are growing and becoming: as independent learners, as problem solvers, and as creative thinkers. Please come in!"

Once inside, you pause momentarily to take in the expanse of people and activities. The children are involved in centers: several boys and girls crowd around a table with the teacher who is helping them cook porridge like "The Three Bears"; others are scattered on the carpet building a block castle for Rumpelstiltskin and labeling the spinning rooms with self-stick note papers; the teacher assistant is recording for another group of youngsters as they compare and contrast the fairy tales they've read so far and insert information about them on a large butcher paper chart; a few children relax on pillows with a collection of fairy tales in various forms and languages near the library.

The classroom is alive with color and writing that represents the children's past and current work. It seems as if literacy is dripping from the walls and ceilings as you bend down under sheets of songs and poems.

Some are familiar renditions illustrated by the children and others seem to be their original compositions. Although few of the children or adults are still or silent, the buzzing hum of activity is soothing and there is a sense of purpose in the air.

Central Premises

More and more early childhood classrooms across the nation resemble the whole language classroom of Chris Brand (a fictitious teacher whose classroom represents a combination of our teaching practices and observations of others). Whole language is a movement that is challenging teachers and administrators to reconsider their early childhood programs and the assumptions about children and learning that are demonstrated through their curriculum.

In this article, we explore four premises of a whole language philosophy that are central to early childhood education: language, active learning, play, and home-school relationships. Then we explore some issues that administrators who are involved in implementing a whole language philosophy need to consider.

Whole language theory and practice builds easily on effective early childhood curriculum because, historically, early childhood has been rooted in child-centered, integrated, and whole-child learning experiences.

Whole language theory grows out

hool, Tucson Ariz., School District except lower right; Marana, Ariz., Unified School District.

of research about the reading process and language development. (See resource list, page 25.) Language is central to thinking and provides teachers with a vehicle for understanding children's growing knowledge, concepts, and belief systems. Authentic, interactive, rich language experiences are absolutely necessary to provide young children with real opportunities to use both oral and written language to express thoughts and comprehend the world.

Undeniably, the most important thinking and learning takes place when children are engaged in talking, reading, writing, and experimenting with ideas that are most significant to their daily lives. This means that children need real purposes for language use, that their purposes must include real audiences, and that the functions for language in the real world should be met in the classroom.

Activities like those taking place daily in Chris Brand's classroom exemplify children's immersion in the world of children's literature, in this case through a set of thematically-related activities about fairy tales.

Young children are fascinated with what is real and what is make-believe. Immersion and discussion of literature help children explore the parameters of fiction and non-fiction. They expand on their imagination and wonderment about the world.

As these children study fairy tales, they use reading, writing, speaking, and listening in an integrated fashion with math (block building), social studies (mapping), science (cooking), and play production with musical accompaniment (fine arts).

The language children need to use to accomplish experiences in various content areas is functional and developmentally appropriate because it builds on existing knowledge. Chris taps the children's knowledge of the fairy tales they've heard at home and seen on video or TV.

Such experiences challenge children's thinking and expand their language into new genres, new topics, and new uses. It is the learning of new ideas and the sharing of knowledge that are important in early childhood, and language is integral for accomplishing these goals.

Bringing Whole Language

BY ROBERT J. MONSON
Superintendent, Westwood, Massachusetts, School District

Whole language demands a major change in the roles of both the child and the teacher. I can think of no innovation in the last 20 years that has required such a dramatically new set of expectations for everyone involved, parents included.

This is the story of how one small, suburban school system is effecting that change.

In March 1989, after 18 months of careful reflection, a 20-member reading committee of teachers recommended a transition to a whole language philosophy for every elementary school classroom in Westwood to take place over a five-year period commencing the following fall.

The committee studied three alternatives — a literature-based reading program, the existing basal program, and a whole language approach — and after much analysis and debate, chose the latter because of its philosophical integrity and the willingness of children to assume a much more active role in learning.

Subsequently, we decided to require all 64 elementary school teachers to make the transition rather than only accept volunteers. Our rationale for a systemic approach was grounded in the belief that all children should have access to a transactional approach to learning, in which they are actively engaged.

Furthermore, the political problems associated with children annually moving back and forth from whole language to basals (e.g., parents comparing teacher styles and expectations) simply were not worth the energy and ultimately would injure teacher morale.

Getting Approval

The teacher committee first sought commitments on three key elements: financial resources, school board endorsement, and administrative support. The following summer the Westwood School Committee adopted a policy on the teaching of reading using the whole language approach, approved a five-year plan for implementation, and created the position of "reading specialist" (half-time teaching, half-time staff development) to demonstrate its support for the initiative.

Since the whole language initiative began, the reading committee has continued to design implementation strategies. Committee members have received training on the Concerns-Based Adoption Model from staff at the Northeast Regional Laboratory in Andover, Mass. (CBAM, developed at University of Texas, helps educators to understand how individuals react to a proprosed innovation.) They now are designing a program assessment plan to measure changes in teachers' beliefs and behaviors as well as to establish markers for program expectations and accomplishments.

A plan to describe the expected changes in instructional behaviors was developed by reading specialists to help teachers envision the transition process. In this, our third year of the initiative, we are developing a list of student learning outcomes for grades 2 and 5 and a portfolio assessment process to more clearly communicate to students and parents our expectations.

A bimonthly parent newsletter, *The Whole Language Journal*, is sent to every home to further assist parents (and senior citizens) in understanding why whole language requires higher expectations of children. We conduct day and evening workshops for parents whenever we introduce a major new component of the program.

Lest readers think otherwise, significant staff resistance was voiced, particularly during the first year of orientation. Initially, about a third of our classroom teachers raised questions about the credibility of the deci-

to a Whole System

sion to move the entire district to whole language rather than move to the traditional intermediate position of a literature-based reading program.

In response to accusations that the superintendent influenced the decision, the reading committee stepped forward to affirm not only their independence in making the decision without administrative interference, but also to reinforce the philosophical and practical reasons why whole language was a better approach for Westwood.

The reading committee's ownership in the decision and their responsibility for the timing and implementation of staff development activities over a five-year period has reduced substantially the vocalized resistance to implementing whole language.

Now in our third year, opposition still is raised (but by a small minority of teachers) as each new set of teacher expectations is established. Most recently, concerns have been expressed over the amount of work required of a portfolio assessment program. The reading committee regularly surveys the faculty to identify concerns and devise a differentiated staff development plan for the various groups of teachers who are at different points of philosophic alignment and various stages of skill development.

Supportive Culture

The most vocal advocates for whole language in Westwood are the children who share classroom experiences with their parents. This is the result of a long-range commitment to create a supportive culture for whole language implementation.

All of our classroom teachers, even those initially opposed, have begun the process of trying whole language techniques with their students. The school board, administrators, and parents consistently have signaled the value they place on risk-taking so all teachers will feel supported as they try out this philosophy.

In addition, administrators, including central-office staff, have been asked to teach several classes using whole language techniques with their students. The school board, administrators, and parents consistently have signaled the value they place on risk-taking so all teachers will feel supported as they try out this philosophy.

Once we made our case to explain why whole language was better for kids of all achievement levels, parents were supportive of early Wednesday afternoon dismissls (17 times over the year) so that teachers could receive staff development support for their transition.

Staff development activities model the transactional approach inherent in the whole language philosophy. Once a month, voluntary after-school support groups, with the help of reading specialists, provide a forum for classroom teachers to discuss concerns about the impact of whole language on their beliefs and behaviors.

Whole language is not the type of innovation that allows a superintendent to receive a two-hour overview before deciding whether to commit a school district to its implementation. Whole language, unlike the basal approach, is not a cookbook style of teaching that is easily transportable to large groups of teachers. Whole language assumes individual teachers are capable of making sound decisions about creating a classroom environment where students can actively construct meaning from text.

This is an innovation that requires a substantive change in the organizational culture of schools. It views teaching as shared work rather than isolated work. It creates role ambiguity for students and teachers, requiring participants to move away from a position of "having the right answers" to one of "asking the right questions."

Whole language demands both top-down facilitation from superintendents and bottom-up commitment from teachers if long-term, internalized, and systemic improvement in literacy education is to occur in America's public schools.

Active Learning

Early childhood educators long have realized the irreplaceable value of active learning experiences that put children in the thick of learning, rather than in an observational, practice, or rote memorization role.

In Chris Brand's classroom, the children plant beans to simulate Jack's beanstalk but at the same time, they explore concepts concerned with biological growth, watering, ecology, and condensation. They make a stone soup like in the story by the same name to learn about steam and conservation of liquids.

As they shop for and prepare different kinds of vegetables for their soup, they discover costs for retailers and wholesalers and talk about the best way to retain the vitamins and minerals in the vegetables they prepare. The children categorize the types of vegetables they bought and then graph which vegetables are the most favored by the children, which are the most nutritious, and why. As they work through these areas, they read books written by professional authors, write letters or postcards, and keep written records.

There is no need to get children *ready* for such experiences. When children are actively involved in answering their own questions and exploring their own wonderment, they become aware they *need* to read, write, and think to solve their problems, to build their knowledge base, and to explore the world.

Since language is most effectively practiced during active learning experiences, children in early childhood whole language programs are moving, acting, drawing, cutting, pouring, measuring, counting, sorting, etc., most of each day, sitting still for only pleasurable experiences such as listening to fairy tales or singing songs.

Theme cycles provide opportunities to organize for active learning experiences. In whole language classrooms, themes are content-rich, integrated, and hands-on. They involve children in experiences tied to unifying and significant concepts.

We have seen young children seriously involved in studying the homeless and opportunities for shelter, Thanksgiving tied to Columbus but also tied to newly arrived immigrants from Cambodia and Haiti, and water conservation in a desert community.

Themes are most effective when they are planned with children to take into consideration their interests and questions about the world through discussion and procedures like webbing. Chris asks the children what they know about a specific topic, what issues they're interested in, and what they would like to learn as part of the planning process.

The fairy tale theme began when Chris discovered that the students knew a few fairy tales ("The Three Bears" and the Disney favorites) but not the wide range of fairy tales that are being written and illustrated in newer publications. The children also seemed to be unaware of the origin of fairy tales, the various versions available, or the universal nature of fairy tales across cultures. The children discover the stories they learn at home about how the world is and came to be also are part of fairy tale and folk traditions.

In this whole language classroom, the world of the school and home are connected when parents and other members in the community are invited to tell the tales they remembered from their childhood. The children come to understand the variety of issues related to fairy tales by their active involvement in building, cooking, mapping, and role playing.

Role of Play

In our present-day world of workaholics, we forget the power of play in our own lives as well as in childhood. Yet even for adults the separation of work from play is an artificial one. There are many of us who love our professional responsibilities but we also know frequently it is during play and recreation we engage in deep thinking about the serious issues of the day. During our time for play we have the time to think and wonder, leading to self-reflection and deeper understandings.

Play is extremely important to the world of the young child. We believe, as so many who have come before us have stated, that "play is the work of children." Play provides opportunities to develop science, math, and social studies concepts as children build blocks, measure their environment, and act out adult activities such as

doctoring, parenting, shopping, etc. It is through play that children explore the parameters of their world, experiment with new ideas, and expand conceptualizations.

Children build confidence in their ability to take on a number of roles in the play society they create. In play settings such as carpentry, wheel toys, water and sand, climbing, finger painting, and clay manipulation, it is

Photos courtesy of Elizabeth Borton Elementary School, Tucson, Ariz., School District

possible to experiment, to take risks, and to explore the unknown.

Imaginations soar as children create new and wondrous worlds with teachers like Chris Brand. Such teachers cultivate the environment to help children recognize how reading, writing, speaking, and listening are part of play experiences.

Administrators need not only to understand the role of play but to encourage early childhood teachers to incorporate play experiences as legitimate and of a high priority in the school curriculum. Play is not a frill or extracurricular activity. Administrators also can help explain to parents the importance of play in the cogni-

tive and linguistic development of their children.

Home-School Connection

As whole language educators come to understand more about how children learn, they are beginning to appreciate the rich learning experiences many young children have in home settings and consider how to adapt such rich experiences to the classroom.

In the home and community, children learn naturally. They learn to speak and listen, to play with peers and siblings, and to complete activities that parents and other family members deem are important with minimal direct teaching and with little or

A Handle on Whole Language

Whole language support groups are developing across the country as teachers and administrators revalue their roles. Rich professional materials are available covering the gamut of whole language educators' needs: research reports, classroom instructional and evaluation ideas, theoretical explanations, strategies for integrating content areas, children's literature, and descriptions of whole language theory in practice.

Superintendents and central-office administrators can play a significant role in whole language groups. First, they can join with teachers as active participants and learners. They also can support the participation of staff in such groups by cooperating with scheduling needs, supplying resources and materials, and serving as a liaison between the school and the community.

A wide variety of books and resource guides are available for those interested in pursuing these ideas related to whole language. *The School Administrator* asked the authors of its whole language articles, as well as the ERIC Clearinghouse on Reading and Communication Skills, for good beginning titles:

- *The Whole Language Catalog,* edited by Kenneth S. Goodman, Lois B. Bird, and Yetta M. Goodman, American School Publishers, [1221 Farmers Lane, Suite C, Santa Rosa, Calif. 95405], 1990.
- *What's Whole in Whole Language,* by Kenneth S. Goodman, Heinemann Educational Books [361 Hanover St., Portsmouth, N.H. 03801], 1986.
- *Whole Language: What's the Difference?* by Carole Edelsky, Bess Altwerger, and Barbara Flores, Heinemann, 1990.
- *Understanding Whole Language: From Principles to Practice,* by Constance Weaver with Diane Stephens and Janet Vance, Heinemann, 1990.
- *Supporting Whole Language,* edited by L. Henke and Constance Weaver, Heinemann, 1992.
- *The Whole Language Kindergarten,* by Shirley C. Raines and Robert J. Canady, Teachers College Press [1234 Amsterdam Ave., New York, N.Y. 10027], 1990.
- *The Whole Language Approach to Reading and Writing Instruction,* Educational Research Service [2000 Clarendon Blvd., Arlington, Va. 22201], 1991.
- *The Whole Language Evaluation Book,* by K.S. Goodman, Y.M. Goodman and W.J. Hood. Heinemann, 1988.
- *Assessment and Evaluation in Whole Language Programs,* edited by Bill Harp, Christopher-Gordon Publishers [480 Washington St., Norwood, Mass. 02062], 1991.
- *The Reading-Writing Connection: A Whole Language Approach,* an annotated resource list edited by Susan Loucks-Horsley, Regional Laboratory for Educational Improvement [290 S. Main St., Andover, Mass. 01810], 1988.
- *The Administrator's Guide to Whole Language,* by G. Heald-Taylor, Richard C. Owen Publishers [P.O. Box 585, Katonah, N.Y. 10536], 1989.
- *Portraits of Whole Language Classrooms: Learning for All Ages,* by H. Mills and J.A. Clyde, Heinemann, 1991.
- *Teaching Reading: Problems and Solutions.* American Association of School Administrators [1801 N. Moore St., Arlington, Va. 22209], 1991.

In addition, the National Council of Teachers of English (1111 Kenyon Road, Urbana, Ill. 61801) provides a resource packet on whole language. The International Reading Association (800 Barksdale Road, P.O. Box 8139, Newark, Del. 19714-8139) has a special-interest group on whole language which publishes a newsletter.

no difficulty. Natural learning needs to be valued by teachers and administrators. In addition, the knowledge and experiences young children bring from their homes need to be understood, accepted, and valued.

The relationship between parents and teachers is critical. Teachers need to realize that parents are experts about their children; they know their children better than anyone, and care deeply about their well-being and success.

Teachers and administrators can organize meetings with parents to discuss mutual concerns about how children learn, the role of language and play in learning, and other specific issues such as invented spelling, early reading, and developing math concepts. Parents can be helped to recognize their role as their children's first teachers as they participate with their children in the natural language experiences that take place daily in the home.

Although parents should be encouraged to read to their children, all kinds of activities can be used to encourage the development of their children's language and learning.

When there are strong bonds between the school and the home, a reciprocal sharing of knowledge can exist between educators and parents who respect one another.

A New Mindset

As school administrators develop holistic views about curriculum and its organization, they will need to consider new ways to evaluate whole language teachers and principals and begin to think differently about how to encourage change within the schools.

When any administrator enters a whole language classroom, he or she must see the world through new lenses. The typical organization of children who sit in straight rows and listen facing a teacher at her desk who controls all the talk in the classroom does not exist.

Instead, the classroom is a buzz of activity. Administrators need to look around carefully at the various kinds of activities in which children are engaged. In some classrooms they may be doing similar kinds of activities at the same time: writer's workshop, research on a social studies or science topic, literature study, or sustained silent reading.

However, in other classrooms, teachers may have children working on a variety of different activities. Centers may be evident or students may each have a plan for their own work to accomplish during a two- or three-day period.

The administrator entering such a dynamic setting will need to refrain from saying to the teacher, "I'll come back when you're teaching." Administrators need to step into such settings and move around the classroom. They should be engaging children in discussions about their projects and encouraging children to share the books they have been reading or the stories or science reports they have been writing and working on.

Teachers and children will be able to provide explanations of why certain activities are occurring and the ways in which the classroom community is involved in continuous planning and evaluation.

The learning experiences in which the children are engaged provide opportunities for evaluating the teacher's awareness of the background and experiences not only of the students but of their homes and community, and families are encouraged to be involved in the ongoing development of their own children's learning.

Empowering All

One of the most exciting and beneficial goals and outcomes of whole language theory in classrooms is the empowerment that occurs as learners take charge of their own learning. Children delight in finding their own voices in the classroom when they have both the power and the responsibility to make decisions, choose materials, ask questions, and read, write, and learn for authentic purposes.

The empowerment of teachers occurs alongside the children's empowerment. Teachers who experience holistic learning and teaching realize the strength of their own knowledge as well as their students. They become professionals in a true sense, not as technicians or transmitters of facts or prescribed curriculum, but confident to support, enrich, and value children's lives. Whole language teachers respect their students as learners. Whole language administrators must value teachers in the same manner.

Therefore, any mandating of a whole language philosophy and program for all teachers or students must be cautioned against. While it is always essential to support and encourage teachers to critically reflect on their teaching, a top-down directive to change toward whole language is counter to the very philosophy set as a goal.

Rather, teacher change must occur slowly, with patience, with learning, and with a vast amount of **support** from administrators. The key to significant change in schools rests with the administrator who respects teachers' decisions about when and how to make changes in their curriculum.

Money must be allocated to support teachers' continuous professional development. Time must be organized for teachers to visit each other's classrooms and other whole language programs. Resources and other materials must be available for teachers when basal programs and packaged curriculum are set aside.

In short, learning for teachers must follow the same principles of whole language that are advocated for children: learning experiences are language-based, authentic, active, and integrated, for real purposes.

A Nurturing Role

We are in the midst of exciting and significant changes in education based in part on the explosion of knowledge about language and learning that has led to a whole language perspective.

The excitement created when teachers and children work together in holistic and empowered situations can be used to make the transformations for which all educators hope: to place children at the center of their educational experience.

As you return to the office of Roosevelt Elementary School before leaving, you observe a book rack at the door of the school office. It's labeled "From Our Young Authors" and you note that all the books are written by the children in Chris Brand's classroom.

You read through a number of the books impressed with the range of topics. Each book has an "About the Author" section on the back page. Some have photographs and others include self-portraits in crayon or paint. One reads: "Tom Sanders loves to read and write. His major interest is in snails. He wants to learn a lot about snails so when he grows up he can become a kindergarten teacher and teach them kids about snails, too."

Kathryn Whitmore is a doctoral candidate in the language, reading, and culture program at University of Arizona's College of Education. Yetta Goodman is a professor of education at University of Arizona.

Voices

*I*t is hoped (whole language) will suit the needs of those who are determined to try out ideas for themselves, to think deeply and to be convinced slowly; those who are prepared to read more widely when in doubt; and those who wish to influence outcomes from an informed conviction which they have tested in their own experience.

Don Holdaway
The Foundations of Literacy

Published by Ashton Scholastic of Sydney, Australia.

In celebration of art...

Strategy Lessons:
Process vs. Product

*"When process learning is the primary goal,
children are learning to learn."*

BY HARRIET W. THOMAS

Far too often, today's educators focus on what students *produce* and not the *process* they go through in learning. Is there a need to reflect not only on *what* we teach, but also on *why* and *how* we teach? Is it our responsibility to look closely at the process, the how and why of learning? The answer to both questions is an emphatic "yes."

Actually, we must do more than just reflect and look at the process. We must change the way we teach. When process-learning is the primary goal, children are learning to learn. They become independent and lifelong learners.

Through reflecting on the differences between product- and process-oriented classrooms, we can focus on changes in our classrooms that will foster process learning. We need to address our models, beliefs and attitudes in how our students learn.

Easily said, but how do we do it? How can we structure our teaching so that students are learning to learn? Are there basic differences in classrooms where process-learning is taking place as opposed to classrooms that focus on the product? If so, what are the differences?

The chart on the opposite page lists some of the differences. But perhaps we can bring them into sharper focus by looking briefly at how two teachers – one concerned with the product, the other with the process – teach the same lesson.

Let's imagine that Miss Ward and Mrs. Clark, both second grade teachers, are dis-

> *"Is it our responsibility to look closely at the process, the how and why of learning?"*

Harriet W. Thomas is a teacher with the Jefferson County (KY) Public Schools.

cussing notes and lesson plan ideas for the day. They are both planning to read Laura Numeroff's *If You Give a Mouse a Cookie* (HarperCollins, 1985).

Miss Ward's Lesson
Miss Ward plans to use the book to acquaint her students with circular sequence.

Structure. Miss Ward will use Velcro-backed characters and props from the book to model the circular-sequential flow of the story. Students working in cooperative groups will discuss why the characters and props were placed in a circle.

Implementation. Students will discuss their reasons and talk about the circular sequence of the story. Time will be given for research. The research assignment will consist of locating other stories or examples of information presented in a circular sequence.

Students can choose any book or source in the room. One available book that tells a story in a circular sequence is *The Round Trip* by Ann Jonas (Greenwillow, 1983). The science textbook also contains an example of circular sequence in the study of evaporation and condensation; a picture graph showing this water cycle presents the sequence in a visual way.

In a large group, students will share examples found in their research and discuss why they follow a circular sequence.

Student response. Students will present a story, or information, in the same circular sequence. They can choose the method of presentation: drawing illustrations, giving an oral report, writing a narrative, acting out the presentation, drawing a diagram, etc. Students

INTEGRATED LANGUAGE ARTS

will then be given time to reflect on what they learned in the lesson.

Mrs. Clark's Lesson

Mrs. Clark thinks Miss Ward's ideas are interesting and good. However, she's afraid that the lesson would take too much time away from other skills and activities she wants to cover that day.

Structure. Mrs. Clark reads the story to the students. The students then discuss what happened first, second, third, etc. Mrs. Clark will ask the students to notice the story's beginning and ending, and how they are the same.

Implementation and response. Mrs. Clark will ask if anyone knows another story like *If You Give a Mouse a Cookie.* After this discussion, the students will be asked to complete a handout. The handout has sentences from the story. The students will number the events as they happened in the story and then draw a picture illustrating each sentence.

Mrs. Clark plans to display the book on a shelf from which students will select books for independent reading the last 15 minutes of the day.

Evaluating the Lessons

It's easy to see that Miss Ward's goal is to have students learn through a process. Mrs. Clark's lesson, although it did involve a good book, failed to focus on the process.

Since accuracy on the skill worksheet was her primary goal, the focus was on the product, not the process. The students were given no choices and the activities were of little value to future learning.

Miss Ward, on the other hand, provided students with a variety of materials, activities and choices. The students learn the skill of sequencing and will be better able to apply this knowledge to future learning.

The students will also be able to recognize the importance of sequencing in their own writing and understand how different authors write.

Students in Mrs. Clark's class will have no opportunity to explore or discover, either on their own or as a group. In Miss Ward's class, however, students will be involved in active learning in a cooperatiuve and non-threatening atmosphere.

Other comparisons could be made, but the point is clear.

Product	Process
Teacher decides what lesson is taught. Lesson is teacher-directed.	Children's needs dictate which lessons are taught. Lesson is child initiated.
Focus is on skill development first, and skills are often developed in isolation.	Skills are taught and embedded in the process. Connections are made to previous knowledge.
Emphasis is on one subject area of the curriculum.	Emphasis is on making connections in an integrated curriculum.
Use of workbooks, worksheets and textbooks.	Use of concrete materials, quality literature and a variety of resources.
The children are passive learners.	The children are active learners.
Learning is rote.	Learning is conceptual.
Instruction provides sequential skill development.	Instruction provides opportunities to solve real-life problems, learning skills as needed.
Teacher's role is director of instruction with a specified goal and product previously determined.	Teacher's role is that of demonstrator who models and leads children in their learning as they progress toward their chosen goal.
Students interact with lesson and materials.	Students interact with each other and the teacher. The interaction takes place in a collaborative, non-threatening, cooperative learning atmosphere.
Activities and materials are the same for all and are selected sequentially by a skills continuum.	Activities and materials are age and developmentally appropriate and vary depending on the child.

We must take a close look at the way we teach. Every step we take toward making process learning our focus and goal will result in more successful, challenging and creative learning for our students.

Learning will be valued and applied to real life experiences. Our responsibilities as educators of lifelong learners will be fulfilled and our goals reached successfully. ↓

Writing in Kindergarten

Helping Parents Understand the Process

Kathleen A. Dailey

As a parent, how would you react to this work from a kindergarten child? Would you respond in the following manner?

"I can't believe Miss Davis let Tommy bring home a paper with so many mistakes."

"Doesn't she take time to spell the words for the children?"

"Shouldn't Tommy learn to make the letters correctly first?"

"How will he learn to spell correctly if she lets him spell like that?"

"He doesn't even know how to read yet and they expect him to write!"

Many parents may have this initial reaction, especially if the teacher has not prepared the parents for such work. Research in homes and schools suggests that the writing process of the child can be enriched by communication between teachers and parents. When parents first encounter the idea of writing programs for kindergartners, they need to be educated about the program. The following research-based answers to some of the most common questions are helpful in

Figure 1. *The flowers are coming out of the ground.*

orienting kindergartners' parents to an early writing program.

How does my child learn to read and write?

Literacy, the process of learning to read and write, begins at home long before children enter school (Ferreiro & Teberosky, 1982; Hall, 1987; Schickedanz, 1986). This process does not officially begin at a particular age; rather, it develops as children gain experience with language and print. The two processes, reading and writing, develop simultaneously.

A variety of activities, which can be a part of daily living in many homes, enhance literacy development. Children learn purposes for reading and writing as the parent and child sing a lullaby, share a picture book, make a shopping list or write a telephone message. Many children *read* environmental print, such as the names on cereal boxes and restaurant signs. Likewise, children learn how a book *works* and realize that print conveys meaning as they partake in a variety of experiences with books. As 2-year-old Ryan sits propped on his mother's lap with a book, she points to the cat and says, "What's that?" "Ki-Ki," says Ryan. Young Ryan gathers meaning from the pictures and the dialogue with his mother. With increased book knowledge, he comes to understand that the black marks on the page tell a story as well as the pictures.

Kathleen A. Dailey is Assistant Professor, Elementary Education Department, Edinboro University of Pennsylvania and Kindergarten Teacher, Miller Research Learning Center (campus laboratory school).

INTEGRATED LANGUAGE ARTS

At the same time, children begin to experiment with different forms of writing that meet their needs and interests. Children may begin to copy letters and words from books, to write lines of squiggle or letters or to ask an adult to make models of letters for them. Children may write the names of family members and spellings of common objects. Writing interests may further develop as children choose to write letters, send postcards to friends, cast their superhero as the main character of their story or write a poem based on a favorite story, such as *In a Dark, Dark Wood* (Melser & Cowley, 1980) (see Figure 2).

The kindergarten reading program should be an extension of reading and writing that began in the home. It should help young children draw upon their past experiences to increase their understanding of how reading and writing function for specific and meaningful purposes (Dyson, 1984; Hall, 1987; Teale, 1982; Teale & Sulzby, 1989).

Do drawing and scribbling help my child learn how to write?

Children's first attempts at authorship are frequently accompanied by a drawing. Drawing is an integral part of the writing process because it is a way for children to plan and organize their written text (Dyson, 1988; Strickland & Morrow, 1989). A drawing can tell a story that written words cannot yet convey for the young child. Parents should accept their children's drawings and encourage them to talk about these drawings. Some researchers encourage parents and teachers to write down what children dictate so they can see their own speech put into words.

Young children will frequently scribble. Scribble drawing takes on a circular form. As children intend these marks to be writing, the scribbles take on a linear, controlled form. A page full of scribbles may be a letter to Grandma or a restaurant menu. When asked to *read* this message, the child may first glance at the picture then point to the scribbles as he or she relays the content of the written work. As

the child's print awareness increases, these scribbled marks become more refined and take on the characteristics of print (see Figures 3 & 4).

How can I encourage my child to write at home?

Research indicates that children engage in literacy events more in the home than in school (Schickedanz & Sullivan, 1984). This evidence supports the importance of parents as writing models. Observational studies of young children reveal that adults involved in writing behaviors such as writing a letter, making a grocery list or writing a check are often a stimulus for a child's early attempts to write (Lamme, 1984; Schickedanz & Sullivan, 1984; Taylor, 1983). When children see adults writing for a variety of purposes, they discover ways in which writing is useful and meaningful.

Parents can create an environment that accepts and values writ-

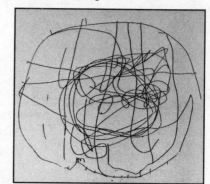

Figure 3. *Random scribbling*

Figure 2. *Poem based on the story, In a Dark, Dark Wood*
On a dark, dark path
In a dark, dark house
On a dark, dark stair
In a dark, dark room
Boo! Ha-ha-ha

Figure 4. *Controlled scribbling*

ing by providing their children with many tools for writing. A variety of unlined paper and many different writing tools (markers, pencils, pens or chalk) are important materials for this craft. Children enjoy a variety of writing media. They may like the feel of writing letters or words in a tray of sand, pudding or jello. They may write using a computer or typewriter. Rich (1985) suggests using a "writing suitcase" as a portable writing station. The suitcase is filled with paper, markers, crayons, plastic letters and stencils. The child has access to the suitcase, is responsible for its contents and is free to add new items. The child is an active learner in the process. The writing that is produced is limited only by imagination.

Aren't paper-and-pencil activities, like workbook pages, the best way of learning to read and write? Children learn through direct participation in meaningful activities. When that learning is a complex process (like reading) rather than a skill (like tying shoes), it is even more important that the conditions of meaningful participation be met. Music is a good analogy. If we want young children to develop their musical abilities, we begin with enjoyment, not worksheets on musical notation. We accept their early efforts as well, realizing that the toddler who bounces in rhythm to a popular song may become a dancer or the child who pounds on a xylophone may play a musical instrument someday.

Reading programs that *teach* children to *read* and *write* through the use of dittos and workbook pages reflect practices that are developmentally inappropriate for young children (Elkind, 1986) for at least two reasons. First, the child's needs are not taken into consideration when the emphasis is on *every* child doing the same thing at the same time. Manuel has recognized the *M* at the beginning of his name and on the McDonald's sign since he was 3 years old. Manuel can write his own name and the word *MOM*. Manuel brings home a paper with neatly circled *M*s. As he hands the paper to his father, Manuel replies, "It was boring!" Molly completed the same paper yet is unable to tell you the letter name. The way and manner in which children learn varies for

Table 1
THE ASSOCIATION BETWEEN LANGUAGE DEVELOPMENT AND WRITING DEVELOPMENT

Language	Writing	Spelling
Babbling	Random scribbling	
Holophrase—one word utterance is used to express a complete thought: "Mama" means "Mommy I want to get up."		One letter spelling—one or two letters represent entire sentences or phrases: *H* = This is my house.
Repetition	Controlled scribbling—the same forms or the same letters are repeated as the child progresses toward mastery of that form.	Writing the same letters or words in order to attain mastery
Expanded vocabulary of frequently used words		Incorporation of conventional spellings with invented spellings
Grammatical rules are applied to speech. "I want up." replaces "Me up."		Transitional spelling—using simple rules to spell
Overgeneralization—internalization of grammar rules, but applied to more cases than those in which they work: "He runned after me."		Overgeneralization—reliance on rules applied in previous spellings, yielding errors due to inconsistencies of the language. "LETUS" (lettuce)
More precise speech		More precise spelling

Adapted from Lamme, 1984.

each individual. Approaches that may be effective for one child may be ineffective for the next.

Second, workbook writing directs the focus away from the child. "When worksheets and phonics lessons are given to young children all the initiative comes from the teacher. When this happens, teachers unintentionally prevent children from developing their own natural initiative" (Willert & Kamii, 1985). On the other hand, activities such as drawing and writing about a trip to the zoo, reading alphabet books and enjoying songs and fingerplays about sounds and letters allow children to take an active role in learning to read and write.

I have difficulty figuring out what my child has written. How can I better understand what she writes?

The writing of children develops in overlapping stages that parallel language development (Table 1).

As children make the transition from scribbling to more conventional forms of writing, they may represent their written work with a random ordering of letters such as

mTEo to represent house. This is followed by stages that reveal the child's understanding of letter-sound correspondence, which is a first step toward reading (Chomsky, 1971). These stages are referred to as "invented spelling" because children apply what they know about sounds and letters to their early writing. It is common, however, for children to be in several stages of spelling development at once and revert to earlier stages as they experiment with writing. The stages of invented spelling development are shown in Table 2.

These early attempts are systematic even though the spelling is unconventional (Richgels, 1987), as shown in the spelling of *monster*, *grass* and *class* (Table 2). This systematic process enables children to take control of their learning and become independent writers.

Should I correct my child's written work?

When a child says "ba" for bottle, parents understand what the child is trying to say and accept the pronunciation at the child's stage of development. Spelling develop-

ment should be treated similarly. Early writing contains many words spelled unconventionally because children experiment with written form at particular stages of development. Children need models who are supportive and patient. When Jane asks, "Mommy, do you spell *tree*, T-R-E?" her mother responds, "That's the way it sounds, but that's not the way it is spelled. It's *T-R-E-E*." This response tells children that there are conventional spellings, but we also accept the way they spell. Criticism of misspelled words makes children fearful of making mistakes. Under these conditions, research shows that they write less and less well, sticking with *safe* known words. What is worse, they learn to dislike writing because they see it as a test rather than as a means of creative expression.

Parents may help children sound out words or spell words for them, but at the same time provide materials that foster independence in writing. Picture dictionaries provide children with an early reference tool. Parents need to show children how the dictionary is set up and how to locate words using the alphabet and picture cues. Parents can help children compile their own personal dictionary of frequently used words, such as objects in the home or names of family members. A set of words on cards serves the same purpose (Ashton-Warner, 1965). An accompanying illustration may help the child use the word cards independently. Understanding spelling development and fostering independence in writing through positive and nurturing practices are essential to a child's healthy attitude toward writing.

My child will write letters correctly one day and reverse them the next. Is that normal?

When parents of young children see a backwards *S* or *2*, they often

Table 2
THE DEVELOPMENT OF INVENTED SPELLINGS

Stage 1	Use of initial consonant to represent an entire word	*M* for monster *G* for grass *C* for class
Stage 2	Initial and final consonants serve as word boundaries	*MR* *GS* *CS*
Stage 3	Inclusion of medial consonant; awareness of blends; may divide blend	*MSTR* *GRS* *CALS*
Stage 4	Initial, final and medial consonants and vowel place-holder. Vowel is incorrect	*MESTR* *GRES* *CLES*
Stage 5	Conventional Spelling	*MONSTER* *GRASS* *CLASS*

Adapted from: Gentry, 1981; Graves, 1983; Lamme, 1984 & Strickland & Morrow, 1989.

worry that their child has a learning disability. Actually, such reversals are very prevalent in kindergarten, 1st and 2nd grade. It is common for children to experiment with reversed writing. Sometimes letters are reversed; sometimes they are placed upside down. These characteristics, including a tendency to write in any direction, are all related (Schickedanz, 1986). Children need practice with directionality and the orientation of printed symbols. Until children have attained consistency in left-to-right and top-to-bottom orientation and formed a mental image of what the letter *b* looks like, for example, they may continue to reverse written symbols. "All exploration is perfectly normal; it is a healthy sign that children are investigating print, getting used to it and figuring out how it works" (Marzollo & Sulzby, 1988, p. 83). If a child consistently reverses written symbols beyond 2nd grade, a parent may want to seek advice. Generally, however, reversals are not a cause for concern at an early age.

What should I look for in my child's writing program?
"Everywhere I look, I see children's written work," comments a visitor to the kindergarten classroom. This atmosphere reflects one in which young writers have been experimenting with different types of print since their first day of school. Each time children sit down to write, they increase their knowledge of written form just through the act itself. At the writing center, children are working in their journals or writing a story. Writing, however, is not limited to one area of the room. In the block area, Erin made a sign that says *CASO* (castle). In the kitchen area, Patrick posted the special food for the day, *APLS* (apples). Meanwhile, the post office clerk is busy delivering letters addressed to Santa Claus (see Figure 5).

Figure 5. *Letter to Santa Claus*
To Santa Claus
You are nice.
Get me a present.
I would like a Barbie.
I like you.

Young children's writing, speaking and action are closely related. Early writing is not only a paper-and-pencil activity, but also a social process. In her observation of children, Dyson (1981) comments, "I saw no quiet, solemn-faced scholars, struggling to break into print. Rather, I saw (and heard) writers using both pencil and voice to make meaning on the empty page" (p. 777). In a writing environment one may observe children engaged in the following activities:

- Asking each other for help
  How did you spell tyrannosaurus?
- Planning and creating
  I'm going to put brontosaurus in the water.
- Rehearsing ideas
  My brontosaurus will be eating plants.
- Questioning each other about their products
  What is your dinosaur doing?
- Sharing and reading their work to each other
  The Brotsrs is RunIng AWAW. (*The brontosaurus is running away.*)
- Evaluating their work
  That was a long sentence. I'll have to make more room on the paper next time.

(Adapted from Lamme, 1984)

In a quality kindergarten writing program, the child's teacher serves as model and facilitator of the writing process, providing the children with an environment rich in opportunities to use and create written materials (Rich, 1985). The teacher observes children write, confers with them and accepts their work. "Teachers who grow writers in their classrooms also regard pieces of writing as growing things to be nurtured rather than as objects to be repaired and fixed" (Bissex, 1981).

What does the teacher do during the writing conference with my child?
The writing conference serves as a personal and meaningful interaction between the child and the teacher; both are learners in the process. Early in the school year, Ms. Hart established a routine for writing conferences. She chose the couch area as a comfortable place where the children can share their written work. Chris knows that his conference with Ms. Hart is every Tuesday. As the other children in the class continue to write, Chris takes his folder, journal, personal dictionary and a pencil and sits with Ms. Hart on the couch. This time together provides Ms. Hart with insights into Chris's writing abilities.

Throughout the writing conference, Ms. Hart asks questions that guide the process (Table 3). This format eventually allows the children to go through the same process independently as they reflect on their own writing. She focuses on the child throughout the conference, allowing the child to take the lead. Through careful observation of written work, the teacher assesses what the child already knows about written language. She may notice, for example, that a child uses letter-sound correspondence correctly for *D* when writing *dog* (*DG*) but confuses *B* and *P* when spelling *boat* (PT). She may have the child write for her during the conference to observe the process firsthand. Ms. Hart keeps detailed records of the child's progress and makes teaching recommendations based on specific needs.

Conclusion

Parents and teachers need to recognize that "... every child who can talk has the capacity to learn to write and also to seize upon its possibilities with enthusiasm" (Smith, 1981, p. 792). Parents and teachers have the responsibility to create an environment for children that develops confidence and success in writing. When parents and teachers understand the processes underlying writing development, they can help children participate in meaningful home and school activities that promote its growth. Thus, home and school partnerships built upon communication and understanding provide children with a firm foundation for successful writing experiences.

Acknowledgment: The author gratefully thanks Mary Renck Jalongo for her assistance in reviewing this article.

References

Ashton-Warner, S. (1965). *Teacher*. NY: Simon and Schuster.

Bissex, G. (1981). Growing writers in classrooms. *Language Arts, 58*, 785-791.

Chomsky, C. (1971). Write first, read later. *Childhood Education, 47*, 296-299.

Dyson, A. H. (1981). Oral language: The rooting system for learning to write. *Language Arts, 58*, 776-791.

Dyson, A. H. (1984). N spell my grandmama: Fostering early thinking about print. *The Reading Teacher, 38*, 262-270.

Dyson, A. H. (1988). Appreciate the drawing and dictating of young children. *Young Children, 43*(3), 25-32.

Elkind, D. (1986). Formal education and early childhood education: An essential difference. *Phi Delta Kappan, 67*, 631-636.

Ferreiro, E., & Teberosky, A. (1982). *Literacy before schooling*. London: Heinemann.

Gentry, J. R. (1981). Learning to spell developmentally. *The Reading Teacher, 34*, 378-381.

Graves, D. (1983). *Writing: Teachers and children at work*. Portsmouth, NH: Heinemann.

Hall, N. (1987). *The emergence of literacy*. Portsmouth, NH: Heinemann.

Lamme, L. L. (1984). *Growing up writing*. Washington, DC: Acropolis.

Marzollo, J., & Sulzby, E. (1988). See Jane read! See Jane write! *Parents, 63*(7), 80-84.

Melser, J., & Cowley, J. (1980). *In a dark, dark wood*. San Diego, CA: The Wright Group.

Rich, S. J. (1985). The writing suitcase. *Young Children, 40*(5), 42-44.

Richgels, D. J. (1987). Experimental reading with invented spelling (ERIS): A preschool and kindergarten method. *The Reading Teacher, 40*, 522-529.

Schickedanz, J. (1986). *More than the ABC's: The early stages of reading and writing*. Washington, DC: National Association for the Education of Young Children.

Schickedanz, J. A., & Sullivan, M. (1984). Mom, what does U-F-F spell? *Language Arts, 61*, 7-17.

Smith, F. (1981). Myths of writing. *Language Arts, 58*, 792-798.

Strickland, D., & Morrow, L. M. (1989). Young children's early writing development. *The Reading Teacher, 42*, 426-427.

Taylor, D. (1983). *Family literacy—Young children learning to read and write*. Exeter, NH: Heinemann.

Teale, W. H. (1982). Toward a theory of how children learn to read and write naturally. *Language Arts, 59*, 555-570.

Teale, W. H., & Sulzby, E. (1989). Emergent literacy: New perspectives. In D. S. Strickland & L. M. Morrow (Eds.), *Emerging literacy: Young children learn to read and write* (pp. 1-15). Newark, DE: International Reading Association.

Willert, M. K., & Kamii, C. (1985). Reading in kindergarten. Direct vs. indirect teaching. *Young Children, 40*(4), 3-9.

Table 3
INAPPROPRIATE AND APPROPRIATE RESPONSES USED DURING WRITING CONFERENCES

Inappropriate Responses	Appropriate Responses
"Allison, will you read this? I can't figure out what it says."	"What are you writing about Allison?"
"What is it?"	"Tell me about your picture."
"Can't you write about something else besides the zoo?"	"Do you like writing about the zoo?"
"Tomorrow, I think you should write about our field trip."	"What do you think you will write about next?"
"The next time I want you to figure out how to spell these words by yourself."	"Allison, how did you go about writing this?"

Adapted from Graves, 1983.

Whole Language – Real World

Remarkable Researchers in First Grade

*It's never too early to help children become lifelong inquirers.
Here's how one teacher does it*

BY MARYANN AND GARY MANNING

Books, books and more books. The reading material you see here is only a small part of Gayle Morrison's classroom library.

First grade researchers work enthusiastically and diligently in Gayle Morrison's classroom. Remarkable? Well, yes – but not unusual.

Like you, we know many remarkable primary grade teachers. They work hard to help their students become lifelong inquirers. They expect their students to be curious, ask questions and then research enthusiastically and diligently to obtain the answers. They create the conditions for children's success as inquirers and researchers as naturally as they create anything else in their classrooms.

Let us share with you the scene in Gayle's educational wonderland at Wilson School in Birmingham, Alabama, as it looked to us when we dropped in. Gayle and her kids were at work as researchers. The students were in groups of three or four and were involved in different activities. For example, two groups were listening to tape-recorded books as they read along. Some were reading books, together or independently, while others were talk-ing about the topic they were researching. All were totally absorbed in their work. Gayle told us that the children select the topics they want to study.

Group book. Students take notes as they find information in books, magazines and other materials. One student usually acts as the secretary who writes down the notes for the group. After completing their note-taking, the entire group reads the notes before deciding on the contents of the book. When this has been done, the students begin writing their group book.

When each group has finished with its draft, Gayle works with them to edit it and then she types it on the computer. Only two sentences are put on each page so there's plenty of room for illustrations. After the pages are illustrated, they are laminated and bound into a book. These books, which children enjoy reading and rereading, are added to the classroom library.

During a recent visit, we saw one of the research groups, the tadpole group, sitting near the aquarium observing two tadpoles. When we asked the children to tell us about them, they explained that tadpoles breathe underwater, and that their tadpoles had grown fatter since they had been in their classroom.

They told us how they examined the tadpoles every day to see if they were getting legs; they had read that the hind legs would come first. Bursting with pride, they showed us the rough draft of their research book on tadpoles. They had the final draft of the book almost completed with illustrations, and were getting ready to bind it.

Maryann and Gary Manning are on the faculty of the School of Education, The University of Alabama at Birmingham, and are Teaching Editors of *Teaching/K-8*.

INTEGRATED LANGUAGE ARTS

Brainstorming topics. Since the group was about to finish its study of tadpoles, except for continued observation of their live specimens, the students had brainstormed topics they wanted to research next. They had narrowed their choices to two: polar bears and Eskimos. When we asked them why they were interested in these topics, one child said she liked the big white polar bear she had seen at the zoo. A boy said he had read about Eskimos and wanted to know more about their houses and what they eat.

We moved to another area of the room and observed the amphibian group listening to a taped book as they followed along with their own copies of the book. They were taking a few notes as they listened. After they finished the book, the children explained that they would listen to the tape at least two more times and would then take more notes.

About then, Gayle came over to the group and asked, "What are some things you've learned about amphibians?" As we walked away, the children were excitely sharing some of their ideas.

Research basket. Later, Gayle saw us looking at the red and yellow basket on the floor by one of the research groups. She explained that she and the children call it their research basket. When Gayle finds articles, books or tapes on a group's topic, she puts them in the basket. The students are also on the lookout for information – for their own group as well as for others.

The basket makes the resources readily available to the students and serves as a place for storing the notes and drafts of their research. Every day, Gayle quickly reviews the work in the baskets of all the groups, which gives her insights about their progress.

The cooperative spirit in this first grade classroom flows to the brim. While we were visiting, for example, a member of the tree group found a book about kangaroos and immediately said to his group that the mammal group should have the book. He walked over and put the book in that group's basket. The mammal group thanked Cedric and kept on working.

Gayle was working with the mammal group at the time, and we heard her ask, "Why is a porcupine a mammal?" Nathan immediately replied, "It has babies." Samantha added, "It comes from Mama's stomach and not from an egg."

How does it happen that first graders

In Gayle Morrison's classroom, everyone is a researcher. Here, she visits a group to ask and answer questions about the group's research project.

develop such skills of inquiry and stay with their line of research over a period of time? It's not easy, but it's well worth the effort.

Gayle has worked continuously for several years at developing first grade researchers, but she was relying mostly on teacher-directed projects. Then, at the 1992 Whole Language Umbrella Conference in Niagara Falls, New York, she heard Kittye Copeland, a multi-age teacher from Columbia, Missouri, describe how her students choose their own topics and find information by themselves.

Gayle realized that her students needed to be more engaged in the process. She had been making many of the decisions that students should be making for themselves. Since Kittye gave her both inspiration and information, Gayle has been getting out of the way of her students' interests.

Developing researchers. Let's reflect on several points that are especially important in developing young researchers:

1. Start researching early in the school year. Gayle began within the first few weeks of school. At the beginning of the year, many of the students, of course, could not read or write, so she encouraged them to work in pairs and help each other. It's fascinating to observe young children figure out meaning when they really want to know about a topic.

2. Build your collection of research materials. A large variety of resources is needed, including books, magazines, records, tapes and real objects. Gayle's classroom library has over 5,000 books, most of which she found

❝ Gayle's classroom library has over 5,000 books, most of which she found at garage sales and thrift stores. Over 2,000 of these are nonfiction. **❞**

The researchers in Gayle's class write with the ease and assurance of much older children. In fact, it's difficult to believe that they're only in first grade.

The class aquarium is definitely the place to be when you're conducting research and writing a group book on tadpoles.

66 *Gayle provides an hour or more every day for students to explore topics that interest them.* 99

at garage sales and thrift stores. Over 2,000 of these are nonfiction. Gayle also puts books and articles on tapes so children can listen to them. Some of the older students in the school make tapes for Gayle's class, which helps build her extensive library of tapes on different topics. Magazines in her classroom include the following: *National Geographic World, Ranger Rick, Highlights for Children, Your Big Back Yard, U*S* Kids* and the *Zoobooks.*

3. Demonstrate how to research. For example, at the beginning of the school year Gayle demonstrated note-taking. One of the topics she selected was "dogs" because she loves dogs and she and the students like to look at pictures of dogs and talk about them. In front of the students, she browsed through several books and magazines that contained information on dogs. The next day, she read aloud from two or three sources, talked aloud about some of the major points and wrote notes on chart paper. She continued this activity for approximately two weeks. She frequently closed the book or magazine before she started to take notes in order to

demonstrate that note-taking is not copying.

4. Provide daily time for researching. If students are to develop as researchers, they must have opportunities to work for extended periods of time. Gayle provides an hour or more every day for students to explore topics that interest them.

5. Facilitate social interaction among the students in the classroom. Students learn by interacting with one another and with the teacher. Thus, teachers like Gayle have classrooms that "hum" with learning. It would be impossible to create a quality learning environment that nurtures inquiry in a quiet and sterile environment.

6. Engage students as researchers. Real engagement occurs when students are involved on a daily basis in studying topics that are important in their world. Gayle's students take responsibility for their own learning as they follow their own interests. They conduct themselves much like researchers in the real world. It's amazing to observe children in Gayle's classroom as they read from magazines and books, listen to tapes, make observations (as they were doing with the tadpoles) and take notes during their research. As the year progresses, the children learn to edit their work and improve in their ability to put their work in book form.

7. Develop a community of learners where everyone is a researcher. You know there's a feeling of community in Gayle's room when you see students help each other find information on their topics. When Cedric found the kangaroo book and put it in the mammal group's basket, he was helping other members of the community. You can also witness the feeling of community when you see the students write in their books. We overheard a conversation between Rachel and Andrea. Andrea said to Rachel, "We have too many 'ands' and we need to put in more periods." The air of community exudes with the cooperation and collaboration between the students and Gayle.

Lifelong inquirers are developed in elementary classrooms as teachers follow students' natural interests. Curiosity aroused by their own questions propels students to learning – now and in the future.

Watching students develop as lifelong inquirers is indeed a pleasure. Teachers like you and Gayle provide students with tools of inquiry that will serve them in the future, and in doing so, help to ensure that the future beckons brightly. ↓

Teach Skills *with a* Strategy

By Regie Routman

Is skills teaching appropriate in the whole language classroom?

Yes—if you teach strategically, says Regie Routman, a nationally recognized author, teacher, and expert on whole language instruction. In this article, excerpted from her latest book, INVITATIONS, Ms. Routman tells how you can teach skills strategically in your classroom.

"I wonder if the kids are really learning anything." Teachers who make the transition from the basal to literature worry a lot about whether or not skills are being taught. Additionally, many teachers feel nervous that they are not teaching enough. We teachers feel guilty spending reading time reading, discussing, and enjoying the literature. We have spent years teaching reading using lots of skills sheets. Without worksheets, where you can "see" skills work, it's hard for teachers to trust that the skills are in the books and that learning is truly occurring. Many of us devise activities to be sure skills teaching occurs.

UNDERSTANDING THE DIFFERENCE BETWEEN *SKILLS* AND *STRATEGIES*

While skills teaching is a necessary part of all good instruction, it is our beliefs about learning combined with our approach, method, context, and timing that determine whether or not we are teaching skills so that they later become useful strategies for the learner.

In discrete skills teaching, the teacher—or the publisher of a program—decides what the learner needs, and the skill is directly taught, often in a predetermined sequence, and then practiced in isolation. The skill, whether it includes word attack, alphabetizing, sequencing, or vocabulary acquisition, is directly taught with an emphasis on practice and automatic, correct responses. The teacher or program controls how much practice or how many exercises students need. Application of the skill to new, meaningful contexts rarely occurs.

In teaching for strategies, however, skills are taught in a broader context because the learner demonstrates a need for specific skills in the instructional/learning setting, perhaps in a guided reading group. The skill is taught because the learner genuinely needs to use it—or the teacher anticipates the

PHOTOGRAPHS BY DONNELLY MARKS/ILLUSTRATIONS BY BETH GLICK

learner's upcoming need to use the skill. The teacher guides the student to self-determine the generalization and think through possibilities in authentic contexts. While the teacher may question and suggest, it is the learner who is encouraged to make deductions and consciously apply what is learned from one context to another.

From Skill to Strategy

A skill—no matter how well it has been taught—cannot be considered a strategy until the learner can use it purposefully and independently. Application of a skill to another context is far more likely to occur when the skill has been taught in a meaningful context that considers the needs of the learners. I have observed that teachers begin to focus on strategies when they begin to change the climate of their classrooms from teacher-dominated to student-centered and when they come to view reading and other language processes as constructive and interactive.

Applying the distinction between skill and strategy to the teaching of sight words, phonics, and vocabulary, we see clearly that merely teaching the skills in isolation and practicing on worksheets has no relation to meaningful teaching. While we may believe that a skill has been covered, until the learner can discover how to utilize the skill in varied reading and writing contexts, skills teaching is largely a waste of time. *The learner must know how and when to apply the skill; that is what elevates the skill to the strategy level.*

Promoting Strategic Teaching

It has taken me many years to become convinced that all the skills are in the literature and that the literature itself can be used as a vehicle to teach skills strategically. Most of us initially need to see concrete evidence of skills teaching, and we use the literature to teach and practice the skills we believe

children need. Even then we must be careful that skills work does not interfere with enjoyment of the story and that our focus on skills results from a genuine need for meaning.

I have observed that after about five years or more, teachers seem to move away from practicing specific skills in literature to promoting strategies in the ongoing context of genuine reading and writing, as the need arises. By becoming careful observers of our students and practicing ongoing evaluation, we can determine what strategies students are using and not using. We need to give ourselves time for this transition. As our own learning theory develops, and as we begin to take ownership of our teaching and rely less on directed instructional programs, we have less of a need for a predetermined skills agenda. ⟶

Self-Evaluation Checks in Teaching for Strategies

Because most of us have had training that emphasizes discrete skills teaching, heightened awareness is necessary to move toward teaching for strategies in reading.

✔ Is your language fostering meaning-based strategies and independence when a student can't read a word, or are you relying only on, "Look at the letters" and "What sounds do those letters make?"

✔ Are you using engaging books with predictable text that support the reader, or are your texts dull and sequentially based for skills?

✔ Are you guiding students to apply strategies, or are you teaching for mastery of skills?

✔ Are you giving students sufficient wait time and encouragement to figure out words and meanings on their own, or are you quick to supply the answer?

✔ Do other students know it is the reader's job to do the work and that they need to give the reader quiet wait time, or do students call out words?

✔ After students have one-to-one matching and some confidence as readers, are you introducing students to unfamiliar text to note what strategies they have under control, or are students reading only books they have already heard?

✔ Are you asking important questions that follow naturally from the text and encourage more than one possibility, or are you looking for only one "right" answer?

✔ Is vocabulary taught in context during and after reading, or are you introducing words in isolation before reading?

✔ Are follow-up activities leading to further enjoyment and engagement with the text or are they merely keeping students busy while others are in group?

Reprinted with permission from Regie Routman: *Invitations* (Heinemann Educational Books, Portsmouth, NH; 1991). Ms. Routman is a language arts resource teacher in Shaker Heights, Ohio. All artwork in this excerpt has been added by INSTRUCTOR.

INTEGRATED LANGUAGE ARTS

HOW TO TEACH PHONICS STRATEGICALLY

In meaningful phonics teaching, connections of sounds and letters are always made in real-life contexts. Beyond the book or story, we lead children to make connections in other contexts—signs, labels, charts, calendars, poems, and children's names.

Even with a natural approach to phonics, it is perfectly acceptable to call attention to sounds and words that we know students will need for reading and writing. In choosing Big Books to read, we are sensitive to the phonics and rhyming words that can be highlighted. For example, I have noticed that the Frank Asch books, some of which are available as Big Books, contain many examples of words with consonant digraphs. *Happy Birthday, Moon* (Prentice Hall, 1982) and *Mooncake* (Prentice Hall, 1983) have lots of words with *th* and *wh*.

Rather than telling students what the sounds and letters are, however, I have found that an inquiry method that has the children "discover" the sounds and rules works best for engaging students in meaningful phonetic associations. I might say, for example, "What do you notice about the words…?" "I see several words that begin with *th*. Who can point to one?" "Can you find any other words with the same sound?" This approach is in direct contrast to that of most commercial phonics programs which tell students the rule or generalization and then present practice examples as skills in isolation rather than in the context of meaningful, continuous text.

FIGURE 1 — A PHONICS CHART IN FIRST GRADE

Making the Transition to More Meaningful Phonics Teaching

Most of us seem to find the transition from prescribed phonics in isolation to teaching meaningful phonics in the context of literature very difficult and slow-going. It may be reassuring to know that most teachers are struggling with making phonics teaching more relevant and applicable to reading and writing. I believe it is critical to remember that before we can change our teaching, we have to carefully re-examine our beliefs in the light of current research and learning theory.

Susan Mears has been a first grade teacher for eight years. In talking about phonics, she describes herself as "struggling awfully" despite the fact that she had done much reading and thinking about phonics teaching:

"I did more phonics in context this year, noting beginning and ending sounds and digraphs in chart poems and Big Books. The kids really like the big charts we made, where they could add their own words, but I am still struggling to find a balance in teaching phonics. I

> *. . . We have to carefully re-examine our beliefs in the light of current research and learning theory.*

find myself feeling pressure from some of the second grade teachers who expect kids to arrive with solid word attack skills. Also, I feel guilty for not giving spelling tests. When I'm teaching all the phonics sounds, I feel as though I'm teaching spelling, too. I still teach phonics separately even though I don't see kids transferring the skills. I notice that every time I pull a sound out of context, two or three kids give me an example of a word that doesn't fit the rule at all. I'm still not comfortable with the way I handle phonics."

Colleen Thompson has been teaching first grade for two years. After a series of workshops on whole language, she began to question the traditional workbook approach to phonics teaching:

"I have continued to teach phonics lessons through the workbooks, but I now see that kids don't transfer that phonics to their reading. I had five kids who learned to read who never did catch on to phonics. I still use the workbooks, but I'm trying to use context more. If I can feel comfortable teaching phonics in context, I'd rather go that way. I saw this year that all the sounds are in the literature books. Next year I plan to spend most of reading time reading. I see I have to work with the parents, too. They use only "sounding out" when working with their kids. If the child can't read the word in isolation, parents think the child is not reading and has just used memorization. I need to make them aware of the other cuing systems."

Opportunities for ongoing phonics teaching and evaluation arise daily in the following contexts:

◆ **Shared reading**
◆ **Shared writing**
◆ **Writing aloud**
◆ **Self-selected writing**
◆ **Guided reading**

Within these contexts, there is nothing wrong with direct, explicit teaching of phonics as long as it is done strategically. Words can be taken out of context as long as they are put back into context before moving on.

Phonics Charts

Making enlarged phonics charts is perfectly appropriate in the whole language classroom. The order of sounds taught and the words used as examples are determined by the teacher and children, as the need arises in the context of reading and writing. This is very different from the use of traditional phonics charts that emphasize rules and use a prescribed sequence and fixed set of words.

For example, after *Who's in the Shed?* (Parkes, 1986) had been enjoyed over and over again during shared book experiences in a first-grade class, I demonstrated for the teacher how the *sh* sound could be reinforced through the book. I asked the children, "Who can find a word that begins with *sh* (I made the sound) on this page?" (Figure 1)

A child was then invited to come up and point to a word. As the child pointed to *sheep* and read it, I used a sliding mask to blend the word parts and highlight the *sh* and the whole word. I then wrote the word on our new *sh* chart, stretching out the sounds and verbalizing as I wrote it. In the same manner, children found *shed* and *she* on that page and subsequent pages, and those words were added to our chart.

It has worked well to tell children, "When you find a word as you are reading, come up and put it here on the chart." Limiting the words to books helps keep the spelling on the charts fairly accurate (we also tell children to write in pencil) and keeps the children from calling out scores of words. Children easily and excitedly work together to fill up our charts, and they develop increasing phonetic awareness and knowledge in the process. Phonics charts are posted in the room for children to add to and refer to. Separate sheets can be hole-punched and put together for easy referral and organization in a large, spiral-bound chart tablet (24 by 16 inches). In the kindergarten classroom, phonics charts may be made with pictures from magazines, with the word written next to each picture.

Personal Phonics Booklets

Some kindergarten and first-grade teachers also have students keep

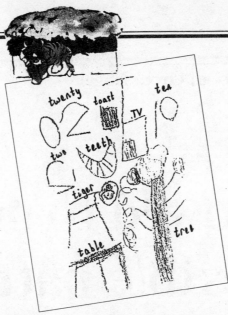

FIGURE 2 — A PAGE FROM A KINDERGARTNER'S PERSONAL PHONICS BOOKLET

their own sound and letter books in which students draw or paste in pictures to represent sounds for letters (figure 2). Sometimes these books are also used to practice handwriting after the teacher has students write optional "tongue twisters" (figure 3).

Some first-grade teachers have students keep lists of words that students notice from their reading to go along with particular letter-sound combinations. Students can always read these words before they examine them phonetically. These booklets serve as personal phonics charts.

Such individual phonics books are appropriate as long as they are a very minor part of the total reading program and students have some ownership over what goes into them. I have noticed that teachers tend to move away from these booklets once they are convinced that children are learning phonics in the normal course of daily reading and writing. One teacher said, "I did the booklets because *I* needed to see the evidence that phonics was being taught."

Phonics: A Suggested Teaching Order

While there is no predetermined order for teaching letter-sound relationships, the following suggested sequence may be helpful when the teacher is trying to decide where to place emphasis first in the early grades. This order is based on my own observations working with young children.

◆ **Beginning consonants**
◆ **Ending consonants**
◆ **Consonant digraphs** (*sh, th, ch, wh*)
◆ **Medial consonants**
◆ **Consonant blends**
◆ **Long vowels**
◆ **Short vowels**

Instruction should always have meaning for the child and not just follow a prescribed sequence.

In determining what letter-sound relationships to highlight, we need to be constantly observant of children's needs and be flexible in our teaching. For example, word endings, especially *–ing*, are often needed early in writing and should be taught as the need arises. It will also be necessary to do repeated demonstrations, individually and in small groups.

Demonstrations of how we are teaching phonics need to occur with parents, too. For parents to understand the meaningful teaching of phonics, we need to educate them about the current research and how we are applying it to the classroom. When parents see that phonics is still being taught and are shown the how and why, they are very supportive. ■

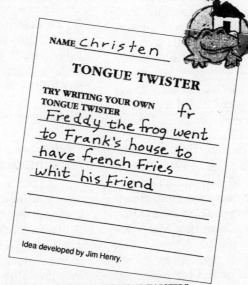

NAME *Christen*

TONGUE TWISTER

TRY WRITING YOUR OWN TONGUE TWISTER *fr*

Freddy the frog went to Frank's house to have french Fries whit his Friend

Idea developed by Jim Henry.

FIGURE 3 — PHONICS "TONGUE TWISTER"

James Flood
Diane Lapp, Sharon Flood, Greta Nagel

Am I allowed to group? Using flexible patterns for effective instruction

At San Diego State University, James Flood and Lapp are professors, Sharon Flood is an instructor, and Nagel is a doctoral student. All four work closely with classroom teachers throughout San Diego County, California.

Classroom reading instruction in the U.S. has been characterized by "ability groups"—instructional groups consisting of children sorted out by their teachers' assessments of their reading achievement—since World War I (Barr, 1989). However, a great deal of research conducted during the past two decades has concluded that ability grouping can create serious problems for students that are social in nature, but cognitive in effect (Allington, 1980; Barr, 1989; Hiebert, 1983; Indrisano & Parratore, 1991). Consequently, recent state and national guidelines have advocated a movement away from ability grouping to an implementation of flexible grouping alternatives (California State Department of Education, 1987a).

Despite such explicit suggestions calling for the implementation of flexible grouping,

many misinterpretations have arisen. For example, Lapp and Flood (1992) observed a prevailing misunderstanding among several teachers that "whole language" instruction necessitated "whole class" instruction. While some educators look at whole class groups as the single alternative to the "old" ability groups, others have espoused collaborative peer groups as the preferred alternative (Schell & Rouch, 1988). Still others cling to ability groups as the only effective way to teach reading. As recently as 1990, in a study of 100 teachers, Nagel, Flood, and Lapp found that 44% still perceived ability groups as "the best way to teach."

The purposes of this article are threefold: (a) an examination of historical perspectives and contemporary research on grouping, focusing specifically on research findings about ability grouping; (b) an investigation of the alternatives to ability grouping; and (c) a model of what flexible grouping patterns look like in the classroom.

Historical perspectives and contemporary research

Various sorts of instructional groups have been considered good and effective at different times throughout the history of reading instruction. Multigrade classrooms gave way to school organizations with one grade per room. Students were often further grouped into levels of ability by classroom. Ability groups became the predominant means of arranging children within classrooms during World War I, along with the advent of IQ tests and achievement tests (Barr, 1989).

Groups that were good for organizing schools or classrooms were not necessarily good for the children, but opinions have varied over the years. In the 1940s, ability groups were seen as good for "slow" children, but bad for "bright" ones (Otto, 1950). Later, authorities declared ability groups to be necessary for "gifted children;" some educational leaders still promote this view (Feldhusen, 1990).

Ability groups have, in spite of any controversy, remained the primary grouping strategy through the 1980s. Studies of elementary ability groups have used a wide variety of methodological approaches and have produced mixed results (Barr, 1989), particularly in analyses that involve short-term observations. However, the research appears to support the notion that ability groups are negative for students in the low groups because the process of grouping in this way labels and sorts them into indelible hierarchies or "castes" (Allington, 1980). Starting in the first grade, students do not escape their placement; they receive differentiated treatment over the years that puts them further and further behind their peers (Hallinan, 1984; Shannon, 1985).

Some of the negative effects of ability grouping include the differences in the amount of silent reading time that children are allotted (Allington, 1980). Low group readers read more words out loud, they are expected to do more drill work in skill materials, they have less exposure to works of literature, and they do far less silent reading than children assigned to high groups (Cook-Gumperz, Simons, & Gumperz, 1981). Further, students in low groups are asked questions that do not expect them to use high levels of thinking (Shake & Allington, 1985).

Situations within low groups shape behavior in negative ways; the amount of teachers' controlling talk is much higher and their expectations for behavior are far lower than their expectations for high group children (Schell & Rouch, 1988). In addition, student attentiveness is less in lower groups (Allington, 1980). In studies focused upon first-grade students, the gaps between ability groups widen during the school years (Weinstein, 1976), because more teacher management and distractions interrupt low groups (Eder, 1981) and lower groups spend less time on meaning-related activities than on decoding words (Hiebert, 1983).

Despite the differences in instruction that occur for groups at various levels, there are also interesting similarities that Barr (1989) observes. For example, she found that both low and high groups read the same materials and participated in many of the same activities at different times throughout the school year. The pacing of specific lessons is not necessarily slower for lower groups; as a matter of fact, when low groups get to a story they may complete it faster than the group that read it several months before.

Alternatives to ability grouping

If static ability groups are not necessarily wise practice, the alternatives need to be examined. Many teachers, aware of the negative research on ability grouping, often ask, "How can I instruct in heterogeneous groups when I know my students have vastly different needs?" For example, at the beginning of the first grade, teachers often have students who are unable to identify the entire alphabet or to read and write any words in the same classroom with students who are quite able to read and write "real" texts.

Teachers wonder how they can use whole group instruction to meet the needs of each student. They are right to wonder. The use of flexible grouping patterns can serve a wide variety of roles as alternatives to ability grouping.

What are effective groups?

Effective groups are groups in which teachers use a variety of grouping patterns to enhance student learning. Many educators have suggested alternatives to ability grouping using a variety of grouping patterns. The patterns that are suggested include: working individually, working in cooperative groups, working in pairs or small groups to develop questions, meeting in small groups to read to each other, reading aloud to the teacher on an individualized basis, and listening as a whole group to a read-aloud piece of literature and working individually. (Au, 1991; California State Department of Education, 1987a, 1987b; Cunningham, Hall, & Defee, 1991).

The most appropriate grouping pattern for each instructional experience can only be determined by analyzing student strengths and needs and matching this information with the choices available to the teacher and student. There must be a successful interaction of three sets of variables to ensure student success: (a) choosing the most appropriate basis for grouping, (b) choosing the most effective format, and (c) choosing the most appropriate materials.

Variables in using flexible grouping patterns

There are many ways to implement flexible grouping. Groups may vary in terms of why they are established and who they will contain, how large they will be, and what materials will be used, but they should always encourage interactions among students as well as between the teacher and students. Teachers can provide scaffolding (appropriate instructional assistance) in a variety of settings.

The chart in Figure 1 delineates three interactive sets of variables that play key roles in instructional decision making.

Figure 1
Flexible grouping variables

Possible bases for grouping learners
  Skills development
  Interest
  Work habits
  Prior knowledge (content)
  Prior knowledge (strategies)
  Task/activity
  Social
  Random
  Students' choice

Possible formats for groups
  Composition: Leadership:
    Individuals   Teacher-led
    Dyads   Student-led
    Small groups (3-4)   Cooperative
    Larger groups (7-10)
    Half-class
    Whole group

Possible materials for groups
  Same material for all groups
  Different levels of material with similar theme
  Different themes within a topic
  Different topics

Bases for grouping

The first category for consideration involves 9 bases for grouping:

(1) Sometimes certain students (including the whole class) have a need for direct instruction in a *skill* that relates to a particular lesson.

(2) Students who share the same *interest* may be placed together (or spread to serve as motivators within separate groups).

(3) The quality of their *work habits* may place students into heterogeneous groups, often because of the modeling provided by some students.

(4) Knowledge of *content* may put children in a group together (or have them spread as experts among several groups).

(5) Knowledge of *strategies* can put certain children in discussion or problem-solving groups because of the modeling they provide.

(6) The *task/activity* criterion may dictate that certain children work together because they succeed best through certain kinds of projects.

(7) *Social* reasons may help place leaders (or followers, talkers) in certain groups.

(8) Sometimes *random* selection techniques (such as numbering off and putting all of the "ones" in one group) are the most useful procedures.

(9) Finally, encouraging *student choice* may be the best basis for forming some types of learning groups.

Formats for grouping

The next group of variables includes possible formats for groups. Although teachers usually interact with students in all situations, they need not always be in directive positions. As indicated in the chart above, groups may vary by their dimensions and then also vary as to their types of leadership.

The six usual sizes of groups include: (1) *individuals,* (2) *dyads* (pairs), (3) *small* groups of 3 or 4, (4) *large* groups of from 7 to 10, (5) *half-class* groups of 15 or so, and (6) *whole* (total class) groups.

The three usual types of leadership include: (1) teacher-led, (2) student-led, and (3) cooperative groups in which the leadership responsibilities are shared among students or between teacher and students.

Materials for grouping

The other major category of variables involves the materials to be used by groups:

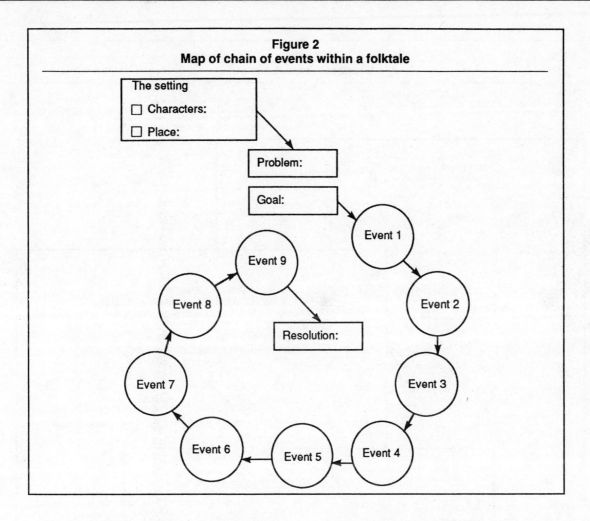

Figure 2
Map of chain of events within a folktale

The setting
☐ Characters:
☐ Place:

Problem:

Goal:

Event 1

Event 2

Event 3

Event 4

Event 5

Event 6

Event 7

Event 8

Event 9

Resolution:

(1) The *same material* for all groups is appropriate in many situations because identical material is often required of all students, as in reading core literature selections.

(2) *Different levels* (types) of similar material may be appropriate when students can learn the same concepts, but may benefit from the support of easier readability or from reading about the subject in their first language.

(3) *Different themes* within a topic may be appropriate, as in learning about the different states of someone's life, or analyzing the different characters of a story.

(4) Having materials that represent *different topics* may be appropriate when individual interests are taken into consideration.

A model of using flexible grouping patterns

Flexible grouping practices can enhance the teaching and learning of reading. Through flexible grouping, each child's needs can be met and each child can develop an understanding of the relations among the language arts.

In the following lesson, in which children read *Why Mosquitoes Buzz in People's Ears,* five different grouping patterns were used and instruction in each of the language arts was emphasized at various stages of the lesson. This lesson was conducted with a heterogeneously grouped third-grade class in a magnet school in San Diego. The 30 children in the class represented a rich mix of ethnic, cultural and linguistic backgrounds and a wide range of reading and writing abilities.

As we explain the way we taught the lesson, we will also explain our decisions for selecting and forming the groups that we used. Many grouping patterns could have been used, and we do not want to suggest that our patterns are either the only ones or the best. The best pattern for you is the one that will best meet your needs and the individual needs of each of your students.

Figure 3
Readers' Theatre scripts

Readers' Theatre for <u>Poor Old Lady</u>
Author unknown

Chacters: Narrator 1   Narrator 4   Narrator 7
             Narrator 2   Narrator 5   Narrator 8
             Narrator 3   Narrator 6

Narrator 1:   Poor old lady, sh
               I don't know why

Narrator 2:   Poor old lady, I

Narrator 3:   Poor old lady, sh
               It squirmed and

Narrator 1:   She swallowed the
               I don't know why

Narrator 2:   Poor old lady, I

Narrator 4:   Poor old lady, sh
               How absurd! she

Readers' Theatre for
<u>Why Mosquitoes Buzz in People's Ears</u>
by Verna Aardema

Chacters: Narrator 1   Iguana   Rabbit   Mother Owl
            Narrator 2   Mosquito   Monkey   King Lion
                         Python   Crow

Narrator 1:   One morning a mosquito saw an iguana drinking
              at a waterhole. The mosquito said ...

Mosquito: Iguana, you will never believe what I saw yesterday.

Readers' Theatre for <u>A Fly Went By</u>
by Mike McClintock

Chacters: Narrator 1   Frog   Cow
             Narrator 2   Cat   Fox
             Fly   Dog   Man
             Boy   Pig   Sheep

Narrator 1:   I sat by the lake. I looked at the sky, and
               as I looked, a fly went by.

Narrator 2:   A fly went by. He said ...

Fly: "Oh, dear!"

Narrator 2:   I saw him shake. He shook with fear

Narrator 1:   And when I saw that fly go past, I asked him
               why he went so fast. I asked him why he
               shook with fear. I asked him why he said ...

Fly: "Oh, dear!"

Step 1: Preparing. As we prepared the children for *Why Mosquitoes Buzz in People's Ears,* we explained to them that this is an African folktale in which events are explained as a chain—as one event occurs it causes another event to happen. Many different aspects of *Why Mosquitoes Buzz in People's Ears* and folktales could be selected for emphasis. For the sake of this lesson, we chose to emphasize an appreciation of the folktale focusing on the "event chain," which explains why mosquitoes buzz in people's ears. We stacked eight books in a row, slightly separating each from the ones next to it. Then we asked the children what would happen if we pushed the first book into the second book. We told them that we could tell the tale of "Why the Last Book Fell" by explaining a chain of events.

Step 2: Reading. We read the folktale aloud to the entire class and discussed the chain of events that led to an understanding of why mosquitoes buzz in people's ears.

Step 3: Explaining. We explained to the children the concept that stories have structures that advance the plot.

Step 4: Assisting/coaching. We assisted/coached the children in completing a map (Figure 2). This further developed their understanding of the structure of a chain of events within a folktale.

Step 5: Explaining. We explained to the children the idea that many folktales have a structure like this. We introduced the concept of Readers' Theatre (for a discussion of Readers' Theatre, see Ratliff, 1980), by explaining to them that they would have the opportunity to perform a Readers' Theatre of a "chain" folktale for the entire class. We showed them the three prepared scripts: *Why Mosquitoes Buzz in People's Ears, Poor Old Lady,* and *A Fly Went By.* The examples in Figure 3 show the first several lines of each of the Readers' Theatre scripts.

Step 6: Assisting. We let the children choose one of the three scripts and assigned them to that group. We asked them to prepare their role, which we assigned to them. We took their reading ability into consideration as we assigned the roles. We asked them to read the entire script together before they started practicing their own parts. We assisted them as they read the script, helping them to develop an overall comprehension of the story.

Step 7: Performing. When they were

ready, we asked the children to perform their Readers' Theatre for the entire class.

Step 8: Explaining. We explained to the children that they would be writing their own "chain" folktale. We prepared them for this writing activity by showing them more models of folktales that use this structure.

Step 9: Assisting/coaching. We assigned each child to a heterogeneous writing group of 7-10 students, ensuring that each group consisted of some proficient writers and some novice writers. We explained that each child would write and illustrate one page of the book. Although they were working on their own page, we assisted/coached them as they composed a whole "chain" folktale which explained a phenomenon. Together they composed, drafted, and revised their folktale before they began the final production (writing and illustrating) of their own page.

Step 10: Sharing. When all the pages were completed, the children bound their books into a whole to be read to the entire class. Samples from a completed tale by one group of third graders are presented in Figure 4. The two pages are the first and last pages of "How Roses Got Their Thorns." Eight children told how a weed and a rose were once great friends, but at a tea party with other roses and weeds, they all got to talking about who was the best rose or weed. The argument ended the party. They were all very angry and they fought with one another. The weeds beat the roses down. A fairy had to come to help them stand again, but they were full of holes. The fairy gave the roses "pointy things" to fill their holes and protect them so they would never have to be hurt again.

The chart in Figure 5 illustrates the effective use of flexible grouping that took place during this lesson.

A final note

Although ability groups have been the preferred instructional format for the teaching of reading in the past, growing evidence has shown that the exclusive use of ability groups for language arts instruction can have a deleterious effect on student learning, particularly for those children assigned to the lowest groups. The alternative to this practice, as proposed here, is the use of flexible grouping patterns. Its practice is based on the theory

Figure 4
Sample tale completed by third graders

Figure 5
Flexible grouping patterns used in the lesson
Why Mosquitoes Buzz in People's Ears

Step	Teacher activity	Student activity	Basis	Format	Materials
1	Preparing for reading	Listening, interacting	Task/activity	Whole group	Same text
2	Reading the folktale	Listening to text	Task/activity	Whole group	Same text
3	Explaining story mapping	Listening, questioning	Task/activity	Whole group	Same text
4	Assisting, coaching map work	Completing story map	Task/activity	Individual	Same text
5	Explaining Readers' Theatre	Listening	Task/activity	Whole group	Same text
6	Assisting in preparing Readers' Theatre	Practicing Readers' Theatre	Student choice	Larger groups (7-10)	Different scripts
7	Listening to performance	Performing Readers' Theatre	Student choice	Larger groups	Different scripts
8	Explaining how to write a folktale	Listening, interacting	Task/activity	Whole group	Different scripts
9	Assisting, coaching folktale writing	Writing folktales	Work habits/ interest	Cooperative small group	Different (their own) scripts
10	Sharing	Sharing folktales	Work habits	Dyads	Different folktales

that every instructional episode demands careful attention to matching students' needs with the most appropriate group experience (including group composition, grouping format, and instructional materials).

Because the use of alternative, flexible groups is relatively new, more research will need to be conducted to further clarify its relative strengths and weaknesses. It is evident that flexible grouping holds promise for the future in classrooms that will, more and more, serve widely diverse needs.

References

Allington, R.L. (1980). Poor readers don't get to read much in reading groups. *Language Arts, 57,* 872-876.

Au, K. (1991, April). A special issue on organizing for instruction. *The Reading Teacher, 44,* 534.

Barr, R. (1989). The social organization of literacy instruction. In *Cognitive and social perspectives for literacy research and instruction: The thirty-eighth yearbook of The National Reading Conference.* Chicago: The National Reading Conference.

California State Department of Education. (1987a). *English-language arts framework for California public schools.* Sacramento, CA: Author.

California State Department of Education. (1987b). *English-language arts model curriculum guide, K-8.* Sacramento, CA: Author.

Cook-Gumperz, J., Simons, H., & Gumperz, J. (1981). *School/home ethnography report.* NIE Grant No. G-78-0082.

Cunningham, P., Hall, D., & Defee, M. (1991). Non-ability grouped, multilevel instruction: A year in a first grade classroom. *The Reading Teacher, 44,* 566-571.

Eder, D. (1981). Ability grouping as a self-fulfilling prophecy: A micro-analysis of teacher-student interaction. *Sociology of Education, 54,* 151-162.

Feldhusen, J. (1990, October). Issue: Should gifted students be educated outside the regular classroom? *ASCD Update, 32,* 7.

Hallinan, M. (1984). Summary and implications. In P.L. Peterson, L.C. Wilkinson, & M. Hallinan, (Eds.), *The social context of instruction: Group organization and group processes.* Orlando, FL: Academic Press.

Hiebert, E. (1983). An examination of ability grouping for reading instruction. *Reading Research Quarterly, 18,* 231-255.

Indrisano, R., & Parratore, J.R. (1991). Classroom contexts for literacy learning. In J. Flood, J. Jensen, D. Lapp, & J. Squire (Eds.), *Handbook of research on teaching the English language arts.* New York: Macmillan.

Lapp, D., & Flood, J. (1992). *Teaching reading to every child,* 3rd ed. New York: Macmillan.

Nagel, G., Flood, J., & Lapp, D. (1990, November). *Cali-*

fornia dreaming? Literature-based English-language arts. A presentation at the National Reading Conference, Miami, FL.

National Governors' Association. (1990). Report on education.

Otto, H.J. (1950). Elementary education III organization and administration. In W.S. Monroe (Ed.), Encyclopedia of educational research (pp. 376-388). New York: Macmillan.

Ratliff, G. (1980). Readers' theatre: The theatrical approach to teaching literature. Montclair, NJ: Montclair State College.

Schell, L.L., & Rouch, R.L. (1988). The low reading group: An instructional and social dilemma. Journal of Reading Education, 14, 18-23.

Shake, M., & Allington, R. (1985). Where do teachers' questions come from? The Reading Teacher, 38, 432-437.

Shannon, P. (1985). Reading instruction and social class. Language Arts, 62, 604-613.

Weinstein, R. (1976). Reading group membership in first grade: Teacher behaviors and pupil experience over time. Journal of Educational Psychology, 68, 103-116.

Reprinted with permision of James Flood and the International Reading Association

Voices

In sum, what is wrong with the transmission model is that it places the teacher or textbook at the center of the educational enterprise and focuses almost exclusively on the input, in the mistaken belief that, to obtain the desired outcomes, what is most important is to ensure that the input is well selected, sequenced, and presented in terms of the educated adult's understanding of what is to be learned.

However, once we give due recognition to the fact that knowledge can only be constructed by individual knowers and that this occurs most effectively when they have an active engagement in all the processes involved, it becomes clear that a different model of education is required — one that is based on a <u>partnership</u> between students and teachers, in which the responsibility for selection and organizing the tasks to be engaged in is shared.

Gordon Wells,
The Meaning Makers: Children Learning Language and Using Language to Learn

Published by Heinemann Educational Books, Inc., 1986.

Priscilla L. Griffith
Mary W. Olson

Phonemic awareness helps beginning readers break the code

Griffith is Assistant Professor in the Department of Childhood/Language Arts/Reading at the University of South Florida, Tampa, Florida. Olson is Professor and Associate Dean of the School of Education at the University of North Carolina at Greensboro.

W hen children learn to speak a language, they naturally become well acquainted with its elementary speech sounds, or phonemes. They pronounce these sounds with every word, and they hear them spoken in every utterance. Despite their remarkable expertise in speech, children ordinarily spend little time thinking consciously about the phonemes they use. Their focus is quite properly on getting meaning and on producing understandable messages. And indeed, phonemic awareness would be irrelevant were it not for the fact that phonemes are the units encoded by the letters of the alphabetic languages used in most of the modern world, the raw material of reading and writing.

The insight that words are composed of smaller units (i.e., phonemes) may be diffi-cult for some children to grasp because phonemes are very abstract units of language. They carry no meaning, and children are accustomed to thinking of words in terms of their meanings, not in terms of their linguistic characteristics. Additionally, there is the problem of producing a phoneme in isolation. Phonemes are not discrete units. The attributes of a phoneme spill over into those that come before it and follow it in a word (Adams, 1990).

Phonemic awareness has been defined as the ability to examine language independently of meaning and to manipulate its component sounds (Cunningham, 1988). And because phonemes are not discrete units, phonemic awareness requires the ability to attend to a sound in the context of the other sounds in the word. There may be several levels of phonemic awareness. The phonemic awareness tasks easiest for children are those requiring them to rhyme words or to recognize rhymes. Blending phonemes and syllable splitting (e.g., segmenting the beginning sound of back, /b/, from the remainder, -ack) are intermediate-level tasks. The most difficult phonemic awareness tasks are those that involve completely segmenting the phonemes in spoken words and manipulating phonemes to form different words (Adams, 1990).

Phonemic awareness skill enables children to use letter-sound correspondences to read and spell words. For example, children segment the phonemes of a word to invent a

INTEGRATED LANGUAGE ARTS

spelling by assigning letters to represent its sounds. Children have to blend sounds together when they use letter-sound correspondences to read words they have never before seen. However, phonemic awareness is *not* synonymous with phonics. It is not learning spelling-to-sound correspondences, and it is not sounding out words. It is an understanding of the structure of *spoken* language. In fact, it is unlikely that children lacking phonemic awareness can benefit fully from phonics instruction (Juel, Griffith, & Gough, 1986) since they do not understand what letters and spellings are supposed to represent.

Phonemic awareness skill enables children to use letter-sound correspondences to read and spell words.

It is important for teachers to understand that phonemic awareness has been shown to be a very powerful predictor of later reading achievement (Juel, 1988; Juel, Griffith, & Gough, 1986; Lomax & McGee, 1987; Tunmer & Nesdale, 1985). In fact, it is a better predictor than more global measures such as IQ or general language proficiency. We know, for example, that poor readers who enter first grade phonemically unaware are very likely to remain poor readers at the end of fourth grade, since their lack of phonemic awareness contributes to their slow acquisition of word recognition skill (Juel, 1988).

In a study comparing whole language and traditional reading instruction, children who began first grade high in phonemic awareness did well regardless of the kind of reading instruction they received. That is, the children in whole language classes who had already developed an awareness of phonemes in spoken words were able to induce letter-sound correspondences without ever receiving explicit phonics instruction. On the other hand, neither type of instruction was any better for

the children who were low in phonemic awareness at the beginning of first grade (Klesius, Griffith, & Zielonka, 1991).

Other studies have shown that phonemic awareness training has a positive effect on the development of children's word recognition and spelling abilities. Bradley and Bryant (1983) provided phonemic awareness training to children over a two-year period of time. The training included rhyme and alliteration activities as well as tasks in which the children were taught to identify the odd word (e.g., bun, *hut*, gun, sun). They concluded that phonemic awareness training had a positive effect on reading success, and the training was especially powerful when combined with explicit instruction in the alphabetic principle. Lundberg, Frost, and Petersen (1988) taught preschool children to attend to the phonological structure of language prior to any explicit instruction about the alphabetic writing system. The phonemic awareness training had a facilitative effect on the acquisition of spelling ability in Grade 1 and word recognition and spelling ability in Grade 2. Ball and Blachman (1991) concluded from an intervention study with kindergarten students that young children can be taught to segment spoken words into phonemes. Furthermore, their research suggests that the most pedagogically useful phonemic awareness training includes letter-name and letter-sound instruction primarily because it makes explicit the relationship between sound segments and letters.

Given these promising research findings, three questions about phonemic awareness that teachers of young children may ask are: (a) Why is phonemic awareness important? (b) How can phonemic awareness be assessed? and (c) What can I do to develop a child's phonemic awareness?

Why is phonemic awareness important?

One of the things we have learned about phonemic awareness is that it plays a very selective, although necessary, role in the reading acquisition process. While phonemic awareness is not needed to speak or understand language (Lundberg et al., 1988), it plays a critical role in learning skills requiring the manipulation of phonemes—specifically word recognition and spelling. It is important for children to overlearn these lower-order processes until they are automatic so that conscious attention will not be diverted from the higher-order processes of comprehending during reading (LaBerge & Samuels, 1974) and composing during writing (Scardamalia, 1981).

The spelling system of the English language is based on the alphabetic principle. Written words are composed of sequences of letters that roughly correspond to the phonemes of spoken words. In order for children to learn to read and spell words they must have an understanding of how spoken language maps onto written language. It appears that some level of phonemic awareness helps a child grasp this understanding. A child who is aware of phonemes is not confused when the teacher starts talking about the sounds that letters stand for in a word, and thus is able to benefit from instruction. Equally important, the child with phonemic awareness can consciously isolate those individual sounds in the context of the other sounds in the word. While children without phonemic awareness may be able to memorize isolated letter-sound correspondences by rote, they will not understand how to actually coordinate letter-sound relationships to read or write novel words.

How can phonemic awareness be assessed in a classroom?

Teachers can use several informal assessment activities to determine whether children have developed enough phonemic awareness to progress rapidly in beginning reading. Adams (1990) suggests that phonemic awareness is not an all-or-nothing trait, something a person either has or doesn't have. Rather, we can distinguish levels of phonemic awareness, reflecting a growing ability to recognize speech as made up of elementary sounds that can be brought under control. Testing for these levels can be accomplished in brief assessment sessions using activities children will enjoy. The assessment tasks in this section are all taken or adapted from a study by Yopp (1988) who compared the reliability, validity, and difficulty of 10 phonemic awareness measures.

Though the tasks are gamelike, it is important to minimize frustration by restricting assessment to no more than one task per sitting. Also keep in mind in planning an assessment that phonemes do not correspond neatly with spellings. Sounds are often represented by combinations of letters; for example, *choose* has 6 letters but only 3 phonemes, /ch/, /oo/, and /z/.

Simple tasks requiring a child to recognize whether pairs of words rhyme enable a teacher to assess phonemic awareness at a rudimentary level. First, prepare a list of 20 pairs of common words, choosing rhyming words for at least half of the pairs (e.g., *fat-cat*). Explain to the child that rhymes are words that sound the same at the end, and show with examples how some words rhyme and others do not. Then pronounce each pair of words, asking the child if they rhyme. Yopp (1988) reported a mean score of 15 correct out of 20 such pairs when a similar assessment was used with kindergarten children.

Blending speech sounds into words is an easy task that requires a slightly higher level of phonemic awareness. A simple game offers a highly reliable measure of blending skill. Prepare a list of 30 short words. The first 10 should have just 2 phonemes (e.g., *is*); the other 20 should be 3- or 4-phoneme words. Divide 10 of these longer words before the vowel (e.g., *m-an*) and segment the others completely (e.g., *sh-i-p*). Tell the child you will say words in a secret language, and he or she will try to guess what word you are saying. The mean score in Yopp's (1988) study for kindergarten children performing this task was 20 words correct.

A higher level of phonemic awareness is needed to isolate speech sounds. While we technically cannot isolate many of the phonemes, it appears advantageous for children to approximate the sounds during early reading instruction. Select 15 3-phoneme common words, targeting sounds in the beginning (*j*am), middle (s*oa*p), and end (boo*k*). Demonstrate for the child how phonemes can be pronounced, showing how *fat* starts with /f/, *teeth* has the /ee/ sound in the middle, and *work* ends with the sound /k/. Then play the game, giving each word and the position of interest, and asking the child to say that sound. On a similar list of words used with the kindergarten children in Yopp's (1988) study, the mean score for this assessment was 9 correct. In Yopp's study, this task was an excellent predictor of readiness for explicit instruction in decoding.

Tasks requiring complete segmentation of

phonemes take the issue a step further. Here the teacher prepares a list of 22 common words, each 2 or 3 phonemes in length. The words should sample a variety of sounds represented by vowels and consonants. First demonstrate how several words can be broken down into sounds, and invite the child to say the words in a secret language of sounds. Don't expect high scores on this more difficult task; Yopp's (1988) mean was 12 correct out of a possible score of 22. The segmentation test, however, was shown to be highly trustworthy, an authentic measure of phonemic awareness, and a good predictor of decoding readiness (Yopp, 1988).

Many of the activities of the early elementary classrooms already incorporate elements that heighten phonemic awareness.

Tests requiring children to remove phonemes from words and to say how the word is transformed (for example, say *cat* without /t/) demand the highest level of phonemic awareness. Such tasks are complex, requiring a child to isolate a speech sound and to hold that sound in memory while performing a second operation. Formal assessment batteries can profitably measure such abilities, thereby increasing their predictive power (Yopp, 1988). Such high-level phonemic awareness, however, seems at least partly a *result* of emergent reading ability, rather than an ability needed to profit from reading instruction.

How can a child's phonemic awareness be developed?

Teachers can help children develop phonemic awareness in many ways. They can expose them to literature that plays with the sounds in language, they can provide extensive writing experiences, and they can provide explicit instruction in sound segmentation and in representing the sounds heard in words.

Note that we intend in this piece only to introduce phonemic awareness to teachers; a complete instructional primer is beyond our scope. Fortunately, many of the activities of the early elementary classroom already incorporate important elements that heighten phonemic awareness. When teachers teach letter names or singing games like "Old MacDonald," they promote conscious awareness of the elementary units of speech. In addition, we suggest a few specific activities below. These should be integrated as much as possible into authentic literacy events.

Literature that plays with the sounds in language. Text can deal playfully with the sounds of language through rhyme and through manipulation of phonemes. In alliteration and assonance, the same sound occurs in two or more words of text. The alphabet book *Animalia* contains many examples of alliteration, the repetition of an initial consonant sound across several words, for example, "Lazy lions lounging in the local library" (Base, 1986). Assonance, the repetition of vowel sounds within words, may be combined with rhyming to create playful text. Some examples are "A leaf, a tree, a green bean green" from *Who Said Red?* (Serfozo, 1988), and "It rains and hails and shakes the sails./Sheep wake up and grab the rails" from *Sheep on a Ship* (Shaw, 1989).

Read rhyming texts to children each day. From repeated readings of rhyming and playful texts, children will develop a repertoire of "old favorites," which can serve as springboards for children to create their own rhymes. For example, the *Jamberry* poem "Hatberry/Shoeberry/In my canoeberry" (Degen, 1983) might become "Tootberry/Hornberry/Can't eat a thornberry."

Don't Forget the Bacon! (Hutchins, 1976) plays with language through the manipulation of phonemes. In this story a child is sent to the store with a shopping list which includes "six farm eggs, a cake for tea, and a pound of pears." As he walks to town he rehearses the list, but he inadvertently switches phonemes in some of the words, changing the shopping list. For example, "a cake for tea" goes through several permutations, evolving by way of "a cape for me" to become "a rake for leaves." Have children role-play the child in the story rehearsing his shopping list. As they do this, they can explore how the sounds in words can be switched.

In addition to pure enjoyment, sound-play books heighten a child's sensitivity to the phonological structure of language. Some children may be able to discover and attend to sounds in language as a result of the linguistic stimulation provided by these kinds of books. Indeed, children who have enjoyed extensive storybook exchanges may develop phonemic awareness without direct instruction.

Writing experiences. Clay (1985) has said that children practice many of the skills of reading in another form when they write. However, the writing must not just be copying letters or words from a chart or chalkboard. It must be going from thoughts to saying words to writing them. At least one study has shown that frequent opportunities to write using invented spellings, which are characteristic of whole language classrooms, enhance writing fluency. Over time daily writing experiences may be beneficial for children lacking phonemic awareness (Griffith & Klesius, 1990). When children write they have to face head-on the problem of mapping spoken language onto written language. Serendipitous to this can be an understanding of the structure of spoken language, because the more children write, the better they become at segmenting sounds in words.

Hearing sounds in words. Listening to text that plays with language and writing with invented spellings are indirect ways to enhance phonemic awareness. With some children it may be necessary to provide more explicit instruction in hearing sounds in words. For such instruction to be effective, children need first to understand that language can be examined independently of meaning (Cunningham, 1988). Lundberg et al. (1988) describe a phonemic awareness training program that began with the segmentation of spoken language into words and syllables. Words and syllables are more directly perceivable and thus more easily available to children than are phonemes. In noncompetitive social situations, the children matched words and syllables to physical movements such as clapping, marching, and walking in place. The rhythmic activities helped the children focus on speech segments separately from meaning.

The use of Elkonin boxes (from the Russian psychologist, D.B. Elkonin) is a procedure prescribed by Clay (1985) as a Reading

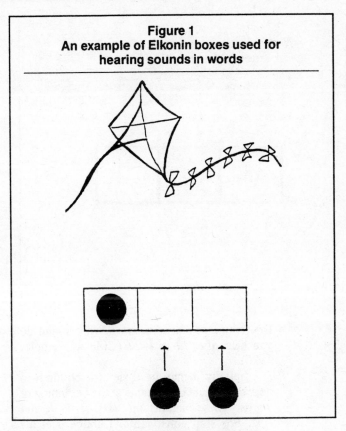

Figure 1
An example of Elkonin boxes used for hearing sounds in words

Recovery strategy to help children think about the order of sounds in spoken words. The teacher prepares a card with a picture of a simple word. Below the picture is a matrix that contains a box for each phoneme (not letter) in the word. Words should be chosen from text with which the children have become thoroughly familiar through multiple oral readings. The use of a whole-to-part sequence of instruction will ensure that children have a context to which they can relate the abstract sounds (Bridge, 1989). An example of these sound segment cards appears in Figure 1.

The teacher slowly articulates the word while pushing counters into the boxes, sound by sound. The child is encouraged to join in the process, perhaps by articulating the word while the teacher moves the counters and later by moving the counters herself. Gradually the responsibility should be transferred to the child. The task can be made more complex by removing the matrix and having only the counters available. Later the picture can be removed. Eventually the child should be able to count the number of sounds in a word and be able to answer questions about the order of sounds in words, for example, What is the

Phonemic awareness

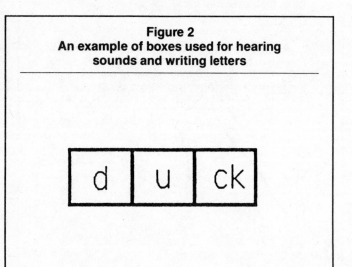

**Figure 2
An example of boxes used for hearing sounds and writing letters**

first sound you hear in *kite*? What sound do you hear after /ī/ in *kite*? (Gillet & Temple, 1990).

Initially it may be easier for children to hear continuant consonants at the beginning of words. These include /m/, /s/, /f/, /sh/, and /th/. For stop consonants, Lundberg et al. (1988) suggest an iterating technique. For example, the teacher might say "/k/ /k/ /k/ kite" to help the child hear the initial phoneme in kite.

A related activity is to use boxes to make the connection between sound segments and letters explicit. Draw a box for each sound in a word the child wants to write. Words should be those the child has not yet learned to spell. Ask questions such as What sounds can you hear? What letters might you see? Where will the letters go? Encourage the child to write the letters she knows and ensure that they go in the correct box. The teacher can help by filling in any letters the child does not know. Figure 2 is an example of boxes used for writing words (Clay, 1985).

Phonemic awareness activities will not be helpful to a child unless they can be placed in a context of real reading and writing. This can be accomplished by relating sound segmentation tasks to the actual things a child does when trying to read or spell a word. For example, writing letters in boxes should be related to the invented spelling process of breaking a word apart and representing the sounds with letters. The value of being able to

hear sounds in words can be emphasized by showing children how it helps them cross-check what they read with the letters they would expect to see in the printed word (Clay, 1985).

In summary, to gain phonemic awareness is to become conscious of the basic sounds of speech. In learning to read and write an alphabetic language, phonemic awareness is critical, since our system of writing maps letters to phonemes. Extensive research has indicated the importance of phonemic awareness as prerequisite for understanding the alphabetic principle, namely that letters stand for the sounds in spoken words. Thus the emergent reader faces the critical tasks of learning to blend phonemes into words and to segment words into phonemes. The ability to perform these tasks can be measured by a sequence of gamelike tasks. More importantly, we can promote phonemic awareness with a series of well-planned activities in the language arts curriculum in kindergarten and first grade. For some children, these activities may be enjoyably superfluous. For others, however, they may bridge a critical gap between inadequate preparation for literacy learning and success in beginning reading.

References

Adams, M.J. (1990). *Beginning to read: Thinking and learning about print.* Cambridge, MA: MIT Press.

Ball, E.W., & Blachman, B.A. (1991). Does phoneme segmentation training in kindergarten make a difference in early word recognition and developmental spelling? *Reading Research Quarterly, 26,* 49-66.

Bradley, L., & Bryant, P.E. (1983). Categorizing sounds and learning to read—A causal connection. *Nature, 301,* 419-421.

Bridge, C.A. (1989). Beyond the basal in beginning reading. In P.N. Winograd, K.K. Wixson, & M.Y. Lipson (Eds.), *Improving basal reading instruction* (pp. 177-209). New York: Teachers College Press.

Clay, M.M. (1985). *The early detection of reading difficulties* (3rd ed.). Portsmouth, NH: Heinemann.

Cunningham, A.E. (1988, April). *A developmental study of instruction in phonemic awareness.* Paper presented at the meeting of the American Educational Research Association, New Orleans, LA.

Gillet, J.W., & Temple, C. (1990). *Understanding reading problems: Assessment and instruction* (3rd ed.). Glenview, IL: Scott, Foresman.

Griffith, P.L., & Klesius, J.P. (1990, November). *The effect of phonemic awareness ability and reading instructional approach on first grade children's acquisition of spelling and decoding skills.* Paper presented at the National Reading Conference, Miami, FL.

Juel, C. (1988). Learning to read and write: A longitudinal study of 54 children from first through fourth grades. *Journal of Educational Psychology, 80,* 437-447.

Juel, C., Griffith, P.L., & Gough, P.B. (1986). Acquisition of literacy: A longitudinal study of children in first and second grade. *Journal of Educational Psychology, 78,* 243-255.

Klesius, J.P., Griffith, P.L., & Zielonka, P. (1991). A whole language and traditional instruction comparison: Overall effectiveness and development of the alphabetic principle. *Reading Research and Instruction, 30*(2), 47-61.

LaBerge, D., & Samuels, S.J. (1974). Toward a theory of automatic information processing in reading. *Cognitive Psychology, 6,* 293-323.

Lomax, R.G., & McGee, L.M. (1987). Young children's concepts about print and meaning: Toward a model of word reading acquisition. *Reading Research Quarterly, 22,* 237-256.

Lundberg, I., Frost, J., & Petersen, O. (1988). Effects of an extensive program for stimulating phonological awareness in preschool children. *Reading Research Quarterly, 23,* 263-284.

Scardamalia, M. (1981). How children cope with the cognitive demands of writing. In C.H. Frederickson & J.F. Dominic (Eds.), *Writing: The nature, development, and teaching of written communication. Vol. 2: Writing: Process, development, and communication* (pp. 81-104). Hillsdale, NJ: Erlbaum.

Tunmer, W.E., & Nesdale, A.R. (1985). Phonemic segmentation skill and beginning reading. *Journal of Educational Psychology, 77,* 417-427.

Yopp, H.K. (1988). The validity and reliability of phonemic awareness tests. *Reading Research Quarterly, 23,* 159-177.

Trade books containing text that plays with sound in language

Allen, P. (1983). *Bertie and the bear.* New York: Putnam.

Barrett, J. (1980). *Animals should definitely not act like people.* New York: Macmillan.

Base, G. (1986). *Animalia.* New York: Abrams.

Degen, B. (1983). *Jamberry.* New York: Harper & Row.

Geisel, T.S. (Dr. Seuss). (1957). *The cat in the hat.* New York: Random House.

Geisel, T.S. (Dr. Seuss). (1960). *Green eggs and ham.* New York: Random House.

Geisel, T.S. (Dr. Seuss). (1963). *Dr. Seuss's ABC.* New York: Random House.

Geisel, T.S. (Dr. Seuss). (1972). *Marvin K. Mooney, will you please go now!* New York: Random House.

Geisel, T.S. (Dr. Seuss). (1987). *I am not going to get up today!* New York: Random House.

Hoberman, M.A. (1982). *A house is a house for me.* New York: Penguin.

Hutchins, P. (1972). *Good-night owl.* New York: Morrow.

Hutchins, P. (1976). *Don't forget the bacon!* New York: Morrow.

Leedy, L. (1989). *Pingo the plaid panda.* New York: Holiday House.

Lord, J.V. (1972). *The giant jam sandwich.* Boston, MA: Houghton Mifflin.

Peet, B. (1962). *Smokey.* Boston, MA: Houghton Mifflin.

Peet, B. (1983). *No such things.* Boston, MA: Houghton Mifflin.

Pomerantz, C. (1974). *The piggy in the puddle.* New York: Macmillan.

Pomerantz, C. (1987). *How many trucks can a tow truck tow?* New York: Random House.

Raffi. (1987). *Down by the bay.* New York: Crown.

Rounds, G. (1989). *Old MacDonald had a farm.* New York: Holiday House.

Serfozo, M.K. (1988). *Who said red?* New York: Macmillan.

Shaw, N. (1986). *Sheep in a jeep.* Boston, MA: Houghton Mifflin.

Shaw, N. (1989). *Sheep on a ship.* Boston, MA: Houghton Mifflin.

Terban, M. (1984). *I think I thought.* Boston, MA: Houghton Mifflin.

Van Laan, N. (1990). *Possum come a-knockin'.* New York: Knopf.

Wadsworth, O.A. (1985). *Over in the meadow.* New York: Penguin.

Reprinted with permission of Priscilla Griffith and the International Reading Association.

Voices

*D*ear children,
    When I was a kid, I had a lot of trouble with spelling. Actually, I could read what I wrote and so could everybody else. The problem was adults. Adults have trouble knowing how to react to poor spelling. You know how a cat's fur will stand up if you lock it in a room with a German shepherd. Many adults get their fur up when they see misspellings. There's nothing really disgusting or gross about misspelled words, but adults think they are bad. And since it's pretty hard to change the way adults think, here are a few tips for keeping your German shepherds (bad spellings) away from your cats (irritated adults).

J. Richard Gentry
Spel . . . Is a Four-Letter Word

Published by Scholastic Professional Books.

The Uses and Abuses *of* Invented Spelling

By REGIE ROUTMAN

Invented spelling does not mean "anything goes,"
says teacher, author, and nationally recognized expert
on whole language Regie Routman.
In this article, she shows how you can get the best
results from invented spelling in your own classroom.

Regie Routman models conferencing for third-grade teacher Dana Bulan. Regie prefers to write conference notes on Post-it notes, which she later gives to the student. This simple technique keeps the child's draft clean of teacher markings.

Invented spelling has gotten a bad name in many classrooms—mainly, I think, because of certain misconceptions surrounding its use. Too many well-intentioned teachers have been operating under the assumption that in a whole language classroom, they are not *allowed* to interfere with children's writing. As a result, students may be writing more and writing more often, but much of their work is illegible, sloppy, and filled with misspellings of basic words. Teachers are growing increasingly frustrated, while some parents have been left to wonder if we are teaching spelling at all. How did all this happen?

In the early stages of the whole language movement, as educators and parents were beginning to understand the developmental nature of all language learning, many believed that kids would learn to spell through immersion in reading and writing with lots of opportunities for practice and experimentation. As with reading, this approach worked fine for some kids—but not for all. Many students still needed strategies to be made explicit for them. When teachers didn't continually model reading and writing processes, provide lots of opportunities for guided practice, and help kids discover and notice features of words, some kids had trouble with reading and spelling despite the use of real literature and the writing process.

As I see it, invented spelling was never meant to be "anything goes." Its purpose was to free kids up to write. In a class of 25 to 30 students, children who are dependent on the teacher to spell every word correctly are unable to freely express themselves. Invented spelling (and with it, the teacher saying, "Do the best you can. That's fine for now. Spell it like it sounds.") allows

REGIE ROUTMAN *is a language arts resource teacher in the Shaker Heights, Ohio, City School District. She is the author of* Transitions: From Literature to Literacy *(Heinemann, Portsmouth, New Hampshire, 1988 and* Invitations: Changing as Teachers and Learners K-12 *(Heinemann, 1991).*

kids to concentrate on their messages without overconcern for correctness. That has allowed even kindergarten children to see themselves as writers early in the school year—and that's a wonderful thing.

But I also believe that we must hold kids accountable for basic standards so they can take pride in their work. Even in daily journal writing, we should have expectations such as legible handwriting, skipping every other line (at least for primary grade children), spelling high-frequency words correctly, and rereading to check for meaning, spelling, and punctuation.

When I am in a classroom in which writing looks a mess and the teacher accepts all invented spellings (even basic words), the students usually do not take writing seriously. The good news, of course, is that it doesn't have to be this way. It is possible to teach spelling and still remain true to the philosophy of whole language. The following strategies and ideas may help you rethink your use of invented spelling.

Use Core Word Lists
Invented spelling recognizes that learning to spell, like learning to talk, is developmental. Children are not expected to get it right immediately. Promotion of invented spelling recognizes and respects that language develops gradually and that learners need lots of time and practice to take risks, make mistakes, and do plenty of reading and writing.

At the same time, while it is unrealistic to expect a first grader to spell all words correctly, it is realistic to expect *some* words to be spelled correctly all

Typical journal writing from a first-grade class in which children write daily, expectations are high, and spelling strategies are taught in context of reading and writing.

It is possible to teach spelling and still remain true to the philosophy of whole language.

the time. Even most kindergarten children can be expected to spell a very small group of often-used words by the end of the school year (words such as *I, me, my,* and *to*). Older children should be inventing only new vocabulary words, uncommon words, and words we wouldn't expect them to be able to spell correctly

Regie saved all of her drafts of this article for INSTRUCTOR and brought them to school so kids could see the many stages that precede a published piece of writing.

at their age or grade level.

In the K–4 elementary building where I am based, teachers in grades 1–4 have worked together to develop core lists of words that we expect students to be able to spell by the time they leave each grade. We developed these core lists because we were concerned about children's misspellings of common words. The lists include words culled from our students' daily writing in addition to days of the week, months, the name of our school and city, and other common words such as *social studies, science, because, enough, through, two, too,* and *to*.

Many words are on more than one grade-level list. We make these core lists available to all parents and students.

Don't Accept Sloppy Drafts

I place the same expectations on children as writers that I place on myself as a writer. I would never expect a colleague to respond to my writing draft without first making sure it was in good form—and that includes legibility, standard spelling, and neatness. Out of respect for the reader, whom I want to focus on the content of the piece, I make sure the draft is easily readable. We should expect no less from our students.

That's one reason why I no longer use the term "sloppy copy" to refer to a draft. Some students have taken the term too literally and use "sloppy copy" as an invitation to turn in messy work with numerous misspellings.

I will not conference with a child until he or she has reread the paper and checked it for basic spelling and punctuation. Also, the paper must be legible, even in the first draft; that is, the writer must be able to read it easily, which brings me to the next strategy.

Make Conferences Count

Recently, I was in a third-grade classroom during writing workshop, modeling conferencing for the teacher. This teacher was exhausted by conferencing because she was assuming most of the responsibility for improving her students' writing. When Damien came up for his conference, I began as I always do. "How can I help you? What would you like out of this conference?"

"Spelling," he said without hesitation. "I want to work on my spelling." (His teacher had already told me he was the poorest writer in the classroom.)

Usually, in a first conference on a piece of writing, students want feedback on content. They might say something like, "I want to know if the beginning brings the reader in," or "I want to know if there are any confusing parts." But Damien was only interested in improving his spelling.

"Read me your piece," I said, while I wondered to myself how he could possibly read it. It was a mess—illegible, very few letters in many words, no punctuation. He began and stumbled along. When he came to the word *president*, he had written only *pt.*

"Damien," I said, "say the word *presi-*

dent slowly. What sound do you hear after the *p*? Good. That's right. Now what do you hear next? Say it slowly."

With continued modeling and questioning, Damien was able to write "prsdnt." Now we could both read it easily. I told Damien I would be glad to help him with his spelling, but first he needed to go back to his seat, reread, and make sure his spelling was his reasonable best and that he had punctuation at the end of his sentences. Even though he was a poor speller, not enough had been expected of him. He knew his teacher would correct his misspellings, so there was no need for him to put forth his best effort.

After the conference, his teacher was relieved. "I thought I had to do it all. It would have taken me 30 minutes to go through his piece, and then I wouldn't have seen any other students. I see that by placing the responsibility on Damien, I will be able to help him more effectively and have more time for other conferences."

Don't Be Afraid To Teach Spelling

While whole language teachers may choose not to teach spelling formally as a separate subject, they *do* teach spelling. They expect their students to spell high-frequency words correctly, to utilize reliable rules and patterns, and to apply spelling strategies in their daily writing. A classroom environment that encourages children to be good spellers provides:

◆ lots of opportunities to write and talk about words;

◆ lots of opportunities to read and talk about words;

◆ lots of spelling references for children (wall charts, personal dictionaries, other children to talk to, classroom dictionaries, print around the classroom, word walls, and so on);

◆ daily writing time, usually as part of writing workshop or journal writing;

◆ a posted core list of words that children and parents know must be spelled correctly;

◆ lots of mini-lessons to see word patterns, develop rules, notice unusual features of words (these lessons arise from what the teacher notices the children need);

◆ lots of playing around with language and noticing special features of words, for example, noticing and commenting on surprising letters found in a word; and

◆ opportunities to share and publish writing.

Underlying all of this is a teacher whose philosophy of how children learn to spell is consistent with the principles of language learning, and who takes the time to effectively communicate the research on learning to spell to parents.

Strive for Balance

Several years ago, most of the K–4 buildings in our school district used a common writing prompt in an attempt to get a handle on what constituted "good" writing across the grades. In an informal look at the invented spelling of students in grades 1–4, I noticed that by the beginning of fourth grade, almost all students were spelling a core of high-frequency words correctly. The message is clear: While students should use invented spelling freely during the primary years, we need to expect most words to be spelled correctly as they get older.

We need to strive for a balance. By over-attending to spelling, students may feel too constrained to write. But by accepting all spelling, even when we know the student can do better, we give the message that spelling is not important.

I believe that everything in writing matters. Of course, we want to emphasize content first, but spelling, handwriting, and general legibility are also important. We need to let our students and their parents know that and keep our expectations for students reasonable and high. Invented spelling is a marvelous tool, as long as we use it appropriately.

> I place the same expectations on children as writers that I place on myself as a writer.

> *A personal educational philosophy evolves from many factors — observing children, demonstration teaching, trying things out, talking with colleagues, keeping up with the research — and will be different for each of us. The important thing is to continue questioning how and why we are doing what we are doing. Does the way we work with children reflect how children learn? Do we have a theory of learning that we can apply to our teaching? Are the children in our classrooms joyful and confident about their learning? A philosophy which is our own gives us empowerment.*
> **Regie Routman**
> **Transitions**
> **Published by Heinemann, Portsmouth, NH 1988**

INTEGRATED LANGUAGE ARTS

The Whole Language Newsletter for Parents

ANTHONY D. FREDERICKS
Associate Professor of Education • York College • York, PA

VOL. 2, NO. 3 FEBRUARY 1993

Teaching with Themes

Greetings! Welcome to another edition of "The Whole Language Newsletter for Parents." In these pages I'll be writing about the wonderful world of whole language, a philosophy of teaching in which reading, writing, listening, and speaking are integrated and taught throughout all the subject areas. I'll explain how it works, what your child is doing in class, and provide you with ideas and strategies you can use at home to promote and extend his or her learning. The intent is not to turn your home into a "school away from school," but rather to assist you in providing a supportive atmosphere - one that can have a positive effect on *what* and *how* your child learns.

To those of you who are new to this newsletter, let me quickly highlight some of the elements of whole language. First, it's not a new program or "fad," but rather a way in which children's literature, writing activities, and communication activities can be used across the curriculum.

Although each whole language classroom is different, there are some elements that tend to appear in most. They include: daily reading, daily writing, literature discussion groups, individualized reading activities, small group work, silent reading, story sharing, thematic units, and opportunities for speaking and listening. Your child's teacher may select all, some, or many of these components to keep pace with the academic needs of each student in the classroom. In addition to a textbook, the teacher may use materials such as magazines, children's literature, and newspapers.

What is distinguishing about whole language is the ability of the teacher to provide youngsters with a natural learning environment based on each child's strengths.

Thematic Units

One learning strategy used in many whole language classrooms is the thematic unit, which consists of well-organized activities, children's books, and other materials that the teacher uses to expand upon a particular theme or concept.

Good thematic units are built around the needs, interests, and abilities of students and allow them to pursue a topic for an extended period of time. For example, in a science unit on "Plants," the teacher may have students read different books about plants, write directions for taking care of plants, grow several varieties in the classroom, invite gardeners in to share information, contact seed companies, create plant-related songs, and observe and write about plants on the school grounds.

A major advantage of the thematic unit is that it provides opportunities for students to engage in hands-on learning activities and be exposed to real-life situations and problems. For example, in presenting lessons on the environment, your child's teacher might have her students read books on the topic, explore local forests or wetlands, visit a local conservation agency, watch a documentary on television, and write a paper about what they learned.

The development of a thematic unit on the environment would allow the class to explore this topic in greater detail than if they relied entirely on a textbook.

Let's take a look at some of the questions parents are asking about thematic units. You may wish to discuss these topics with your child's teacher as well.

Where do thematic units come from?

Thematic units come from a variety of sources. Many are available commercially to teachers and can be purchased as books or handbooks through local bookstores or education catalogs (see "Recommended Books" below).

Teachers can also develop their own thematic units; many have been designed by teams of teachers working together to select appropriate literature and create the activities. Regardless of the source, thematic units will be tailored to the needs, interests, and abilities of the students.

Aren't thematic units a collection of "fun time" activities?

Well-written thematic units include a series of carefully designed and selected activities that involve students in making decisions, solving problems, asking questions, and conducting research.

Good units also familiarize students with a host of ideas that revolve around the theme, provide them with the skills needed to express their own ideas, and help them apply their learning to real-life situations. The activities are not random, but rather represent a logical ordering of assignments in a meaningful context.

Won't my child miss important work in his or her textbooks?

Thematic units do not replace textbooks (often referred to as "basals"). Instead, thematic units offer a way for teachers to organize objectives around a theme and use a variety of materials, including the basals, to make learning more meaningful. Since basals often form the backbone of subject areas, it seems natural to supplement those basals with additional literature and thematic activities.

Recommended books for parents and other adults

Anthony D. Fredericks, Anita Meinbach, and Liz Rothlein. *Thematic Units: An Integrated Approach to Teaching Science and Social Studies.* (HarperCollins Publishers, New York, 1993).

Marjorie Kostelnik, Donna Howe, Kit Payne, Barbara Rohde, Grace Spalding, Laura Stein, and Duane Whitbeck. *Teaching Young Children Using Themes (Ages 2–6).* (Scott, Foresman and Co., Glenview, IL, 1991).

Christine C. Pappas, Barbara Kiefer, and Linda Levstik. *An Integrated Language Perspective in the Elementary School.* (Longman, White Plains, NY, 1990).

What will be the ultimate effect on my child's standardized test scores?

Several recent educational reports have called for a more "integrated approach" to learning (theme teaching is one such approach) to help prepare students for the 21st century. What the students learn through such teaching strategies, however, can't always be measured with traditional standardized tests.

With thematic teaching, therefore, test scores will generally not go up or down to any appreciable degree. Yet the information the students learn will stay with them for longer periods of time because they have been given opportunities to use what they have learned in practical, everyday situations.

What about homework?

You may notice that your child will be doing a different kind of homework while involved in a thematic unit. For example, your child may be asked to assemble a collage of sea animals for a unit on the oceans of the world; create a poster, display, mobile, diorama, or photographic essay on a tropical rain forest for a unit on the environment; or interview people in the neighborhood or community for a group project on race relations.

The biggest difference between thematic-unit homework and traditional homework is more "active" assignments in the latter. Less time is spent looking up words in a dictionary or reading a chapter in a textbook and more time is spent "creating" or "doing" things. That's not to say that more traditional forms of homework are eliminated; they are enhanced through opportunities to use the material in a more productive way.

What are some thematic unit principles that I can use at home with my child?

Here are some ideas you may want to consider incorporating into your family's routines:

- Provide your child with a variety of literature centered around a particular theme. If, for example, your child is interested in horses, obtain books and videos from your local library on that topic.
- Discuss some of the thematic unit-based activities your child is involved in. Ask questions that will allow your child to explain, in detail, some of these activities. Be sure you discuss the relationship between those activities and what may take place in the outside world.
- Ask your child to create a display or model of some of the projects accomplished in school. If possible, your child may be able to take photographs of the projects completed at school to share with family members.
- Talk with your child's teacher about appropriate supportive activities that family members can use to enhance a particular thematic unit. Teachers have often discovered that many of the assignments accomplished in school can also be tackled at home.

More whole language activities for families

- Have your child interview grandparents or other relatives and then transcribe the information into a small booklet for display in the family bookcase.
- Give your child old magazines or travel brochures about your state or region. The assignment: put together a collage of interesting places, each of which should include a written description.
- Suggest that your child create the journal of an imaginary ancestor as he or she traveled to America. What would be some of the adventures encountered by this person?
- Schedule a "family read-in." Invite all family members to gather in a central location to read silently for a designated period of time (15 minutes, for example). Afterwards, share some of the things each of you learned while reading.
- Have your child write an imaginary letter to "Dear Abby" about a real or fictional family problem or situation. Take time to discuss your child's letter.
- Help your child to create a wordless picture book about a recent event in his or her life. Plan to discuss your child's choice of pictures. ↓

Reprinted with permission of the publishers, Early Years, Inc., Norwalk, CT 06854. From the Feb. 1993 issue of Teaching/K-8.

Developing an Integrated Language Curriculum: One District Shows How

by Deborah Sumner

"The vision is simple. We want all students to love language, reading, writing and speaking. We have chosen not to use a common basal in order to provide teachers the freedom to do what they do best — develop the potential of each individual child.

"Teaching is an art. The talent of the artist inspires young minds to enjoy exciting literature and to be expressive and articulate through pen and speech. The work of the artist is never quite finished, never quite good enough . . . ."

From the introduction to Contoocook Valley (ConVal) School District's *Integrated Language Curriculum*

ConVal's *Integrated Language Curriculum* outlines grade level expectations in reading, writing, listening and speaking for the district's readiness through eighth grade students. Shaped with an understanding of children's developmental stages and individual differences among students and teachers, the document guides, but does not constrain. It remains in draft form with the expectation of continuing review and change.

The 2,800-student ConVal School district is comprised of eight small towns located in southwestern New Hampshire's Monadnock region. Teachers in ConVal have been gradually developing an integrated language program since the early 1980s. Their growing interest and experience first with writing process, then with literature-based reading evolved into a more holistic approach to teaching language skills and processes. Currently, all elementary classrooms integrate language teaching, although variations in teacher experience and styles are expected.

An Evolving Curriculum

Three language arts consultants completed the first draft of the language curriculum during the 1989-90 school year after extensively reviewing research and getting input from middle school and high school students, teachers, parents and administrators.

The curriculum "put into print what we had been doing," in the district for years, said Paula Flemming, one of the two current language arts consultants. The district developed the written curriculum to guide new teachers and those who needed more help in integrating the language areas.

Teachers in ConVal have been gradually developing an integrated language program since the early 1980s. Their growing interest and experience first with writing process, then with literature-based reading evolved into a more holistic approach to teaching language skills and processes.

The district began implementing the first draft of the curriculum during the 1990-91 school year and a Core Team of teachers representing different grade levels began working with the language arts consultants to review and revise the initial draft.

Changes approved by the school board in the spring of 1991 included

the title — from "Essential Skills Curriculum" to "Integrated Language Curriculum." The current draft represents a compromise among the educational community's various constituent groups, Flemming noted.

Although she was among those who would have preferred an emphasis on teaching students strategies to learn phonics, the curriculum includes a phonetic analysis strand for grades 1-4. Still, the spirit of compromise is evident.

"Teach (phonics) WITHIN THE CONTEXT of reading and writing," the curriculum guide states. "Generally, phonics workbooks are not an appropriate context. However, to meet the needs of individual students, a variety of adaptations may be used as necessary."

In addition to grade level expectations for each of the four language areas (with activities integrated when possible), the current framework includes a list of core and protected books to be used only at certain grade levels and recommendations for the amount of time teachers should spend on reading, writing, handwriting, spelling and reading aloud.

Curriculum revision continues as an ongoing process. Some members of the Core Team are currently questioning whether it's appropriate to restrict core books for use at specific grade levels.

"It's a philosophical question," Flemming said. Should students of a particular grade level all have experience with certain books or not? It's a question staff will continue to grapple with during the 1993-94 school year.

Study, research and library skills also need to be added to the curriculum, but integrated into what is already there, not as separate strands, she said.

Supporting Change

Flemming recommends that districts moving toward developing an integrated language curriculum plan on three to five years to make the change. Teachers need time, resources, support, and inservice opportunities, she said. As individuals deepen their understanding, faculty meetings should allow time for teachers to share ideas and react to professional reading.

In the ConVal School District, students learn language skills and processes as part of an integrated curriculum.

If an integrated language program through the district is an important goal, the question becomes, "how do we help people move toward that goal — help, not push?" Flemming asked.

In ConVal, the language consultants do everything they can to help develop a stronger language program. They find resources for teachers to use in the classroom, lead workshops, work directly with students, write curriculum, review assessment practices, and provide an extra person to help coordinate major projects, such as a published book the district's 250 fourth graders researched, wrote, edited, and illustrated as part of their New Hampshire studies.

"We say we'll do anything except bathrooms and windows," Flemming quipped.

Teachers know that the consultants are there to support, not evaluate them.

"People can say 'this is really stupid,' or 'I can't do it,' and we work from there . . . .

"All change is a gradual process," she added. "In working with individuals, adults or children, we realize that not everyone is in the same place at the same time."

"How do I use big books?" one experienced teacher wanted to know. "How do I plan integrated themes?" another asked.

The teacher as artist continues to grow, learn, refine skills, and improve ways to help children develop their full potential as language users.

ConVal's *Integrated Language Curriculum* is a compromise, but it also reflects the current consensus of the educational community. As individuals deepen and broaden their understanding of language learning and teaching, the curriculum will continue to evolve and accommodate that learning. Like an artist's work, the language curriculum is "never quite finished, never quite good enough."

Excerpts from the **Integrated Language Curriculum** *have been reprinted on the following pages with permission of the ConVal School District. Complete copies of the readiness through eighth grade guide are available for $50 (including shipping and handling).*

Contact: ConVal School District
Attn: Denise
SAU I
Rt. 202N
Peterborough, NH 03458
(603) 924-7333

INTEGRATED LANGUAGE ARTS

INTEGRATED LANGUAGE CURRICULUM
Developed by the ConVal School District

FIRST GRADE SKILLS

READING

GENERAL CHARACTERISTICS:
- Enjoys books and rereading familiar books.
- Participates in reading patterned and predictable text with familiar language.
- Predicts vocabulary.
- Uses background experiences.

VOCABULARY:
- Reads the first 100 words on the High Frequency Word List.
- Predicts vocabulary to fill a space left in speech or writing, provided contextual clues are strong and the language is familiar.

PHONETIC ANALYSIS:

Teach *within the context* of reading and writing. Generally, phonics workbooks are not an appropriate context. However, to meet the needs of individual students, a variety of adaptations may be used as necessary.
- Cross-checks one source of cues (semantic, syntactic or phonetic) with another set of cues.
- Recognizes words with upper or lower case letters in the initial positions of words.
- Reads words *in context* with the following symbol/sound associations:
    Consonants in initial and final position except soft *c* and *g*.
    Consonant blends: bl, fl, pl, sl, br, cr, dr, fr, gr, tr, str, sm sn, sw, pr, cl, gl, tw, sp, spr.
    Consonant digraphs: ch, sh, th, wh.
- Reads words with:
    Suffixes: -s, -ed, -ing, -er, -'s
    Prefixes: a- (away), be-
    Contractions: -n't, -'ll
    Abbreviations: Mr., Mrs., Ms.
- Reads simple compound words.
- Understands that final *e* is silent.

COMPREHENSION
- Discusses meaning of a story.
- Infers words in cloze-type activities where the language and story are familiar. (Cloze is an activity where words are left out of text, and students complete the gaps.)
- Retells some details from a familiar story.
- Retells major events of a story in sequence.
- Understands cause and effect in a familiar story.
- Compares / contrasts books.
- Follows a single written direction.
- Uses the text and illustrations to sample, predict, and confirm.
- Knows that the same story is in the same book each time and is not one made up in one's head.
- Dramatizes, illustrates, and retells stories which have been read.

Memory is still important but is used much more in conjunction with cues supplied by the book and language.

ORAL READING:
- Recognizes end punctuation.
- Takes risks and makes approximations.
- Reruns and reads on when meaning has been lost.
- Makes some self-corrections.
- Matches language to print.
- Finger or voice points. (Pauses between each word, no phrasing, no expression)

SILENT READING:
- Students "read" continuously for a minimum of 10 minutes per day.

WRITING

FLUENCY:
- Has confidence as a writer.
- Writes an average of 40 words during a writing session. Fluctuation from day to day is to be expected.

COMPOSITION:
- Writes daily for 30 minutes. Drawing, mini-lessons and sharing are part of this activity.
- Writes five or more related sentences using sight vocabulary and invented spelling.
- Reads what they have written.
- Revises one or more words during or after a conference.
- Edits for those specifics listed under mechanics and spelling and for those items on the student's personal editing list.

MECHANICS:
- Consolidates previous level.
- Capitalizes:
    First and last name of own name
    Names of persons

HANDWRITING:
- 50 minutes each week devoted to letter formation — demonstration and/or practice.
- Appropriately uses upper and lower case letters most of the time.
- Writes on lined paper.

SPELLING:
- Spells own first and last name.
- Spells a few of the most frequently used words.
- Represents all consonant sounds in writing with correct letter except for soft *c* and *g*.

SPEAKING

- Expresses needs.
- Asks questions or makes statements at appropriate times.
- Responds appropriately to questions.
- Maintains the subject line in conversation.
- Shares experiences in a group.
- Uses complete sentences when appropriate.
- Retells a story including sequence, major characters, and important details.
- Uses specific vocabulary for objects. (book, puzzle, scissors)
- In an oral context, predicts words and meanings.
- Participates in drama, discussion, and role playing associated with books.

First Grade Sight Words
ConVal School District

the	be	which	into	now
of	this	she	time	find
and	have	do	has	long
a	from	how	look	down
to	or	their	two	day
in	one	if	more	did
is	had	will	write	get
you	by	up	go	come
that	words	other	see	made
it	but	about	number	may
he	not	out	no	part
was	what	many	way	
for	all	then	could	
on	were	them	people	
are	we	these	my	
as	when	so	than	
with	your	some	first	
his	can	her	water	
they	said	would	been	
I	there	make	called	
at	use	like	who	
	an	him	oil	
	each		its	

Second Grade Sight Words
ConVal School District

In addition to the words listed in grade 1, students will be able to correctly spell the following:

over	say	see	try
new	great	put	kind
sound	where	end	hand
take	help	does	picture
only	through	another	again
little	much	well	change
work	before	large	off
know	line	must	play
place	right	big	spell
years	too	even	air
live	means	such	away
me	old	because	animals
back	any	turned	house
give	same	here	point
most	tell	why	page
very	boy	asked	letters
after	following	went	mother
things	came	men	answer
our	want	read	found
just	show	need	study
name	also	land	still
good	around	different	learn
sentence	form	home	should
man	three	us	American
think	small	move	world

SECOND GRADE SKILLS
READING

GENERAL CHARACTERISTICS:
- Enjoys social aspect of reading: partners, small groups.
- Uses background experiences.
- Is becoming comfortable with print.
- Chooses reading as an activity.

VOCABULARY:

Teachers will share other meanings of words which students encounter in reading when students do not understand the contextual meaning. For example, "We will *store* the books in the closet," when the student is not aware of the meaning of *store* as a verb.

- Predicts vocabulary to fill a space left in speech or writing, provided contextual clues are strong and the language is familiar.
- Identifies a word that means the opposite of a given word.
- Identifies synonyms.

PHONETIC ANALYSIS:

Teach *within the context* of reading and writing. Generally, phonics workbooks are not an appropriate context. However, to meet the needs of individual students, a variety of adaptations may be used as necessary.

- Cross-checks one source of cues (semantic, syntactic or phonetic) with another set of cues.
- Takes risks and makes approximations.
- Reads words *in context* with the following symbol/sound associations:

    Consonants including soft *c* and *g*

    Consonant blends and digraphs

    Suffixes: -ly, -y, -er, -est, -y changed to -ies and -ied, -en, -n, -ful, -ness, -self

    Prefixes: un-

    Contractions: -'m, -'ve, -'d, -'re

    Dropped silent *e* (hoped)

    Double consonant (sitting)

    Silent *b* and *k*

    Short and long vowel sounds including *y*

    Vowel combinations: oo ow ar or er

COMPREHENSION:
- Reads for meaning.
- Infers words in cloze-type activities where the language is familiar.
- Self-corrects more often.
- Uses the text and illustrations to sample, predict, and confirm. Gives less importance to illustrations as more reliance is placed on text itself.
- Draws conclusions.
- Predicts outcomes.
- Finds proof.
- Identifies main idea.
- Follows plot sequence.
- Compares/contrasts books.
- Follows printed directions.
- Infers the motive, traits or feelings of characters.

- Dramatizes, illustrates, and retells stories which have been read.
- Locates information:
    Table of contents
    Page numbers
    Titles
    Specific details
- Library skills are to be taught within an integrated unit.

ORAL READING:
- Begins to read in chunks of language and with more expression.
- Self-corrects.
- Reads distinctly.

SILENT READING:
- Reads continuously for 20 minutes per day.
- Begins to feel comfortable reading silently. Subvocalization or lip movement is acceptable.

WRITING

FLUENCY:
- Has confidence as a writer.
- Writes an average of 100 words during a writing session. Fluctuation from day to day is to be expected.

COMPOSITION:
- Writes daily for 45 minutes. Drawing and sharing are part of this activity.
- Produces pieces of 5 or more related sentences. Time and sequence are indicated in many of the writings. There is a flow from beginning to end although all parts may not be fully developed.
- Participates in teacher and/or peer conferences, revises one or more words, phrases or sentences to expand, change or clarify. This process will require more than one writing session.
- Edits for those specifics listed under mechanics and spelling and for those items on the student's personal editing list.

MECHANICS:
- Consolidates previous levels.
- Capitalizes:
    First and last names
    First word in opening sentence
    Names of months and days

HANDWRITING:
Demonstration and practice for individual students who need it.
Cursive writing will be introduced in the third term. 50 minutes each week devoted to letter formation — demonstration and/or practice.

SPELLING:
Teachers will encourage fluent writers to correctly spell those words from previous formal spelling lessons. However, teachers need to be sensitive to reluctant writers. Students who have mastered the words at their grade level may go on to the words of the next grade level. (Teachers may also need to provide other alternatives to excellent spellers.)
- Represents all consonant sounds in writing with correct letter including soft *c* and *g*.
- Spells correctly the first 200 words on the High Frequency Word List when editing writing.
- Shows understanding of the following generalizations when editing:
    Use of two vowels in a word to represent a long vowel sound. The two vowels may not be

correct, but indicate a beginning awareness of spelling patterns. For example, *rain* might be spelled *rane* or *rayn*.

The letter *q* is always followed by *u* in common English words.   queen   quiet

No English words end in *v*.   love   glove

When students learn spelling generalizations, they should probably learn them inductively with the help of the teacher. A generalization taught by rote usually is of little value to students as they will seldom apply it. Generalizations cannot be considered a central approach to spelling, but if they are approached reasonably and are derived inductively, they are of advantage to many learners. Not all students need to learn these generalizations, but teachers do. A clear understanding of the generalization will make it possible to diagnose a student's spelling needs. (Blake, 1970)

SPEAKING

- Expresses needs.
- Expresses self fluently.
- Asks questions or make statements at appropriate times.
- Responds appropriately to questions.
- Maintains the subject line in conversation.
- Shares experiences in a group.
- Uses complete sentences when appropriate.
- Retells a story including sequence, major characters, and important details.
- Extends vocabulary toward finer conceptualizations. For example, refines *animal* to *squirrel*, *tree* to *pine* or *boat* to *canoe*.
- Participates in drama, discussion, and role-playing associated with books.

THIRD GRADE SKILLS

READING

GENERAL CHARACTERISTICS:
- Increases in confidence and competence.
- Comfortable with print.
- Attends minimally to print detail.

VOCABULARY:
- Predicts vocabulary to fill a space left in speech or writing, provided contextual clues are strong and the language is familiar.
- Derives new meanings from using simple forms of the following clues:
    Syntactic
    Semantic
    Contextual
    Picture
- Identifies a word that means the same as a given word.
- Identifies a word that means the opposite of a given word.

PHONETIC ANALYSIS:

Teach *within the context* of reading and writing. Generally, phonics workbooks are not an appropriate context. However, to meet the needs of individual students, a variety of adaptations may be used as necessary.
- Cross-checks one source of cues (semantic, syntactic or phonetic) with another set of cues.

- Takes risks and makes approximations.
- Reads words *in context* with the following symbol/sound associations:
    - Suffixes: -tion -able -ish -less -ment -ty -able   *f* changed to *v* before *es*
    - Prefixes: dis- com- pre- mis- con- pro- re-
    - Contractions:
    - Abbreviations: Dr.
    - Vowel combinations: ar, er, ir, or, ur, are, air, ear, oar, au, ou, aw, ew, ow, al, el, ul, oo, oi, oy
    - Symbol/sound associations for: kn, wr, gn
- Knows that a syllable has only one vowel sound and distinguishes between vowel – letters and vowel – sounds.

COMPREHENSION:
- Reads for meaning.
- Uses background experiences.
- Infers words in cloze-type activities where the language and story are familiar.
- Maintains meaning through longer and more complex sentence structures and various kinds of prose and poetry.
- Draws logical conclusions.
- Predicts outcomes.
- Connects text to personal experiences.
- Finds proof.
- Identifies main idea.
- Follows plot sequence.
- Compares/contrasts books and authors.
- Follows printed directions.
- Dramatizes, illustrates, and retells stories which have been read.
- Interacts with content.
- Infers the motives, traits or feelings of characters.
- Reads:
    - For pleasure.
    - To obtain an answer to a question.
    - To obtain a general idea of content.

ORAL READING:
- Reads for a purpose.
- Reads fairly fast, but may have self-corrections and reruns.
- Puts expression into reading.

SILENT READING:
- Has automatic recognition of many words.
- Reads continuously for 20 minutes per day.
- Reads at or below the rate of speech.
- Comprehends material read.

WRITING

FLUENCY:
- Has confidence as a writer.
- Writes an average of 115 words during a writing session. Fluctuation from day to day is to be expected.

Minimum output will be an average of one piece each week for a total of 36 pieces. Pieces might include reading journal entries, learning logs, poems, personal narratives, stories, letters.

COMPOSITION:
- Writes daily for 45 minutes. This may happen during the language block and/or during content area studies.

- Produces pieces of more than five sentences. The writing has a beginning, middle, and end. The story parts may be loosely connected and may not have clear transitions. The writer will include at least three details which contribute to descriptions and/or the communication of thoughts and feelings.
- Participates in teacher and/or peer conferences, revises at least one part of the writing. This process will require more than one writing session.
- Edits for those specifics listed under mechanics and spelling and for those items on the student's personal editing list.
- Brings seven pieces of writing to final copy. These may be generated in any content area. Bringing a piece of writing to final copy contains the following steps:
  1. Student revises first drafts in an attempt to achieve clarity, meaning, and a well-crafted piece of writing. This may be done alone or with others.
  2. Student edits last drafts for those items listed under spelling and mechanics in the previous grade levels and for those spelling words and mechanical elements learned in the present grade level. Students with individualized editing check lists will edit for those specific terms.
  3. The teacher edits the student-edited draft either alone or with the student.
  4. The student produces a final draft which is neat and legible. Single line cross-outs, carets and the use of correction fluid are acceptable in this final copy. The student works for an error-free copy, but in the copying process new errors may emerge. The teacher uses his/her judgment as to whether or not it is necessary for that student to redo the final copy.
- Students will compose, edit, and bring to final copy:
  A personal narrative.
  A thank you letter for a real purpose.

MECHANICS:
- Consolidate previous levels.
- Capitalize:
  (Initial in a name) Names
  First word in a sentence
- Punctuate:
  Period at end of sentence
  Question mark
  Exclamation point
  Periods after initials
  Apostrophes to indicate contractions on the first 500 words on the High Frequency Word List
- Use Comma:
  In dates
  Between city and state
  Between items in a series

HANDWRITING:
50 minutes each week devoted to demonstration and/or practice of formation of cursive letters. There will be a gradual implementation of cursive writing to meet the expectation that most of the student's writing will be in cursive with the exception of spelling tests and rough drafts. Beginning in the third term most of a student's writing will be in cursive. Teachers recognize that there will be a temporary loss of quality and quantity of writing during this transition period.

SPELLING:
Teachers will encourage fluent writers to correctly spell those words from previous formal spelling lessons. However, teachers need to be sensitive to reluctant writers. Students who have mastered the words at their grade level may go on to the words at the next grade level. (Teachers may also need to provide other alternatives to excellent spellers.)

Students spell correctly the first 500 words on the High Frequency Word List when editing their writing. (See "spelling generalizations" for second grade.)

"Learning to read and to write ought to be one of the most joyful and successful of human undertakings."

"Children learn to listen and to speak in an unbreakable unity of function." [1] Reading and writing are two sides of an integrated learning process. We approach these skills together — and term them literacy learning. Reading is a developmental process starting early in childhood and continuing throughout life.

The essence of reading is to gain meaning from text, and children learn to read by reading. Therefore we teach reading strategies through quality children's literature, rich in human meaning. The joy of reading a novel is superior to using a commercial series for language learning.

The essence of writing is to communicate ideas in written form. Techniques of grammar and spelling are taught after children experience the thrill of expressing themselves in writing. We believe phonics skills need to be taught in order for children to spell correctly and we incorporate these skills as the child is ready.

"Children taught in this way take pride in their work, take pride in themselves, and take joy in communicating from their own writing and reading." [2]

1. Don Holdaway, *The Foundations of Literacy* (Sydney, Australia: Ashton Scholastic, 1979).

2. Marlene J. McCracken and Robert A. McCracken, *Reading, Writing, and Language, A Practical Guide for Primary Teachers* (Winnipeg, Canada: Peguis Publishers Limited, 1979) Foreword, viii.

INTEGRATED LANGUAGE ARTS

Jay Buros

3 Cue Systems

Meaning
(semantic)

Structure
(grammar/syntax)

Visual
(shapes • sounds • graphophonic)

9:00–9:40	Miss Minor	ART Ms. Robinson	GYM Miss Taylor	MEETING Moe	GYM Miss Taylor
9:40–10:15		OPENING	SHARING		CALENDAR
10:15–10:30			SNACK		
10:30–10:45		NOISY OR SILENT	RECESS– IN AUTUMN READING REST OF YEAR		
10:45–11:45			WRITING		
11:45–12:10			LUNCH		
12:15–12:40			RECESS		＊ DUTY
12:40–2:05		INTEGRATED DAY WHOLE LANGUAGE wed ½ group library (3:00) others share writing.			
2:05–2:40			PLAY child's choice		
2:40–	EARLY BUS!	Share outcome of "Play".			Readiness Schedule J. Buros
3:00–	EVERYONE LEAVES	TO GO HOME.			
	MONDAY	TUESDAY	WEDNESDAY	THURSDAY	FRIDAY

Jay Buros

WHOLE LANGUAGE

1. WARM-UP
   - Songs
   - Poems
   - Nursery Rhymes
   - Jingles
   - Cheers
2. OLD STORY
   - Have a child choose the story
3. NEW STORY
   a. Big Book
   b. Good literature on opaque projector or overhead
   c. Student made Big Book
   d. Teacher published Big Book
   e. Song/Poem, chant on chart paper
4. OUTPUT/DEMONSTRATIONS — Student participation in relationship to new story
   1. Wall Chart
   2. Student made, published Big Book
   3. Student made small books (copy of large book)
   4. Murals
   5. Puppets
      - hand (made out of socks)
      - popsicle stick
   6. Flannel board characters and magnetic board characters
   7. Play of story
   8. Innovation of new story (Creating a new story together — probably after it has been read 8-10 times)
   9. Mobile of all the characters in the story
   10. Personal writing about the story — mine and the children's
   11. Field trips to make story come alive
   12. Invite people — to make story come alive (example: teddy bear collector to talk with children)
   13. Share book with a larger audience

Jay Buros

Whole Language Block

Monday	Tuesday	Wednesday	Thursday	Friday
	← Warm-up →			
	← Children choose "old" story →			
	← New story — song — poem — rhyme Teacher's choice from observation of children →			
	← Demonstration by teacher — Output by children →			

Jay Buros

ARE YOU READY FOR PUBLICATION?

Today's Date: _____

Your first and last name: _____

The title of your book: _____

Dedicated to: _____

Circle the size type you want. _____

Large Type   Small Type

Do you want pictures in your book?_____

    If you do, circle where you want the pictures to be.

        Left page (The writing will be on the right page.)

        Top half of the page.

        Bottom half of the page.

        Only one or two pictures...Where do you want them?

        All pictures will be drawn on special paper. Get it from your teacher.

What color cover do you want?_____

NOW: 1. Attach **About The Author** to your writing.
         2. Clip your writing and this form together.
         3. Put it on the **manuscript** desk.

CONGRATULATIONS!

Jay Buros

_____ **Observation**

_____ **Date**

I looked at: _____

A picture of what I saw:

Here are things I noticed: _____

_____

_____

① (The Dream) ———

Benchmarks (back plan — include span of time)

④

② If you achieved it how would you know?

A.

B.

C.

D.

E.

F.

⑤ Methods you will try. "Be flexible."

③ Where are you today? (in each area listed under ②)

A.

B.

C.

D.

E.

F.

Jay Buros

Why Whole Language

By Jay Buros

What do you want children to accomplish by the end of the year?

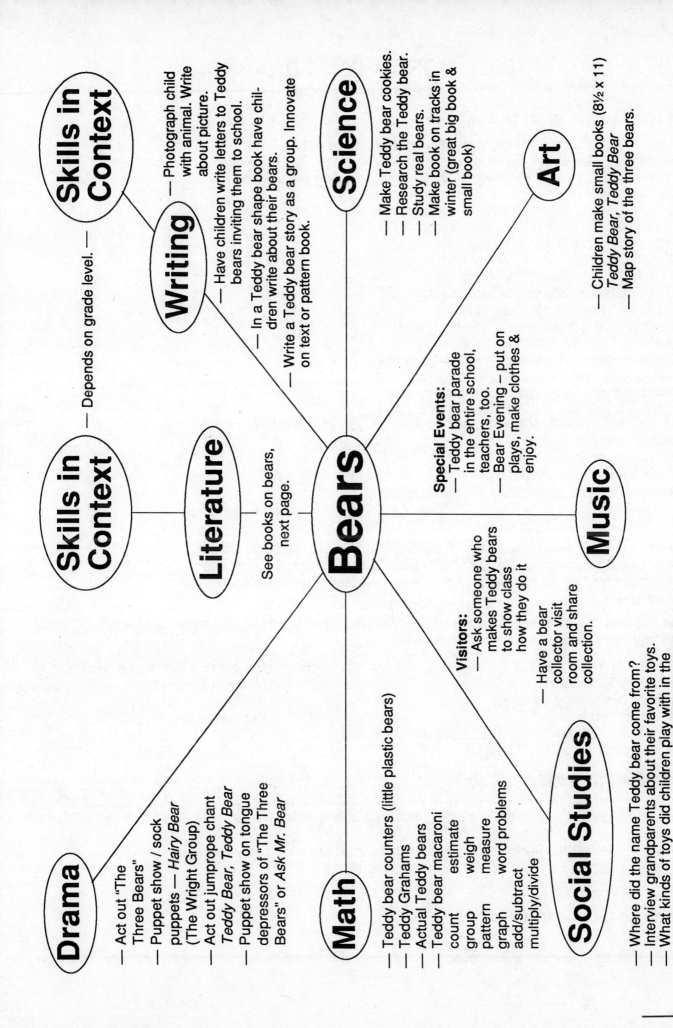

Skills in Context
— Depends on grade level.

Writing
— Photograph child with animal. Write about picture.
— Have children write letters to Teddy bears inviting them to school.
— In a Teddy bear shape book have children write about their bears.
— Write a Teddy bear story as a group. Innovate on text or pattern book.

Science
— Make Teddy bear cookies.
— Research the Teddy bear.
— Study real bears.
— Make book on tracks in winter (great big book & small book)

Art
— Children make small books (8½ x 11) *Teddy Bear, Teddy Bear*
— Map story of the three bears.

Skills in Context

Literature
See books on bears, next page.

Bears

Special Events:
— Teddy bear parade in the entire school, teachers, too.
— Bear Evening — put on plays, make clothes & enjoy.

Music

Visitors:
— Ask someone who makes Teddy bears to show class how they do it
— Have a bear collector visit room and share collection.

Drama
— Act out "The Three Bears"
— Puppet show / sock puppets — *Hairy Bear* (The Wright Group)
— Act out jumprope chant *Teddy Bear, Teddy Bear*
— Puppet show on tongue depressors of "The Three Bears" or *Ask Mr. Bear*

Math
— Teddy bear counters (little plastic bears)
— Teddy Grahams
— Actual Teddy bears
— Teddy bear macaroni

count   estimate
group   weigh
pattern   measure
graph   word problems
add/subtract
multiply/divide

Social Studies
— Where did the name Teddy bear come from?
— Interview grandparents about their favorite toys.
— What kinds of toys did children play with in the olden days?

Jay Buros

INTEGRATED LANGUAGE ARTS

BIBLIOGRAPHY . . . BEARS!

Compiled by Jay Buros

** A to Z Subject Access to Children's Picture Books. by Caroline Lima, Bowker Co.

* Asch, Frank. *Happy Birthday Moon, Mooncake*. Prentice Hall.
* Berenstein, Stan & Jan. *Bears in the Night, The Bike Ride*. Random House.
  Brustlein, Janice. *Little Bears Pancake Party*. Lothrop, Lee & Shepard.
  Carlstrom, Nancy. *Jesse Bear, What Will You Wear?*
  Cauley, Lorinda. *Bryan, Goldilocks and the Three Bears*. Putnam's Sons.
  Craft, Ruth. *The Winter Bear*. Atheneum.
* Dabcovich, Lydia. *Sleepy Bear*. Dutton.
  Douglas, Barbara. *Good As New*. Lothrop, Lee & Shepard Co., NY.
  DuBois, William. *Bear Party*. Viking.
* Duvoisin, Roger. *Snowy and Woody*. Knopf.
* Flack, Marjorie. *Ask Mr. Bear*. Puffin.
* Freeman, Don. *Beady Bear, Corduroy*. Puffin.
  Galdone, Paul. *The Three Bears*. Seabury.
  Ginsburg, Mirra. *Two Greedy Bears*. Macmillan.
* Kennedy, Jimmy. *The Teddy Bears' Picnic*.
* Kraus, Robert. *Three Friends*. Windmill Books.
  Kuratomi, Chizuko. *Mr. Bear Goes to Sea*. Judson.
* Martin, Bill. *Brown Bear, Brown Bear, What Do You See?* HRW Press.
* Waber, Bernard. *Ira Sleeps Over*.
* Wahl, Jan. *Humphrey's Bear*.
* Ward, Lynn. *The Biggest Bear*.
  Yolen, Jane. *The Three Bears Rhyme Book*. HBJ.

CHARTS

Teddy bear, teddy bear, turn around. Teddy bear, teddy bear, touch the ground.
Teddy bear, teddy bear, go upstairs. Teddy bear, teddy bear, say your prayers.
Teddy bear, teddy bear, turn out the light. Teddy bear, teddy bear, say goodnight,
"Goodnight!"

One little, two little, three little Teddy bears, four little, five little, six little Teddy bears, seven little, eight little, nine little Teddy bears, ten little Teddy bears and _____.

ME AND MY TEDDY BEAR
Me and my Teddy bear
Have no worries have no cares.
Me and my Teddy bear
Just _____ and _____ all day.
   (play)   (play)

Music: **Unbearable Bears** by Kevin Roth
Marlboro Records
845 Marlboro Spring Rd.
Kennet Square, PA 19348

BEARS ARE SLEEPING (Sung to "Frere Jacques" from *More Piggyback Songs*)
Bears are sleeping, bears are sleeping. In their dens, in their dens.
Soon it will be spring, soon it will be spring. Wake up bears, wake up bears!

TEDDY BEAR SONG (Sung to: Mary Had A Little Lamb from *More Piggyback Songs*)
(child's name) has a Teddy bear, Teddy bear, Teddy bear.
_____ has a Teddy bear. It's _(brown)_ and _(furry)_ all over.

I'M GOING ON A BEAR HUNT

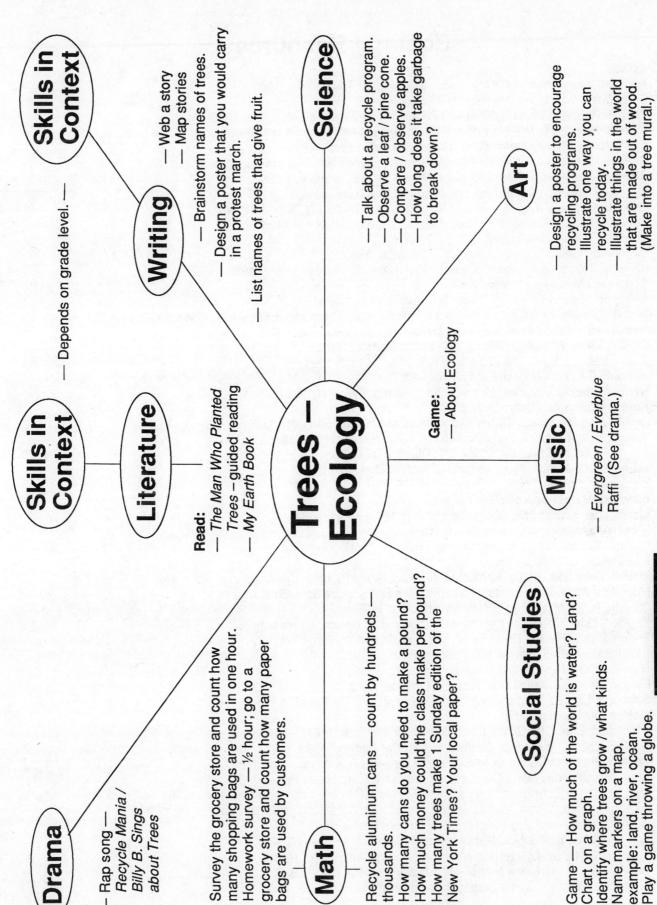

Trees – Ecology

Skills in Context — Depends on grade level. —

Writing
— Web a story
— Map stories
— Brainstorm names of trees.
— Design a poster that you would carry in a protest march.
— List names of trees that give fruit.

Science
— Talk about a recycle program.
— Observe a leaf / pine cone.
— Compare / observe apples.
— How long does it take garbage to break down?

Art
— Design a poster to encourage recycling programs.
— Illustrate one way you can recycle today.
— Illustrate things in the world that are made out of wood. (Make into a tree mural.)

Skills in Context

Literature

Read:
— *The Man Who Planted Trees* — guided reading
— *My Earth Book*

Game:
— About Ecology

Music
— *Evergreen / Everblue*
Raffi (See drama.)

Drama
— Rap song —
*Recycle Mania /
Billy B. Sings
about Trees*
— Survey the grocery store and count how many shopping bags are used in one hour.
— Homework survey — ½ hour; go to a grocery store and count how many paper bags are used by customers.

Math
— Recycle aluminum cans — count by hundreds — thousands.
— How many cans do you need to make a pound?
— How much money could the class make per pound?
— How many trees make 1 Sunday edition of the New York Times? Your local paper?

Social Studies
— Game — How much of the world is water? Land?
— Chart on a graph.
— Identify where trees grow / what kinds.
— Name markers on a map, example: land, river, ocean.
— Play a game throwing a globe.

Jay Buros

INTEGRATED
LANGUAGE ARTS

Ecology Resources

Books:

* Applehof, Mary. *Worms Eat My Garbage*. Michigan Flower Press, 1982.
* Bare, Edith. *This Is the Way We Go To School*.
  Bonnet, Robert L. *Earth Science — 49 Science Fair Projects*. Tab Books, 1990.
* Brandenberg, Aliki. *The Story of Johnny Appleseed*. NY: Simon and Schuster.
  Byars, Betsy. *The Summer of the Swans*. NY: Puffin Press, 1970.
  Caduto, Michael and Bruchac, Joseph. *Keepers of the Earth*. Fulcrum Inc., 1988.
* Cherry, Lynn. *A River Ran Wild*. NY: Harcourt, Brace Jovanovich, 1992.
  _____. *The Great Kapok Tree*. NY: Harcourt, Brace Jovanovich, 1990.
* Child, Lydia Maria. *Over the River and Through the Wood*. NY: Scholastic, 1974.
* Cook, Janet. *How Things Are Made*. Belgium: Usborne Pub. Ltd., 1989.
* Cooney, Barbara. *Island Boy*.
* Dabcovich, Linda. *Busy Beavers*. NY: Scholastic, 1988.
* dePaola, Tomie. *The Legend of Bluebonnet*. NY: G.P. Putnam's Sons, 1983.
* Donahue, Mike. *The Grandpa Tree*.
  Elkington, Hailes Hill. *Going Green*. NY: Puffin Books, 1990.
  Fiarotta, Phyllis. *Ships, Snails, Walnut Whales: Nature Crafts for Children*. NY: Workman Pub. Co.
* Giono, Jean. *The Man Who Planted Trees*. Chelsea Green Pub., 1985.
* Glaser, Linda. *Wonderful Worms*. The Millbrook Press, 1992.
  Goble, Paul. *I Sing for the Animals*. NY: Bradbury Press, 1991.
* Hallinan, P.K. *I'm Thankful Each Day!* Ideals Pub.
  Herman, Marina. *Teaching Kids to Love the Earth*. Pfeifer-Hamilton, 1991.
* Holling, Holling, C. *Paddle to the Sea*.
  Javna, John. *50 Simple Things Kids Can Do to Save the Earth*. NY: Universal Press.
* Jeffers, Susan. *Stopping by Woods on a Snowy Evening*. NY: Dutton, 1978.
* _____. *Brother Eagle, Sister Sky*. NY: Dial Books, 1991.
  Jeunesse, Gallimard. *The Earth and Sky*. NY: Scholastic, 1992.
* Kindersley, Dorling. *My First Green Book*. NY: Alfred Knopf, 1991.
  Lankford, Marg. *Hopscotch Around the World*.
* Lionni, Leo. *Tico and the Golden Wings*. NY: Alfred Knopf, 1964.
* Lobel, Arnold. *Ming Lo Moves the Mountain*.
* Locker, Thomas. *The Land of the Gray Wolf*. NY: Dial Books, 1991.
* MacDonald, G. *Little Island*.
* Maeno, Itoko. *Mother Nature Nursery Rhymes*, Santa Barbara, CA: Advocacy Press, 1990.
* McLerran, Alice. *The Mountain that Loved the Bird*. Picture Book Studio, 1985.
* Orbach, Ruth. *Apple Pigs*. NY: Philomel Books, 1976.
  Paulsen, Gary. *The Night the White Deer Died*. NY: Delacorte Press, 1978.
* Pearce, Fred. *The Big Green Book*. NY: Grosset and Dunlap, 1991.
  Pinnington, Andrea. *Nature*. NY: Random House, 1991.
* Ray, Deborah Kogan. *Little Tree*. NY: Crown Pub., 1987.
* Ryland, Cynthia. *When I Was Young in the Mountains*.
  Schwartz, Linda. *My Earth Book*. Santa Barbara, CA: The Learning Works, 1991.
* Siebert, Diane. *Hartland*.
* Silverstein, Shel. *The Giving Tree*. NY: Harper and Row, 1964.
* Soutter, Perroti, Andrienne. *Earthworm*. Creative Editions, 1993.
* Speare, Elizabeth George. *The Sign of the Beaver*. NY: Dell Pub. Co., 1983.
* Starr, Susan Bryer. *I Was Good to the Earth Today*. Starhouse Pub., 1992.
  Swartz, Linda. *Earth Book for Kids*. Santa Barbara, CA: The Learning Works Inc., 1990.
* Taylor, Barbara. *Green Thumbs Up!* (Experiments and Activities) NY: Random House, 1954.
* _____. *Hear! Hear!* (Experiments) NY: Random House, 1990.
* _____. *Over the Rainbow*. (Experiments) NY: Random House, 1992.
* _____. *Up, Up and Away!* (Experiments) NY: Random House, 1991.
* Udry, Janice May. *A Tree Is Nice*. NY: Harper and Row Pub., 1986.
* Van Allsburg, Chris. *Just a Dream*. Boston: Houghton Mifflin Co., 1990.

Jay Buros

Walker, Colin. *The Great Garbage Mountain.*

_____. *Oceans of Fish.*

_____. *We Need Energy.*

_____. *Our Storehouse Earth.*

_____. *Our Changing Atmosphere.*

_____. *Forests Forever.*

_____. *Food Farming.*

_____. *Ecology — Plants and Animals.*

_____. *The Environmental Teacher Guide*, Bothell, WA: The Wright Group, 1992.

White Deer of Autumn. *Ceremony in the Circle of Life.* Beyond Word Pub. Co., 1983.

* Wildsmith, Brian. *Squirrels.* Toronto: Oxford University Press, 1974.

* _____. *The Trunk.*

* Winter, Jeanette. *Follow the Drinking Gourd.*

Wolfman, Ira. *My World and Globe.* NY: Workman Pub., 1991.

Wood, Douglas. *Old Turtle.*

* Yolen, Jane. *Encounter.*

* _____. *Owl Moon.* NY: Philomel Books, 1987.

* Young, Ed. *Birches.* NY: Holt and Co., 1988.

GAME:

About Ecology
Earthwood, Inc.
Keyport, NJ 07735

MUSIC:

Recycle Mania / Billy B. Sings About Trees
P.O. Box 5423
Takoma Park, MD 19912
301-445-3845

PUZZLES, PROJECTS, FACTS AND FUN:

The Learning Works
P.O. Box 6187
Santa Barbara, CA 93160

Jay Buros

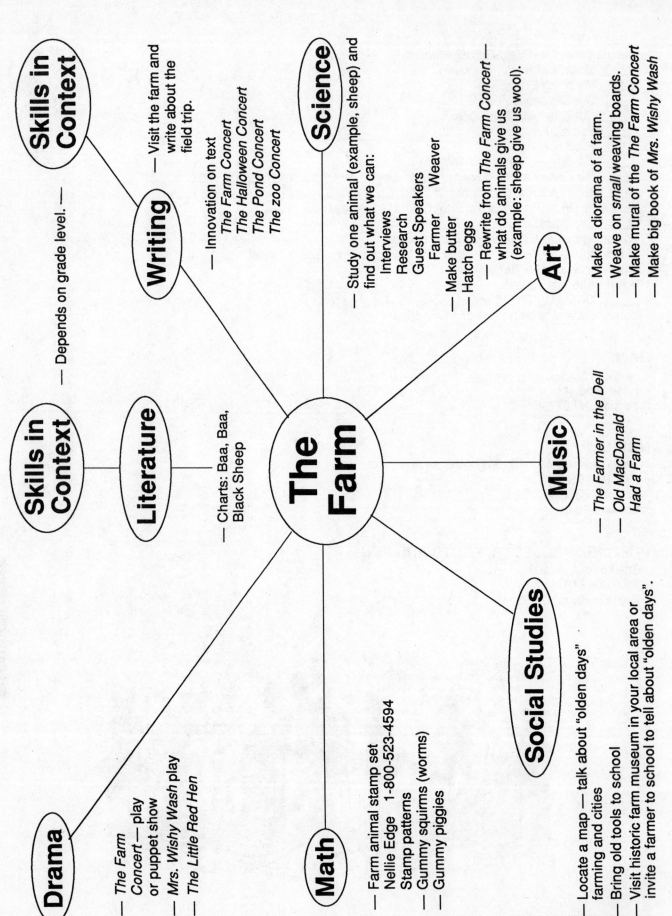

The Farm

Skills in Context

Writing
— Depends on grade level. —
— Visit the farm and write about the field trip.
— Innovation on text
  The Farm Concert
  The Halloween Concert
  The Pond Concert
  The zoo Concert

Skills in Context

Literature
— Charts: Baa, Baa, Black Sheep

Drama
— *The Farm Concert* — play or puppet show
— *Mrs. Wishy Wash* play
— *The Little Red Hen*

Math
— Farm animal stamp set
  Nellie Edge 1-800-523-4594
— Stamp patterns
— Gummy squirms (worms)
— Gummy piggies

Social Studies
— Locate a map — talk about "olden days" farming and cities
— Bring old tools to school
— Visit historic farm museum in your local area or invite a farmer to school to tell about "olden days".

Music
— *The Farmer in the Dell*
— *Old MacDonald Had a Farm*

Art
— Make a diorama of a farm.
— Weave on *small* weaving boards.
— Make mural of the *The Farm Concert*
— Make big book of *Mrs. Wishy Wash*

Science
— Study one animal (example, sheep) and find out what we can:
  Interviews
  Research
  Guest Speakers
    Farmer   Weaver
— Make butter
— Hatch eggs
— Rewrite from *The Farm Concert* — what do animals give us (example: sheep give us wool).

Jay Buros

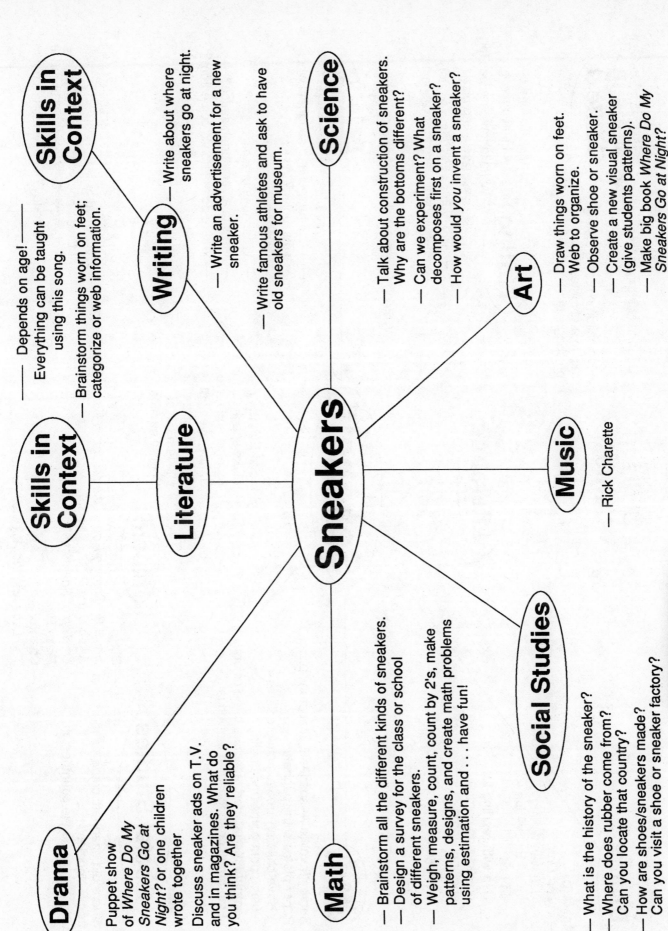

Sneakers

Skills in Context
— Depends on age!
Everything can be taught using this song.
— Brainstorm things worn on feet; categorize or web information.

Writing
— Write about where sneakers go at night.
— Write an advertisement for a new sneaker.
— Write famous athletes and ask to have old sneakers for museum.

Science
— Talk about construction of sneakers. Why are the bottoms different?
— Can we experiment? What decomposes first on a sneaker?
— How would *you* invent a sneaker?

Skills in Context

Literature

Drama
— Puppet show of *Where Do My Sneakers Go at Night?* or one children wrote together
— Discuss sneaker ads on T.V. and in magazines. What do you think? Are they reliable?

Math
— Brainstorm all the different kinds of sneakers.
— Design a survey for the class or school of different sneakers.
— Weigh, measure, count, count by 2's, make patterns, designs, and create math problems using estimation and . . . have fun!

Social Studies
— What is the history of the sneaker?
— Where does rubber come from? Can you locate that country?
— How are shoes/sneakers made?
— Can you visit a shoe or sneaker factory?

Art
— Draw things worn on feet. Web to organize.
— Observe shoe or sneaker.
— Create a new visual sneaker (give students patterns).
— Make big book *Where Do My Sneakers Go at Night?*

Music
— Rick Charette

Jay Buros

INTEGRATED LANGUAGE ARTS

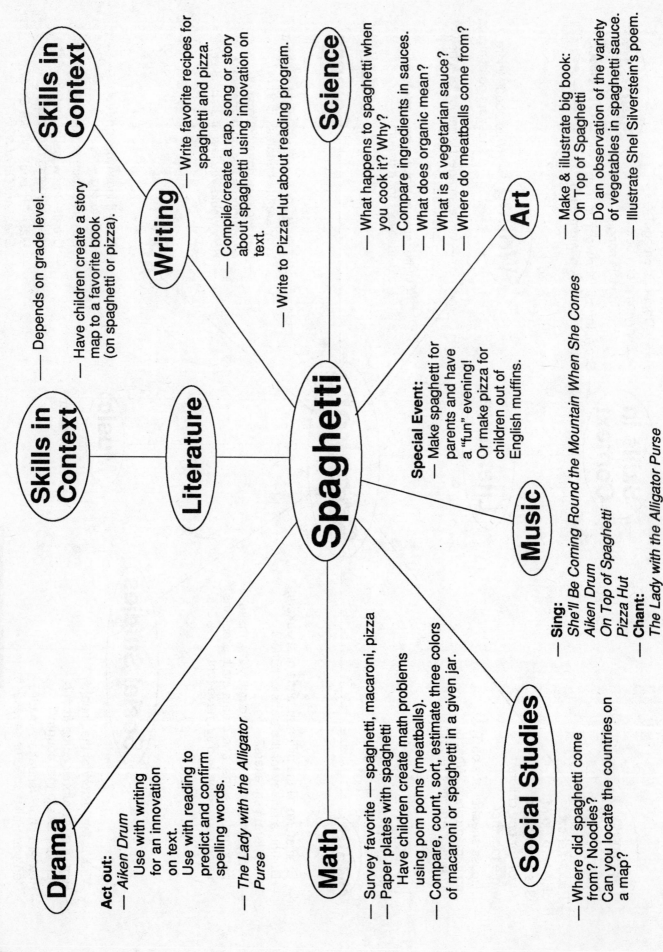

Skills in Context

Writing

— Depends on grade level.
— Have children create a story map to a favorite book (on spaghetti or pizza).
— Write favorite recipes for spaghetti and pizza.
— Compile/create a rap, song or story about spaghetti using innovation on text.
— Write to Pizza Hut about reading program.

Science

— What happens to spaghetti when you cook it? Why?
— Compare ingredients in sauces.
— What does organic mean?
— What is a vegetarian sauce?
— Where do meatballs come from?

Art

— Make & illustrate big book: On Top of Spaghetti
— Do an observation of the variety of vegetables in spaghetti sauce.
— Illustrate Shel Silverstein's poem.

Skills in Context

Literature

Spaghetti

Special Event:
— Make spaghetti for parents and have a "fun" evening! Or make pizza for children out of English muffins.

Music

Sing:
She'll Be Coming Round the Mountain When She Comes
Aiken Drum
On Top of Spaghetti
Pizza Hut
Chant:
The Lady with the Alligator Purse

Drama

Act out:
— *Aiken Drum*
  Use with writing for an innovation on text.
  Use with reading to predict and confirm spelling words.
— *The Lady with the Alligator Purse*

Math

— Survey favorite — spaghetti, macaroni, pizza
  Paper plates with spaghetti
— Have children create math problems using pom poms (meatballs).
— Compare, count, sort, estimate three colors of macaroni or spaghetti in a given jar.

Social Studies

— Where did spaghetti come from? Noodles? Can you locate the countries on a map?

FAVORITE SONGS, POEMS, AND RHYMES

HEY THERE NEIGHBOR!
Hey there, neighbor!
What do you say?
It's going to be a wonderful day!
Clap your hands and boogie on down.
Give 'em a bump and pass it around!
(or sit on down)

HI! MY NAME IS JOE!
Hi! My name is Joe and I work in the button
   (doughnut) factory.
I have a wife, a dog, and a family!
One day my boss came to me and said,
"Hey Joe, are you busy?"
I said, "No."
He said, "Well, then work with your right hand."
   • Repeat each time adding one more body part: left
      hand, right foot, left foot, head
   Last line, last time:
I said, "YES!!!"

TONY CHESTNUT
Toe knee chestnut
Nose eye love you.
Toe knee nose.
Toe knee nose.
Toe knee chestnut nose I love you . . .
That's what toe knee nose.

HI DEE HAY! HI DEE HO!
Leader: *Hi dee hay! Hi dee ho!*
Group: **Hi dee hay! Hi dee ho!**
Leader: *Igglee wigglee wogglee wo!*
Group: **Igglee wigglee wogglee wo!**
Leader: *Raise your voices to the sky.*
Group: **Raise your voices to the sky.**
Leader: *Mrs. _____ 's class is walking by*
Group: **Mrs. _____'s class is walking by.**
Leader: *Count off!*
Group: **1, 2, 3, 4, 5**
Leader: *Break it on down now!*
Group: **6, 7, 8, 9, 10 . . .**
Leader: *Let's do it all once again!*

RISE RUBY RISE!
Down in the valley two by two.
Down in the valley two by two.
Down in the valley two by two.
Rise Ruby Rise!

2nd verse:
We can do it your way two by two.
We can do it your way two by two.
We can do it your way two by two.
Rise Ruby Rise!

3rd verse:
We can do it my way two by two.
We can do it my way two by two.
We can do it my way two by two.
Rise Ruby Rise!

COPY CAT
Let's play copy cat just for fun
Let's copy _____, she's the one.
Whatever she does we'll do the same,
'cause that's how you play the Copy Cat Game.

OH! MY AUNT CAME BACK
Oh! my aunt came back,
Oh! my aunt came back
from _____ .

And she brought me back
And she brought me back

_____ .

Old Japan	old hand fan
Old Algiers	a pair of shears
Belgium too	some gum to chew
London Fair	a rocking chair
Holland too	some wooden shoes
Timbuktu	a nut like you

"Whatever you can do or dream
you can begin it. Boldness has
genius, power, and magic in it."
Goethe

Jay Buros / Kathryn L. Cloonan

SING ME A STORY — READ ME A SONG

INTEGRATING MUSIC INTO THE WHOLE LANGUAGE CLASSROOM
By Kathryn L. Cloonan

PURPOSE

1. Instill a love for reading and music.
2. Make use of simple, delightful materials that have rhythm, rhyme, repetition.
3. To give children early successes in reading.
4. Give children an opportunity to make the connection between print and what they say and sing.
5. Build sight vocabulary by frequently seeing words in meaningful, predictable context.
6. Enrich decoding/reading skills through meaningful print.

STEPS

SHARE IT — Sing Lots of Songs Often
PRINT IT — Print a Favorite on Chart Paper
ILLUSTRATE IT — Make a Big Book, Make Mini Books
READ IT — Let the Children Read It

RESOURCES

Record and Tapes
Sing Me a Story, Read Me A Song, Kathryn Cloonan
Whole Language Holidays — Stories, Chants and Songs, Kathryn Cloonan
Peter, Paul and Mommy, Peter, Paul and Mary
Elephant Show Record, Sharon, Lois and Bram
Special Delivery, Fred Penner
The Cat Came Back, Fred Penner
Learning Basic Skills Through Music, Hap Palmer
We All Live Together, Volumes 1, 2, 3 & 4, Greg Scelse and Steve Millang
Doing the Dinosaur Rock, Diane Butchelor
You'll Sing a Song and I'll Sing a Song, Ella Jenkins
Singable Songs for the Very Young, Raffi
More Singable Songs for the Very Young, Raffi

Resource Books
Sing Me a Story, Read Me a Song, Book I, Kathryn Cloonan. Rhythm & Reading Resources, 1991.
Sing Me a Story, Read Me a Song, Book II, Kathryn Cloonan, 1991.
Whole Language Holidays, Books I and II, Kathryn Cloonan. Rhythm & Reading Resources.

SONGS

WE HAVE A FRIEND
We have a friend and
her name is Amy
Amy is her name
Hello, Amy-Hello, Amy
Hello, Amy
We're so glad you're here.
Innovation:
    Change names of children

TWINKLE TWINKLE LITTLE STAR
Twinkle, twinkle little star
How I wonder what you are.
Up above the world so high.
Like a diamond in the sky.
Twinkle, twinkle little star
How I wonder what you are.

HICKORY, DICKORY DOCK
Hickory, Dickory Dock
The mouse ran up the clock
The clock struck one
The mouse ran down
Hickory, Dickory Dock
Innovations:
    The clock struck 2, 3, 4, etc.

BAA, BAA, BLACK SHEEP
Baa, Baa Black Sheep
Have you any wool?
Yes sir, yes sir three bags full.

One for my master
One for the dame
One for the little boy
that lives down the lane.

Baa, Baa, Black Sheep
Have you any wool?
Yes sir, yes sir three bags full.
Innovation:
    Color Words
    Baa, Baa, Purple sheep, etc.

BINGO
There was a farmer
Had a dog and Bingo was his name-o.
B I N G O
B I N G O
B I N G O
And Bingo was his name-o.

ON A SPIDER'S WEB
One elephant went out to play
On a spider's web one day.
He had such enormous fun
He asked another elephant to come.

Two elephants went out to play
On a spider's web one day.
They had such enormous fun
They asked another elephant to come.

Three elephants, four elephants,
Five elephants, six elephants,
Seven elephants, eight elephants,
Nine elephants................

Ten elephants went out to play
They had such enormous fun
They asked everyone to come.
Innovations: Change with theme or
    holidays — black cat, Christmas elf,
    leprechaun, dinosaur, Panda bear,
    etc.

FIVE SPECKLED FROGS
Five green and speckled frogs
Sat on a speckled log
Eating the most delicious bugs.
    YUM!   YUM!
One jumped into the pool
where it was nice and cool
Then there were four green speckled
    frogs.
Four...etc., Three...etc.,
Two...etc., One...etc.
Then there were NO green speckled
    frogs.

THE WHEELS ON THE BUS

The wheels on the bus go
    round and round
    round and round
    round and round
The wheels on the bus go
    round and round
All through the town.
Innovations:
1. doors...open and shut
2. children...up and down
3. wipers...swish, swish, swish
4. babies...wah, wah, wah
5. snakes...Sss, Sss, Sss
6. bears...growl, growl, growl, etc.

I KNOW AN OLD LADY

I know an old lady who swallowed a fly
I don't know why she swallowed a fly...
perhaps she'll die.

I know an old lady who swallowed a
    spider
(that wiggled and jiggled and tickled
    inside her)
She swallowed the spider to catch the fly
But I don't know why she swallowed a
    fly
perhaps she'll die.

I know an old lady who swallowed a
    bird
She swallowed the bird to catch the
    spider
(that wiggled and jiggled and tickled
    inside her)
She swallowed the spider to catch the fly
But I don't know why she swallowed a
    fly
perhaps she'll die.

I know an old lady who swallowed a cat
She swallowed the cat to catch the bird
She swallowed the bird to catch the
    spider
(that wiggled and jiggled and tickled
    inside her)
She swallowed the spider to catch the fly
But I don't know why she swallowed
    the fly
perhaps she'll die.

I know an old lady who swallowed a dog
She swallowed the dog to catch the cat
She swallowed the cat to catch the bird
She swallowed the bird to catch the
    spider
(that wiggled and jiggled and tickled
    inside her)
She swallowed the spider to catch the fly
But I don't know why she swallowed
    the fly
perhaps she'll die.

I know an old lady who swallowed a goat
She swallowed the goat to catch the dog
She swallowed the dog to catch the cat
She swallowed the cat to catch the bird

She swallowed the bird to catch the
    spider
(that wiggled and jiggled and tickled
    inside her)
She swallowed the spider to catch the fly
But I don't know why she swallowed
    the fly
perhaps she'll die.

I know an old lady who swallowed a
    horse
She's Full, of course!
Innovations: Change the animals she
    swallowed

TEN IN THE BED

There were ten in the bed
And the little one said,
"Roll over, Roll over"
So they all rolled over and one fell out
      And they gave a little scream
      And they gave a little shout

Please remember to tie a knot in your
    pajamas
Single beds were only made for
1,2,3,4,5,6,7,8,
Nine in the bed etc.
Eight etc., Seven etc.
Six-five-four-three-two...etc.
One in the bed and the little one said,
"I've got the whole mattress to myself"
(repeat last line three more times)
    GOOD-NIGHT!

LITTLE COTTAGE IN THE WOODS

"Little cottage in the woods" (Touch
fingertips of both hands together to
form a triangle shape for the house.)
"Little man by the window stood."
(Form "glasses" shapes with forefinger
and thumb of each hand making a
circle — put hands up to eyes in that
shape, against face.) "Saw a rabbit
hopping by" (Make rabbit "ears" by two
fingers held up on one hand and "hop"
them about.) "Frightened as could be."
(Arms held crossed across chest,
"shake" in mock fear.) "Help me, help
me, help me, he said." (Raise arms
overhead and down several times.)
"Before the hunter shoots me dead:
(Form "guns" with forefingers and
"shoot.") "Come, little rabbit, come
inside" (Beckon with hand.) "And
happy we will be." (Stroke the back of
one hand with the other as though
tenderly petting a rabbit.)

LITTLE SKUNK

Oh! I stuck my head in a little skunk's
hole — and the little skunk said, "God
bless your soul." Take it out! Take it
out! Take it out! Remove it! But I didn't
take it out and the little skunk said, "If
you don't take it out you'll wish you

had." Take it out! Take it out! Take it
out! Psssss — I removed it.

MICHAEL FINNAGIN

There once was a man named Michael
    Finnagin
He had whiskers on his chin-a-gain
The wind came along and blew them in-
    again
Poor old Michael Finnagin...begin-
    again.

There once was a man named Michael
    Finnagin
He went fishing with a pin-again
Caught a whale that pulled him in-
    again
Poor old Michael Finnagin...begin-
    again.

There once was a man named Michael
    Finnagin
He was fat and then grew thin-again
Ate so much he had to begin again
Poor old Michael Finnagin...begin-
    again.

TINY TIM

I had a little turtle,
His name was Tiny Tim
I put him in the bathtub
To see if he could swim.
He drank up all the water.
He ate up all the soap.
And now he's home sick in bed
With a bubble in his throat.

THE ANTS GO MARCHING

The ants go marching one by one
Hurrah! Hurrah!
The ants go marching one by one
Hurrah! Hurrah!
The ants go marching one by one
the little one stops to suck his thumb
And they all go marching down —
into the ground — to get out — of the
    rain —
BOOM, BOOM, BOOM, BOOM,
BOOM, BOOM, BOOM, BOOM
two by two.....tie his shoe
three by three.....climb a tree
four by four.....shut the door
five by five.....jump and dive
six by six.....pick up sticks
seven by seven.....wave to heaven
eight by eight.....climb the gate
nine by nine.....look behind
ten by ten.....pat a hen

GOOD-BYE

We have a friend and her name is Amy.
Amy is her name. Good-bye, Amy,
    good-bye Amy
Good-bye, Amy, we'll see you
    tomorrow.
Innovation: Change names of children.

Kathryn L. Cloonan

HOLIDAY SONGS

TRICK OR TREAT
They'll be Trick or Treating here on
   Halloween, **Trick or Treat!**
They'll be Trick or Treating here on
   Halloween, **Trick or Treat!**
They'll be Trick or Treating here,
They'll be Trick or Treating here,
They'll be Trick or Treating here on
   Halloween, **Trick or Treat!**

2. They'll be knocking at our doors on
   Halloween, **Knock! Knock!**
3. Ghosts will all go "Boo!" on Halloween, **Booooooooo!**
4. Black cats all meow on Halloween,
   Meeeeeeeeeeow!
5. We will all have fun on Halloween,
   Hurray!

ONCE I HAD A PUMPKIN
Once I had a pumpkin, a pumpkin, a
   pumpkin
Once I had a pumpkin with no face at all.
With no eyes and no nose and no mouth
   and no teeth.
Once I had a pumpkin with no face at all.

Then I made a Jack-o-Lantern, Jack-o-
   Lantern, Jack-o-Lantern.
Then I made a Jack-o-Lantern . . . with
   a big funny face.
With big eyes and a big nose and a big
   mouth and big teeth.
Then I made a Jack-o-Lantern . . . with
   a big funny face.

DOG HAIR STEW
© 1991 Kathryn L. Cloonan

Ten black cats were left by themselves
on Halloween night with nothing to do.
So they decided to make their own
Dog Hair Stew.

First they got a very large pot
And filled it with water that was
   extremely hot.
Their goal was to make a horrible brew
More horrible even, than last year's stew.

Cat #1 flicked his tail in a wave
And said, "Here's some slime from a
   nearby cave."
"And here's some juice from a
   skunkweed plant."
Said Cat #2 as he joined in the chant.

Cat #3 said, "Heh, Heh, wait till you see
   what I brought.
The eyes of two dead fish I finally got!"
"Let me add some bat liver oil,"
   meowed Cat #4,
A skinny cat named "Skin and Bones."

Cat #5 said, "Here's a couple of frogs
   and a snake.
This is my very favorite stew to make."
One by one the cats came by
Adding secret ingredients with a meow
   and a cry.

The oldest cat carefully stirred it round
   and round
While the fire crackled with an ominous
   sound.
The 10th cat hissed with eyes aglow,
"Here's the hair of a dog so stir it in
   slow."

Now the cats they pranced and danced
   around their Dog Hair Stew
Then drank every drop of their mysterious brew.
Then all at once the cats gave a very
   loud wail
And their hair stood up straight from
   their head to their tail.

"Happy spooky Halloween!", they said
   with a wink,
"Dog Hair Stew is our favorite drink!"
And for the rest of the year
They had nothing to fear . . .

For each time a dog was seen,
Their hair stood up straight and they
   looked so mean
Not a dog would dare
give them a scare.

And the cats would wink an eye and
   say,
A little Dog Hair Stew on Halloween
   day
Keeps even the meanest dogs away.

SCAT THE CAT
I'm Scat the Cat
I'm sassy and fat
And I can change my colors
Just like that! (Snap)

THIS IS THE CANDLE
This is the candle
This is the candle
That glowed in the jack-o-lantern.

This is the mouse
That lit the candle
That glowed in the jack-o-lantern.

This is the cat
That chased the mouse
That lit the candle
That glowed in the jack-o-lantern.

This is the ghost
That said "BOO!" to the cat
That chased the mouse
That lit the candle
That glowed in the jack-o-lantern.

This is the moon
That shown on the ghost
That said "BOO!" to the cat
That chased the mouse
That lit the candle
That glowed in the jack-o-lantern.
That shouted **"Happy Halloween!"**

ONE LITTLE SKELETON
One little skeleton, hopping up and
   down
One little skeleton, hopping up and
   down
One little skeleton, hopping up and
   down
For this is Halloween!

2. Two little bats, flying through the air.
3. Three little pumpkins, walking in a
   row.
4. Four little goblins, skipping down
   the street.
5. Five little ghosties, popping in and out.

FIVE LITTLE PUMPKINS
Five little pumpkins sitting on a gate.
The first one said, "My, it's getting late!"
The second one said, "There are bats in
   the air".
The third one said, "I don't care!"
The fourth one said, "Let's run, let's run."
The fifth one said, "Halloween is fun!"
OOOOOOOOOOOOO went the wind.
Clap out went the lights.
And five little pumpkins rolled out of
   sight.

BRAVE LITTLE PILGRIM
The brave little Pilgrim went looking for
   a bear.
He looked in the woods and everywhere.
The brave little Pilgrim found a big bear.
He ran like a rabbit! Oh! what a scare!

FIVE FAT TURKEYS
Five fat turkeys are we.
We slept all night in a tree
When the cook came around
We couldn't be found

Let's fly to the tallest tree
There we'll be safe as safe can be.
From the cook and the oven you see
It surely pays on Thanksgiving days
To sleep in the tallest trees!!

WE WISH YOU A MERRY CHRISTMAS

We wish you a Merry Christmas
We wish you a Merry Christmas
We wish you a Merry Christmas
and a Happy New Year!

Let's all do a little jumping
Let's all do a little jumping
Let's all do a little jumping
And spread Christmas cheer.

Let's all do a little twirling
Let's all do a little twirling
Let's all do a little twirling
And spread Christmas cheer.

Let's all do a little clapping
Let's all do a little clapping
Let's all do a little clapping
And spread Christmas cheer.

We wish you a Merry Christmas
We wish you a Merry Christmas
We wish you a Merry Christmas
and a Happy New Year!

S.A.N.T.A.

There was a man who had a beard
   and Santa was his name-o.
S.A.N.T.A.
S.A.N.T.A.
S.A.N.T.A.
And Santa was his name-o!

There was a man who had a beard
   and Santa was his name-o.
S.A.N.T.**Ho!**
S.A.N.T.**Ho!**
S.A.N.T.**Ho!**
And Santa was his name-o!

(Leave off one more letter and
   replace it with a "Ho" until the
   final verse is "Ho, Ho, Ho, Ho,
   Ho.")

FIVE LITTLE REINDEER

Five little reindeer prancing up and
   down
Five little reindeer prancing up and
   down
Five little reindeer prancing up and
   down
For Christmas time is near.

2. Four little Santa elves trimming
   up a tree . . .
3. Three little jingle bells ring, ring,
   ringing . . .
4. Two little snowflakes twirling in
   the night . . .
5. One little sleigh speeding through
   the snow . . .

MY DREIDEL

I have a little dreidel.
I made it out of clay.
And when it's dry and ready
My "dreidel" I shall play.

chorus
Oh dreidel, dreidel, dreidel
Oh little top that spins
The children all are happy
When Hanukkah begins.

My dreidel's always playful
It loves to spin all day.
A happy game of dreidel
My friends and I shall play
(repeat chorus)

OH VALENTINE!
© 1991 Cloonan

Oh Valentine! Oh Valentine!
I hope that you'll be mine.
I took my time and wrote this
   rhyme
Especially for you.

Oh! Valentine! Oh! Valentine!
I hope that you'll be mine.
With crayons, paper, and some glue
I've made this card for you.

Oh Valentine! Oh Valentine!
I hope you'll be mine.
And on this very special day
There's just one thing to say . . .
"I love you!"
"Happy Valentines Day!"

HERE'S A LETTER
Here's a letter, here's a letter.
One for you.
One for you.
Guess what's in the letter.
Guess what's in the letter.
I love you!
I love you!
*(Verses two & three are done in a
   round)*

ONE LEPRECHAUN WENT OUT TO PLAY

One leprechaun went out to play
On a bright St. Patrick's day.
He had such enormous fun
He asked another leprechaun to
   come.

Two leprechauns went out to play
On a bright St. Patrick's day.
They had such enormous fun
They asked another leprechaun to
   come.

Three, four, five, six, seven, eight,
   nine

Ten leprechauns went out to play
On a bright St. Patrick's day.
They had such enormous fun
They asked everyone to come!

LITTLE PETER RABBIT
Little Peter Rabbit
Had a fly upon his nose.
Little Peter Rabbit
Had a fly upon his nose.

Little Peter Rabbit
Had a fly upon his nose.

And he swished until it flew away.
(repeat)

Kathryn L. Cloonan

A TEDDY BEAR'S MERRY CHRISTMAS

Teddy Bear, Teddy Bear
Touch your knee.

Teddy Bear,
Teddy Bear
Trim the tree.

Teddy Bear,
Teddy Bear
Touch your wrist.

Teddy Bear,
Teddy Bear
Make your list.

Teddy Bear,
Teddy Bear
Touch your feet.

Teddy Bear,
Teddy Bear
Eat, Eat, Eat!

Teddy Bear,
Teddy Bear
Touch your toe.

Teddy Bear,
Teddy Bear
It's Mistletoe!!!

Kathryn L. Cloonan

Daily Schedule

Time	Activity	
8:50	Welcome	Get Organized
9:00	Creative writing/Independent Study	
9:20	Group Time — Plannning the Day, Current Events	
9:30	Super Readers	
9:40	Literature Block	
10:00	Recess/Snack	
10:15	Guided Writing	
10:30	Language Arts	

Mini Groups by Interest	Independent Reading Centers Buddy Reading	Literature Extenstion Reenforcement

Time	Activity	
11:30	Story, Songs, Sharing	
11:45	Lunch & Recess	
12:15	Read Aloud	
12:30	Math	
1:00	Thematic — Social Studies & Science	
2:00	Art	Music	P.E.
2:30	Centers	
3:00	Clean Up, Story, Songs, Discuss the Day, Plan for Tomorrow	
3:20		

Kathryn L. Cloonan

WHOLE LANGUAGE — THE COMPLETE CYCLE

By Kathryn L. Cloonan

WHOLE LANGUAGE STEPS

1. Share a Piece of Literature...
   - Story — oral as well as written.
   - Song
   - Flip Chart
   - String Story
   - Big Book
   - Flannel Board Story
   - Student Made Book
2. Personalize It   READ IT!
3. Put It Into Print   READ IT!
4. Model It   READ IT!
5. Make a Big Book   READ IT!
6. Expand It — Recreate It
   - Mini Books
   - Puppets
   - Bulletin Board Stories
   - Mobiles
   - Wall Stories
   - Overhead Transparency Stories
   - Tutorette Stories
   - Masks, Plays, Etc.
   - Innovations
7. Make The Writing Connection
   - Slot Stories
   - Signs
   - Posters
   - Letters to a Character in the Story
   - Letter to the Author
   - "News" Article
   - Adding Another Chapter
     - Different Ending, etc.
   - Writing Their Own Stories

Kathryn L. Cloonan

WHOLE LANGUAGE AT HOME

MAKING A READING AND WRITING CONNECTION FUN!

1. Encourage reading, writing, listening and discussing ideas at home.

2. Develop confidence and self-esteem by encouragement and praise.

3. Surround your whole family with a variety of types of literature: magazines, newspapers, encyclopedias, books.

4. Be a model — show your family you read for your own enjoyment.

5. Read to your family — no matter how old they are, they will still enjoy hearing a story.

When Reading With Your Children...

6. Keep it fun and stress free.

7. Read your children's favorite over and over if they ask — you are allowing them to hear the "music or rhythm" of the story called the story structure.

8. Stop before a predictable word and let your child fill in the word — you are giving him an opportunity to use the pictures and the sense of the story as strategies for reading.

9. Encourage your child to read along with you — it's good rehearsal before he tries it on his own.

When Your Child Is Reading To You...

10. Let your child decide on the book she/he wants to read to you.

11. Remember that even reading pictures is reading.

12. Overlook mistakes — he is still getting good practice on all the words he is reading correctly — and feeling successful, too.

13. Tell your child the word he is having trouble with — he learns from hearing the correct word and seeing it at the same time.

14. When helping your child figure out a word...
    a. Just point to the words and give him an opportunity to self-correct.
    b. Ask him what word would make sense.
    c. Point to the beginning letter and see if he can think of a word that begins with this letter sound and also makes sense.
    d. If your child has tried and can't figure it out, tell him the word.

15. Encourage your child to make a writing connection...
    a. Add a new ending to the story.
    b. Write a letter to the author.
    c. Write an "ad" telling friends at school about the book.
    d. Write to one of the characters in the story, i.e., Dear Big Bad Wolf,...
    e. Write his or her own story.

INTEGRATED LANGUAGE ARTS

Kathryn L. Cloonan

MAKING THE WRITING CONNECTION
By Kathryn L. Cloonan

HOW TO ENCOURAGE YOUR CHILDREN'S WRITING

HAVE A WRITING ENVIRONMENT...

1. Make available easy access to paper — different sizes, colors, and shapes, too.

2. Make available easy access to markers, crayons, pencils and pencil sharpeners.

3. Have a message board or chalk board where children see the importance of writing by giving and receiving messages.

4. Model — write notes, have a special writing time when everyone writes.

5. Look for any excuse to encourage writing. Have your child: write to Grandmother, write Mom a note, make a list of chores he's done, keep a photo album and write a little bit about his favorite pictures.

6. Treat any creative attempt as special.

7. Have correct spellings around for the child to refer to — label things in the home, label drawers in his bedroom.

8. Have your child draw a picture and write about it.

9. Listen to your child read his writing.

10. Use "Post-it" paper to write what the child was trying to say on the back.

WHAT DO YOU SAY WHEN

YOUR CHILD SAYS:

YOU SAY:

"I don't know how...."

"Do the best you can..."

"How do you spell..."

"Use your inventive spelling."

"Sound it out and write down some clues."

"Don't worry about correct spelling...
just get those great ideas down first."

"I don't know how to use inventive spelling..."

"What are you trying to say?"
"What sounds do you hear?"

"What does this say?"
(When they show you their inventive spelling.)

"What do you want it to say?"

"Does this really spell..."

"It's close. Remember the neat thing about
inventive spelling is you're always right."

"Can you read this?"

"You're giving me lots of clues.
Read it to me won't you?"
(Point out a good clue.)

Kathryn L. Cloonan

Writing the Right Way!

Benefits	Process	Purpose

Writing

Encourages self-expression

Makes letter-sound connections

Builds fluency in ideas

Getting great ideas down on paper

Conference I

Makes the connection between
their ideas and the printed word

Supports inventive spelling/
corrective spelling

Communicating ideas

Learning new skills in
- phonics   • decoding skills
- grammar   • spelling
- punctuation • sight words

Conference II

Builds self-confidence by acceptance

Enhances creativity

Increases communication skills
through making choices and decisions

Creating, planning, and expressing
ideas for a finished product

Publishing

Encourages further efforts
Builds self-respect and self-concept

Modeling correct spelling, punctuation,
sentence formation, and publishing

Illustrating

Builds the connection between print and
ideas

Encourages sight vocabulary

Increasing comprehension

Encouraging creativity

Reading

Builds sight vocabulary

Enhances decoding strategies

Builds reading fluency

Encourages a love for reading and writing

Building sight vocabulary

Decoding through meaningful context
and phonetic clues

Celebrating

Celebrating with an Authors' Tea

Encourages a love for reading and writing

Enhances acceptance of others

Increases awareness of "presenting" to others

Enriches sight vocabulary

Builds a collection of readable materials

Encourages learning more about a subject

Builds self-confidence

Enriches organizational and planning skills

Models respect and love for literature

Gives *all* children an arena for success

Offers a completed reading and writing cycle that
is relevant to children

Kathryn L. Cloonan

AUTHOR'S PLANNING PAGE

Name: _____

Title: _____

Dedicated to: _____

Because: _____

About - Me - The Author: _____

_____

_____

I would like my book:

    Handwritten   _____

        or

    Typed   _____

I would like the words this size:

VERY LARGE   LARGE   SMALL

I would like the color of the cover to be: _____

1. I have chosen my paper: _____

2. I have talked with my Publisher: _____

3. I have a picture of me: _____

4. I have done my illustrations: _____

5. My book is all put together: _____

I DID IT!!!

R.E.A.L. Reading
for
Upper Grades

I. Share a Piece of Literature

A. Book Groups
Students choose book group to be in

B. Author's Study
Class is reading a variety of same author's work

C. Story Types

Mysteries

Fables, Myths

Nursery rhymes

Folklore

Folk songs

Fantasy

Science fiction

Nonfiction

Humor

D. Thematic Units

Space

Insects

Ocean

Pets

Dinosaurs

E. Historical Collections

Pilgrims,

Civil War

Settlement of state

Kathryn L. Cloonan

SCHEDULING

Daily Schedule

9:00-9:40	Special
9:40-10:00	Circle: news and poems
10:00-10:10	Snack
10:10-10:20	Focus of the morning
10:20-11:00	Language activity based on focus.
11:00-11:40	Math
11:40-12:40	Lunch, recess
12:40-1:10	Sharing, read aloud
1:10-2:15	Reading/writing/sharing
2:15-2:50	Continuation of reading/writing, activity or free time

What I Wanted to see:

Nurturing, caring environment

1. Teacher a coach rather than dictator.

2. Children feel safe and can take chances.

3. Children have choices and learn to take control of their learning.

4. Teach $500 concepts rather than "cover" the curriculum.

5. Each child has a positive self image and is proud of his/her activities.

6. Children are learning through doing.

7. Each child has the feeling that he/she is a reader and writer.

What do I want to happen? How can I foster that in my room?

1. Coach, not direct
   a. my desk not the focus
   b. children's areas most attractive
2. Kids have control
   a. materials available
   b. books available
   c. workspace for individuals, pairs and groups
   d. booklists, book report forms, observation sheets and paper available
   e. room for children to move around easily
3. Children's positive self image
   a. places to display kids' work
   b. child able to be self-sufficient
4. Room run easily with little effort
   a. ease of movement
   b. transitions
   c. materials I need ready to go and moveable

INTEGRATED LANGUAGE ARTS

Sandy Cook

Examples of Literacy Profiles In Reading

The Ministry of Education in Victoria, Australia, developed literacy profiles to facilitate monitoring and reporting of teachers' observations of student proficiency in reading and writing. The literacy profiles are not assessment instruments; they are descriptive bands sequenced in terms of an ordered scale to report student proficiency and progress over time.

READING BAND A

Concepts about Print
Holds book the right way up.
Turns pages from the front to the back.
On request, indicates the beginning and end of sentences.
Distinguishes between upper and lower case letters.
Indicates the start and end of books.

Reading Strategies
Locates words, lines, spaces, letters.
Refers to letters by name.
Locates own name and other familiar words in a short text.
Identifies known, familiar words in other contexts.

Responses
Responds to literature (smiles, claps, listens intently)
Joins in familiar stories.

Interest and Attitudes
Shows preference for particular books.
Chooses books as a free time activity.

READING BAND B

Reading Strategies
Takes risks when reading.
"Reads" books with simple repetitive language patterns.
Uses pictures for clues to meaning of text.
Asks others for help with meaning and pronunciation of words.
Consistently reads familiar words and interprets symbols within a text.
Predicts words.
Matches known clusters of letters to clusters in unknown words.
Uses knowledge of words in the environment when "reading" and "writing".
Recognises base words within other words.
Names basic parts of a book.
Makes a second attempt at a word if it doesn't sound right.

Responses
Selects own books to "read".
Describes connections among events in texts.
Writes, role plays and/or draws in response to a story or other form of writing (e.g. poem, message).
Creates ending when the text is left unfinished.
Recounts parts of text in writing, drama, or art work.
Retells using language expressions from reading sources.
Retells with approximate sequence.

READING BAND C

Reading Strategies
Rereads a paragraph or sentence to establish meaning.
Uses context as a basis for predicting meaning of unfamiliar words.
Reads aloud showing understanding of purpose of punctuation marks.
Uses picture cues to make appropriate responses for unknown words.
Uses pictures to help read a text.
Finds where another reader is up to in a reading passage.

Responses
Writing and art work reflect understanding of text.
Retells, discusses and expresses opinions on literature, and reads further.
Recalls events and characters spontaneously from text.

Interest and Attitudes
Seeks recommendations for books to read.
Chooses more than one type of book.
Chooses to read when given free choice.
Concentrates on reading for lengthy periods.

READING BAND D

Reading Strategies
Reads materials with a wide variety of styles and topics.
Selects books to fulfil own purposes.
States main idea in a passage.
Substitutes words with similar meanings when reading aloud.
Self-corrects, using knowledge of language structure and sound-symbol relationships.
Predicts, using knowledge of language structure and/or sound-symbol to make sense of a word or phrase.

Responses
Discusses different types of reading materials.
Discusses materials read at home.
Tells a variety of audiences about a book.
Uses vocabulary and sentence structure from reading materials in written work as well as in conversation.
Themes from reading appear in art work.
Follows written instructions.

Interest and Attitudes
Recommends books to others. Reads often.
Reads silently for extended periods.

Excerpted from page 86 of *English Profiles Handbook*, © 1991, Victoria Ministry of Education, Australia. The *English Profiles Handbook* is printed and distributed in the United States by Touchstone Applied Science Associates (TASA), Inc. Reproduced with permission.

Available from: TASA, P.O. Box 382, Brewster, NY 10509, 1-914-277-8100, $18 plus shipping.

Sandy Cook

Friendship Theme

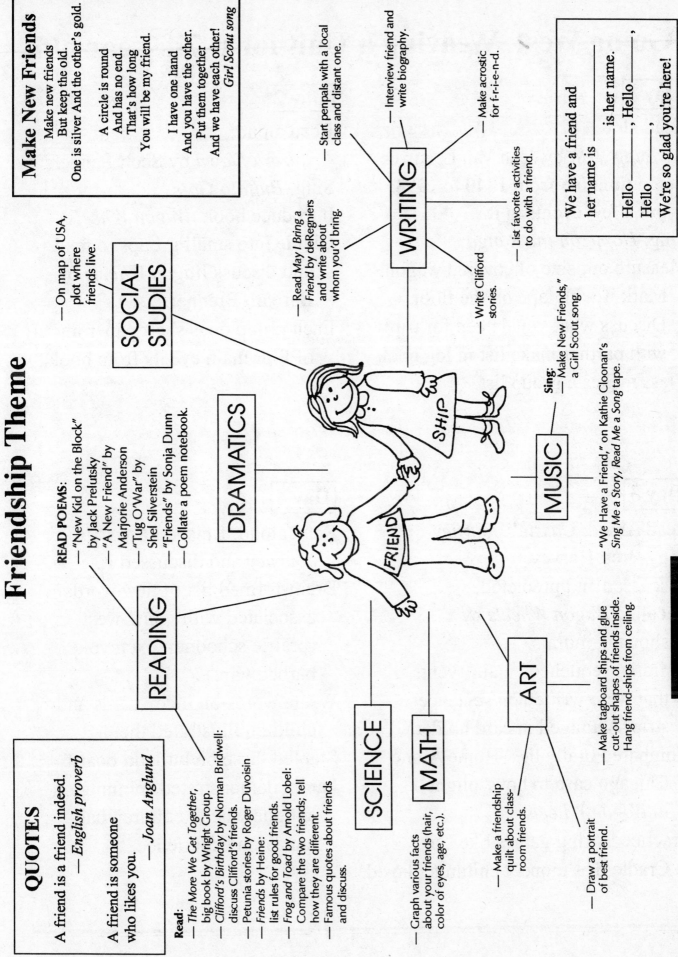

QUOTES

A friend is a friend indeed.
— *English proverb*

A friend is someone
who likes you.
— *Joan Anglund*

READING

READ POEMS:
— "New Kid on the Block"
by Jack Prelutsky
— "A New Friend" by
Marjorie Anderson
— "Tug O'War" by
Shel Silverstein
— "Friends" by Sonja Dunn
— Collate a poem notebook.

Read:
— *The More We Get Together,*
big book by Wright Group.
— *Clifford's Birthday* by Norman Bridwell:
discuss Clifford's friends.
— Petunia stories by Roger Duvoisin
— *Friends* by Heine:
list rules for good friends.
— *Frog and Toad* by Arnold Lobel:
Compare the two friends; tell
how they are different.
— Famous quotes about friends
and discuss.

SOCIAL STUDIES

— On map of USA,
plot where
friends live.

WRITING

— Interview friend and
write biography.

— Make acrostic
for f-r-i-e-n-d.

— Start penpals with a local
class and distant one.

— List favorite activities
to do with a friend.

— Read *May I Bring a
Friend* by deRegniers
and write about
whom you'd bring.

— Write Clifford
stories.

We have a friend and
her name is _____ is her name.
Hello _____, Hello _____,
Hello _____,
We're so glad you're here!

DRAMATICS

MUSIC

Sing: — Make New Friends,"
a Girl Scout song.

— "We Have a Friend," on Kathie Cloonan's
Sing Me a Story, Read Me a Song tape.

SCIENCE

— Graph various facts
about your friends (hair,
color of eyes, age, etc.).

MATH

— Make a friendship
quilt about class-
room friends.

ART

— Make tagboard ships and glue
cut-out shapes of friends inside.
Hang friend-ships from ceiling.

— Draw a portrait
of best friend.

Ann Lessard

Going West: Weaving a Unit for 6-7-8-year-olds

Day 1

Read aloud:
  Going West by Jean Van Leeuwen
Begin timeline from 1840 to 1993;
  put a few events in it
Sing: *Home on the Range*
Measure out size of covered wagon.
  Mark it with tape on the floor.
  Discuss what you'd need for trip;
  with partner make list in log book
Class makes a group list.

Day 2

Read aloud:
  Aurora Dawn by Scott Sanders
Sing: *Buffalo Gals*
Introduce book: *Wagon Wheels*
Divide into small groups to read
  and discuss *Wagon Wheels* by
  Barbara Brenner.
Each group does shelf paper mural
  of four main events from book.

Day 3

Read Aloud: *Cassie's Journey*
  by Brett Harvey.
Discussed and predicted.
Recalled *Wagon Wheels* by
  showing murals.
Children sequenced main events
  that were written on sentence
  strip. Arranged in card holder.
Compared orally the "Home Alone"
  Chicago case to boys' plight
  in *Wagon Wheels*.
Practiced string games like Cats'
  Cradle that pioneer children played.

Day 4

Read aloud: finished *Cassie's
  Journey* and discussed it.
Brainstormed list of new words
  associated with going west
  (prairie schooner, oxen yoke,
  barbed wire)
Wrote words on index cards and
  children illustrated them.
Stapled these on bulletin board.
Parent demonstrated spinning on
  antique wheel; children had
  hands-on experience.

Ann Lessard

Day 5

Read aloud: *On the Banks of Plum Creek* by Laura Ingalls Wilder

Children choose "west" book to read with partner.

Used notebooks for partners to write three sentences about book while first grader drew a picture

Continued *On the Banks* each day

Day 6

Read aloud: *If You Traveled West in a Covered Wagon* by Ellen Levine

Put out piles of wagon wheel pasta, pipe cleaners, small boxes, pieces of sheeting, staplers, tongue depressors

Each child made a covered wagon

Day 7

Read aloud: more of *If You Traveled West*

Finished covered wagons and made some possessions to put inside

With partner started stories about a trip westward they might take. Wrote in notebooks.

Day 8

Read aloud: *My Prairie Year* by Brett Harvey

Song: *Down in the Valley*

Quilt demonstration by parent; then made paper square for quilt

Pasted them on mural paper leaving a border.

Read aloud: *Sam Johnson and the Blue Ribbon Quilt* by Lisa Ernst

Day 9

Read aloud: *The Quilt Story* by Johnston and dePaola

Shared stories written about trip westward. Focused on which possessions you took and what you really needed.

Read supply list and discussed limit of 2,000 pounds

Each team made a new list of what they'd take

Day 10

Read aloud: *Dakota Dugout* by Ann Turner

Compared sod houses with one in *On the Banks of Plum Creek*

Planned four murals of trip westward:

1 Town in East
2 Traveling in Covered Wagon
3 Sod House and Stable
4 Frontier Town

Began painting

Ideas for Newspaper Unit

1. List ways families use the newspaper.

2. Read *Weekly Reader*, local paper, Sunday paper and contrast style and content.

3. Each student writes her daily news; collate into a class newspaper.

4. Use copies of real newspaper; read headlines and predict news that follows.

5. Students read front page and circle words they can read or list unfamiliar ones.

6. List names of various sections and read a section aloud and discuss.

7. Students start writing a chosen section (all doing the same or in assigned groups).

8. Select editorial committee which decides which writing will be used in class paper.

9. Look at bylines and discuss news sources.

10. Invite actual reporter, editor to speak to class.

11. Make press hats and allow class reporters to set up interviews.

12. Visit a real paper as the presses roll.

13. Print and distribute own paper.

14. Share newspaper with other classes.

Ann Lessard

My name is _____ .

The date is _____ .

The title of my book is _____

_____ .

The author of my book is _____

_____ .

I liked it because _____

_____ .

Here is a picture about my book.

Name _____ Date _____

Title: _____

Author: _____

Illustrator: _____

Who was in this book? _____

_____

What did they do? _____

_____

Where did they do it? _____

_____

When did they do it? _____

_____

How did you like this book? _____

_____

My Weekly Reading Log
by Ann Lessard

My name: _____ The date: _____

Monday

1. _____

2. _____

3. _____

alone? _____

with partner? _____

Tuesday

1. _____

2. _____

3. _____

alone? _____

with partner? _____

Wednesday

1. _____

2. _____

3. _____

alone? _____

with partner? _____

Thursday

1. _____

2. _____

3. _____

alone? _____

with partner? _____

Friday

1. _____

2. _____

3. _____

alone? _____

with partner? _____

How did you do?

SDE Reproducible Page
For Classroom Use

Ann Lessard

INTEGRATED LANGUAGE ARTS

HOME SCHOOL STRENGTHENING THE CONNECTION

Dear _____,

You're invited to my Authors' Tea

on _____ at _____ . I'll be

reading my new book.

I need to bring _____ .

Love,

_____

STORY MAP

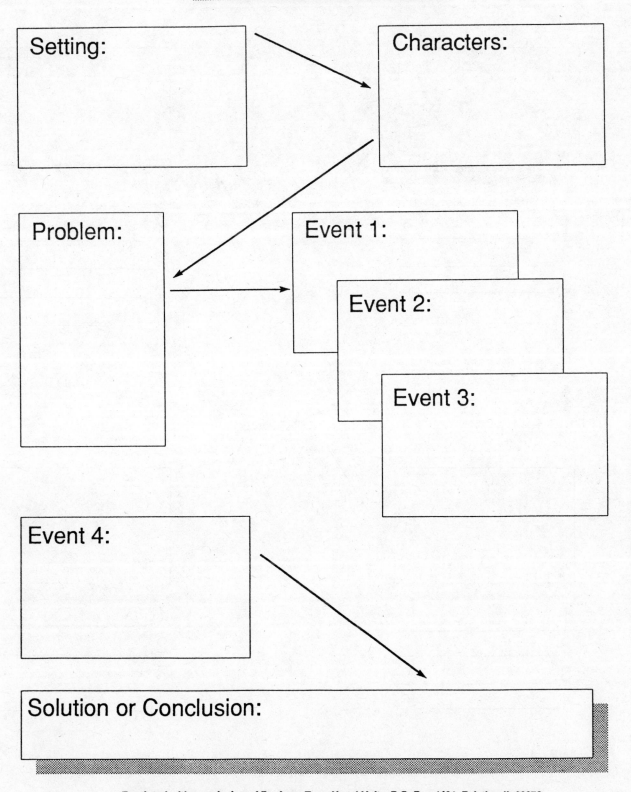

Setting:

Characters:

Problem:

Event 1:

Event 2:

Event 3:

Event 4:

Solution or Conclusion:

Reprinted with permission of Dr. Anne Troy, Novel Units, P.O. Box 1461, Palatine, IL 60078

INTEGRATED
LANGUAGE ARTS

CHARACTER WEB

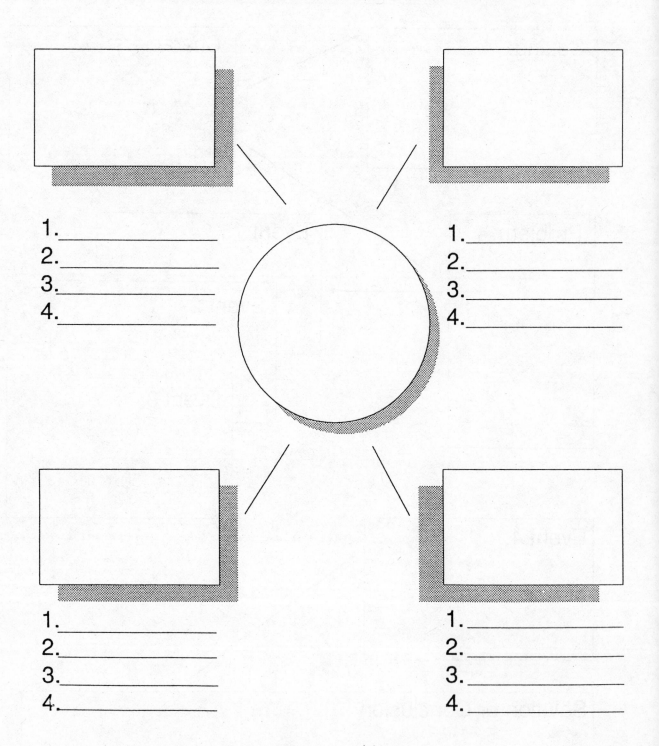

1._____
2._____
3._____
4._____

1._____
2._____
3._____
4._____

1._____
2._____
3._____
4._____

1._____
2._____
3._____
4._____

Character Web
Great Gray Owl by Orin Cochrane

BEAUTIFUL

MIGHTY

WISE

KIND

DEADLY

POWERFUL

Character Chart
Good Dog Carl by Alexandra Day

Clever	●					**Not Clever**
Happy			●			**Unhappy**
Friendly	●					**Unfriendly**
Careful				●		**Careless**
Loving	●					**Unloving**

CHARACTER ANALYSIS CHART

Character Trait	Evidence	How Trait is Revealed

Jean Mann

Pop-up Books

1.   Fold paper in half and cut
2 parallel lines on fold.

2. 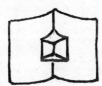 Fold cut out section back and crease.

3. 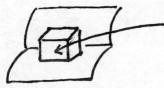 Open paper up, hold like tent,
push cut out through,
fold paper and press firmly.

4. 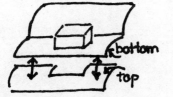 Glue picture to pop-up,
write words above or below.

5.  To connect pages of book,
glue bottom of first page
to top of second page.
Continue in same manner.

6. To make a cage, simply cut strips
in cut out section as shown.

For more ideas on pop-up books, see *How to Make Pop-ups* by Joan Irvine.
Published by Beech Tree Books.

INTEGRATED
LANGUAGE ARTS

SDE Reproducible Page
For Classroom Use
Jean Mann

TRIARAMA

1. Fold a square piece of paper diagonally both ways.

2. Make a cut ½-way up one fold.

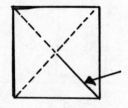

3. Fold ½ of cut section under other cut section.

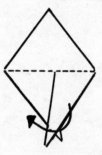

4. Attach together with glue, staple, or clip. This will form a half shell.

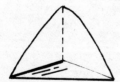

Suggested Materials for Writing

Organize a writing center or area where materials are available at all times for children to use. Separate materials in different containers to make it easy for children to choose what is appropriate for them.

A. **Writing utensils (vary sizes to accommodate different fine motor abilities)**
pencils
pens
colored pencils
crayons
markers
crayons, paints, brushes
(try covering coffee cans with wall paper and separate utensils in them)

B. **Paper (use different sizes, weight, color)**
lined
unlined
story-book
drawing
stationery
graph
computer

C. **Organizing writing**
folders (manila, duo-tang) for keeping current work in
folders for permanent work
dish tubs for younger children (put student's name on front; paper, utensils in tub)
corrugated cardboard boxes (to store past work)
plastic milk crates for folders
box for "finished papers"

D. **Additional supplies at hand**
stapler
staple remover
erasers
rulers
scissors
glue
tape
paper clips
paper punches
paper fasteners
date stamp and pad

E. **Other**
tape recorder
typewriter/computer
dictionaries
reference books

Jean Mann

Reading and Writing Workshop

Mini-lesson: Whole or small group together with teacher. (In beginning of year can be used for procedural). Teacher-centered, orally-based group instruction where teacher models a lesson for a skill, strategy or a convention. Provides a common frame of reference.

Independent time: Students have the opportunity to practice what was taught in the mini-lesson in the context of meaningful content, providing an immediate follow-up. Teacher has the chance to see how lesson is used by students and can plan for effective follow-up.

Sharing: Closure to reading or writing time. Coming back together as a group to talk, see how things went, discuss problems, and share what students did.

Jean Mann

Developmental Stages of Spelling

(Richard Gentry)

Pre-communicative:

Semi-phonetic:

Phonetic:

Transitional:

Conventional:

Jean Mann

LOOK-COVER-WRITE-CHECK

1.   Student **LOOKS** at word in middle column.

2.   Student visualizes word in mind.

3.   Student **COVERS** word by folding over right hand flap.

4.   Student tries to **WRITE** the word from visual memory in left column.

5.   Student **CHECKS** and corrects if necessary by looking at original word.

HAVE-A-GO

Jean Mann

WHOLE LANGUAGE
DEFINITION

Whole Language is a child-centered, holistic philosophy of learning and teaching which recognizes that language learning is both contextually and socially determined, and is constructive in nature. It provides children with a wide range of meaningful language and literary experiences across the entire curriculum, includes evaluation and parent involvement and facilitates the development of responsible, cooperative and caring individuals for whom language is a source of increasing empowerment.

From: Norma Mikleson, University of Victoria, Centre for Whole Language, Victoria, Canada
Presentation April 30, 1989 International Reading Association, New Orleans

WHOLE LANGUAGE
THE BASIC PRINCIPLES

1. The program is child-centered — it begins with the language, thoughts and knowledge of the child. The child is the curricular informant.

2. The program is not hierarchial or arbitrarily sequenced. However, skills are taught.

3. The learner is surrounded with language at various levels. Literature is a basis for the program.

4. Choice is allowed. Autonomy is developed.

5. The program is functional. Thoughtful use of language is encouraged.

6. Language is owned, social.

7. Multiple opportunities for expression and support are provided.

8. Students monitor their own learning.

9. Content subjects continue to be taught — but language in all its forms is emphasized.

10. The teacher is a learner too. S/he is a researcher — a participant observer.

11. The child is trusted and respected.

12. The program is holistic and integrated.

13. Parents are co-learners, co-teachers, and colleagues.

14. Evaluation is an integral on-going component. Self-evaluation is important.

15. There is a strong research base.

John T. Poeton

COMPONENTS OF A WHOLE LANGUAGE PROGRAM

A Balanced WHOLE LANGUAGE Program
Should Include The Following Components:

Reading to Children

Shared Book Experience

Uninterrupted Sustained Silent Reading (USSR)

Guided Reading

Individualized Reading

Language Experience

Children's Writing

Modelled Writing

Sharing Time

Content Area: Reading, Writing, Talking, Listening

Evaluation and Assessment Procedures Including:

Logs, Portfolios, Self-Evaluation

and Kid Watching

Revised by: John Thomas Poeton

John T. Poeton

Directed Reading and Guided Reading

In recent articles pertaining to reading there has been much made of a new term called "guided reading." Here are some comparisons between guided reading and a term which has been a part of pre-service reading instruction since 1960 — directed reading.

Directed	Guided
The focus is on:	
author's meaning and it is often found in the teacher's guide	reader constructs own meaning
literal questions often based on content and recall	reading strategies, process
prepared script, teacher professional plan	interactive responsive to the learner
answer questions after reading	making predictions before reading
follow-up enrichment activities	"preparing the soil" dialogue interaction before reading
the text at hand	the learner as a life long reader

Developed by Mike Hagan of San Jose, California with a group of teachers.
Reprinted with permission of Mike Hagan.

John Poeton

INTEGRATED LANGUAGE ARTS

Literature Study

Name _____   Date _____

During the week of _____ I agree to read the book entitled:

_____

This book has a total of _____ pages. I will pace myself according to the schedule below:

Mon	Tue	Wed	Thu	Fri	Sat	Sun

I kept closely to my planned schedule.   YES ☐   NO ☐

I finished the book on time.   YES ☐   NO ☐

I did not finish my book. I am on page _____ .

Child's Signature _____

Teacher's Signature _____

Parent's Signature _____

Next book proposed _____

Next literature study date _____

John T. Poeton

Responses to Literature

Some suggestions for student responses:

1. What you liked or disliked and why
2. What you wished had happened
3. What you wish the author had included
4. Your opinion of the characters
5. Your opinion of the illustrations, tables, and figures
6. What the text reminds you of
7. What you felt as you read
8. What you noticed about how you read
9. Questions you have after reading

Types of teacher responses:

1. Share your own ideas and responses.
2. Provide information.
3. Develop students' awareness of reading strategies.
4. Develop students' awareness of literary techniques.
5. Model elaboration.
6. Challenge students to think in new ways.

John Poeton

Sample Writing Survey

Name _____ Date _____

1. Do you consider yourself an author? Why or why not?

2. Do you think most people like to write?

3. Do your parents write? If so, what do they usually write?

4. Who is your favorite author today? Why?

5. Who are your "old" favorite authors?

6. Are there any books by favorite authors that have changed the way you write?

7. How do you decide what you are going to write about?

8. What are some of your favorite topics to write about?

9. When and where do you like to write?

10. What helps you to write better?

John Poeton

Literacy Portfolio

Topic: _____

List the activities you did.

What was your favorite?

Why?

What did you learn?

What do you want to learn next?

Write a note or draw a picture about this topic.

Ellen Thompson

Writing Club
Conference Recording Sheet

Date: _____

Name of story: _____

I shared with: _____

_____

_____

_____

Group comments: _____

_____

_____

_____

_____

_____

Author comments: _____

_____

_____

_____

_____

_____

Circle all that apply:

I will: write more   revise   have a content conference

        have an editing conference   stop here

Linda J. Pils

Soon anofe you tout me: Evaluation in a first-grade whole language classroom

Pils teaches first grade at Northside School in Middleton, Wisconsin. In this article, she shares evaluation strategies implemented in her whole language classroom.

Last year, on the last day of first grade, Courtney handed me a small book that she had made as a gift. It read, "First I didnt know how It would be like to have you. But less then one week I had alredy started to like you. First I didn't know how to read very well. Soon anofe you tout me." I had my report card. Courtney had just provided me with all the evaluation that I needed about my efforts to change the way that I had previously taught reading to children.

I had embraced the whole language philosophy because it allowed me to teach children at their levels and enable them to become independent learners. I had abandoned workbooks for journals, Ditto sheets for key words, and basal readers for trade books and reading/writing workshops. I still taught phonics, strategies for decoding, and comprehension, but they would be only one lane on the literacy highway, and often there were many detours along the way. Meaning and natural language became the basis of my curriculum, and literature, oral language, drama, and writing became my major building blocks.

However, during my transition, I struggled with ways to piece all of the parts together to make a snug fit. If I used alternative methods for reading instruction, then I could not rely on the formal assessments which were part of the basal program I used previously. How should I evaluate children's progress and the program itself, and how should I demonstrate to parents and administrators the progress which had been made?

This article is a story of changes: changes in perspective, attitude, and responsibility. In it I describe the assessments that were implemented in my classroom in order to evaluate my students' progress and guide their acquisition of literacy abilities. First, I describe my classroom and the literacy events that occur in it. Next, I share the new perspective on evaluation that I have acquired and various special ways I gather and respond to information about my students.

My classroom

I have always believed that children should be surrounded by good literature, so the jump from a classroom with lots of read-aloud time, literature follow-up activities, and sustained silent reading to a literature based/ whole language classroom was not a broad one. But as I read articles, attended conferences, and shared ideas with colleagues, my understanding of why these activities were important changed. I came to realize that these activities were not the fluff but the substance of the reading program. I changed my basal reading program to one which included a wide variety of literacy activities. These began with our class meeting and continued with reading, writing/sharing, and read-aloud blocks (see daily schedule figure). Thematic units were implemented to integrate the subjects of math, science, and social studies. The following is a brief description of some of these literacy activities.

● *Key words and sentences*. I use a key word program based on Sylvia Ashton-Warner's work as described by Johnson (1987). Three to four times a week the children dictate words which I write on tagboard strips. The children copy their words into a key word booklet, draw a picture, and write a story. These words are also used as a resource for writing and reading.

● *Daily news*. As we complete our calendar activities, I ask the children for sentences about yesterday, today, and tomorrow. I write down the today sentences on a piece of large, lined story paper. I use these daily news stories in various ways, for example, as a source of words for decoding lessons.

● *Buddy reading*. In this time, children select their reading material and sit alone or with a buddy and read. Initially I assigned buddies, usually a strong reader with a child of lesser ability. Now we alternate between assigned and self-chosen buddies.

● *Reading workshop*. In reading workshop, small groups of children look at and talk about books that have been placed in a large container. There are books of varying levels and interests in each container, multiple copies of books that have been read aloud, and others that the children have selected.

● *Writing workshop*. Working in pairs or alone, the children write about themselves and the world around them. They write fiction and nonfiction; they write humorously and poignantly. I model the writing process with a class story. Parent helpers, trained in process writing, assist in the publishing stage, and the published books are kept in our class library.

New forms of assessment

In the past, I would rely on basal tests to assess my students' growth in reading, but in my new environment, those tests were not useful. Instead, I began to examine students' work. For example, I would analyze the children's journal entries and make some judgments about their word identification abilities. For instance, Kristi wrote in her journal, "I wis I had a hamsdr his name is cdls. I wd pl wt hma" (I wish I had a hamster. His name is Cuddles. I would play with him.). This told me Kristi could formulate a complete idea in a

---

Daily schedule

Class meeting
8:10-8:40: Calendar, weather report, class business, poetry helpers (we read 2-3 poems), music, and daily news.

Reading block
8:40-9:30: Shared reading (big books), skill follow-up on a book previously read, daily news independent work, key words, story mapping, small group or individual conferences.

Writing/sharing block
9:45-11:05: Buddy reading, writing workshop, journals, publishing center, reading workshop, formal and informal dramatics, sharing time.

Read alouds
11:45-12:15: Read alouds and silent reading.

Math, science, and social studies
12:15-2:45: Large and small group, centers, special classes, end-of-the-day meeting.

paragraph; she was aware of syntax, spacing between words, beginning and ending sounds, and some medial vowels and consonants; she used some standard spellings; and she understood the components of sentence structure and was beginning to capitalize and use periods appropriately.

In contrast, Bobby's entry on the same date was "IWTOM" (I went to Madison). He understood that writing is a meaningful activity and that letters are the basis for written communication. He relied on beginning sounds and understood the left-to-right convention in written language.

The information from these journals gave me a much richer picture of these two very different children. How I assisted them was determined by where they were in the reading/writing process. In working with Kristi, I began stressing vowel sounds and word families in her key words; in her journal writing we talked about how to expand her story and about the possibility of making a "Cuddles" chapter book. In planning for mini-lessons, I included different uses of capital letters, for if Kristi were ready to expand her knowledge, there were other children who could also benefit from such a lesson.

Bobby was ready for other things. Bobby was selected to be our song leader during our morning meeting. He pointed to the words as we sang them, which made him aware of the spaces between words and the need for them. In our big book lessons, I used a variety of cloze activities. I covered up the ends of words with small sticky notes, sometimes covering the entire word and, at other times, just the endings of specific words. Bobby could predict which words were appropriate and then check his predictions as individual letters were shown. This activity stressed the ends of words and involved him in the process. When I assisted Bobby with his journal, I encouraged him to write all of an unknown word with the use of boxes to designate each letter. He usually knew the first letter, and we worked together to formulate the rest.

Clipboards and labels

My classroom paraphernalia now includes a clipboard with strips of blank mailing labels attached. Each morning I date several of these labels and write names and observations that I make as I walk around the room discussing each child's work, progress, and problems. At the end of the day, I place the labels on sheets of paper in a three-ring binder which is divided into sections for each child in my class. As I reread these anecdotal records, it is easy to spot patterns of behavior, problems that I need to address, and recent achievements. My anecdotal records take many forms:

- 8-30 Ben: Rarely raises hand during meeting, but always attentive.
- 9-30 Ben: "I like doing daily news because it's so easy sometimes."
- 10-30 Ben: Tells story of The Three Little Pigs to Chris.
- 10-30 Ben: "Look, *at* is in my last name."
- 8-23 Amy: Very interesting story in journal, re: eagles nesting; good beginning and ending sounds.
- 10-17 Amy: Running record taken of daily news, self-corrected *monkeybars*. Says she read three books at home that we've read in school.
- 10-30 Amy: "Eleven minus seven equals four, it's a rhyme!"
- 9-24 Stacy: "I can read *Hop on Pop* all by myself."
- 10-5 Stacy: Stacy and Alan very good buddies, Stacy helps Alan with words. She read all of helper chart when she selected her job.

What do I learn as I meander around the room observing students and taking notes? On October 2, I learned that Danny said, "Oh, goody!" when I announced that it was buddy reading time. This was from a boy who cried daily for the first month of school and said "I can't" to every new activity or lesson. On November 20, I learned that Richard read *Noisy Nora* by Rosemary Wells perfectly; he held the book up as I do to show the pictures, even though no one was listening. I learned that Crystal was reading the song that we had learned at Halloween, a song put on sentence strips. She sang aloud as she pointed to each word with the pointer.

These observations, made on a daily basis, gave me a clear picture of the progress these children were making. All teachers observe children, but now I am using my observations in a more coherent, organized way.

ASSESSMENT

Portfolios

As a means to assemble and analyze the large amount of data I began to gather on my students, I initiated literacy portfolios for each student. I placed a variety of materials in these literacy portfolios, including the following:

Writing samples. At the beginning of the year after we had brainstormed ideas, I asked each child to write a story about what she or he did during the summer. I compared these initial stories to other writings done later on during the year. I analyzed the stories for sentence structure, number of known words, punctuation, and content. Some children could write one sentence in invented spelling about what they had done over the summer. Bobby wrote "I W Rg A The P" (I went raking at the park). Other children like Brian and Shannon could only draw what they enjoyed during the summer.

Some children develop their understanding of the code in great leaps. Others make minute but steady steps. For example, it took a month for Danny to change from "I can't" to initiating his own drawing and dictating the story. It took another month to write "I" every day on the first line of his journal. On November 20 after making the illustrations for his first book, Danny asked me to write the words: "I am learning to read." By December, Danny was writing his own stories independently. By gathering and analyzing Danny's writing samples, I was able to guide his development as a writer.

Number of words read aloud in one minute. In September, each child was asked to read aloud an excerpt from *Frog and Toad All Year* by Arnold Lobel. The selected passage was long enough so that no child could finish reading it in less than a minute (Kramer, 1990). I calculated the number of words read aloud in one minute. The children read the same selection again in January and May, and the results were tabulated. This assessment, which took less than an hour to administer to all 24 children in the class, provided important feedback to both me and my children regarding their developing competence as readers.

Ten-minute writing sample. I also keep track of how many words each child can write in a 10-minute period at 3-month intervals throughout the year. The children and I com-

Some children develop their understanding of the code in great leaps. Others make minute but steady steps.

pare these totals, giving us evidence of their development as writers.

Lists of books read and to be read. Each child keeps a list of books read during buddy reading time. As we confer, this list is a starting point for our talks, and it assists me in making suggestions for interesting or challenging follow-up titles. We also keep a list of books or authors that each child would like to read. These often are titles that other children have mentioned in reading workshop, in sharing time, or during read alouds.

Challenge Cards. Lists of unknown words and their sources are placed on Challenge Cards. These are discussed at reading conferences. I examine these words for miscue patterns and initiate mini-lessons as needed for individuals or groups of students.

Conference records. In reading and writing conferences, the children and I discuss what interests them in their readings, how books or themes are alike or different, and what they are currently writing about. They read favorite passages and talk about authors. They discuss problems and how to solve them. We keep a check list that contains items such as "I use capital letters at the beginning of sentences," and "I can write from left to right."

Conclusion

In previous years, I was in charge of the learning and the evaluation that occurred in my classroom. Now the children share responsibility for their learning, and they participate in its evaluation.

Parents also participate. For instance, at a fall conference with Laura's parents, we discussed what kinds of growth they could expect to see, what stages would probably come next. They read her journal and her book list and listened to a tape of Laura reading. I learned about Laura's interests and hobbies from the completed parent survey. They did not hear about what Laura could not do; we discussed what she *could* do.

At first my evaluation was episodic. There was a flurry of activity prior to each conference or reporting period. Now assessments are done every day. This makes me more aware of my students' development and any possible problems. We can work on a difficult area immediately, individually or in a small group. The children do not need to stop their reading or writing to be evaluated. Their reading and writing *is* the evaluation; it is not a separate phenomenon.

In *Leo the Late Bloomer* by Robert Kraus, Leo's father watches Leo for signs of blooming.

> "Are you sure Leo's a bloomer?" asked Leo's father. "Patience," said Leo's mother, "A watched bloomer doesn't bloom." So Leo's father watched television instead of Leo....Then one day, in his own good time, Leo bloomed! He could read! He could write! ...He also spoke. And it wasn't just a word. It was a whole sentence. And that sentence was..."I made it!"

In a whole language classroom, kids bloom just like Leo, and the reason that they bloom is that we trust them to learn. Teachers bloom in such classrooms, too, not because they are super teachers but because teachers can rely on themselves and not the faraway editors of standardized tests to legitimize observations of children.

I am trusted to observe and evaluate. Yetta Goodman (1989, p. 5) states it succinctly when she writes, "Once teachers begin to take account of what they know about learning, language, and conceptual development ...their reflective thinking grows and takes on new dimensions."

Move over, Leo.

References

Goodman, Y.M. (1989). Evaluation of students. In K.S. Goodman, Y.M. Goodman, & W.J. Hood (Eds.), *The whole language evaluation book* (pp. 3-14). Portsmouth, NH: Heinemann.

Johnson, K. (1987). *Doing words.* Boston: Houghton Mifflin.

Kramer, C.J. (1990). Documenting reading and writing growth in the primary grades using informal methods of evaluation. *The Reading Teacher, 44,* 356-357.

ASSESSMENT

When Your Principal Asks: What Should Principals See Teachers Doing When Evaluating Whole Language Teachers?

by Bill Harp

As the school year drew to a close, you, the principal, and your colleagues had a lively discussion about what principals should see children doing when evaluating the work of whole language teachers. That conversation in the spring led to two goals for this fall: you would refine the list of things the principal should see children doing when evaluating the work of a whole language teacher, and you would attend to the things the principal should see the teacher doing.

In your enthusiasm about the topic of what the principal should see teachers doing, you volunteered to lead a task force of teachers who will answer the question. The principal has scheduled your presentation for a faculty meeting in two weeks. What will you say?

You are reminded of Ken Goodman's (1986) statement that whole language teachers believe there is something special about human learning and human language. They believe all children have language and the ability to learn language, and they reject negative, elitist, racist views of linguistic purity that would limit children to arbitrary "proper" language. Instead, they view their role as helping children to expand on the marvelous language they already use. Whole language teachers expect children to learn and are there to help them do it.

Teachers are Set Directors rather than Educational Technocrats

In whole language classrooms the teacher spends more time on creating an environment in which children are free to communicate, explore, experiment and take risks than in direct instruction. When the principal walks into the whole language classroom he or she should have the feeling that the room is foremost the children's, rather than the teacher's.

Teacher Relatively Invisible

The teacher may, at first, be difficult to find when the principal enters the room. He or she is likely to be kneeling at eye level with a child, discussing a writing piece. The teacher may well be on the floor working an experiment with a group of children, or doing guided reading activities. In short, the teacher is more likely to have melded into the group of children rather than be positioned in front of them, lecturing. This is not to say that whole class instruction is inappropriate in whole language classrooms — it just isn't the norm.

Attention Focused on Activities of Children

The attention of the principal should be drawn to the activities of the children as evidence that the classroom is student centered and teacher guided rather than teacher directed. You are reminded of the difference between reading a story to children and telling them to write about it as opposed to reading a story to children and asking "What would you like to do with this story now?" The second way of handling children's responses puts them in charge of their learning and leads to a far greater variety of responses than you would ever think of on your own.

Teacher Creates Ways for Children to Behave as Real Readers and Real Writers

The teacher has created an environment that invites children to use reading and writing for authentic purposes: to communicate, to persuade, to inform, to entertain — both as receiver and responder. For example, children do not write pretend addresses inside rectangles printed on paper. They address envelopes because they have mail to send to someone for important reasons. When children have read a piece they respond the way real readers respond to literature. They don't get out the papier-mache and create a three-dimensional representation of a character. Instead they tell someone about the book, they read another book by the same author, they recommend the book to a friend, they research something that piqued their curiosity, or they do nothing. They respond to the literature the way real readers respond.

Children Behave as Real Learners

The teacher has created a learning environment that invites children to explore, to experiment, to investigate — to take responsibility for their own learning. Real learners assess what they already know, determine what they need to learn, and plan strategies for learning. The principal observing the work of a whole language teacher should see evidence that the teacher has handed over much of the responsibility for learning to children. Thematic and other units should begin, for example, with a discussion of what the children already know about the topic (maybe charting the information) and concluding with planning for how they will learn what they want to learn.

There should also be evidence that the teacher understands that his or her function is to create an environment that will take the child further along the learning path than the child could achieve by him or her-self — Vygotsky's (1978) notion of the Zone of Proximal Development. Whole language teachers understand that there is a distance between what learners can accomplish on their own and what they can reach through the help of a teacher and others. This distance is what Vygotsky called the zone of Proximal Development. In creating a classroom environment the whole language teacher plans for cooperative/collaborative learning links from children to children and from children to teacher.

The Teacher is Focused on Strategies as Opposed to Basic Skills

The whole language teacher rec-ognizes the importance of teaching basic skills when needed, but the focus of attention is on the degree to which children are mastering strate-gies in a classroom that is process oriented, rather than product ori-ented in literacy.

Knows which Strategies Children Use

The teacher can engage the prin-cipal in conversation about the fact, for example, that Roberto is now making predictions when he reads, and that he has a strategy for reread-ing when he cannot confirm those predictions. The teacher can tell which children are learning to sample from the myriad of cues on the printed page to make predictions. He or she can offer evidence that chil-dren are integrating what they read with what they already know. Those children who have strategies for dealing with unfamiliar words can be identified.

Basic Skills are Taught in the Context of Authentic Literacy Experiences

Rather than making extensive use of workbooks or work sheets, the teacher will teach and reinforce knowledge of "basic skills" as chil-dren are making real use of language to communicate. For example, the teacher might point out and discuss certain text features while introducing an enlarged text story. Review of the "short /a/ sound" might be made as the title to a story is being discussed or as a child inquires about how to spell "attic." The teacher is well aware of the basic skills that have been learned and that need to be re-inforced, but those needs are met in real communicative contexts, not in artificial drill and practice lessons.

The Teacher is a Learner

Evidence should exist in both classroom practice and professional development activities that the teacher is a learner. The whole lan-guage teacher operates from a solid knowledge base that is soundly rooted in language development, linguistics, psycholinguistics, socio-linguistics, anthropology, and edu-cation. Whole language teachers are professionals who carefully critique their own work, collaborate with other professionals, and take respon-sibility for their success and failures. They expect to be granted profes-sional freedom to perform in the best ways they know, and they expect to be held accountable. All of this should be taken into account when evaluat-ing the work of a whole language teacher.

The Teacher Is Able to Engage in Conversation about Developmental Processes

Discussions of "grade level" have given way in whole language class-rooms to discussions of the uses of processes and strategies. Instead of looking at artificial grade boundaries placed over curriculum, teachers are looking at children coming to liter-acy in developmental ways.

Knows How Children Are Using the Cueing Systems

The teacher will be able to engage in conversation about children, for example, who in the fall were rely-ing primarily on graphophonic cues with little attention to creating meaning. The teacher will now be able to describe how those children are making increasingly more mis-cues that have semantic and syntac-tic acceptability. The whole language teacher is an observer of children. He or she will be able to describe ways in which children are making increasingly more sophisticated use of the cueing systems in reading.

Knows How Children Are Using the Writing Process

The teacher will be able to share writing portfolios with the principal and document ways in which each child's writing is advancing. It will be possible to document that, instead of grading writing pieces, the proc-ess of writing is evaluated. The edit-ing group or editing committee is the primary responder, and children write several ever-improving drafts.

The teacher can describe where each child is along a developmental continuum in the movement from emerging reader and writer to devel-oping reader and writer to maturing reader and writer.

You are confident that your group will offer good answers to the ques-tion of what the principal should see the teacher doing in a whole lan-guage classroom. You even feel a rush of excitement about how far your group can move evaluation of teachers if you combine this work with the work you did in the spring on what the principal should see children doing in whole language classrooms. You have a long way to go, but you've made a good start.

References

Goodman, K. (1986). *What's Whole in Whole Language?* Portsmouth, NH: Heinemann Educational Books.

Vygotsky, L. (1978). *Mind in Society*. M. Cole, V. J. Steiner, S. Scribner, and E. Souberman, editors. Cambridge, MA: Harvard Uni-versity Press.

ASSESSMENT

Reprinted from *Teachers Networking*, Volume 11, Number 1, by permission of Richard C. Owen Publishers, Inc., 135 Katonah Ave., Katonah, NY 10536.

———271

Lynn K. Rhodes
Sally Nathenson-Mejia

Anecdotal records: A powerful tool for ongoing literacy assessment

Rhodes and Nathenson-Mejia are faculty members in the Language, Literacy, and Culture program at the University of Colorado at Denver where they work with teachers on issues of classroom assessment.

A great deal of attention is being paid to the assessment of process in addition to product in reading and writing. Observing the process a student uses provides the teacher with a window or view on how students arrive at products (i.e., a piece of writing or an answer to a comprehension question). This allows the teacher to make good decisions about how she or he might assist during the process or restructure the process in order to best support more effective use of strategies and students' development as readers and writers. Anecdotal records can be written about products or can include information about both process and product. As process assessment, resulting from observation, anecdotal records can be particularly telling.

Observations of students in the process of everyday reading and writing allow teachers to see for themselves the reading and writing and problem-solving strategies students use and their responses to reading and writing. Genishi and Dyson (1984), Jaggar (1985), Pinnell (1985), Y. Goodman (1985), Galindo (1989), and others discuss the need to observe children while they are involved in language use. Goodman notes:

> Evaluation provides the most significant information if it occurs continuously and simultaneously with the experiences in which the learning is taking place.... Teachers who observe the development of language and knowledge in children in different settings become aware of important milestones in children's development that tests cannot reveal. (Goodman, 1985, p. 10)

When teachers have developed a firm knowledge base that they can rely on in observations of students' reading and writing, they usually prefer recording their observations in anecdotal form. This is because the open-ended nature of anecdotal records allows teachers to record the rich detail available in most observations of literacy processes and products. The open-ended nature of anecdotal record taking also allows teachers to determine what details are important to record given the situation in which the student is reading/writing, previous assessment data, and the instructional goals the teacher and student have established. In other words, what is focused on and recorded depends upon the teacher, the student, and the context, not on the predetermined items on a checklist.

Taken regularly, anecdotal notes become not only a vehicle for planning instruction and documenting progress, but also a story about an individual. The definition of an anecdote is "a short narrative (or story) concerning a particular incident or event of an interesting or amusing nature" (*The Random House Dictionary of the English Language*, 1966). A story is "a way of knowing and remembering information—a shape or pattern into which information can be arranged.... [Story] restructures experiences for the purpose of 'saving' them" (Livo, 1986, p. 5). Anecdotes about events in the reading/writing life of a student tell an ongoing story about how that child responds to the classroom's literacy environment and instruction. Since stories are how we make sense of much of our world, anecdotal records can be a vehicle for helping us make sense of what students do as readers and writers. In addition, teachers find that telling the story accumulated in anecdotal records is a natural and easy way to impart information about students' literacy progress to parents and others who care for the children.

In short, anecdotal records are widely acknowledged as being a powerful classroom tool for ongoing literacy assessment (Bird, 1989; Cartwright & Cartwright, 1974; Morrissey, 1989; Thorndike & Hagen, 1977). In this article we will provide information about techniques for collecting and analyzing anecdotal records. In addition, we will review uses of anecdotal records including planning for instruction, informing parents and students, and generating new assessment questions.

Techniques for writing anecdotal records

Reflecting about techniques for writing anecdotal records can positively affect both the content of the records as well as the ease with which they are recorded. Thorndike and Hagen (1977) suggest guidelines for the content of anecdotal records that teachers may find helpful:

1. Describe a specific event or product.
2. Report rather than evaluate or interpret.
3. Relate the material to other facts that are known about the child.

We have found these points particularly helpful if teachers feel that the content of their previous anecdotal records has not been useful to them. Below we have included an example of an anecdotal record for a first grader, Eleanor. Note how Eleanor's teacher uses detailed description to record how Eleanor is starting to understand sound/letter relationships but is still confused about word boundaries and sentences.

Eleanor
STRDAIPADENBSNO
(Yesterday I played in the snow)
STRDA = yesterday
I = I
PAD = played
EN = in
B = the (said "du" and thought she was writing "D")
SNO = snow
Showed her how to stretch her words out like a rubberband—doing it almost on own by SNO. E does have a fairly good grasp of sound/letter relationships. However, has a hard time isolating words and tracking words in sentences in her mind. That may hold up progress for awhile. Asked her—at end—what she did in writing today that she hadn't done in previous writing. She said, "I listened to sounds." Told her to do it in her writing again tomorrow.

Taken regularly, anecdotal notes become not only a vehicle for planning instruction and documenting progress, but also a story about an individual.

Instead of recording the descriptive detail found in Eleanor's anecdotal note, the teacher might have written, "Eleanor sounded out words in writing for the first time today and will continue to need lots of help to do so." A general conclusion such as this is not as useful to instructional planning or to documenting progress as the detailed description in the note written by Eleanor's teacher. However, we believe that Thorndike and Hagen's points should be treated as guidelines, not as strict rules. We find that it is sometimes helpful to evaluate or interpret what has been observed.

ASSESSMENT

Anecdotes about events in the reading/writing life of a student tell an ongoing story about how that child responds to the classroom's literacy environment and instruction. Since stories are how we make sense of much of our world, anecdotal records can be a vehicle for helping us make sense of what students do as readers and writers. In addition, teachers find that telling the story accumulated in anecdotal records is a natural and easy way to impart information about students' literacy progress to parents and others who care for the children.

For example, read the sample anecdotal record below written about Katie, a fourth grader.

Katie

I asked if I could read more of the poetry book she had written at home over the last two years. (She had read selected poems to her classmates earlier.) She showed me a poem she didn't want to read to the class "because they wouldn't understand." (It's quite serious and deep.) Poetry doesn't look like poetry though she reads it as poetry—could use a formatting lesson.

The teacher's comment, "could use a formatting lesson," in Katie's note provides useful evaluation and interpretation as long as it is supported by a description of the event or product itself. The comment "Poetry doesn't look like poetry though she reads it as poetry," is the description that supports the interpretive comment.

Observational guides can be valuable complements to anecdotal recording because they serve to remind teachers what might be observed. If teachers find an observation guide helpful, they may want to post for themselves a list of the kinds of observations that might be recorded anecdotally. The table illustrates such a guide resulting from teachers' brainstorming. The list is displayed in a place in the classroom where the teachers can easily consult it, especially when they feel they need to improve the content of their notes.

In addition to increasing the content value of anecdotal notes, teachers also are concerned about increasing the ease with which anecdotal notes can be recorded. In part, ease of recording emanates from the classroom environment the teacher has established. Classroom routines that encourage students to be increasingly independent and responsible as readers and writers enable teachers to more easily record anecdotal records than classrooms in which literacy tasks are more teacher directed. Once students are familiar with and secure about the structure and behaviors demanded in routines such as Sustained Silent Reading, Author's Circle, Literature Circles, Writers' Workshop, and Readers' Workshop, teachers can find the time to work with and record observations of individuals or groups.

In addition to encouraging student independence and responsibility in literacy situations, it is easier to write anecdotal notes as teachers discover recording techniques that fit their styles and busy classroom lives. It is useful to carry a clipboard to a variety of classroom settings, using such complementary recording tools as sticky notes to transfer information to a notebook sectioned off by students' names. Teachers can take notes on a prearranged list of children each day, labeling sticky notes with the date and the names of students to be observed. This technique makes it possible to take notes on every child a minimum of once a week in each curricular area in which notes are taken. Students can keep records too. Following a conference, the teacher might ask the student to record a summary statement of what they worked on together, what the student learned, or what the student still had questions about or wanted help with. Students can use sticky notes too so that their notes may be placed in the notebook along with the teacher's notes.

Teachers can take notes on groups as well as on individuals. For example, in working with a group of Chapter 1 students, one teacher noted that all five students were having difficulty putting the information they were gathering from books into their own words as they took notes. Instead of writing the same information five times, she wrote it once and put the note in a spot in her notebook reserved for notes about the group. When a note is taken in a group, but applies only to selected students in the group, the note can be photocopied for the file of each student to whom it applies.

Analyzing anecdotal records

Good techniques for recording anecdotal notes must be matched with good techniques for analyzing those notes if the potential for anecdotal records is to be realized. Effective analysis techniques include making inferences from the notes, looking for developmental trends or patterns within individuals and across children, identifying both strengths and weaknesses in learning and teaching, and making time for analysis.

Making inferences. Teachers continually make inferences about students' reading and writing on the basis of observations. Looking back at the sample anecdotal record on Eleanor, you can see that Eleanor's teacher made one of her inferences explicit: "E does have a fairly good grasp of sound/letter relationships." Because the teacher observed that Eleanor was able to consistently produce letters that matched the sounds she heard, she was able to infer that Eleanor had developed knowledge of sound/letter relationships.

Katie's teacher doesn't explicitly infer anything in the first anecdotal record but it is

---

Teacher-generated observation guide

- functions served in reading/writing
- engagement in reading/writing
- what appears to impact engagement in reading/writing
- what aspects of text student attends to
- interactions with others over reading/writing
- interactions with materials
- insightful or interesting things students say
- hypotheses students are trying out in reading/writing
- misconceptions students have
- miscues students make while reading
- changes students make in writing
- how students use text before, during, and after reading
- how a lesson affects students' reading/writing
- comparisons between what students say and what they do
- plans students make and whether/how plans are amended
- how, where, and with whom students work
- what students are interested in
- what students say they want to work on in their reading/writing
- what students say about reading/writing done outside of school
- how students generate and solve problems in reading/writing
- ideas for reading/writing lessons and materials
- how students "symbol weave" (use multiple symbolic forms)
- how students theorize or talk about reading/writing
- how one reading/writing event relates to another
- how students use a variety of resources in reading/writing

possible for us to hypothesize that Katie may think she is different from many of her classmates with regard to what she thinks and writes. An analysis of other anecdotal records on Katie may lead the teacher to uncover a pattern in Katie's responses that confirms her hypothesis.

Identifying patterns. Patterns of behavior can be uncovered for individuals and groups by reading and rereading anecdotal records looking for similarities and differences. For example, the following two notes were taken during a reading period in a second-grade classroom in which the majority of the students elect to read in pairs or small groups. What pattern of behavior do you see?

> Brooke & Larry reading a Nate the Great story together—switching off at each paragraph. Brooke jumps in to correct Larry or give him a word at the slightest hesitation.

> Aaron & Shawn reading—switching off after every 2 pgs. Shawn loves the story—keeps telling Aaron the next part will be funny & chuckling as he reads aloud. Shawn is the leader in this situation. He interrupts with immediate help when Aaron hesitates with a word.

In recording and reviewing these notes, the teacher noticed that she had observed the same problem in both pairs of readers: one reader would take over the responsibility for working out words from the other reader. Since she had notes on only two pairs of students, however, the teacher interviewed the class the next day, focusing on what they did to help classmates who encountered difficult words to find out whether the pattern she had uncovered in these two situations was a more general problem. Differing patterns in language use, both oral and written, can be seen through regular anecdotal record keeping.

To illustrate with another example, a second-grade teacher, one of our practicum students, was concerned about Raul, who was new to the United States. She felt he was gaining more control over written and oral English, but she had nothing to document his progress. Moreover, she did not want to push him too hard if he wasn't ready, or cause him to lag behind. The following are excerpts from anecdotal records Sally took as the practicum supervisor while observing Raul working with his peers, none of whom spoke his native Spanish. These notes demonstrate not only his interaction with print, but also his use of oral language.

> The boys begin reading through the questions. Raul looks at the book and says, "Que es esto?" (What is this?). No one answers him.

> They are sitting next to a chart that has all their names on it. They proceed to copy each others' names from the chart. Raul says to the group, "You can get my name from the chart."

> T [the teacher] comes over to see what they are doing. She asks which question they are on. Raul replies, "Where do they live? Water." T reminds them to write the answer in the appropriate square.

Using these and other notes, the teacher was able to see patterns in Raul's use of language on two levels, interacting with print, and interacting with peers. Getting no response when he initiated interaction in Spanish, Raul proceeded to use English to read from the chart, read from the book, speak to his classmates, and respond to his teacher. Together the teacher and Sally were able to plan for how his use of English could continue to be encouraged in context-laden situations without worrying about pushing him too fast.

Identifying strengths and weaknesses. Anecdotal records can be analyzed for both strengths and weaknesses in students' reading and writing. Katie's anecdotal record, which we discussed already, reveals that she writes poetry for herself outside of school and that she has a sense of audience. These are strengths. The record also reveals an area in which Katie can grow—formatting the poetry she writes. A look back at Eleanor's note also reveals strengths and weaknesses. For example, the teacher discovered that Eleanor has graphophonic knowledge not previously revealed in her writing and that she could verbalize what she learned during the conference with the teacher. The teacher also discovered that Eleanor had previously been using random strings of letters in her writing because she had such difficulty tracking words in sentences in her mind.

Finding time for analysis. Finally, just as it is important to find time to *record* anecdotal records, it is important to find time to *analyze* anecdotal records. Some analysis occurs concurrently with recording anecdotal notes and is recorded along with a description of the event that was observed. However, other analysis follows the recording of notes. We recommend that teachers try two things to make time for such analysis. First, use the start of each instructional planning period for an analysis of anecdotal records for individuals and groups. This will serve to focus planning time so that it may be used more efficiently. Second, if teachers meet on a regular basis with other teachers, analyzing anecdotal records can be a fruitful part of the meeting. For example, if a classroom teacher and Chapter 1 teacher both take anecdotal records on the same child, they can analyze both sets of notes together by comparing individual notes and looking for shared patterns and trends. If a group of teachers from the same grade level meets regularly, an analysis of one another's notes may uncover a great deal to talk about, including how best to adapt teaching to students' needs.

Uses of anecdotal records

Analysis of anecdotal records allows teachers to find patterns of success and difficulty for both individuals and groups of students. Students who have a need for particular information or for particular kinds of reading and writing opportunities can be grouped together and provided with the information or opportunities meeting their needs. In addition to instructional planning, the records also can be used to inform students and parents about progress and the value of various instructional and learning contexts. Finally, anecdotal records can help teachers generate new assessment questions.

Instructional planning. To extend what Genishi and Dyson say about oral language to written language (1984), anecdotal records on children's social behaviors and responses to written language can help teachers plan stimulating situations for the reluctant as well as the enthusiastic reader/writer. Using the set of anecdotal notes taken in the second-grade classroom during buddy reading discussed previously, we will show how the earlier analysis we provided can lead naturally to an instructional plan.

To review, the teacher noted that students in the buddy reading activity were taking reading responsibility away from their classmates when they hesitated or showed any sign of difficulty with reading words. When she interviewed the class the next day to glean more information about why this happened, she found that few students knew any options for helping partners with difficult words except to tell them the words. These assessment data helped the teacher plan lessons to demonstrate

how to help readers retain responsibility for figuring out difficult words. For example, she talked to the children about the strategies she used with them—providing plenty of wait time, suggesting that they read on, suggesting that they reread, and so on. Then she demonstrated each of these strategies with a child and made a list of the strategies for the children to refer to. Finally, she ended the next several reading sessions early so that the children could share with her and each other the strategies they used to successfully figure out their own words and to assist peers in figuring out words they didn't know. The children also shared problems they encountered and talked about how to solve them.

Analysis of anecdotal records allows teachers to find patterns of success and difficulty for both individuals and groups of students.

During the week the class focused on improving their strategies, the teacher observed pairs as they read, provided individual coaching for some, recorded more anecdotal notes, and used the notes to couch her lessons in detailed examples. In short, though the original anecdotal records and class interview were the basis of her first lesson, the anecdotal notes taken *after* the lessons began became equally important in planning ongoing instruction to further develop the students' strategies and understanding.

Informing. In addition to using anecdotal records for planning ongoing instruction, teachers also may use them to periodically inform others, including the students themselves, about students' strengths, weaknesses, and progress. Reviewing anecdotal records with students helps them see the growth they have made as readers and writers, and helps them gain a sense of progress over time and learn to pinpoint where improvements need to be made. To illustrate, one Chapter 1 teacher who involved students in generating instructional goals claimed that the process of writing anecdotal records affected the students' attention to the goals they had set: "The children seem to get more focused faster since I started carrying a clipboard and taking notes. It seems to remind them about the goals they decided to work on."

Anecdotal records also can help teachers create support systems for students outside the classroom. Report cards, parent conferences, and staffings are all situations in which instructional planning can take place on the basis of the teacher's analysis of anecdotal records. Specific examples pulled from anecdotal records help parents or other school personnel see the child in the same way as the teacher who has collected the anecdotal records. They can augment the home or test information provided by others and provide clues about what contexts are and are not supportive of the child's learning in school.

Generating new questions. Analyzing anecdotal records and using them to plan instruction encourages teachers to generate new questions that lead full circle to further assessment of students and of teaching itself. One teacher commented, "As I review kids' notes, sometimes even as I write them, I realize what else I need to find out." Bird (1989) commented that anecdotal records "not only guide [a teacher] in her instructional decision making but also provide her with a frequent opportunity for self-evaluation, enabling her to assess her role as a teacher" (p. 21).

We agree, and find that the use of anecdotal records to inform instruction helps teachers become more aware of how their instruction is interpreted by students. Teachers are able to see how they can influence students' interactions with each other as well as with books and other materials through specific instructional practices. To illustrate, below are some assessment questions generated by the teacher who recorded the anecdotal notes on pairs of students who were reading together in her classroom:

• What effect will the planned lessons have on students' interactions over words during reading?

• What other interactions do students have with each other over *ideas* in the story when they read together? (Her notes about Shawn led her to wonder this.)

• Do different pairings during reading make a difference in how readers interact with each other? What kinds of pairings are optimal?

• In what other situations is Shawn a leader? What can be done to further encourage that side of him?

The teacher has come full circle. Her original anecdotal notes were analyzed and used to plan instruction. But the notes also led to more focused assessment of individuals as well as assessment of a wider range of students and incidents. Her analysis and instructional planning led her to consider new assessment questions, questions not only about the students' reading but also about the effect of her teaching on their reading. For this teacher and for others who have realized the potential of anecdotal records, these "stories" are the basis from which they assess both their students' learning and their own teaching.

Conclusion

Anecdotal records are a powerful tool for collecting information on an ongoing basis during reading and writing and for evaluating the products of instruction. Keeping anecdotal records on a regular basis can enhance a teacher's classroom observation skills. Teachers report that they see and hear with more clarity when using anecdotal records, by focusing more intensively on how children say things and how they interact with each other.

Anecdotal records are advantageous not only for planning instruction but for keeping others informed of children's progress in reading and writing and for focusing future assessment. When teachers discover the value of anecdotal records and figure out techniques to embed them in classroom literacy events and planning, anecdotal record keeping becomes a natural and important part of teaching and learning.

References

Bird, L.B. (1989). The art of teaching: Evaluation and revision. In K. Goodman, Y. Goodman, & W. Hood (Eds.), *The whole language evaluation book* (pp. 15-24). Portsmouth, NH: Heinemann.

Cartwright, C.A., & Cartwright, G.P. (1974). *Developing observational skills*. New York: McGraw-Hill.

Galindo, R. (1989). "Así no se pone, Sí" (That's not how you write, "sí"). In K. Goodman, Y. Goodman, & W. Hood (Eds.), *The whole language evaluation book* (pp. 15-24). Portsmouth, NH: Heinemann.

Genishi, C., & Dyson, A.H. (1984). *Language assessment in the early years*. Norwood, NJ: Ablex.

Goodman, Y. (1985). Kidwatching. In A. Jaggar & M.T. Smith-Burke (Eds.), *Observing the language learner*. Newark, DE: International Reading Association.

Jaggar, A. (1985). On observing the language learner: Introduction and overview. In A. Jaggar & M.T. Smith-Burke (Eds.), *Observing the language learner* (pp. 1-7). Newark, DE: International Reading Association.

Livo, N. (1986). *Storytelling: Process and practice.* Littleton, CO: Libraries Unlimited.

Morrissey, M. (1989). When "shut up" is a sign of growth. In K. Goodman, Y. Goodman, & W. Hood (Eds.), *The whole language evaluation book* (pp. 85-97). Portsmouth, NH: Heinemann.

Pinnell, G.S. (1985). Ways to look at the functions of children's language. In A. Jaggar & M.T. Smith-Burke (Eds.), *Observing the language learner* (pp. 57-72). Newark, DE: International Reading Association.

The Random House Dictionary of the English Language. (1966). New York: Random House.

Thorndike, R.L., & Hagen, E.P. (1977). *Measurement and evaluation in psychology and education* (4th ed.). New York: John Wiley and Sons.

Reprinted with permision of Lynn K. Rhodes and the International Reading Association.

Voices

*W*hole language assumes that learning is a process of outgrowing our present selves. Learners can't do that by answering other people's questions; they can only do that by asking their own. It is this notion of learning as a question-asking process which makes the difference between educative and miseducative experiences (Dewey, 1938). Educative experiences propel learning forward and outward; miseducative experiences keep learning at rest.

Standardized testing, however, is based on a behavioral model of learning because it sees literacy and literacy learning in terms of convention and control, not purpose, function, and self-selection. It assumes that a one-to-one correspondence exists between teaching and learning; that is, it assumes that what gets taught is what gets learned. Standardized testing seeks answers, not questions, from students. It privileges its own questions over those that individuals can generate themselves.

William P. Bintz and *Jerome Harste*
Assessment and Evaluation in Whole Language Programs, edited by Bill Harp

ASSESSMENT

PORTFOLIO ASSESSMENT

By Susan Black

*If your school is considering portfolio assessment as an
alternative to traditional tests, take note: The new approach
has problems of its own*

ALONG WITH BOOK BAGS AND LUNCH BOXES, many students now tote something new to school—portfolios of their work. The use of portfolios is becoming increasingly popular in U.S. schools as teachers look for alternatives to traditional tests to measure student progress. But so new is the portfolio concept that there isn't yet much research to guide educators in setting up new systems. And that should signal a go-slow approach.

In fact, one recent research report from the RAND Corp., evaluating Vermont's portfolio assessment program, points to some serious problems with portfolios that should serve, according to report author Daniel Koretz, as a "warning call for people to be a little more cautious."

Portfolios appeal to educators for good reason, though. Researchers have long noted that traditional tests, standardized or otherwise, have clear limitations. According to Joan L. Herman and S. Golan, for example, the content of the tests too often determines what is taught. These researchers (along with many others) find that tests "narrow the curriculum" to basic skills rather than higher-order thinking skills. Another researcher, Lorrie Shepard, reports that even when students do well on tests (often because teachers "teach to the test"), it doesn't mean they've learned anything valuable. Most likely, Shepard says, what they've learned is to take tests well.

Many teachers, for their part, maintain there's little match between what they teach and what tests measure. Teachers who stretch children's minds beyond simple memorization and who emphasize group problem solving and cooperative learning protest that stan-

Susan Black is an education consultant who lives in Penn Yan, N.Y.

dardized tests don't reflect their students' real knowledge and abilities.

Portfolios are one answer in the search for alternative ways to assess students' performance. Portfolios are supposed to represent what students know—to show, over time and in a variety of ways, the depth, breadth, and development of student's abilities, according to researchers Lorraine Valdez Pierce and J. Michael O'Malley.

But as any teacher who's tried portfolios will attest, deciding to use them is the easy part; it's much harder to ensure portfolios accurately record and measure student performance. Some state education departments and research labs do offer workshops and booklets on portfolio assessment. But teachers usually find it's best to experiment and develop their own strategies to fit their subject areas and their classrooms. The work of Ohio State University researcher Robert Tierney and his public school teacher colleagues encourages teachers along those lines.

But even under supportive circumstances, the change from traditional testing to portfolios isn't always easy. Judith Arter, a researcher with the Northwest Regional Educational Laboratory, says few teachers who are excited about the possibilities of using portfolios have worked out exactly what they mean by portfolios or how they should be used. And, says Arter, most teachers haven't anticipated or addressed the fallout issues that can accompany portfolio assessments.

Using portfolios without a clear plan can lead to misunderstandings with parents, administrators, and students. Teachers might also find some tasks bewildering, such as setting acceptable standards for student work, coordinating assessments with grading requirements, and storing archives. If teachers feel overwhelmed with the planning details, they might forsake their good intentions. And if that happens, student portfolios might end up in the circular file.

The Vermont experience

In one of the best known portfolio programs, Vermont teachers helped the state department of education design a statewide system of portfolio assessment as one way of evaluating the results of a new writing program. The portfolios are now used in grades four and eight, with grade 11 to be added soon. A typical Vermont fourth-grader's portfolio contains these pieces: (1) a table of contents listing the pieces the student has selected; (2) the best piece of writing as chosen by the student; (3) a letter—written by the student to the teacher and other reviewers—about the best piece, explaining why the student chose it and the process used to produce the final draft; (4) a poem, short story, play, or personal narrative; (5) a personal response to an event, program, or item of interest; and (6) a prose piece from any subject area other than English or language arts.

Vermont, which also uses portfolios to evaluate students' math progress, is a pioneer in implementing the approach, beginning in 1988. But the state is also a pioneer in coming face-to-face with the problems associated with portfolios. The evaluation by the RAND Corp., released in December, showed rater reliability—that is, the odds that two different teachers would rate a portfolio the same way—to be very low. The recommendations put forth in the report include improving training for teachers in how to score portfolios accurately and making changes in the scoring system itself, which the report suggests might be too complex. The report's author, Daniel Koretz, says Vermont is actively looking at instituting some of the changes and that RAND will continue its evaluation.

Koretz, a resident scholar at RAND, says those who begin using portfolios often want to accomplish two things: Improve what goes on in the classroom, and find a good assessment tool. But, he says, those two goals can be at odds with each other. Improving what goes on in the classroom often means broadly training every teacher in rating student work. Assessing students accurately, on the other hand, could well require training only a small number of teachers at a time, but training them carefully and thoroughly.

The question that needs to be addressed, Koretz says, "is how to compromise between a powerful educational intervention and a decent assessment program."

Koretz also says it's important for school districts that opt for portfolio assessment to put in place a means for assessing the program. "People ought to have realistic expectations about how quickly [implementing a portfolio system] can be done and how it will come out the first time," he says. "A lot of people around the country have unrealistic expectations."

Making way for portfolios

Before moving toward the use of portfolios, other researchers agree, teachers must first think through their reasons for using this alternative assessment approach. Do they want to improve curriculum and teaching, or to assess student work—or perhaps both? (See the box on this page for a list of possible purposes for portfolios.)

Teachers also must define exactly what they mean by portfolios. Judith Arter defines a portfolio as "a purposeful collection of student work that exhibits to the student and others effort, progress, or achievement in a given area or areas." F. Leon Paulson and Pearl R. Paulson emphasize process over product in their definition: "A portfolio is a carefully crafted portrait of what someone knows or can do." Teachers might find someone else's definition suitable, or they might choose to write their own.

Then there are the nitty-gritty decisions. What should be included in a portfolio? Who should select the contents? Should a portfolio reflect only a student's best work, or should it represent a spectrum of accomplishments and efforts? Should bulky items (such as science

---

WHY USE PORTOLIOS?

Here are some reasons to use portfolios, as set down by English and language arts teachers in California. These reasons are excerpted from *Testing for Learning*, by Ruth Mitchell, and adapted from *Portfolio News*, published by Portfolio Assessment Clearinghouse, c/o San Dieguito Union High School District, Encinitas, Calif.

1. As a teaching tool
— to provide students ownership, motivation, a sense of accomplishment, and participation.
— to involve students in a process of self-evaluation
— to help students and teachers set goals
— to build in time for reflection about students' accomplishments
— to aid in parent conferences

2. Professional development of teachers
— to study curriculum and effective teaching practices
— to allow for better staff communication
— to reduce the paper load
— to identify school strengths and needs for improvement
— to build a sequence in writing instruction

3. Assessment
— to serve as an alternative to standardized testing
— to serve as a college application and high school placement vehicle
— to replace competency exams
— to serve as a grade or end-of-year culminating activity
— to provide program evaluation
— to supplement or substitute for state assessment tests

4. Research
— to examine growth over time and progress in students' writing
— to look at the revision process.

SELECTED REFERENCES

Alexander, L., et. al. "The Nation's Report Card: Improving the Assessment of Student Achievement." Cambridge, Mass.: National Academy of Education, 1987.

Althouse, S.M. "A Pilot Project Using Portfolios to Document Progress in the School Program." Paper presented at the annual meeting of the International Reading Association, May 1991.

Arter, J. "Curriculum-Referenced Test Development Workshop Theory: Using Portfolios in Instruction and Assessment." Portland, Ore.: Northwest Regional Educational Laboratory Nov. 1990. ERIC Document No. ED 335 364.

Ballard, L. "Portfolios and Self-Assessment." *English Journal*, Feb. 1992, 81, 46-48.

Cooper, W. and Brown, B.J. "Using Portfolios to Empower Student Writers." *English Journal*, Feb. 1992, 81, 40-45.

Herbert, E.A. "Portfolios Invite Reflection — from Students and Staff." *Educational Leadership*, May 1992, 58-61.

Herman, J.L. "What Research Tells Us About Good Assessment." *Educational Leadership,* May 1992, 74-78.

Herter, R.J. "Writing Portfolios: Alternatives to Testing." *English Journal,* Jan. 1991, 90-91.

Hetterscheidt, J., et. al. "Using the Computer as a Reading Portfolio." *Educational Leadership,* May 1992, 73.

Knight, P. "How I Use Portfolios in Mathematics." *Educational Leadership,* May 1992, 71-72.

Koretz, D., et al. *The Reliability of Scores from the 1992 Vermont Portfolio Assessment Program, Interim Report.* Washington, D.C.: RAND Institute on Education and Training, Dec. 1992.

Mitchell, R. *Testing for Learning.* New York: The Free Press (Macmillan, Inc.), 1992.

New York State United Teachers. "Multiple Choices: Reforming Student Testing in New York State. A Report of the NYSUT Task Force on Student Assessment." Jan. 1991.

Paulson, F.L., and Paulson, P.R. "The Ins and Outs of Using Portfolios to Assess Performance (Revised)." Expanded paper presented at the joint annual meeting of the National Council of Measurement in Education, April 1991.

Paulson, F.L., and Paulson, P.R. "The Making of a Portfolio." Prepublication Draft, Feb. 1991, 1-11.

Shepard, L. "Will National Tests Improve Student Learning?" *Phi Delta Kappan,* Nov. 1991, 232-238.

Tierney, R.J., Carter, M.A., and Desai, L.E. *Portfolio Assessment in the Reading-Writing Classroom.* Norwood, Mass.: Christopher-Gordon Publishers, Inc., 1991.

Valencia, S.W. "Alternative Assessment: Separating the Wheat from the Chaff." *The Reading Teacher,* 1990. 43, 60-61.

Wiggins, G. "The Case for Authentic Assessment." ERIC Clearinghouse on Tests, Measurement, and Evaluation, Dec. 1990.

Yunginger-Gehman, J. "A Pilot Project for Portfolio Assessment in a Chapter 1 Program." Paper presented at the Annual Meeting of the International Reading Association, May 1991.

projects) be considered? What should the school keep for its permanent records? How should teachers communicate students' achievement to parents? How should teachers evaluate portfolios? What other kinds of assessment should be used, if any?

Answers to some of these questions can be found in research. Judith Arter notes that portfolio contents should be chosen according to their purpose. She finds that, in general, teachers either require certain items from each student or, with students, choose samples of work that reflect growth and development in a specific subject area.

F. Leon Paulson and Pearl R. Paulson find portfolios should be more than just collections of students' work. Portfolios, they say, ought to include students' narratives about how they produced the contents and about what they learned. Students' written reflections about their learning might be among the most valuable pieces in the portfolios, these researchers say.

The Paulsons maintain that "students own their portfolios," so they—not teachers—should create their collections and review their selections. They suggest that portfolios should tell a student's story, and anything that helps tell that story could be included—classroom assignments, finished or rough drafts, work students develop specifically for the portfolio to show their interests and abilities, self-reflections, and observations and comments by teachers or parents.

In her report, Sharon Althouse provides diagrams to guide teachers, students, and parents as they choose items for students' reading and writing portfolios. (Althouse's study found that teachers and students most often selected *writing* samples for portfolios.)

California math teacher Pam Knight encourages her algebra students to choose from their semester's worth of classwork and homework to construct well-balanced portfolios. Knight's students are likely to include long-term projects, daily notes, journal entries about difficult test problems, scale drawings, best and worst tests, and homework samples.

In some remedial programs, students design portfolios that align with their individual education plans. In Pennsylvania's Eastern Lancaster County School District, for example, teachers first identify two or three goals for each student in Chapter 1 reading and math. (Students may add goals of their own.) Portfolios are likely to include written compositions, records of books read, examples of drafts and revisions of written work, samples of math processes and problems, and original math story problems.

Teachers and researchers also report successful ventures using portfolios with high school science and social studies students. Missouri teachers use computer portfolios to capture their fifth-graders' reading progress. In Wyoming, elementary students use laser disk technology to record their verbal ability, physical accomplishments, artistic achievement, and self-assurance. Lorraine Valdez Pierce and J. Michael O'Malley describe how elementary and middle school students learning English as a second language use portfolios to show oral language and reading skills.

Other concerns

Time and grades are among the other issues to consider before going ahead with portfolios. Managing portfolios takes time, that precious classroom commodity. But, researchers report, teachers who change from traditional assessment to portfolio assessment are more likely to manage their time without frustration if they change teaching styles at the same time. Rather than continuously assigning and grading workbook lessons, teachers should prompt students to learn through writing and exchanging ideas. Teachers can more efficiently and effectively guide instruction through cooperative learning groups. And teachers should hold conferences with their students to reinforce and motivate their learning and, when necessary, to reteach prerequisite skills.

Then there's the sticky issue of grades. How can teachers assign unit grades or report card grades (usually required by the district office, and perhaps by the state education department) when they're assessing students' portfolios for effort, progress, and insight as well for as specific achievement? Some districts are experimenting with new kinds of report cards—using checklists and narratives, for example—that more closely reflect their new assessments.

It's imperative that teachers inform and educate students and parents about new grading systems. Even when they're pleased with their portfolios and their teachers' comments, some students demand familiar letter grades—especially when they're accustomed to earning A's and B's. Sometimes parents give portfolio assessment systems cool receptions because they don't understand the new evaluation reports. They might prefer their children's report cards to look just like the ones they used to bring home from school.

It's important to discuss a new portfolio assessment system with students and parents. In Sharon Althouse's Pennsylvania pilot project, students doubted their parents would understand the portfolios, even when teachers enclosed letters explaining the new assessment plan. And, Althouse reports, students often changed the contents of their portfolios when they knew their parents would examine their selections. Though parents expressed appreciation and approval of the portfolio system, they provided skimpy answers or no answers at all to a short survey about the new method.

Finally, other considerations might arise. In high schools, students and parents might object to portfolio assessment on the grounds that college admissions offices require grades and class rankings. And at any grade level, serious questions remain about the objectivity of portfolio assessment. Any program of portfolio assessment must address the possibility that assessments might be biased on the basis of race, sex, or cultural orientation or overly generous so as to bolster students' self-esteem.

A successful start

If your school or school district is considering using portfolio assessments, what can you do to help the new approach succeed? You can begin by setting agendas for staff planning and staff development. The Northwest Regional Educational Laboratory (NWREL) proposes tackling these topics: purpose, curriculum and instruction, content, assessment, management and logistics, and staff development. Specific questions to discuss, NWREL researchers say, include: What are the purposes for using portfolios? How will portfolios reflect the school's curriculum? How must instruction change to support portfolio assessments? What is acceptable in a student portfolio? Who owns the portfolio, and who chooses the contents? What other types of student assessment will the school use? How will portfolio assessments be coordinated among grade levels? How will assessments be communicated to parents?

You need to invest time and effort helping teachers *before* they begin using portfolio assessments, but you also need to offer support to teachers who might encounter problems *after* they've started up their new system. Peer coaching—pairing teachers who are reluctant or uneasy about using student portfolios with teachers who easily are incorporating the new method in their classrooms—might help teachers who want to throw in the towel and return to traditional testing alone. Workshops at which teachers examine models and then work out their own plans can also help get portfolio assessments off to a smooth start.

It's a long and often rocky road to institutionalize any innovation in education. Even when teachers are eager to accept a new plan, you can bet the process will be one of fits and starts. When it comes to developing portfolio assessments, you'll need to encourage teachers not to give up when they face difficult issues. But you'll also have to remind them—and yourself—to go slow with this new approach to assessment. ▣

> *You need to invest time and effort helping teachers before they begin using portfolio assessments, but you also need to offer support to teachers who might encounter problems after they've started up their new system*

ASSESSMENT

READING: READINESS LEVEL

Vocabulary:
Reads by sight:
  Own name in print
  A personal sight vocabulary (high interest)
  20 words from the basic sight vocabulary

Word Meaning:
Understands **beginning** and **end** in relation to:
  print
  speech
When listening, predicts:
  outcome
  vocabulary, word, rhyme

Comprehension:
Knows that:
  reading makes sense
  print represents the sounds of the language
Has a reading attitude.
  Listens well to stories.
  Has a desire to read:
    Looks at books on his/her own
  Is interested in words and symbols.

Auditory:
Identifies:
  beginning sounds
  ending sounds
  rhymes
Discriminates the major consonant sounds.

Visual:
Has correct directional habits:
  looks at books from front to back
  looks at books from left page to right page
  begins left top
  proceeds left to right
  proceeds top to bottom
Identifies:
  word
  letter

Auditory/Visual:
Matches spoken and printed words when some
  one reads
Knows most letter names:
  upper case
  lower case

Oral Reading:
Attacks words using context and initial letter
  checked by sense

WRITING: READINESS

Fluency:
Writes independently
Has confidence as a writer

Composition:
Expresses thoughts in writing
Writes telling sentences
Talks about what he/she has written
Revises one or more words during conferences

Mechanics:
Capitalizes:
  First name and initial of last name
  I

Handwriting
Tries to make recognizable letters

Spelling:
Own first name
Uses major consonants: b, d, j, k, l, m, n, p, s, t, z
  for the beginnings of words

SPEAKING

Expresses his/her needs

Asks questions

Responds appropriately to questions

Maintains the subject line in conversation

Shares experiences in a group

Uses complete sentences

Uses specific vocabulary for objects

  (book, puzzle, scissors)

EVALUATION

EVALUATION SHOULD:

• be ongoing and integrated, built into the daily process

• give a child positive feedback

• make self-evaluation valuable; a child knows best about him/ or herself

• represent individual growth

• emphasize change, progress, growth

• encourage independence in the learner and the teacher

• be innovative, creative, dynamic

• be able to be modified and changed according to the individual or situation

• be consistent with language development: reading for meaning, writing for communication

• be holistic, not fragment language

• be "user" friendly

• be natural, in context

• not be judgmental

• be useful

• value what people know and make a bridge between what they know and don't know

Ways to evaluate — Things to observe

Levels box
Sight words
Observe during S.S.R., work time

Things to observe

Do they:

look at pictures or print?

choose familiar or unfamiliar?

choose to read during free time?

follow written directions?

finish what they start?

make good or bad choices, books or activities?

share books with others?

look for same title, author, subject, illustrator?

get books from the library?

enjoy reading?

use multiple strategies to figure out words?

proofread their work?

read aloud with expression?

respond in sharing groups?

interact with books?

self-initiate projects?

read outside of school?

Are they:

overwhelmed by print? Still look at pictures?

independent?

peer teachers?

critical thinkers?

Sandy Cook

ASSESSING PROGRESS

FIRST GRADE

Midyear Expectations

Reading:

Can see him/herself as a reader
Reads 50 sight words
Sustains reading for 15 minutes
Fluent at third pre-primer
Uses picture and beginning sound cues
Can focus and participate in shared reading and discussion for 10 minutes
Can generally retell a story
Can draw a picture about a book read

Writing:

Writes for 15-20 minutes at a sitting
Gaining confidence as a writer
Writes two related thoughts
Can read back what he/she has written during the process
Uses inventive spelling
Has concept of word; leaves spaces between words
Shares writing willingly

Third Term Expectations

Reading:

Knows 75 sight words
Reads 15-20 minutes on his/her own
Uses picture cues, beginning and ending sounds
Can skip unknown words and go on
Can focus and participate in shared reading and discussion for 15 minutes
Can retell a story with details
Can write a sentence about what he/she has read

Writing:

Writes for 20-30 words at a sitting
Writes three or four sentences that are related
Reads what he/she has written after a period of time
Uses inventive spelling, beginning and ending sounds and some sight words
Begins to use punctuation
Writes 15-20 minutes at a sitting
Begins to revise after teacher conference

End of Year Expectations

Reading:

Fluent at 1.9 level test
Knows 100 sight words
Sustains 20 minutes reading on his/her own
Uses picture; beginning and ending sound cues
Can skip unkown word and go on, can reread for meaning
Realizes that print constructs meaning
Can focus and participate in shared reading and discussion for 20-25 minutes
Can retell a story with details
Can write about his/her reading

Writing:

Writes for 40 words at a sitting
Writes four or five sentences
Can read back own writing
Uses inventive spelling, beginning and ending sounds, and some sight words
Begins to use capital letters
Begins to use classroom units as ideas for writing
Begins to use punctuation
Can revise a few words after a teacher conference

SECOND GRADE

	First Term			Third Term	
	Sept.	Oct.	Nov.	Sept.	March
Writing Samples (words written in ½ hr.)	_____	_____	_____	_____	_____
Average for class	_____	_____	_____	_____	_____
Percentage of words correctly spelled in writing samples.	_____	_____	_____	_____	_____
Spelling test — approximate grade equivalents (Morrison McCall)	_____	_____	_____	_____	_____
Class Average on Morrison McCall	_____	_____	_____	_____	_____

First Term Profile

Social:
   takes turns and listens to others
   listens and focuses in group discussion
      (15-20 minutes)

Reading:
   knows about 125 sight words
   reads on own for 20 minutes
   uses picture clues plus beginning/ending sounds
   can skip unknown word and go back
   can retell a story read with some details
   can focus and participate in shared reading
   can write two or three sentences about a book s/he's read

Writing:
   writes 40-50 words daily
   can write four or five related sentences
   can read what s/he's written
   uses invented spelling with correct beg/ending
      and vowel sound
   is using capital at beginning for names and self;
      periods at end
   can write for 20-25 minutes
   beginning to add or delete words

Third Term Profile

Social:
   takes turns and listens to others
   listens and focuses in group discussions
      for 15-20 minutes

Reading:
   knows about 200 sight words
   reads on own for 20 minutes
   uses picture clues plus beginning/ending sounds
   can skip unknown word and go back
   can retell a story read s/he's read with some details
   can focus and participate in shared reading
   can write two/three sentences about a book
      s/he's read

Writing:
   writes 60-70 words daily
   can write four or five related sentences
   can read what s/he's written
   uses invented spelling with correct beg/ending
      and vowel sound
   is using capital at beginning of name and self;
      periods at end
   writes for 30-35 minutes
   begins to add/delete words for clearer menaing

Ann Lessard

Month of_____

Writing

fluency_____
composition_____
capitals_____
punctuation_____
handwriting_____
spelling_____

Child's name_____

Reading

sight words_____
word analysis_____
comprehension_____
verifies_____
draws conclusions_____
sequences_____
oral _____ silent _____

Month of_____

Writing

fluency_____
composition_____
capitals_____
punctuation_____
handwriting_____
spelling_____

Child's name_____

Reading

sight words_____
word analysis_____
comprehension_____
verifies_____
draws conclusions_____
sequences_____
oral _____ silent _____

Month of_____

Writing

fluency_____
composition_____
capitals_____
punctuation_____
handwriting_____
spelling_____

Child's name_____

Reading

sight words_____
word analysis_____
comprehension_____
verifies_____
draws conclusions_____
sequences_____
oral _____ silent _____

Month of_____

Writing

fluency_____
composition_____
capitals_____
punctuation_____
handwriting_____
spelling_____

Child's name_____

Reading

sight words_____
word analysis_____
comprehension_____
verifies_____
draws conclusions_____
sequences_____
oral _____ silent _____

Created by Ann Lessard

Developing Writing Fluency

Kindergarten → First Grade

Yes, I can ...	Dates checked			
Draw picture and tell about it.				
Draw picture and write random marks.				
Draw picture and write letters.				
Begin to leave spaces.				
Write the first letters in words.				
Write the first and last letters in words.				
Write some middle letters.				
Write some whole words.				
Use a period.				
Use capital letters correctly.				
Write sentences.				

Second Grade

Yes, I can ...	Dates checked			
Use capital letters at beginning.				
Put periods at end.				
Use a capital I for myself.				
Write two sentences that go together.				
Write three sentences the go together.				
Spell sight words correctly.				
Use spelling dictionary to correct words.				
Can change or add words to make meaning clearer.				
Can write four or more sentences that go together.				

ASSESSMENT

INDEPENDENT READING RECORDS AND EVALUATIONS

A. Children's Independent Reading Log

Date	Title	Author	Opinion (Easy — E; Medium — M; Hard — H)

B. Reading Journals (Following independent silent reading)

1. Journals for written summary of material read during s.r. (list date, title, author)

2. Journals of blank pages for non-readers who will summarize their book in picture form.

3. Journals for specific information requested by teacher.

   Examples: Who is the most important character in the book?
   What is the story about?
   How did the story end?
   How did you feel while reading the story?

C. Teacher's conference log (individual conferences take place during s.r. time)

Student	Date	Title	Author

1. Questions: ex.   Who are some of the characters?
   What is the story about?
   Where does it take place?
   What did you like best about the story?

2. Oral Reading by student: small passage chosen in advance. If non-reader, explanation of chosen picture in book.

3. Independent incidental instruction on any skill or concept that may be needed at that moment. (Ex. explanation of vocabulary word or specific skill within a word that child is struggling with)

D. Student vocabulary list. List of words with meaning and context which child would like to make his/her own.

E. Sharing Time

1. Group or whole class discussions and sharing of books.

2. Group activities, drama, projects, as follow-up to books.

3. Audience reading.

Jean Mann

Independent Reading Conference Records

Name: **Date:**
Title: **Author:**
BME

Characters:

Setting:

Main idea:

Ending:

Feelings:

Specific questions:

Liked/disliked:

Vocabulary:

Skills:

Strategies:

Conventions:

Oral reading:

General comments:

Writing Group Conference

Name: **Date:**

Topic:

Comments:

Questions:

Sample use of folder for record-keeping

Books_____(name)_____
has written

1. My cabin   9-16

2. My New House   10-5 (P.)

3. Louisiana   10-21

4. Thanksgiving dinner   11-16

Front Cover

Spelling/Vocabulary

too   Christmas

to   Louisiana

two   ocean

Back Cover

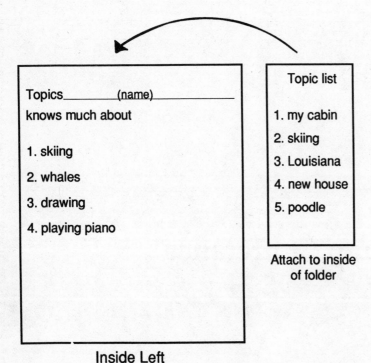

Topics_____(name)_____
knows much about

1. skiing
2. whales
3. drawing
4. playing piano

Inside Left

Topic list

1. my cabin
2. skiing
3. Louisiana
4. new house
5. poodle

Attach to inside
of folder

Things_____(name)_____
knows

capitals
periods
quotation marks
ai

Inside Right

Jean Mann

Writing —
Sample teacher's conference record

Child's name _____Kevin_____

Date	Title	Skills used correctly	Skills taught
1-19	"ski getaway"	Quotes Apostrophes on possessives Edited for spelling, checked circled words.	capitals for Title words work on paragraphs
1-25	"Future" (poem)	Rhyming words at ends of 2nd and 4th	stanzas

ASSESSMENT

Sample Record-keeping for Writing Conferences
— Status of Class —

week of____	Monday	Tuesday	Wednesday	Thursday	Friday
Andy	"White Tail Deer"		"The War"	c.c.⁺ "The War" good info spaces	"The War" P
Nathaniel	"The Swamp"	"The Swamp" e.c. "ed" [2 subjects]	"The Swamp" caps/periods P	"Abominable Snowman"	g.c. !
Lara	"Apple Bear In The Snow s.c. vowels aio	"Skiing"	"Gina Coming Over"		To be published
Julie	"Ice Cream" (Flavors)	"Colors" (Picture book)	"Hearts"	"Rainbows"	"Ice Cream" c.c.
Trevor	"The Cabin"		"The Cabin" s.c. silent "e" ai (main) quotes	Skiing	g.c.
Amanda	"Julie Going To My House" c.c.⁺ good content	"Everything In The World"			

concepts written in <u>black</u> are concepts taught during conference

concepts written in <u>blue</u> show that a child is using a concept previously taught, but inconsistently

concepts written in <u>red</u> are mastered and used consistently

Suggested Symbols:

cc	content conference	EV	evaluation conference
sc	skills conference	1D	first draft
ec	editing conference	2D	second draft
gc	group conference	P	publish

Jean Mann
(Adapted with permission from Paula Flemming)

Profiles

1. **Personal:** Surveys that ask questions about students' lives, their interests, hobbies, families, experiences, etc.
"Rapping," sharing to begin the day. Provides a chance to get to know one another. Gives teacher a chance to find out what motivates students and gives ideas for exciting curriculum.

2. **Reading:** Surveys that elicit information about attitudes and interests in reading. Listening to students read individually. Choose a short, comfortable but challenging passage for a student to read to you. Copy that passage on a sheet of paper so that you can read along with the child and take notes on strategies, body language, visual habits, etc.

3. **Writing:** Provide about 10 minutes and ask students to write about anything they want to. Tell them to include everything they know. Spend 5 or 10 minutes afterward with each child conferencing. With each student, make a list on the front of a writing folder all the things that the student has demonstrated he/she knows as a writer.

4. **Spelling:** Dictate two spelling lists (not tests) to the class. One could be a list of developmental words appropriate for the grade, the other a list of commonly used sight words for the grade. Take time to meet with each child and go over the lists. Ask students which they think they spelled correctly, which they aren't sure of, how else they could have spelled a word. Look for strategies and problem solving.

5. **Kid Watching:** Observe children as they work and play. Keep anecdotal records to remember important things you have seen. Look for learning styles, behavior, social interaction, development, etc.

Jean Mann

Language Learning

What do I believe an effective language learner does?

or

What do I believe a reader and writer can do?

Knowledge and skills children need to become effective language users:

1. Sense of audience when communicating

2. Control of conventions appropriate to language context (surface features)

3. Control of a range of registers / genres

4. Vocabulary acquisition and use appropriate to the context

5. Control of grammatical options

6. Confidence in using language in different contexts

7. Comprehension of what's been heard or read

Guidelines for Selecting Authentic Material

Material Should:

• reflect important themes and ideas

• be rooted in real-world experiences and have application to the world — both inside and outside of school

• be sensitive to the developmental progression of students

• allow students to engage in higher order thinking

We must also think differently about the nature of the content we use for assessment.

John Poeton

Evaluation

What do we value about literacy?

What should we focus on?

Evaluation does not only happen at the end; it starts at the beginning of process and then remains on-going throughout.

Whole language assessment travels primarily three basic avenues:
- collecting samples of student work
- using checklists to log skills and behaviors
- writing anecdotal and other records

Because it is **shared assessment,** the student is aware of his/her progress.

Whole language evaluation is:
- learner referenced (rather than norm-referenced or criterion-referenced)
- focused on what learners know (not on what they don't know)
- continuous, on-going and cumulative
- process oriented (but considers product)
- non-competitive
- generative (it teaches)
- involved with self-evaluation for the teacher and the child

Whole language evaluation:
- takes many forms
- must reflect the way children have been taught
- never violates the integrity of language (keeps the language whole)
- makes everyone involved

Whole language evaluation looks at development over time.

John Poeton

Cumulative Evaluation
of Literature Study Participation

Name _____

Book _____

	Always		Sometimes		Never
	A	B	C	D	E
Participated in discussion					
Completed reading on time					
Brought book to group					
Completed assignments					

Overall Grade _____

Comments:

Teacher's Signature _____

Student's Signature _____

Parent's Signature _____

Mastery of Narrative/Expository

Student Name _____

Narrative

Expository

Date	Observer	

PRESCHOOL

		tells a simple story
		listens to a story
		engages in dramatic play
		identifies who/what in a story

KINDERGARTEN/FIRST

		moral of story
		has concept of plot (beginning, middle, end)
		author's craft (as listener)
		describes setting
		has concept of setting
		has concept of character (major/minor)

SECOND/THIRD

		concept of theme
		author's craft (as reader — character motivation, reader response, purpose)
		compares/contrasts characters
		knows relationship of setting to plot
		visualizes setting
		analyzes and extends a theme
		recognizes complex plots
		uses cause and effect

FOURTH/FIFTH

		character dynamics/personification
		author's craft (as writer)
		reconstructs a setting
		episodic analysis (rising/falling action)

Expository

date	observer	
		takes part in large group investigation
		creates a picture that informs
		differentiates between fiction/non-fiction

		presents an informative piece
		uses a variety of sources
		uses conventions (table of contents, title page, bibliography)
		finds author's voice

		Understands appropriate resource and format
		organizes and interprets information
		understands forms of expository
		identifies author's purpose

Reprinted with permission of Mike Hagan

John Poeton

Reading Strategies

Date	observer	Name	self-assessed
		Reading is supposed to make sense. When it doesn't make sense any more I need to stop and find out why.	
		Think about what you already know about the topic. You probably know some of the things the author knows.	
		Try to guess what will happen next. Do this often while reading, and check your guesses now and then to see if they were right.	
		Skip a word if it's too hard. Read ahead to figure out what's happening. The whole story is more important than a few of the words.	
		Look at the pictures for information.	
		When something doesn't make sense, go back and read it again. Learn how to fix your own mistakes.	
		Reading is just like talking. Think about the way English works.	
		Try to read several words together sometimes, like "Once upon a time."	
		Sound it out. Think about what you know about letter names and sounds.	
		Read different things different ways. Sometimes readers skip through a piece, sometimes they read from the beginning. Use the table of contents.	
		Try to imagine what the character or the place looks like. Try to make a movie in your head.	

(A reading strategy is signed and dated when it is observed being used consistently. A strategy is self-assessed when a child is aware of using it.)

Reprinted with permission of Mike Hagan

John Poeton

Portfolios

The following list gives some perspective concerning the variety of tools that can be incorporated into a portfolio:

checklists	interviews
taped recordings	questionnaires
projects / photos	journal entries
reports	samples of work
chart records	planning / evaluation sheets
conference records	gummed labels / sticky notes
running records	skill logs
parent reports	computer logs

Evaluation encompasses more than just the student — if learning is not optimal, it could be the fault of the student, the teacher or the program. Sometimes a problem in one of these areas can promote problems in others.

Features of an Entire Portfolio

- Reveal the **power** of the reader and writer

- Show the **versatility** of the reader and the writer

- Reflect **effort** — revisions

- Use of **process** — include pieces at all stages of completion

- **Self-reflection** — students' perceptions about their own reading and writing

ASSESSMENT

Meaning-Based Evaluation

Portfolio evidence might include:

- self-assessment
- samples of student writing, in many subject areas:
  rough drafts, journals, reading logs, research reports
- lists of books read and pieces published
- checklists, strategies, skills, genres
- home surveys, parent conferences
- teacher observations, anecdotes, notes
- audiotape, videotape
- interviews, conferences with learner
- running records, miscue analysis
- scores, standardized test results, progress report forms

Portfolio evaluation should be:

ongoing	updated regularly
instructive	provide insights into instructional strategies, the responsibility of the teacher
manageable	easy to implement
informative	provide information on progress to student, parents, teachers, administrators
evolving	subject to revision, re-thinking
comprehensive	describe a range of attitudes, understandings, and behaviors
selective	based on evaluation priorities, regularly revised
collaborative	items are included during teacher/student conferences
articulated	provide useful information to successive teachers
individualized	based on goals set by the learner, with focus on self-evaluation
supportive	positive, based on what student can do rather than deficit model
consistent	reflective of the learning theory upon which the classroom environment is based

John Poeton

Evaluation
A Portfolio Approach

I. Reading Literacy

Awareness — checklist

Activity — Booklog

Analysis of strategies

PLUS

Comprehension

a. written
b. oral
c. illustrations
d. cloze

Expansion Activities

II. Writing and Spelling

Awareness — checklist

Activity — writing folder

Analysis of strategies

PLUS

Publishing projects

III. Self-evaluation

Kathryn L. Cloonan

ASSESSMENT

Whole Language Professional Books

Bibliography
Compiled by SDE Presenters

If you would like help locating any of the books, contact Crystal Springs Books, 1-800-321-0401.

Allen, JoBeth, and Mason, Jana, eds. *Risk Makers, Risk Takers, Risk Breakers.* Portsmouth, NH: Heinemann, 1989.

Alvermann, Donna et al. *Using Discussion to Promote Reading Comprehension.* Newark, DE: International Reading Association, 1989.

Andrasick, Kathleen. *Opening Texts.* Portsmouth, NH: Heinemann, 1990.

Atwell, Nancie. *In the Middle.* Portsmouth, NH: Heinemann, 1987.

_____. *Coming to Know: Writing to Learn in the Middle Grades.* Portsmouth, NH: Heinemann, 1990.

_____. *Workshop 1: Writing and Literature.* Portsmouth, NH: Heinemann, 1989.

_____. *Workshop 2: Beyond the Basal.* Portsmouth, NH: Heinemann, 1990.

_____. *Workshop 3: The Politics of Process.* Portsmouth, NH: Heinemann, 1991.

_____. *Side by Side: Essays on Teaching to Learn.* Portsmouth, NH: Heinemann, 1991.

Baghban, Marcia. *Our Daughter Learns to Read and Write.* Newark, DE: International Reading Association, 1985.

Barrett, F.L. *A Teacher's Guide to Shared Reading.* Toronto, Ont.: Scholastic TAB, 1982.

Barron, Marlene. *I Learn to Read and Write the Way I Learn to Talk.* Katonah, NY: Richard C. Owen Publishers, 1990.

Barton, Bob. *Tell Me Another.* Portsmouth, NH: Heinemann, 1986.

Baskwill, Jane. *Connections — A Child's Natural Learning Tool.* Toronto, Ont.: Scholastic TAB, 1990.

Baskwill, Jane, and Steven. *The Language Arts Sourcebook: Whole Language — Grades 5 and 6.* Toronto: Scholastic, 1991.

Baskwill, Jane, and Whitman, Paulette. *Moving On: Whole Language Sourcebook for Grades 3 and 4.* Toronto, Ont.: Scholastic TAB, 1988.

_____. *Whole Language Sourcebook — Grades K-2.* Toronto: Scholastic TAB, 1986.

_____. *A Guide to Classroom Publishing.* Toronto: Scholastic TAB, 1988.

Bayer, Ann Shee. *Collaborative-Apprenticeship Learning.* Katonah, NY: Richard C. Owen Publishers, 1990.

Bean, Wendy, and Bouffler, Christine. *Spell by Writing.* Portsmouth, NH: Heinemann, 1988.

Bird, Lois Bridge. *Becoming a Whole Language School: The Fair Oaks Story.* Katonah, NY: Richard C. Owen Publishers, 1989.

Bissex, Glenda. *GNYS AT WRK.* Cambridge, MA: Harvard University Press, 1980.

Bissex, Glenda, and Bullock, Richard, eds. *Seeing for Ourselves.* Portsmouth, NH: Heinemann, 1987.

Bixby, Mary, and Pyle, Donelle et al. *Strategies That Make Sense! Invitations to Literacy for Secondary Students.* Katonah, NY: Richard C. Owen Publishers, 1987.

Blake, Robert, ed. *Whole Language — Explorations and Applications.* New York: New York State English Council, 1990.

Booth, David. *Spelling Links.* Ontario: Pembroke Publishers, 1991.

Bosma, Bette. *Fairy Tales, Fables, Legends, and Myths.* New York: Teacher's College Press, 1987.

Britton, James, ed. *English Teaching: An International Exchange.* Portsmouth, NH: Heinemann, 1984.

Brown, Hazel, and Mathie, Vonne. *Inside Whole Language: A Classroom View.* Portsmouth, NH: Heinemann, 1991.

Buchanan, Ethel. *For the Love of Reading.* Winnipeg, Man.: The C.E.L. Group, 1980.

_____. *Spelling for Whole Language Classrooms.* Winnipeg, Man.: The C.E.L. Group, 1989.

Buncombe, Fran, and Peetoom, Adrian. *Literature-Based Learning: One School's Journey.* New York: Scholastic, 1988.

Buros, Jay. *Why Whole Language?* Rosemont, NJ: Programs for Education, 1991.

Butler, Andrea, and Turbill, Jan. *Towards a Reading-Writing Classroom.* Portsmouth, NH: Heinemann, 1984.

Butler, Dorothy. *Cushla and Her Books.* Boston: The Horn Book, 1980.

Calkins, Lucy McCormick. *Lessons from a Child: On the Teaching and Learning of Writing.* Portsmouth, NH: Heinemann, 1983.

_____. *The Art of Teaching Writing.* Portsmouth, NH: Heinemann, 1986.

_____. *Living Between the Lines.* Portsmouth, NH: Heinemann, 1991.

Cambourne, Brian. *The Whole Story.* New York: Scholastic, 1988.

Cambourne, Brian, and Turbill, Jan. *Coping with Chaos.* Portsmouth, NH: Heinemann, 1988.

Cambourne, Brian, and Brown, Hazel. *Read and Retell.* Portsmouth, NH: Heinemann, 1990.

Clay, Marie. *"Concepts about Print" Tests.* Portsmouth, NH: Heinemann, 1980.

_____. *Observing Young Readers.* Portsmouth, NH: Heinemann, 1982.

_____. *Reading: The Patterning of Complex Behaviour.* Portsmouth, NH: Heinemann, 1980.

_____. *What Did I Write?.* Portsmouth, NH: Heinemann, 1975.

_____. *Becoming Literate.* Portsmouth, NH: Heinemann, 1991.

_____. *Reading Recovery: A Guidebook for Teachers in Training.* Portsmouth, NH: Heinemann, 1993.

Clifford, John. *The Experience of Reading — Louise Rosenblatt and Reader-Response Theory.* Portsmouth, NH: Heinemann,1991.

Collis, Mark, and Dalton, Joan. *Becoming Responsible Learners.* Portsmouth, NH: Heinemann, 1991.

Cochrane, Orin, ed. *Questions & Answers About Whole Language.* Katonah, NY: Richard C. Owen Publishers, 1992.

Cochrane, Orin et al. *Reading, Writing, and Caring.* Katonah, NY: Richard C. Owen Publishers, 1985.

Crafton, Linda. *Whole Language: Getting Started, Moving Forward.* Katonah, NY: Richard C. Owen Publishers, 1991.

Cullinan, Bernice. *Children's Literature in the Reading Program.* Newark, DE: International Reading Association, 1987.

Cutting, Brian. *Talk Your Way to Reading.* Auckland, New Zealand: Shortland Publications, 1985.

_____. *Getting Started in Whole Language.* Auckland, New Zealand: Applecross, 1989.

Dakos, Kalli. *What's There to Write About?* New York: Scholastic, 1989.

Davidson, Merrilyn et al. *Moving on with Big Books.* Auckland, New Zealand: Ashton Scholastic, 1989.

DeFord, Diane et al. *Bridges to Literacy.* Portsmouth, NH: Heinemann, 1991.

Department of Education, Victoria. *Beginning Reading.* Victoria: Department of Education, 1984.

Department of Education, Wellington, New Zealand. *Reading in Junior Classes.* New York: Richard C. Owen Publishers, 1985.

Dewey, John. *The Child and the Curriculum and the School and Society.* Chicago: Phoenix Books, combined edition, 1956.

Dudley-Marling, Curt, and Searle, Dennis. *When Students Have Time to Talk.* Portsmouth, NH: Heinemann, 1991.

Edelsky, Carole; Altwerger, Bess; and Flores, Barbara. *Whole Language: What's the Difference?* Portsmouth, NH: Heinemann, 1990.

Eisele, Beverly. *Managing the Whole Language Classroom.* Cypress, CA: Creative Teaching Press, 1991.

Ferreiro, Emilia, and Teberosky, Ana. *Literacy Before Schooling.* Portsmouth, NH: Heinemann, 1979.

Fisher, Bobbi. *Joyful Learning: A Whole Language Kindergarten.* Portsmouth, NH: Heinemann, 1991.

Five, Cora Lee. *Special Voices.* Portsmouth, NH: Heinemann, 1991.

Freeman, Yvonne, and Freeman, David. *Whole Language for Second Language Learners.* Portsmouth, NH: Heinemann, 1992.

Froese, Victor, ed. *Whole Language: Theory and Practice.* Scarborough, Ont.: Prentice-Hall, 1990.

Fulwiler, Toby, ed. *The Journal Book.* Portsmouth, NH: Heinemann, 1987.

_____. *Programs That Work: Models and Methods for Writing Across the Curriculum.* Portsmouth, NH: Heinemann, 1990.

Furniss, Elaine, ed. *The Literacy Agenda.* Portsmouth, NH: Heinemann, 1991.

Gamberg, Ruth et al. *Learning and Loving It — Theme Studies in the Classroom.* Portsmouth, NH: Heinemann, 1988.

Garvey, Catherine. *Children's Talk.* Boston: Harvard Press, 1984. (Part of The Developing Child series).

Geller, Linda Gibson. *Word Play and Language Learning for Children.* Urbana, IL: National Council of Teachers of English, 1985.

Gentry, Richard. *Spel . . . Is a Four-Letter Word.* New York: Scholastic, 1987.

Gentry, J. Richard, and Gillet, Jean Wallace. *Teaching Kids to Spell.* Portsmouth, NH: Heinemann, 1993.

Glover, Mary, and Sheppard, Linda. *Not on Your Own — The Power of Learning Together.* New York: Scholastic, 1990.

Gollasch, Fredrick, ed. *Language and Literacy — The Selected Writings of Kenneth S. Goodman, Vol. 1.* Boston: Routledge & Kegan Paul, 1982.

_____. *Language and Literacy — The Selected Writings of Kenneth S. Goodman, Vol. 2.* Boston: Routledge & Kegan Paul, 1985.

Goodman, Kenneth. *What's Whole in Whole Language?* New York: Scholastic, 1986.

Goodman, Kenneth et al. *Language and Thinking in School: A Whole-Language Curriculum.* Katonah, NY: Richard C. Owen Publishers, 1987.

_____. *Report Card on Basals.* New York: Richard C. Owen Publishers, 1988.

Goodman, Yetta. *How Children Construct Literacy.* Newark, DE: International Reading Association, 1990.

Goodman, Yetta; Hood, Wendy; and Goodman Kenneth. *Organizing for Whole Language.* Portsmouth, NH: Heinemann, 1991.

Graves, Donald. *A Researcher Learns to Write.* Portsmouth, NH: Heinemann, 1984.

_____. *Discover Your Own Literacy.* Portsmouth, NH: Heinemann, 1990.

_____. *Experiment with Fiction.* Portsmouth, NH: Heinemann, 1989.

_____. *Investigate Nonfiction.* Portsmouth, NH: Heinemann, 1989.

_____. *Writing: Teachers and Children at Work.* Portsmouth, NH: Heinemann, 1983.

_____. *Build a Literate Classroom.* Portsmouth, NH: Heinemann, 1991.

Graves, Donald, and Stuart, Virginia. *Write from the Start.* New York: New American Library, 1985.

Greenwood, Barbara. *The Other Side of the Story.* Toronto, Ont.: Scholastic Tab, 1990.

Gunderson, Lee. *A Whole Language Primer.* New York: Scholastic, 1989.

Hall, Nigel, and Robertson, Anne. *"Some Day You Will No All About Me: Young Children's Explorations in the World of Letters."* Portsmouth, NH: Heinemann, 1991.

Hancock, Joelie, and Hill, Susan, eds. *Literature-Based Reading Programs at Work.* Portsmouth, NH: Heinemann, 1988.

Hansen, Jane. *When Writers Read.* Portsmouth, NH: Heinemann, 1987.

Hansen, Jane; Newkirk, Thomas; and Graves, Donald, eds. *Breaking Ground: Teachers Relate Reading and Writing in the Elementary School.* Portsmouth, NH: Heinemann, 1985.

Harste, Jerome, and Short, Kathy. *Creating Classrooms for Authors:The Reading-Writing Connection.* Portsmouth, NH: Heinemann, 1988.

Harste, Jerome; Woodward, Virginia; and Burke, Carolyn. *Language Stories and Literacy Lessons.* Portsmouth, NH: Heinemann, 1984.

Hart-Hewins, Linda, and Wells, Jan. *Read It In The Classroom!* Portsmouth, NH: Heinemann, 1992.

Harwayne, Shelley. *Lasting Impressions: Weaving Literature into the Writing Workshop.* Portsmouth, NH: Heinemann, 1992.

Hayes, Martha. *Building on Books.* Bridgeport, CT: First Teacher Press, 1987.

Heald-Taylor, Gail. *Administrator's Guide to Whole Language.* Katonah, NY: Richard C. Owen Publishers, 1989.

Heard, Georgia. *For the Good of the Earth and Sun: Teaching Poetry.* Portsmouth, NH: Heinemann, 1989.

Holdaway, Don. *Independence in Reading.* New York: Scholastic, 1980.

_____. *The Foundations of Literacy.* New York: Scholastic, 1979.

_____. *Stability and Change in Literacy Learning.* Portsmouth, NH: Heinemann, 1984.

Holly, Mary Louise. *Writing to Grow: Keeping a Personal-Professional Journal.* Portsmouth, NH: Heinemann, 1989.

Hornsby, David; Sukarna, Deborah; and Parry, Jo-Ann. *Read On: A Conference Approach to Reading.* Portsmouth, NH: Heinemann, 1986.

_____. *Teach On.* Portsmouth, NH: Heinemann, 1993.

Hubbard, Ruth. *Authors of Pictures, Draughtsmen of Words.* Portsmouth, NH: Heinemann, 1989.

Hubbard, Ruth and Brenda Power. *The Art of Classroom Inquiry.* Portsmouth, NH: Heinemann, 1993.

Infant Education Committee. *Beginning Reading.* Victoria: Education Department, 1984.

Jagger, Angela, and Smith-Burke, eds. *Observing the Language Learner.* Newark, DE: International Reading Association, 1985.

Jewell, Margaret, and Zintz, Miles. *Learning to Read Naturally.* Dubuque, IA: Kendall-Hunt, 1986.

Johnson, Paul. *Literacy Through the Book Arts.* Portsmouth, NH: Heinemann, 1993.

Johnson, Terry, and Louis, Daphne. *Literacy through Literature.* Portsmouth, NH: Heinemann, 1987.

_____. *Bringing It All Together.* Portsmouth, NH: Heinemann, 1990.

Jorgensen, Karen. *History Workshop.* Portsmouth, NH: Heinemann, 1993.

Karelitz, Ellen Blackburn. *The Author's Chair and Beyond.* Portsmouth, NH: Heinemann, 1993.

Kitagawa, Mary, and Kitagawa, Chisato. *Making Connections with Writing.* Portsmouth, NH: Heinemann, 1987.

Kobrin, Beverly. *Eyeopeners! How to Choose and Use Children's Books about Real People, Places and Things.* New York: Penguin, 1988.

Lamme, Linda. *Highlights for Children, Growing up Reading.* Reston, VA: Acropolis Books, 1985.

_____. *Growing Up Writing.* Reston, VA: Acropolis Books, 1984.

Landsberg, Michele. *Michele Landsberg's Guide to Children's Books.* New York: Penguin, 1988.

Lloyd, Pamela. *How Writers Write.* Portsmouth, NH: Heinemann, 1987.

Lynch, Priscilla. *Using Big Books and Predictable Books.* New York: Scholastic, 1987.

McClure, Amy; Harrison, Peggy; and Reed, Sheryl. *Sunrises and Songs.* Portsmouth, NH: Heinemann, 1990.

McConaghy, June. *Children's Learning Through Literature.* Portsmouth, NH: Heinemann, 1990.

McCracken, Robert and Marlene. *Stories, Songs and Poetry to Teach Reading and Writing.* Chicago: American Library Association, 1986.

_____. *Reading, Writing and Language: A Practical Guide for Primary Teachers.* Winnipeg, Man.: Peguis, 1979.

McKenzie, Moira. *Journeys into Literacy.* Huddersfield: Schofield & Sims, 1986.

McTeague, Frank. *Shared Reading in the Middle and High School Years.* Portsmouth, NH: Heinemann, 1992.

McVitty, Walter. *Word Magic — Poetry as a Shared Adventure.* PETA (Heinemann), 1985.

_____. *Children and Learning.* PETA (Heinemann), 1984.

_____. *Getting It Together: Organizing the Reading-Writing Classroom.* Portsmouth, NH: Heinemann, 1986.

Meek, Margaret. *The Cool Web.* New York: Atheneum, 1978.

_____, ed. *Opening Moves.* London: University of London Institute of Education, 1983.

Miller, Joan. *Sharing Ideas: An Oral Language Programme.* Melbourne: Nelson Publishing Co., 1988.

Mills, Heidi, and Clyde, Jean Anne. *Portraits of Whole Language Classrooms*. Portsmouth, NH: Heinemann, 1990.

Moffett, James, and Wagner, Betty Jane. *Student-Centered Language Arts, K-12,* Fourth Edition. Portsmouth, NH: Boynton/Cook, 1991.

Mooney, Margaret. *Developing Life-Long Readers.* Katonah, NY: Richard C. Owen Publishers, 1988.

Morris, A. *Learning to Learn from Text.* Reading, MA: Addison-Wesley, 1984.

Murray, Donald. *Learning by Teaching.* Portsmouth, NH: Boynton-Cook, 1982.

Myers, Miles. *The Teacher-Researcher: How to Study Writing in the Classroom.* Urbana, IL: National Council of Teachers of English, 1985.

NCTE & IRA. *Cases in Literacy.* International Reading Association and National Council of Teachers of English, 1989.

Newman, Judith, ed. *Whole Language: Theory in Use.* Portsmouth, NH: Heinemann, 1985.

_____. *The Craft of Children's Writing.* Portsmouth, NH: Heinemann, 1985.

_____, ed. *Finding Our Own Way.* Portsmouth, NH: Heinemann, 1990.

Newkirk, Thomas. *More Than Stories.* Portsmouth, NH: Heinemann, 1989.

_____. *Nuts and Bolts.* Portsmouth, NH: Heinemann, 1993.

Newkirk, Thomas, and McLure, Patricia. *Listening In.* Portsmouth, NH: Heinemann, 1992.

Nova Scotia Department of Education. *Language Arts in the Elementary School.* Curriculum Development Guide No. 86, 1986.

Olson, Janet. *Envisioning Writing.* Portsmouth, NH: Heinemann, 1992.

Paley, Vivian. *Molly Is Three.* Chicago: University of Chicago, 1986.

_____. *Wally's Stories.* Boston: Harvard Educational Press, 1981.

Parker, Robert P., and Davis, Francis, eds. *Developing Literacy: Young Children's Use of Language.* Newark, DE: International Reading Association, 1983.

Parry, Jo-Ann, and Hornsby, David. *Write On: A Conference Approach to Writing.* Portsmouth, NH: Heinemann, 1988.

Parsons, Les. *Response Journals.* Portsmouth, NH: Heinemann, 1989.

_____. *Writing in the Real Classroom.* Portsmouth, NH: Heinemann, 1991.

_____. *Poetry, Themes, and Activities.* Portsmouth, NH: Heinemann, 1992.

Peetboom, Adrian. *Shared Reading: Safe Risks with Whole Books.* Toronto, Ont.: Scholastic TAB, 1986.

Perl, Sondra. *Through Teachers' Eyes.* Portsmouth, NH: Heinemann, 1986.

Peterson, Ralph. *Grand Conversations.* New York: Scholastic, 1990.

_____. *Life in a Crowded Place: Making a Learning Community.* Portsmouth, NH: Heinemann, 1992.

Pigdon, Keith, and Woolley, Marilyn. *The Big Picture: Integrating Children's Learning.* Portsmouth, NH: Heinemann, 1993.

Pinnell, Gay Su. *Teachers and Research — Language Learning in the Classroom.* Newark, DE: International Reading Association, 1989.

Raines, Shirley C., and Candy, Robert J. *The Whole Language Kindergarten.* New York: Teachers College Press, 1990

Raphael, Ray. *The Teacher's Voice: A Sense of Who We Are.* Portsmouth, NH: Heinemann, 1985.

Rief, Linda. *Seeking Diversity: Language Arts with Adolescents.* Portsmouth, NH: Heinemann, 1992.

Romano, Tom. *Clearing the Way.* Portsmouth, NH: Heinemann, 1987.

Routman, Regie. *Transitions: From Literature to Literacy.* Portsmouth, NH: Heinemann, 1988.

_____. *Invitations: Changing as Teachers and Learners, K-12.* Portsmouth, NH: Heinemann, 1991.

Roy, Susan, ed. *Young Imagination.* New South Wales: Primary English Teaching Association, 1988.

Sampson, Michael. *Literacy and Language Instruction.* Lexington, MA: Ginn Press, 1987.

_____. *The Pursuit of Literacy.* Dubuque, IA: Kendall-Hunt, 1986.

_____. *Pathways to Literacy.* New York: Holt, Rinehart & Winston, 1991.

Schell, Leo. *How to Create an Independent Reading Program.* New York: Scholastic, 1991.

Schickedanz, Judith. *Adam's Righting Revolutions.* Portsmouth, NH: Heinemann, 1990.

Schwartz, Susan. *Creating the Child-Centered Classroom.* Katonah, NY: Richard C. Owen Publishers, 1991.

Shafer, Robert E., and Staab, Claire. *Language Functions and School Success.* New York: Scott Foresman, 1983.

Shannon, Patrick. *The Struggle to Continue.* Portsmouth, NH: Heinemann, 1990.

_____. *Broken Promises.* Portsmouth, NH: Heinemann, 1989.

_____. *Becoming Political.* Portsmouth, NH: Heinemann, 1992.

Shedlock, Marie. *The Art of the Storyteller.* New York: Dover Press, 1951.

Short, Kathy, and Burke, Carolyn. *Creating Curriculum.* Portsmouth, NH: Heinemann, 1991.

Short, Kathy, and Pierce, Kathryn, eds. *Talking About Books,* Portsmouth, NH: Heinemann, 1990.

Silko, Leslie Marmon. *Storyteller.* New York: Seaver Books, 1981.

Sloan, Peter and Ross Latham. *Teaching Reading Is...* Melbourne: Nelson, 1981.

Smith, Frank. *Essays into Literacy.* Portsmouth, NH: Heinemann, 1983.

_____. *Insult to Intelligence.* Portsmouth, NH: Heinemann, 1986.

_____. *Joining the Literacy Club.* Portsmouth, NH: Heinemann, 1988.

_____. *Psycholinguistics and Reading.* New York: Holt, Rinehart & Winston, 1978.

_____. *Reading Without Nonsense.* New York: Teachers College Press, 1978.

_____. *Understanding Reading.* Hillsdale, NJ: Lawrence Erlbaum Publishers, 1986.

_____. *Writing and the Writer.* New York: Holt, Rinehart & Winston, 1982.

Somerfield, Muriel. *A Framework for Reading.* Portsmouth, NH: Heinemann, 1985.

Stephens, Diane. *What Matters? A Primer for Teaching Reading.* Portsmouth, NH: Heinemann, 1990.

Strickland, Dorothy. *Emerging Literacy: Young Children Learn to Read and Write.* Newark, DE: International Reading Association, 1989.

Taylor, Denny. *Family Literacy.* Portsmouth, NH: Heinemann, 1983.

_____. *Learning Denied.* Portsmouth, NH: Heinemann, 1990.

Taylor, Denny, and Dorsey-Gaines, Catherine. *Growing Up Literate.* Portsmouth, NH: Heinemann, 1988.

Temple, Charles et al. *The Beginnings of Writing.* Boston: Allyn & Bacon, 1988.

Tough, Joan. *Talk for Teaching and Learning.* Portsmouth, NH: Heinemann, 1981.

Tovey, Duane, and Kerber, James, ed. *Roles in Literacy Learning.* Newark, DE: International Reading Association, 1986.

Turbill, Jan, ed. *No Better Way to Teach Writing!* Portsmouth, NH: Heinemann, 1982.

_____. *Now, We Want to Write.* Portsmouth, NH: Heinemann, 1983.

Vail, Priscilla. *Common Ground: Whole Language and Phonics Working Together.* Rosemont, NJ: Programs for Education, 1991.

Van Manen, Max. *The Tone of Teaching.* Portsmouth, NH: Heinemann, 1986.

Vygotsy, Lev. *Mind in Society.* Cambridge, MA: Harvard University Press, 1978.

_____. *Thought and Language.* Cambridge, MA: MIT Press, 1986.

Ward, Geoff. *I've Got a Project.* Australia: PETA, 1988. (Distributed in the United States by Heinemann, Portsmouth, NH.)

Watson, Dorothy. *Whole Language: Inquiring Voices.* New York: Scholastic, 1989.

Weaver, Constance. *Reading Process and Practice.* Portsmouth, NH: Heinemann, 1988.

RESOURCES

_____. *Understanding Whole Language.* Portsmouth, NH: Heinemann, 1990.

Weaver, Constance, and Henke, Linda, eds. *Supporting Whole Language.* Portsmouth, NH: Heinemann, 1992.

Wells, Gordon. *The Meaning Makers.* Portsmouth, NH: Heinemann, 1986.

Wilde, Jack. *A Door Opens: Writing in Fifth Grade.* Portsmouth, NH: Heinemann, 1993.

Wilde, Sandra. *You Kan Red This!* Portsmouth, NH: Heinemann, 1991.

Wittels, Harriet, and Greisman, Joan. *How to Spell It.* New York: Putnam, 1982.

Wollman-Bonilla, Julie. *Response Journals.* New York: Scholastic, 1991.

Assessment

Anthony, Robert. *Evaluating Literacy.* Portsmouth, NH: Heinemann, 1991.

Barrs, Myra et al. *The Primary Language Record: Handbook for Teachers.* Portsmouth, NH: Heinemann, 1989.

Batzle, Janine. *Portfolio Assessment and Evaluation.* Cypress, CA: Creative Teaching Press, 1992.

Baskwill, Jane, and Whitman, Paulette. *Evaluation: Whole Language, Whole Child.* Toronto, Ont.: Scholastic, 1988.

Belanoff, Pat, and Dickson, Marcia, eds. *Portfolios: Process and Product,* Portsmouth, NH: Heinemann, 1991.

Clay, Marie. *An Observation Survey of Early Literacy Achievement.* Portsmouth, NH: Heinemann, 1993.

Cochrane, Orin, and Cochrane, Donna. *Whole Language Evaluation for Classrooms.* Bothell, WA: The Wright Group, 1992.

Daly, Elizabeth, ed. *Monitoring Children's Language Development.* Portsmouth, NH: Heinemann, 1992.

Eggleton, Jill. *Whole Language Evaluation.* Hong Kong: Applecross LTD, 1990.

Goodman, Kenneth, ed. *The Whole Language Evaluation Book.* Portsmouth, NH: Heinemann,1988.

Goodman, Yetta et al. *Reading Miscues Inventory: Alternative Procedures.* New York: Richard C. Owen Publishers, 1987.

Graves, Donald, and Sustein, Bonnie, eds. *Portfolio Portraits.* Portsmouth, NH: Heinemann, 1992.

Harp, Bill, ed. *Assessment and Evaluation in Whole Language Programs.* Norwood, MA: Christopher Gordon, 1991.

ILEA/Centre for Language in Primary Education. *The Primary Language Record: Handbook for Teachers.* Portsmouth, NH: Heinemann, 1989.

Johnston, Peter. *Constructive Evaluation of Literate Activity.* New York: Longman, 1992.

Parsons, Les. *Response Journals.* Portsmouth, NH: Heinemann, 1990.

Picciotto, Linda. *Evaluation: A Team Effort.* Ontario: Scholastic, 1992.

Tierney, Robert J.; Carter, Mark A.; and Desai, Laura E. *Portfolio Assessment in the Reading-Writing Classroom.* Norwood, MA: Christopher Gordon, 1991.

Traill, Leanna. *Highlight My Strengths.* Reed Publications, 1993.

Parent Involvement

Baskwill, Jane. *Parents and Teachers — Partners in Learning.* Toronto, Ont.: Scholastic, 1990.

Butler, Dorothy, and Clay, Marie. *Reading Begins at Home.* Portsmouth, NH: Heinemann, 1982.

Clay, Marie. *Writing Begins at Home.* Portsmouth, NH: Heinemann, 1988.

Doake, David. *Reading Begins at Birth.* Toronto, Ont.: Scholastic, 1988.

Hill, Mary. *Home: Where Reading and Writing Begin.* Portsmouth, NH: Heinemann, 1989.

Lipson, Eden. *Parent's Guide to the Best Books for Children.* New York: Times Books, 1988.

Mooney, Margaret. *Reading to, with, and by Children.* Katonah, NY: Richard C. Owen Publishers, 1990.

Northeastern Local School District. *Every Child is a Promise: Early Childhood At-Home Learning Activities.* Springfield, OH, 1986.

_____. *Every Child is a Promise: Positive Parenting.* Springfield, OH, 1986.

Rich, Dorothy. *Mega Skills.* Boston: Houghton Mifflin, 1988.

Taylor, Denny, and Strickland, Dorothy. *Family Storybook Reading.* Portsmouth, NH, 1986.

Trelease, Jim. *The New Read-Aloud Handbook.* New York: Penguin Books, 1989.

_____. *Hey! Listen To This: Stories to Read Aloud.* New York: Penguin Books, 1992.

Wlodkowski, Raymond, and Jaynes, Judith H. *Eager to Learn.* San Francisco: Jossey-Bass, 1990.

Great Idea Books

Beierle, Marlene, and Lynes, Teri. *Book Cooks: Literature-Based Classroom Cooking, 4-6.* Cypress, CA: Creative Teaching Press, 1992.

Bruno, Janet. *Book Cooks: Literature-Based Classroom Cooking, K-3.* Cypress, CA: Creative Teaching Press, 1991.

Cherkerzian, Diane. *The Complete Lesson Plan Book.* Peterborough, NH: Crystal Springs Books, 1993.

Cloonan, Kathryn. *Sing Me a Story, Read Me a Song, Book I.* Beverly Hills, FL: Rhythm & Reading Resources, 1991.

_____. *Sing Me A Story, Read Me a Song, Book II.* Beverly Hills, FL: Rhythm & Reading Resources, 1991.

_____. *Whole Language Holidays, Book 1.* Beverly Hills, FL: Rhythm & Reading Resources, 1992.

_____. *Whole Language Holidays, Book 2.* Beverly Hills, FL: Rhythm & Reading Resources, 1992.

Cochrane, Orin, ed. *Reading Experiences in Science.* Winnipeg, Man.: Peguis, 1985.

Drutman, Ava Deutsch, and Huston, Diane L. *150 Surefire Ways to Keep Them Reading All Year.* New York: Scholastic, 1992.

Frank, Marjorie. *If You're Trying to Teach Kids How to Write, You've Gotta Have This Book.* Nashville, TN: Incentive Publications, 1979.

Gilbert, Labritta. *Do Touch: Instant, Easy Hands-on Learning Experiences for Young Children.* Mt. Ranier, MD: Gryphon House, 1989.

Haack, Pam, and Merrilees, Cynthia. *Write on Target.* Peterborough, NH: The Society for Developmental Education, 1991.

_____. *Ten Ways to Become a Better Reader.* Cleveland, OH: Modern Curriculum Press, 1991.

Hall, Mary. *Daily Writing Activities.* Frank Schaffer.

Hopkins, Lee. *Pass the Poetry Please.* New York: Harper & Row, 1987.

Huck, Charlotte and Hickman, Janet, eds. *The Best of the Web.* Columbus, OH: Ohio State University, 1982.

Irvine, Joan. *How to Make Pop-ups.* New York: Beech Tree Books, 1987.

_____. *How to Make Super Pop-Ups.* New York: Beech Tree Books, 1992.

Johnson, Paul. *A Book of One's Own.* Portsmouth, NH: Heinemann, 1992.

Kovacs, Deborah, and Preller, James. *Meet the Authors and Illustrators: 60 Creators of Favorite Children's Books Talk about Their Work.* New York: Scholastic, 1991.

McCracken, Marlene and Robert. *Themes.* Winnipeg, Man.: Peguis, 1984-87.

Raines, Shirley C., and Canady, Robert J. *Story Stretchers.* Mt. Ranier, MD: Gryphon House, 1989

_____. *More Story Stretchers.* Mt. Ranier, MD: Gryphon House, 1991

_____. *Story Stretchers for the Primary Grades.* Mt. Ranier, MD: Gryphon House, 1992.

Ritter, Darlene. *Literature-Based Art Activities.* Cypress, CA: Creative Teaching Press, 1991.

Salmon, Linda. *Applause.* Tucson, AZ: Zephyr Press, 1992.

Stangl, Jean. *Is Your Storytale Dragging?* Carthage, IL: Fearon Teaching Aids, 1989.

Spann, Mary Beth. *Literature-Based Seasonal and Holiday Activities.* New York; Scholastic, 1987.

Suid, Murray. *Writing Hangups.* Monday Morning Books.

Poetry In Motion

Bibliography
Compiled by Bob Johnson and John Poeton

If you would like help locating any of these books, contact Crystal Springs Books 1-800-321-0401.

Adoff, Arnold. *Chocolate Dreams.* New York: Lothrop, 1989.

_____. *Greens.* New York: Lothrop, 1988.

Bagert, Brod. *If Only I Could Fly.* Baton Rouge, LA: Juliahouse, 1984.

Behn, Harry. *The Little Hill.* New York: Harcourt Brace Jovanovich, 1949.

Baskwill, Jane. *Pass the Poems, Please.* Wildfire, 1989.

Blake, Quentin. *All Join In.* Boston: Little, Brown, & Co., 1990.

Booth, David. 'Till All the Stars Have Fallen. New York: Viking, 1989.

Ciardi, John. *Doodle Soup.* Boston: Houghton Mifflin, 1985.

_____. *Fast and Slow.* Boston: Houghton Mifflin, 1975.

_____. *You Read to Me, I'll Read to You.* New York: Harper & Row, 1987.

_____. *The Monster Den or Look What Happened at My House—and to It.* Honesdale, PA: Boyds Mills Press, 1991.

Cole, William. *Poem Stew.* New York: Harper & Row, 1983.

Dakos, Kalli. *If You're Not Here Please Raise Your Hand.* New York: Four Winds, 1990.

Fleischman, Paul. *Joyful Noise.* New York: Harper & Row, 1988.

_____. *I Am Phoenix.* New York: Harper & Row, 1985.

Frost, Robert. *You Come Too.* New York: Holt, Rinehart & Winston, 1959.

Gander, Father. *Nursery Rhymes.* Santa Barbara, CA: Advocacy Press, 1985.

Giovanni, Nikki. *Spin a Soft Black Song.* New York: Farrar, Straus & Giroux, 1987.

Greenfield, Eloise. *Honey, I Love.* New York: Harper & Row, 1978.

_____. *Nathaniel Talking.* New York: Writers & Readers Publishing, 1989.

Hadjusiewicz, Babs. *Poetry Works.* Cleveland, OH: Modern Curriculum Press, 1990.

Halloran, Phyllis. *I'd Like to Hear a Flower Grow.* Oregon Ciry, OR: Reading, 1989.

Hopkins, Lee Bennett. *Creatures.* San Diego, CA: Harcourt Brace Jovanovich, 1986.

_____. *Dinosaurs.* San Diego, CA: Harcourt Brace Jovanovich, 1990.

_____. *The Sea Is Calling Me.* San Diego, CA: Harcourt Brace Jovanovich, 1986.

_____. *The Sky Is Full of Song.* New York: Harper & Row, 1987.

Hughes, Shirley. *Out and About.* New York: Lothrop, 1988.

Janeczko, Paul. *The Place My Words Are looking For.* New York: Bradbury, 1990.

Jeffers, Susan. *Robert Frost, Stopping by Woods on a Snowy Evening.*

Kennedy, X. J. *Ghastlies, Goops and Pincushions.* New York: McElderry, 1989.

_____. *Fresh Brats.* New York: McElderry, 1990.

Koch, Kenneth. *Talking to the Sun.* New York: Henry Holt, 1985.

Koeppen, Peter. *A Swinger of Birches, Poems of Robert Frost for Young People.*

Larrick, Nancy. *Cats Are Cats*. New York: Philomel, 1988.

_____. *When the Dark Comes Dancing*. New York: Philomel, 1983.

_____. *Mice are Nice*. New York: Philomel, 1990.

Lee, Dennis. *Alligator Pie*. New York: Macmillan, 1974.

_____. *Jelly Belly*. New York: Macmillan, 1983.

_____. *Garbage Delight*. New York: Macmillan.

Livingston, Myra Cohn. *Worlds I Know*. New York: Atheneum, 1986.

_____. *Celebrations*. New York: Holiday House, 1985.

_____. *There Was a Place and Other Poems*. New York: McElderry, 1990.

Lobel, Arnold. *The Random House Book of Mother Goose*. New York: Random House, 1986.

_____. *Whiskers and Rhymes*. New York: Greenwillow, 1985.

_____. *The Book of Pigericks*. New York: Harper & Row, 1988.

McNaughton, Colin. *There's an Awful Lot of Weirdos in Our Neighborhood*. New York: Walker & Co., 1987.

Merriam, Eve. *A Poem for a Pickle*. New York: Morrow, 1989.

_____. *A Sky Full of Poems*. New York: Dell, 1964.

_____. *You Be Good and I'll Be Night*. New York: Morrow, 1988.

Milne, A.A. *Now We Are Six*. New York: Dutton, 1988.

_____. *When We Were Very Young*. New York: Dutton, 1988.

Moss, Jeff. *The Butterfly Jar*. New York: Random House, 1989.

O'Neill, Mary. *Hailstones and Halibut Bones*. New York: Doubleday, 1990.

Prelutsky, Jack. *The New Kid on the Block*. New York: Greenwillow, 1984.

_____. *The Baby Uggs Are Hatching*. New York: Greenwillow, 1982.

_____. *My Parents Think I'm Sleeping*. New York: Greenwillow, 1985.

_____. *Nightmares*. New York: Greenwillow, 1976.

_____. *Poems of a Nonny Mouse*. New York: Greenwillow, 1989.

_____. *The Random House Book of Poetry for Children*. New York: Random House, 1983.

_____. *Rolling Harvey Down the Hill*. New York: Greenwillow, 1980.

_____. *Ride a Purple Pelican*. New York: Greenwillow, 1986.

_____. *The Sheriff of Rottenshot*. New York: Greenwillow, 1982.

_____. *Tyrannosaurus Was a Beast*. New York: Greenwillow, 1989.

_____. *What I Did Last Summer*. New York: Greenwillow, 1984.

_____. *Circus*. New York: Greenwillow, 1989.

_____. *Underneath a Blue Umbrella*. New York: Greenwillow, 1990.

_____. *For Laughing Out Loud*. New York: Greenwillow, 1991.

Ryder Joanne. *Inside Turtle's Shell*. New York: Macmillan, 1985.

Silverstein, Shel. *A Light in the Attic*. New York: Harper & Row, 1981.

_____. *Where the Sidewalk Ends*. New York: Harper & Row, 1974.

Singer, Marlyn. *Turtle in July*. New York: Macmillan, 1989.

Sneve, Virginia. *Dancing Teepees.* New York: Holiday, 1989.

Stopple, Libby. *A Box of Peppermints*. Austin, TX: American Universal Artforms, 1975.

Viorst, Judith. *If I Were in Charge of the World*. New York: Atheneum, 1983.

Voake, Charlotte, ill. *Over the Moon — A Book of Nursery Rhymes*. New York: C.N. Potter Books, 1985.

Wood, Nancy. *Many Winters*. New York: Doubleday, 1974.

Worth, Valerie. *All the Small Poems*. New York: Farrar, Straus & Giroux, 1987.

Yolen, Jane. *Dinosaur Dances*. New York: Putnam, 1990.

Zolotow, Charlotte. *Some Things Go Together*. New York: Harper & Row, 1987.

Voices

"(Childhood) is the time when the human brain can set to work on language, on taste, on poetry and music, with centers at its disposal that may not be available later on in life. If we did not have childhood, and were able to somehow jump catlike from infancy to adulthood, I doubt very much that we would turn out human.

Lewis Thomas
The Fragile Species: Notes of an Earth Watcher

Publications / Special Interest Groups

Children's Literature

AAP Reading Initiative News
Association of American Publishers
220 East 23rd St.
New York, NY 10010

Booklinks
American Library Association
50 Huron St.
Chicago, IL 60611

The Bulletin
Council on Interracial Books for Children
1841 Broadway
New York, NY 10023

The Bulletin of the Center for Children's Books
University of Illinois Press
54 E. Gregory Dr.
Champaign, Il 61820

CBC Features
350 Scotland Rd.
Orange, NJ 07050

Chapters
Hodge-Podge Books
272 Lark St.
Albany, NY 12210

Children's Book Council
568 Broadway, Suite 404
New York, NY 10012

Children's Literature and Reading
(special interest group of the
International Reading Association)
Membership: Miriam A. Marecek
10 Merchant Rd.
Winchester, MA 01890

Children's Literature in Education
Human Sciences Press, Inc.
233 Spring St.
New York, NY 10013-1578

The CLA Bulletin
Journal of the Children's Literature Assembly, NCTE
Membership: Marjorie R. Hancock
2037 Plymouth Rd.
Manhattan, KS 66502

The Five Owls
2004 Sheridan Ave. S.
Minneapolis, MN 55408

The Hornbook Magazine
14 Beacon St.
Boston, MA 02105

*Journal of the Children's Literature
Council of Pennsylvania*
101 Walnut St.
Harrisburg, PA 17101

The Kobrin Letter (reviews nonfiction books)
732 Greer Rd.
Palo Alto, CA 94303

Literacy Matters
Instructional Materials Laboratory
CETE/Ohio State University
1900 Kemy Rd.
Columbus, OH 43210

The New Advocate
Christopher Gordon Publishers, Inc.
480 Washington St.
Norwood, MA 02062

Perspectives
College of Education and Allied Professions
The University of Toledo
Toledo, OH 43606

Telltales
P.O. Box 614
Bath, ME 04530

The WEB (Wonderfully Exciting Books)
The Ohio State University
Room 200 Ramseyer Hall
29 West Woodruff
Columbus, OH 43210

Early Childhood
(See Developmental Education Resources)

General Education — Classroom Focus

Creative Classroom
Children's Television Workshop
P.O. Box 53152
Boulder, CO 80321-3152

Instructor Magazine
Scholastic, Inc.
730 Broadway
New York, NY 10003

Learning
1111 Bethlehem Pike
Springhouse, PA 19477

Teaching Pre-K-8
40 Richards Ave.
Norwalk, CT 06854

General Education — Issues/Research Focus

*The American School Board Journal /
Executive Educator*
National School Boards Association
1680 Duke St.
Alexandria, VA 22314

Democracy and Education
The Institute for Democracy and Education
College of Education
199 McCracken Hall
Ohio University
Athens, OH 45701-2979

Education Week
4301 Connecticut Ave. NW #250
Washington, DC 20008

Educational Leadership
Journal of the Association for Supervision and
Curriculum Development (ASCD)
1250 N. Pitt St.
Alexandria, VA 22314-1403

The Elementary School Journal
University of Chicago Press
P.O. Box 37005
Chicago, IL 60637

Phi Delta Kappan
Eighth and Union
P.O. Box 789
Bloomington, IN 47402

Principal
National Association of Elementary School
Principals (NAESP)
1615 Duke St.
Alexandria, VA 22314-3483

The School Administrator
American Association of School Administrators
1801 North Moore St.
Arlington, VA 22209

Teacher Magazine
Subscription Services
P.O. Box 2091
Marion, OH 43305-2091

Teaching Voices
The Massachusetts Field Center for Teaching
and Learning
University of Massachusetts
100 Morrissey Blvd.
Boston, MA 02125

TIP (Theory into Practice)
Subscription Dept.
174 Arps Hall
1945 N. High St.
Columbus, OH 43210

Language *(See also Whole Language, this section)*

Language Arts
National Council of Teachers of English
1111 Kenyon Rd.
Urbana, IL 61801

Literacy
The Journal of the International Institute
of Literacy Learning
Box 1414
Commerce, TX 75428

Primary Voices K-6
National Council of Teachers of English
1111 Kenyon Rd.
Urbana, IL 61801-1096

The Reading Teacher
International Reading Association
P.O. Box 8139
Newark, DE 19714-8139

(IRA also publishes *Journal of Reading, Reading
Today, Reading Research Quarterly; lectura y
yida* — a Spanish language journal.)

Teachers As Readers Project
AAP Reading Initiative
American Association of American Publishers
220 East 23rd St.
New York, NY 10010

Math and Science

Arithmetic Teacher
National Council of Teachers of Mathematics
1906 Association Dr.
Reston, VA 22091

NatureScope
National Wildlife Federation
1412 16th St.
Washington, DC 20036

Science and Children
National Science Teachers Association
1742 Connecticut Ave. NW
Washington, DC 20009-1171

Whole Language

Spotlight on Whole Language
A Newsletter of the ASCD Whole Language Network
Hofstra University
Hempstead, NY 11550-1090

Teachers Networking
The Whole Language Newsletter
Richard C. Owen Publishers
135 Katonah Ave.
Katonah, NY 10536

Whole Language Assembly of NCTE
Paul Crowley
614 B Dufranedue
Sebastopal, CA 95472

The Whole Idea
The Wright Group
19201 120th Ave. NE
Bothell, WA 98011-9512

Whole Language Network
Teaching K-8
40 Richards Ave.
Norwalk, CT 06854

The Whole Language Teachers Association
Newsletter
P.O. Box 216
Southboro, MA 01772

WLSIG Newsletter
Whole Language Special Interest Group of the IRA
Membership: Grace Vento Zogby
125 Pro... Blvd.
Utica, NY 13501

Whole Language Umbrella
President: Jerome Harste
Whole Umbrella Office
Indiana University
3024 Education Building
Bloomington, IN 47405
812-856-8281

Whole Language Hotline

In the fall of 1991, the Center for the Expansion of Language and Thinking (CELT) began sponsoring a crisis hotline to support teachers and administrators who come under attack for their child-centered practices. For further information, contact:

The Center for Establishing Dialogue (CED)
325 E. Southern Ave.
Suite 14
Tempe, AZ 85282 • 1-602-929-0929

Paperback Book Clubs

Scholastic, Inc.
P.O. Box 7502
Jefferson City, MO 65102
1-800-325-6149

The Trumpet Club
P.O. Box 604
Holmes, PA 19043
1-800-826-0110

Troll Book Club
2 Lethbridge Plaza
Mahwah, NJ 07430
1-800-541-1097

Weekly Reader Paperback Club
P.O. Box 16628
Columbus, OH 43216

Authors' Addresses (Compiled by Sandy Cook)

Jerry Pallota
P.O. Box 760
Needham, MA 02192

Russell Hoban
c/o Harper & Row
Harper Junior Books
10 East 53rd St.
New York, NY 10022

Nonny Horgrogian
c/o Macmillan Pub. Co.
Children's Book Dept.
866 Third Ave.
New York, NY 10022

Mercer Mayer
E.P. Dutton
c/o Children's Marketing
2 Park Ave.
New York, NY 10016

Judith Viorst
c/o Atheneum
115 Fifth Ave.
New York, NY 10003

Thomas P. Lewis
c/o Harper & Row
Harper Junior Books
10 East 53rd St.
New York, NY 10022

Harry Allard
Houghton Mifflin Co.
215 Park Ave. South
New York, NY 10003

Verna Aaedema
E.P. Dutton
c/o Children's Marketing
2 Park Ave.
New York, NY 10016

Dr. Margaret Musgrave
Community College of Baltimore
English Dept.
2901 Liberty Heights Ave.
Baltimore, MD 21215

Bernard Waber
Houghton Mifflin Co.
215 Park Ave. South
New York, NY 10003

Tomie dePaola
Box 444 RFD #1
New London, NH 03257

Materials

Compiled by Kathryn Cloonan and Jay Buros

Big Book Materials
Sticky pockets, colored cotton balls — Demco Library
    Supplies and Equipment, 1-800-356-1200

Velour paper — Dick Blick Art Supply,
    1-800-345-3042

Grommets — Hardware stores

Alphabet stickers — Childcraft, 1-800-631-6100

"Scribbles" Glitter Glue — Arts and crafts stores or
    Duncan Hobby, 1-209-291-2515

Binding Machines and Spiral Binding
Quill Office Products
P.O. Box 1450
Lebanon, PA 17042-1450
(717) 272-6100

General Binding Corporation
One GBC Plaza
Northbrook, IL 60062
(708) 272-3700

Scholastic, Inc.
1-800-325-6149

Book Racks/Easels
Fixturecraft Corp.
443 East Westfield Ave.
P.O. Box 292
Roselle Park, NJ 07204-0292
1-800-275-1145

Chart Paper/Sentence Strips
New England Supply
P.O. Box 158
Springfield, MA 01101

J.L. Hammett Company
P.O. Box 9057
Braintree, MA 02184-9057
1-800-333-4600

Computer Programs
Magic Slate
Sunburst Communications
101 Castleton
Pleasantville, NY 10570
1-800-321-7511

Letters, Labels, Lists
MECC
6160 Summit Dr. N.
Minneapolis, MN 55430-4003
1-800-685-MECC

Print Shop
Broderbund
500 Redwood Blvd., P.O. Box 6121
Novato, CA 94947
1-800-521-6263

SuperPrint
Scholastic
P.O. Box 7502
Jefferson City, MO 65102
1-800-325-6149

Evaluation Tapes
15 minute tapes to evaluate oral reading
World Class Tapes
1-800-365-0669

Highlight Tape
Available through Crystal Springs Books
1-800-321-0401

Kinesiology
Techniques to help children make
right/left brain connections
Educational Kinesiology Foundation
P.O. Box 3396
Ventura, CA 93006
1-800-356-2109

Metal Shower Curtain Rings
Department Stores

Plastic Rings/Bird Bands
Farm Feed Stores

Plastic Slide Mounts
"Lott 100" — photo stores or
Arel Inc., St. Louis, MO 63110

Ribbons and Awards
Hodges Badge Company, Inc. — 1-800-556-2440

Stencil Machines
Ellison Educational
P.O. Box 8209
Newport Beach, CA 92658-8209
1-714-724-0555

Tutorettes
Audiotronics — 1-800-821-6104
Language Masters — 1-800-771-4466

Wikki Stix
Available through Crystal Springs Books
1-800-321-0401

Videos

*Big Books: Practical Strategies. (*Available from Scholastic, Inc.)

Butler, Andrea. *Language, Learning and Literacy.*

_____. *Whole Language — A Framework for Thinking.*

_____. *The Elements of a Whole Language Classroom.*

_____. *Shared Book Experience.* (All four available from Rigby Education)

Calkins, Lucy McCormick. *The Writing Workshop: A World of Difference.* (Heinemann)

Hansen, Jane, and Graves, Donald. *The Writing and Reading Process: A Closer Look.*

_____. *The Writing and Reading Process: A New Approach to Literacy.* (Both available from Heinemann)

Harste, Jerome.*The Authoring Cycle: Read Better, Write Better, Reason Better.* (Heinemann)

Learning Through Literature, Grade K-3.

Learning Through Literature, Grade 4-6. (Both available from Scholastic, Inc.)

Martin, Bill. In-service and classroom videos. (DLM Teaching Resources)

Natural Language Learning. (Scholastic, Inc.)

Big Book Publishers

Curriculum Associates, Inc.
Holt Impressions
Modern Curriculum Press
Richard C. Owen Publishers, Inc.
Rigby Education

Scholastic, Inc.
Sundance
Whole Language Consultants
The Wright Group

Addresses of Video and Big Book Order Departments:

Crystal Springs Books
Route 202
P.O. Box 577
Peterborough, NH 03458
1-800-321-0401
in NH 1-603-924-9380

Curriculum Associates, Inc.
5 Esquire Rd.
N. Billerica, MA 01862-2589
1-800-225-0248

DLM Teaching Resources
P.O. Box 4000
One DLM Park
Allen, TX 75002

Heinemann
361 Hanover St.
Portsmouth, NH
1-800-541-2086

Holt Impressions
6277 Sea Harbor Dr.
Orlando, FL 32887
1-800-782-4479

Modern Curriculum Press
13900 Prospect Rd.
Cleveland, OH 44136
1-800-321-3106

Richard C. Owen Publishers, Inc.
P.O. Box 585
Katonah, NY 01536
1-800-336-5588

Rigby Education
P.O. Box 797
Crystal Lake, IL 60014

1-800-822-8661

Scholastic, Inc.
P.O. Box 7502
Jefferson City, MO 65102
1-800-325-6149

Sundance
P.O. Box 1326
Newtown Road
Littleton, MA 01460
1-800-343-8204

Whole Language Consultants
#6-846 Marion St.
Winnipeg, Manitoba
Canada R2J OK4
1-204-235-1644

The Wright Group
19201 12th Ave. NE
Bothell, WA 98011-9512
1-800-523-2371

More Than Books
Expanding Children's Horizons Through Magazines

Publication Subscription Address	Interest Area/Age Group	Publication Subscription Address	Interest Area/Age Group
Boys' Life Boy Scouts of America P.O. Box 152079 1325 Walnut Hill Lane Irving, TX 75015-2079	General Interest 7-17	*Dolphin Log* The Cousteau Society 870 Greenbrier Circle, Suite 402 Chesapeake, VA 23320	Science/Ecology 7-15
* *Chickadee* Box 304, 255 Great Arrow Ave Buffalo, NY 14207-3024	Science/ Nature 4-9	*Faces* 7 School St. Peterborough, NH 03458-1454	World Cultures 8-14
* *Child Life* P.O. Box 7133 Red Oak, IA 51591-0133 Submissions: P.O. Box 567 1100 Waterway Blvd. Indianapolis, IN 46206	Health/General Interest 9-11	* *Highlights for Children* 2300 West Fifth Ave. P.O. Box 269 Columbus, OH 43272 Submissions: 803 Church St. Honesdale, PA 18431	General Interest 2-12
* *Children's Album* P.O. Box 6086 Concord, CA 94524	Writing/Crafts 8-14	* *Humpty Dumpty's Magazine* P.O. Box 7133 Red Oak, IA 51591-0133 Submissions: (*see Child Life*)	Health/General Interest 4-6
* *Children's Digest* P.O. Box 7133 Red Oak, IA 51591-0133 Submissions: (*see Child Life*)	Health/General Interest 8-10	*Images of Excellence* Images of Excellence Foundation P.O. Box 1131 Boiling Springs, NC 28017	Social Studies 10-13
* *Children's Playmate* P.O. Box 7133 Red Oak, IA 51591-0133 Submissions: (*see Child Life*)	Health/General Interest 6-8	* *Jack and Jill* P.O. Box 7133 Red Oak, IA 51591-0133 Submissions: (*see Child Life*)	General Interest 6-8
Classical Calliope 7 School St. Peterborough, NH 03458-1454	World History 9-16	* *Kid City* P.O. Box 51277 Boulder, CO 80321-1277	General Interest 6-9
Cobblestone 7 School St. Peterborough, NH 03458-1454	American History 8-14	* *Kids Life and Times* Kids Life P.O. Box D Bellport, NY 11713 Submissions: Children's Television Workshop One Lincoln Plaza New York, NY 10023	Entertainment/Education 6-12
* *Creative Kids* P.O. Box 637 Holmes, PA 19043 Submissions: P.O. Box 6448 Mobile, AL 36660	Student Art/Writing 8-14		
* *Cricket* Box 51144 Boulder, CO 80321-1144 Submissions: Open Court Publishing P.O. Box 300 Peru, IL 61354	Literature/Art 6-12	*Koala Club News* San Diego Zoo Membership Dept. P.O. Box 271 San Diego, CA 92112	Animals 3-15
		Ladybug Cricket Country Lane Box 50284 Boulder, CO 80321-0284	Literature 2-7

Publication Subscription Address	Interest Area/Age Group	Publication Subscription Address	Interest Area/Age Group
* *The McGuffey Writer* 400 A McGuffey Hall Miami University Oxford, OH 45056	Student Writing 5-18	*Scienceland* 501 Fifth Ave. Suite 2108 New York, NY 10017-6165	Science 5-11
* *Merlyn's Pen* The National Magazine of Student Writing P.O. Box 1058 East Greenwich, RI 02818	Student Writing 12-16	*Seedling Short Story* International P.O. Box 405 Great Neck, NY 11022	Short Stories 9-12
National Geographic World P.O. Box 2330 Washington, DC 20077-9955	Science/General Interest 8-14	*Sesame Street Magazine* P.O. Box 52000 Boulder, CO 80321-2000	General Interest 2-6
* *Odyssey* 7 School St. Peterborough NH 03458-1454	Space Exploration/ Astronomy 8-14	* *Skipping Stones: A Multi- Cultural Children's Forum* P.O. Box 3939 Eugene, OR 97403-0939	Culture/Environment All ages
Owl Box 304 255 Great Ave. Buffalo, NY 14207-3024	Science/Nature 8-13	*Sports Illustrated for Kids* P.O. Box 830607 Birmingham, AL 35283-0607	Sports 8-13
Penny Power Consumers Union 256 Washington St. Mt. Vernon, NY 10553	Consumer Education 8-14	* *Stone Soup* The Magazine by Children P.O. Box 83 Santa Cruz, CA 95063	Student Writing/Art 6-13
Plays 120 Boylston St. Boston, MA 02116-4615	Drama 6-18	*Storyworks* Scholastic 730 Broadway New York, NY 10003	Literature 8-11
* *Prism* 2455 E. Sunrise Blvd. Ft. Lauderdale, FL 33304	Student Writing 11-18	*3-2-1 Contact* P.O. Box 51177 Boulder, CO 80321-1177	Science 8-14
Ranger Rick National Wildlife Federation 8925 Leesburg Pike Vienna, VA 22180-0001	Science 6-12	*Turtle* P.O. Box 7133 Red Oak, IA 51591-0133	Health/General Interest 2-5
* *Read Magazine* Field Publications 4343 Equity Dr. P.O. Box 16630 Columbus, OH 43216 Submissions: 245 Long Hill Rd. Middletown, CT 06457	Student Writing 12-15	*U.S. Kids* P.O. Box 50351 Boulder, CO 80321-0351	Health/General Interest 5-10
		Voices of Youth P.O. Box JJ Sonoma, CA 95476	Student Writing / Art 14-18
* *Reflections* P.O. Box 368 Duncan Falls, OH 43734	Poetry 4-18	*Your Big Backyard* National Wildlife Federation 8925 Leesburg Pike Vienna, VA 22180	Animals/Conservation 3-5
School Mates 186 Route 9W New Windsor, NY 12550	Chess 7 and up	*Zoo Books* 3590 Kettner Blvd. San Diego, CA 92101	Wildlife 5-14

*encourages children's submissions

Great Songs and Where to Get Them!

Compiled by John and Janet Poeton

Peter & Mary Alice Amidon
6 Willow St.
Brattleboro, VT 05301
802-257-1006

*Things Are Going My Way & Traditional Songs
   for Children
All I Really Need
The Pretty Planet—Songs for the Earth
This Longest Night—Songs of Christmas,
   Chanukah, and the Winter Solstice*

Bev Bos
Turn the Page Press
203 Baldwin Ave.
Roseville, CA 95678

*Thumbprints   Handed Down
Thumbprints, Too   Come on Over
Hand in Hand   I'll Tell you a Story* (Storytelling)

The Burlington Children's Space
250 Main St.
Burlington, VT 05401
(802) 658-1500

*The Children's Tape — A Collection of
   Our Favorite Songs and Stories*

Nancy & John Cassidy
Klutz Press
Palo Alto, CA 94306

Kids' Songs (book and tape)

Rick Charette
Crystal Springs Books   Pine Point Record Co.
Northgate, Route 202   P.O. Box 901
P.O. Box 577   N. Windham, ME 04062
Peterborough, NH 03458   207-892-7175
1-800-321-0401

*Alligator in the Elevator
Where Do My Sneakers Go at Night?
Bubble Gum
I've Got Super Power
Chickens on Vacation
An Evening with Rick Charette* (video)

Jon Gailmor
Green Linnet Records
43 Beaver Brook Rd.
Danbury, CT 06810-6210

*Generations
Gonna Die with a Smile If It Kills Me
Dirt
Passing Through*

Red Grammar
Smilin' Atcha Music
81B Sugarloaf Mountain Rd.
Chester, NY 10918
914-469-9450

Teaching Peace

Bill Harley
Round River Records
301 Jacob St.
Seekonk, MA 02771
508-336-9703

*50 Ways to Fool Your Mother
Monsters in the Bathroom
You're in Trouble
Come on Out and Play
I'm Gonna Let It Shine*

John Langstaff
Revels Records
Box 502
Cambridge, MA 02139

*Let's Make Music
Songs for Singing Children*

Fred Penner / Raffi
Troubadour Records, Ltd.

A Children's Sampler

Rosenshontz
Lightyear Entertainment
350 Fifth Ave., Suite 5101
New York, NY 10118
1-800-229-STORY

*Family Vacation   It's the Truth
Share It   Tickles You
Rock 'n Roll Teddy Bear   Uh -Oh*

Sharon, Lois & Bram
Elephant Records   Silol/Alcazar, Inc.
P.O. Box 101 Station Z   P.O. Box 429, Main St.
Toronto, Ontario   Waterbury, VT 05676
Canada M5N 2Z3   1-800-342-0295

Mainly Mother Goose

Pam Beall / Susan Nipp
Price Stern Sloan, Inc.
Los Angeles, CA

*Wee Sing America
Wee Sing Together*

Will Wright & Jim Reiman
Rooster Records
RFD 2
Bethel, VT 05032

Childhood's Greatest Hits

Please add more and let us know about them.

Great Stories and Where to Get Them!
Compiled by John and Janet Poeton

Marcia Lane

Tales on the Wind
Stories and Songs for Children
Box 3103
Albany, NY 12203

Joe Hayes

Coyote and Native American Folk Tales
Silo/Alcazar, Inc.
P.O. Box 429 Main Street
Waterbury, VT 05676
1-800-342-0295

Jay O'Callahan

Vineyard Video Productions
Elias Lane
West Tisbury, MA 02575
508-693-3584

Titles:
A Master Class in Storytelling
Orange Cheeks
Six Stories About Little Heroes
Herman & Marguerite

Laura Simms

Laura Simms Tells Stories Just Right for Kids
Kids Records
Box 670 Station A
Toronto, Ontario
Canada M5W 1G2

Odds Bodkin

Wisdom Tree Records
P.O. Box 410
Bradford, NH 03221

Titles:
The Earthstone: A Musical Adventure Story
The Teacup Fairy: Very Old Tales for Very Young Children
Giant's Cauldron: Viking Myths of Adventure
With a Twinkle in Your Eye: Funny Folk Tales
    from Everywhere
The Wise Little Girl: Tales of the Feminine
Dark Tales of the Supernatural

INDEX

"Magazines you can use across the curriculum"

Grades 4–9

Over 250 back issues available!

Theme Packs:

Teachers tell us that they rely increasingly on theme units that incorporate reading and writing skills into content areas. Our theme packs with teacher's guides can greatly reduce the time spent preparing such units. The guides, based on the content of nine issues, contain discussion questions, vocabulary lists, art ideas, student project ideas, writing ideas, and additional suggestions for the teacher. They devise activities attuned to the spectrum of abilities encountered in a typical class, teach research skills, incorporate literature, and encourage outside reading of nonfiction.

Each theme pack includes nine issues and a teacher's guide, all boxed in an attractive slipcase: $36.95 each. Teacher's guides

Colonial Life (TU01)

Westward Expansion (TU02)

Native Americans (TU03)

Art History (TU04)

Black History (TU05)

U.S. Government (TU06)

Notable Women in American History (TU07)

Literature (TU08)

Environment (TU09)

Multicultural America (TU10)

Ancient Civilizations (TU11)

Exploration and Discovery (TU12)

Westward Expansion II (TU13)

Native Americans II (TU14)

Science/Technology (TU15)

Geography (TU16)

Egypt (TU17)

Family (TU18)

WORDSONG

. . . because poetry lies at the heart of children's language learning!

Bernice Cullinan, Ph.D., Editor in Chief, Wordsong
      Past president, International Reading Association
      Author, *Literature and the Child*

STREET RHYMES AROUND THE WORLD
edited by Jane Yolen
illustrated by seventeen international artists
$16.95

"Thirty-two chants and rhymes from seventeen nations . . . might have you wishing you could be wisked away to learn the games that children play in other lands."
    Hungry Mind Review

" . . . [a] cheerful, colorful volume . . . a lively, visual multicultural feast."
    Booklist

ISRAEL

Bo elai parpar nechmad.
Sher etzlee al kaf hayad.
Sher tannuch al tirah . . .
Veta'oof bechazarah.

Come to me, nice butterfly,
Rest in the palm of my hand.
Sit, rest, don't be afraid . . .
And fly away again.

—*Hebrew finger game*

Alef
Beys
Giml
Dolid
Kokh mir in
a tepl fleysh.
Nisht keyn sakh.
Nisht keyn bisl.
Nor a fule shisl.

A
B
C
D
Cook for me
A pot of meat.
Not a lot,
Not a little,
But a whole bowl full.

—*A coming-out rhyme in the
Yiddish language, which was
once popular among Jewish
children and adults in Eastern
Europe, many of whom
immigrated to Israel*

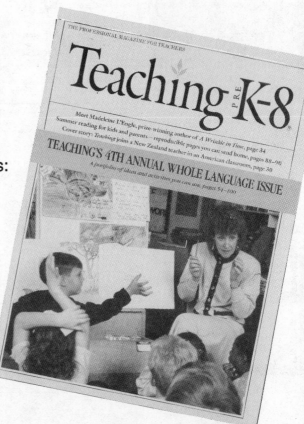

RIGBY

For your complimentary copy of the Rigby 1993-1994 catalog please call 800/822-8661.

- -

Please complete the form below and return to us for your FREE Rigby catalog.

MR. MRS. MS. _____

Position: _____   Send this catalog to my **SCHOOL/BUSINESS**

Send this catalog to **MY HOME**   **- OR -**   School/Business Name: _____

Home street address: _____   School street address: _____

City: _____ Zip: _____   City: _____ Zip: _____

RIGBY ● P.O. Box 797 ● Crystal Lake, IL   60039-0797

LITERACY PLUS

Integrated Language Arts

"It's language arts **PLUS CRITICAL THINKING**, so your students understand more and achieve more..."

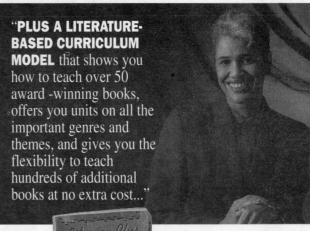

"**PLUS A LITERATURE-BASED CURRICULUM MODEL** that shows you how to teach over 50 award -winning books, offers you units on all the important genres and themes, and gives you the flexibility to teach hundreds of additional books at no extra cost..."

"**PLUS A UNIQUE VOCABULARY AND SPELLING COMPONENT** that enhances the natural process of learning new words from literature and other sources, with strategies that help you teach a wide range of students, including bilingual and ESL."

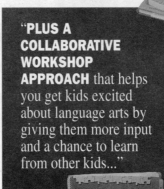

"**PLUS A COLLABORATIVE WORKSHOP APPROACH** that helps you get kids excited about language arts by giving them more input and a chance to learn from other kids..."

Find out how Literacy Plus can help you make the transition to the new integrated language arts. Call or write Zaner-Bloser today.

Zaner-Bloser

2200 West Fifth Avenue • P.O. Box 16764
Columbus, Ohio 43216-6764 • 1(800)421-3018

To Our Friends and Customers,

Our goal at Crystal Springs Books is to provide you with the best books and material available to elementary school educators. We have designed our current offering to reflect the exciting changes taking place in classrooms throughout the country. Specifically, we've included selections which provide scores of ready-to-use classroom ideas. Also, you will find many wonderful professional books to guide and support you as you develop a child-centered environment where all students can learn and grow together.

If you need any further information about the products in this catalog, please call us toll-free at **1-800-321-0401**. And remember, though we feel all our products are among the best you can find, you must be the final judge. We will gladly refund any purchase if you are not completely satisfied.

Wendy, Betsy, Lorraine
Rob, Ryan, Putnam

Sincerely,

Lorraine Walker

Lorraine Walker
Crystal Springs Books Manager

P.S. If you're ever in the Monadnock Region of southern New Hampshire, stop in and visit our warehouse store in Peterborough. Call us at **1-800-321-0401** for directions.

Return Policy

We guarantee **100% satisfaction** on any books or materials we sell. Returned items will be accepted within **30** days as long as they are in saleable condition.

Ordering Information

Individuals:
Orders must be prepaid using check or credit card.

Prompt Shipping:
All in stock orders to the 48 contiguous states are shipped **UPS** within 48 hours. A street address is required for delivery.

3 Easy Ways to Place Your Order

Choose one of the following:

1.) Call **1-800-321-0401** with credit card or purchase order number.

2.) Mail your order to:

**Crystal Springs Books
PO Box 577
Peterborough, NH 03458**

3.) FAX orders to 603-924-6688.

Schools:
Orders may be prepaid or purchase orders are accepted.

Shipping, Handling, and Insurance Charge:

Up to $24.99	$3.50
$25 – 49.99	$5.00
$50 – 79.99	$8.00
$80 – 500.00	10% of order

FREE shipping for orders over $500

Ten Ways to Become a Better Reader
by Cindy Merrilees and Pamela Haack

Ten Ways to Become a Better Reader is especially valuable for parents and teachers who are searching for classroom-proven, practical advice on making the transition from traditional reading groups to whole-group reading.

Although the title says there are 10 ways to become a better reader, there is really only one — read! This book includes ideas and activities that encouraged Merrilees and Haack's students to do just that. 48 pp.   1221   **$7.95**

Write On Target
by Cindy Merrilees and Pamela Haack

Write On Target offers a wealth of easily implemented ideas to help generate student interest in writing and meet the needs of a wide range of learners.

Experienced classroom teachers, Cindy and Pam give suggestions for writing individual student books, whole-group big books, journals, and creative writing booklets. They also explain how they solved the most frequently encountered problems of students writing every day. 63 pp.   1120   **$8.95**

Story Stretchers, More Story Stretchers, *and* Story Stretchers for the Primary Grades
by Shirley C. Raines and Robert J. Canady

Each book offers 450 ways to expand the impact and interest of 90 popular children's picture books. The activities are arranged in chapters with suggestions for integrating them into childhood curriculum units.

Raines and Canady offer a wealth of ideas for extending the book experiences through math, art, circle time, science, creative dramatics, snack time, music and movement activities — and more.

All three books are a wonderful resource for teachers, parents, and children's librarians.

Story Stretchers 251 pp.
   1119   **$14.95**
More Story Stretchers 254 pp.
   1245   **$14.95**
Story Stretchers for the Primary Grades 256 pp.
   3078   **$14.95**

Beginning In Whole Language: A Practical Guide
by Kristin Schlosser and Vicki Phillips

A compendium chock full of reproducible materials, activities, and ideas for putting whole language to work: board games, poetry cubes, big books, journal writing, and more. Illustrated with actual classroom photos. (K-2) 112 pp.   3140   **$12.95**

Why Whole Language
by Jay Buros

Based on Jay Buros' extensive experience as a teacher and consultant, this book explains the whole language approach through a detailed examination of classroom techniques. *Why Whole Language* provides information to help you set up a whole language classroom, find appropriate materials, integrate the curriculum through themes, and develop parental support. 119 pp. P022   **$8.95**

Celebrate with Books
by Imogene Forte and Joy MacKenzie

What better way to celebrate special times than with a good book? This collection of seasonal and holiday thematic literature units will provide you with loads of fun and easy-to-do projects and activities to celebrate well-chosen pieces of literature all year long. It's the perfect complement to today's literature-driven curriculum. (1-4) 143 pp.   3160   **$12.95**

I Can Read! I Can Write!
by Terri Beeler

Immerse young readers in a print-rich environment and turn your classroom into a laboratory for learning. This book contains practical suggestions for using environmental print — the print we see all around us — to promote literacy and foster an appreciation of the written word. (PreK-2) 79 pp. 3475   **$9.95**

Read! Write! Publish!
by Barbara Fairfax and Adela Garcia

Simple instructions and diagrams show you and your students how to make 20 different books. Motivating writing activities and literature suggestions accompany each book idea. The language arts take on new meaning as budding authors write for "publication." (1-5) 70 pp. 3306   **$7.95**

Alternatives to Worksheets
by Karen Bauer and Rosa Drew

At last, a book of meaningful child-centered activities for teachers who want alternatives to worksheets. Directions are simple and the format is teacher-friendly. Contains 40 activities with hundreds of variations for seatwork. (K-4) 96 pp.   3103   **$8.95**

Transitions: From Literature to Literacy
by Regie Routman

Transitions provides support, encouragement, and ideas to teachers who are looking for alternatives to a reading program emphasizing skill-oriented basal texts and worksheets.

Drawing from her own experience, Routman describes an existing literature-based, whole language program that has worked well for students and teachers and offers suggestions of how any elementary classroom can benefit from the transition from standardized texts to literature. She presents material designed to demonstrate the alternatives available, to stimulate thinking, and to give teachers, parents, and administrators the knowledge and procedures that are necessary to make a change. Heinemann 352 pp. 1132 **$18.95**

Invitations: Changing as Teachers and Learners
by Regie Routman

Invitations is an invaluable, practical, easy-to-read text that has been written to support and encourage K-12 educators as they translate whole language theory into practice. This remarkably complete and well-organized resource provides specific strategies for the daily management and educational issues teachers think about and struggle with in their efforts to make teaching more relevant for their students and themselves. Heinemann (K-12) 644 pp. 3023 **$26.50**

150 Surefire Ways to Keep Them Reading All Year
by Ava Drutman and Diane Houston

Dozens of book-related classroom activities: games, contests, display and storage ideas, author birthdays, school-wide read-alouds, lots more. (K-6) 112 pp. 3076 **$12.95**

The New Read-Aloud Handbook
by Jim Trelease

Jim Trelease shows you how to raise a reader and bring your family closer at the same time. He explains: • how to begin reading aloud — and which books to choose; • how reading aloud awakens children's imaginations, improves their language skills, and opens new worlds of enjoyment; • how to coax children away from the television; • how time shared reading together is valuable to parents and children; • how individuals across America have raised reading scores and united communities. 290 pp. 1097 **$10.95**

Reading, Writing and Caring
by O. Cochrane, D. Cochrane, S. Scalena and E. Buchanan

Educational theory and research can lead to new classroom strategies, but if these new strategies don't work in a real classroom then they don't pass the final test.

The ideas and strategies outlined in this book have all been successfully used by classroom teachers. Children from various backgrounds have found success and enjoyment of learning through the use of this whole language approach. 216 pp. 1102 **$15.95**

Hey! Listen to This: Stories to Read Aloud
edited by Jim Trelease

Trelease brings together forty-eight read-aloud stories that parents and teachers can share with children ages 5–9. From folktales (*Uncle Remus, The Pied Piper of Hamelin,* and *The Indian Cinderella*) to classic favorites by such wonderful children's authors as Roald Dahl (*James and the Giant Peach*), E. B. White (*Charlotte's Web*), Beverly Cleary (*Ramona the Pest*), C. S. Lewis (*The Lion, the Witch and the Wardrobe*), and L. Frank Baum (*Ozma of Oz*). In addition, Trelease has written a special introduction to each story and makes suggestions for further reading. (K-3) 414 pp. 3296 **$11.00**

Read Aloud Anthology

98 stories for all grades and all occasions: holidays, seasons, special people, other cultures, and countries. Includes 50 quick ideas for reading motivation, story starters, and other strategies. (1-6) 192 pp. 3145 **$12.95**

Meet the Authors and Illustrators: 60 Creators of Favorite Children's Books Talk about their Work
by Deborah Kovacs and James Preller

Anno, Eric Carle, E.B. White, Chris Van Allsburg, Bruce Degen, and dozens of other favorite children's authors and illustrators provide easy-to-read profiles, with bibliographies, extension activities, index of authors, and illustrators by birthdate. (K-6) 142 pp. 3074 **$19.95**

Teaching with Caldecott Books: Activities that Cross the Curriculum
by Christine B. Moen

Use such Caldecott winners as *On Market Street, Strega Nona, Where the Wild Things Are, Frog and Toad Are Friends, Jumanji, The Snowy Day,* and nine more to promote language acquisition. Includes model lessons plus critical thinking questions, teaching tips, and extension activities. (K-3) 179 pp. 3304 **$14.95**

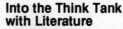

Reading & Writing

Literature-Based Seasonal and Holiday Activities
by Mary Beth Spann

28 favorite children's books (*Sarah Morton's Day; Angelina's Christmas; Arthur's Valentine; Our Martin Luther King Book*) are the springboards for games, arts and crafts projects, writing ideas, recipes, and other creative activities. Includes reproducible game boards. (K-3) 112 pp.
3075 **$12.95**

Linking Literature & Writing
by Shirley Cook & Kathy Carl

This whole language resource contains stimulating activities to use with selected children's books. Organized by month to provide activities for the whole year, this title "links" 174 favorite children's books to writing. (1-4) 240 pp. 4001 **$14.95**

Incorporating Literature into the Basal Reading Program
by Judith Cochran

Finally, a commonsense approach that does not "throw the baby out with the bath water." This jumbo handbook is so well organized and researched you can't go wrong. It's all here, from daily lesson plans to adapting basal program worksheets. This important work will certainly become the nucleus of reading programs everywhere! (K-6) 160 pp. 4004 **$14.95**

Into the Think Tank with Literature
by Jo Ann Pelphrey

Teach your beginning readers to expand their thinking skills. Lesson plan outlines present a story or rhyme with activities that take into account the varied needs of K-3 readers. Follow-up activities range from hands-on projects to role playing and student interaction. Let literature take your class into a think tank. (K-3) 160 pp.
4000 **$14.95**

Linking Literature & Comprehension
by Shirley Cook

This power-packed resource provides stimulating activities in conjunction with 125 carefully selected children's books. These comprehension activities are arranged in a monthly thematic format to supplement your year-round reading program. (K-4) 240 pp. 4002 **$14.95**

Teaching Through Themes
by Gare Thompson

Hands-on guide to choosing themes, selecting the literature, and building the themes into a year-round literature program, plus specific teaching and assessment strategies. Includes 6 model themes with bibliographies. (1-6) 176 pp. 3251 **$15.95**

Insights to Literature
by Judith Cochran

Here are two complete reading programs designed to accompany widely acclaimed books. Each piece of literature is presented through an individual unit and teacher's guide. Reproducible units contain comprehension questions and activities for each book chapter along with journal writing activities. The teachers' guides contain pre/post reading questions and activities that touch on all areas of the curriculum. Everything is correlated to Bloom's Taxonomy with a simple-to-use symbol indicating the thinking skills level. The Primary Grades edition features 3 wordless books, 21 picture books, and 5 novels. The Middle Grades version is designed to accompany 10 popular books. Don't miss these exciting and complete resources.
(Primary) 240 pp. 4005 **$14.95**　　(Mid. Grades) 240 pp. 4006 **$14.95**

If You're Trying to Teach Kids How to Write, You've Gotta Have this Book!
by Marjorie Frank

This is the handbook at the top of every required resource list. Why? The title says it all! This is a favorite how-to book for understanding and working with the whole writing process, an at-your-fingertips source of ideas for starting specific activities, and a ready-when-you're-in-need manual for solving writing problems. If you've ever said, "How do I get kids to write on their own?" "I have this kid who just won't!" "I just don't have time," or "I always run out of ideas by October," then this book is for you! (K-6) 232 pp. 4007 **$12.95**

Story Journal
by Shirley Cook

Shirley Cook is from the team that brought you the very popular LINKING LITERATURE & WRITING resource. By request, she has produced this new middle grades format just for you! Seventeen wonderful books are the theme for daily journal writing activities. Each activity introduces new vocabulary words and provides thought-provoking writing stimulators for every book. At the end of each unit, you will find extended activities to integrate literature with the curriculum and to exercise creative thinking. (4-8) 240 pp.
3165 **$14.95**

Assessment and Evaluation in Whole Language Programs
Edited by Bill Harp

Examines the basic principles of whole language assessment and evaluation practices. This book includes strategies for assessment in primary, intermediate, special education, bilingual, and multicultural settings.

"A scholarly, yet practical work that not only examines the growing research base that supports whole language, but offers realistic suggestions for tackling the many thorny issues involved in the assessment and evaluation of students." 232 pp.   2075   **$16.25**

(An Observation Study and Reading Recovery replace Marie Clay's The Early Detection of Reading Difficulties)

An Observation Survey of Early Literacy Achievement
by Marie M. Clay

An Observation Survey introduces teachers to ways of observing children's progress in the early years of learning about literacy, and leads to the selection of children for whom supplementary teaching is necessary. 120 pp.   3422   **$15.00**

Reading Recovery
A Guidebook for Teachers in Training
by Marie M. Clay

Reading Recovery is a guidebook for training teachers to deliver an early intervention program designed to reduce literacy problems in an education system. Children entering this program are those from ordinary classes who have the most difficulty in reading and writing after one year at school.   *(Due September 1993)*   3423   **$15.00**

Sand *and* Stones — "Concepts About Print" Tests
by Marie M. Clay

Diagnostic tools which can be used with the new entrant or non-reader because the child is asked to help the examiner by pointing to certain features as the examiner reads the book. Heinemann.

Sand (20 pp.)   1107   **$3.50**   *Stones* (20 pp.)   1117   **$3.50**

Portfolio Assessment and Evaluation
by Janine Batzle

This book contains useful and practical information about assessment strategies and answers the questions teachers have about portfolio assessment. • How do I assess students' progress without standardized tests? • What is a portfolio? • How do I set up and use portfolios in the classroom? • What goes in a portfolio? • Who is involved in assessment? • Where and how should assessment take place? (K-6) 125 pp.   4014   **$15.00**

Evaluation in the Literature-Based Classroom: Whole Language Checklists

Reproducible, hole-punched assessment sheets for individual, group, and class evaluation for grades K-3 and 4-6. Includes instructions, plus rationales. (K-6) 38 pp.   3288   **$7.95**

Evaluation: Whole Language, Whole Child
by Jane Baskwill and Paulette Whitman

Manageable alternatives to traditional testing procedures, alternatives that are simple and clear as practiced by experienced whole language teachers. (K-6) 44 pp.   3111   **$7.95**

Evaluation: A Team Effort
by Linda Picciotto

Specific how-to's for teacher, parent, and student involvement in the evaluation process. Includes sample student work, suggested reporting, and recording techniques. (K-3) 64 pp. 4015   **$9.95**

Cooperative Learning

Cooperative Learning: Getting Started
by Susan Ellis & Susan Whalen

Hands-on guide to this key learning strategy. Includes solutions to possible problems, outlines of six different classroom models, and other specific how-to's. (K-6) 72 pp.   4016   **$9.95**

Cooperative Learning Lessons for Little Ones
by Lorna Curran

This is the only comprehensive book on cooperative learning lessons and activities for primary grades. The teacher's manual has 36 lessons which focus on language development and social skills. Adaptions of structures for young children make cooperative learning possible for primary students who have not yet mastered the reading and writing skills. The lessons are based on children's literature. Blackline masters are included. (K-2) 153 pp.   3114   **$15.00**

Cooperative Learning
by Spencer Kagan

Included are step-by-step instructions for 100 structures and hundreds of activities to get started. The book provides comprehensive information on the development of social skills, conflict resolution, classroom set-up and management, scoring and recognition, lesson planning, cooperative sports, and cooperative learning research. (all grades) 376 pp. 3113   **$25.00**

The Cooperative Learning Guide & Planning Pak for Primary Grades
by Imogene Forte & Joy MacKenzie

Keep interest high and learning fun. This resource comes complete with primary thematic units and projects for the entire year. Included in a bonus section are quick-and-easy cooperative activities and planning, recordkeeping, and study guide worksheets. (1-4) 144 pp.   4017   **$12.95**

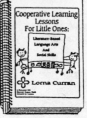

Creative Resources for the Early Childhood Classroom
by Judy Herr and Yvonne Libby

An entire year of activities for the preschool classroom in one volume. Organized on a theme basis, 57 themes and their activities include gardens, construction tools, zoo animals, hats, and much more. Each unit includes a flow chart, theme goals, concepts for the children to learn, vocabulary words, how to integrate the themes into learning centers, and resource books. Also includes a thorough discussion on how to plan a curriculum using a thematic approach. 567 pp. plus appendix. 3117 **$31.95**

Get Ready, Set, Grow!
by Eileen Morris and Stephanie Crilly

This comprehensive, completely tested calendar-book provides 44 weeks worth of learning activities — plus summer-fun ideas! All activities are carefully sequenced and organized into special thematic units that include:
• indoor/outdoor play
• art activities
• essential learning skills
• rhythm and music
• snacks and recipes
• storytime
• and more!
108 pp. 3374 **$11.95**

Kindergarten Readiness Checklists & Guide
by Anthony Coletta, Ph.D.

Now there's an effective way to gather the parent input you need when determining grade placement and designing an appropriate curriculum. Dr. Coletta's checklists cover a range of developmental factors that can affect a child's performance in kindergarten and are designed so that parents can complete them quickly and easily. The helpful guide provides valuable background information on kindergarten readiness, a framework for evaluating checklist and assessment results, and new information on the readiness goal.
Guide (32 pp.) 3209 **$4.95**
Checklists (pkg. of 25) 3210 **$14.95**

Joyful Learning: A Whole Language Kindergarten
by Bobbi Fisher

Bobbi Fisher discusses whole language theory and offers practical, applicable advice on such topics as shared reading, the reading and writing process, math manipulatives, dramatic play, assessment, and communication with parents. A valuable resource for curriculum planners and administrators. Heinemann. 243 pp.
3025 **$19.50**

KinderUnits
by Esther Howard and Dianne Faulk

A complete resource of thematic units designed specifically for young learners. *KinderUnits* promotes the development of skills such as visual discrimination, sorting, classifying, and counting, while including content in the areas of art, health, language arts, math, music, science, and social studies. Complete with snack suggestions, field trips, and party ideas. 128 pp. 3158 **$11.95**

Positively Kindergarten: A Classroom-proven, Theme-based, Developmental Guide for the Kindergarten Teacher
by Beth Lamb, Ph.D. and Phyllis Logsdon, Ph.D.

Positively Kindergarten offers information for understanding the developmental philosophy and stages of children; organizing the classroom and the school day; planning and using theme units; and working with peers, parents, and administrators. 146 pp. P038 **$14.95**

The Whole Language Kindergarten
by Shirley C. Raines and Robert J. Canady

This practical volume includes an abundance of whole language activities within the classical content areas of reading, writing, science, art, music, and mathematics. It offers clear suggestions on how to interest children in books and print; how to structure group-work to emphasize whole language philosophy; and how parents can reevaluate their roles to better understand and effect classroom change. In addition, each chapter contains examples of kindergartens where programs have been implemented and describes how the changes were organized, as well as how the children reacted.
272 pp. 3095 **$20.50**

How to Make Pop-Ups *and* How to Make Super Pop-Ups
both by Joan Irvine

Anyone can make pop-ups. Find a piece of paper, a pair of scissors, some crayons, and a little glue. In minutes make greeting cards that talk, rockets that fly, or a zoo full of animals.

Both books feature: • easy-to-follow directions; • step-by-step instructions; • illustrations for each pop-up creation; • projects for all levels and abilities; • ideas for birthday cards, invitations, holiday decorations, gifts — and more! Great ideas to use for making books for the classroom.

Pop-Ups 93 pp. 1043 **$6.95**
Super Pop-Ups 96 pp. 3297 **$6.95**

A Book of One's Own
by Paul Johnson

A comprehensive guide to book art. By developing skills such as writing, story construction, design, illustration, binding methods, and paper technology, the author shows how book making can enhance many different areas of the curriculum. Heinemann. 119 pp. 3107 **$18.50**

Book Cooks:
Literature-Based Classroom Cooking

Stir up a batch of eager readers. 35 recipes for your favorite books, easy preparation, tips on managing classroom cooking, and integrated learning activities for student cooks.

Book Cooks — (K-3) 80 pp. 3166 **$9.98**
Book Cooks — (4-6) 80 pp. 3276 **$9.98**

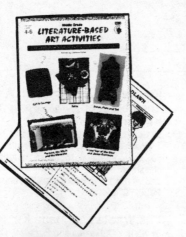

Is Your Storytale Dragging?
by Jean Stangl

Read original stories such as "Nibble, Nibble," "Pam's Magic Trick," and "The Unexpected, Disappearing Guest." Simple props enliven these fold-and-cut paper stories, stringboard stories, and flip chart stories! (PreK-3) 80 pp. 2062 **$8.95**

Literature-Based Art Activities

Fun-to-make art projects inspired by 45 favorite children's books. Common classroom art materials are used to create these original projects. Each project includes a list of related literature titles and integrated learning activities. What a way to build a lifelong love of literature!

Grades K-3, 104 pp. 3079 **$9.98**
Grades 4-6, 104 pp. 3128 **$9.98**

Teacher's Holiday Helper
by Lynn Brisson

Fresh and easy to use, you'll find hats, ornaments, greeting cards, booklets, certificates, and worksheets ready to reproduce and make. Save time, save money. (K-6) 96 pp. 3279 **$9.95**

Teacher's Bag of Tricks
by Patty Nelson

Here's a "bag of tricks" no elementary teacher should be without! It's filled with 101 instant lessons, activities, puzzles, and more, for language arts, math, science, art, and general classroom enrichment. (K-6) 80 pp. 3248 **$8.95**

Math

Integrating Beginning Math & Literature
by Carol A. Rommel

Now you can integrate children's literature and mathematics throughout the entire school year with fun-filled, high-interest activities. Thirty-one favorite books are used to involve children in active exploration of beginning math concepts in a "whole learning" environment. (K-3) 180 pp. 4008 **$8.95**

600 Manipulatives and Activities for Early Math
by Diane Peragine

More than 600 cut-out-and-use multi-purpose manipulatives and lessons for reinforcing such concepts as big/bigger/biggest; shapes; the numerals zero-ten; adding and subtracting; classifying; categorizing. (K-2) 176 pp. 3302 **$19.95**

Making Multiplication Easy: Strategies for Mastering the Tables through 10
by Meish Goldish

Dozens of games, puzzles, songs, and reproducibles that replace rote methods of teaching. Fun, creative strategies work with children of all abilities. Includes take-home ideas, review activities, answer key. (2-4) 64 pp. 3077 **$7.95**

Teaching Thinking and Problem Solving in Math
by Char Forsten

How to utilize cooperative learning, graphing, logic, working backwards, estimating, making a table, drawing a picture, and other proven strategies to build problem-solving skills. Includes cross-curricular applications. Geared to the new math standards. (2-6) 96 pp. 3094 **$10.95**

Math Medley
by Sylvia Gay & Janet Hoelker

Fresh out of ways to teach your young students beginning math concepts? Everyday household items are utilized as manipulatives for the 210 hands-on math activities contained in this book. Allow your students to begin to understand mathematical concepts spontaneously and with enjoyment! (Pre K-1) 64 pp. 4009 **$7.95**

Do-It-Yourself Math Stories
by Allyne Brumbaugh

Add students' names and their choice of numbers and you have 20 personalized math adventure stories that involve addition, subtraction, multiplication, division, and problem solving. Developed to meet today's new math guidelines. (2-5) 96 pp. 3143 **$10.95**

A Collection of Math Lessons from Grades 1 through 3
by Marilyn Burns and Bonnie Tank

A Collection of Math Lessons from Grades 3 through 6
by Marilyn Burns

A Collection of Math Lessons presents practical, classroom-tested ideas for teaching mathematics through problem solving. Using classroom vignettes, Marilyn Burns presents exciting and practical lessons for promoting thinking and reasoning, implementing cooperative learning groups, using concrete materials, and integrating writing into math instruction. Each book includes helpful illustrations and many samples of children's work.
(1-3) 193 pp. 2071 **$14.95**
(3-6) 176 pp. 2072 **$14.95**

Science

Integrating Science & Literature
by Judith Cochran

Every literature selection in this resource becomes a springboard for scientific exploration. Each unit includes a teacher's guide, a science activities page, student activity pages, and a thematic activities page, all with clear, easy instructions. All activities are keyed to Bloom's Taxonomy and are linked to other areas of the curriculum. (K-4) 144 pp. 4010 **$12.95**

Hug A Tree: And Other Things to Do Outdoors with Young Children
by Robert E. Rockwell, Elizabeth A. Sherwood, and Robert A. Williams

Each of the learning experiences in *Hug A Tree* has a suggested age level, a clear description of what will be done, and suggestions for follow-up learning. Special emphasis is placed on using natural environments for learning lan-guage, spatial and mathematical relationships, and much more. (Pre K-2) 108 pp. 2061 **$9.95**

Bugs to Bunnies: Hands-On Animal Science Activities for Young Children
by Kenn Goin, Eleanor Ripp, and Kathleen Nastasi Solomon

This complete resource features hundreds of hands-on activities to teach young children, ages 4-7, the science of animals and help answer their most frequently asked questions. The book includes over 200 activity ideas in eight units on "all about animals," insects, spiders, amphibians, reptiles, fish, birds, and mammals.

Each unit is filled with stories, easy-to-use activity ideas for large and small groups, and reproducible worksheets. (Pre K-2) 192 pp. 2057 **$14.95**

202 Science Investigations
by Marjorie Frank

These fun investigations cover life, physical, earth, and space science. Perfect for individual or group activity and complete with "no-fail" directions. Also includes glossary of science words and symbols. (K-6) 240 pp. 4011 **$14.95**

Add Some Music

Kathie Cloonan has used favorite children's and holiday songs to produce two series. Integrating music into a whole language classroom gives children reading success they can sing about. Her books contain ideas and patterns for making big books, mini books and class books to accompany the songs on her cassettes.

Sing Me a Story, Read Me a Song:

Book 1	1012	**$9.95**
Book 2	1242	**$9.95**
Cassette	1166	**$11.95**

Whole Language Holidays:

Book 1	3223	**$9.95**
Book 2	3224	**$9.95**
Cassette	1263	**$11.95**

Art

Rainbow

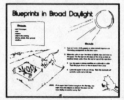
Puddles

I Can Make a Rainbow
by Marjorie Frank

Hundreds of delightfully-illustrated rainbow-colored pages contain step-by-step instructions for unique art experiences with most every art medium! Highly recommended. (K-6) 300 pp. 3361 **$16.95**

Puddles & Wings & Grapevine Swings
by Imogene Forte & Marjorie Frank

A perfect companion to . . . RAINBOW. 304 brightly-colored pages are filled with activities, games, & art projects using easy-to-find, natural materials. Includes crafts for all seasons; things to grow; things to do with sticks, stones, sand & mud; weather & ecology experiments; recipes for fun & food . . . and more! Suitable for indoors or out! (K-6) 304 pp. 3360 **$16.95**

Pick up a Poem Series

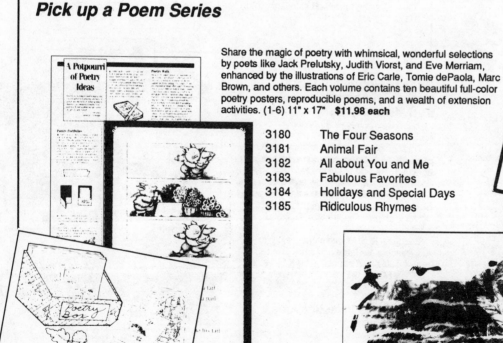

Share the magic of poetry with whimsical, wonderful selections by poets like Jack Prelutsky, Judith Viorst, and Eve Merriam, enhanced by the illustrations of Eric Carle, Tomie dePaola, Marc Brown, and others. Each volume contains ten beautiful full-color poetry posters, reproducible poems, and a wealth of extension activities. (1-6) 11" x 17" **$11.98 each**

3180	The Four Seasons
3181	Animal Fair
3182	All about You and Me
3183	Fabulous Favorites
3184	Holidays and Special Days
3185	Ridiculous Rhymes

Arnold Lobel

Michael Flanders

Eric Carle

Poetry Place Anthology

More than 600 poems to celebrate the seasons and scores of holidays...to inspire art projects, bulletin boards, and creative dramatics...to give a lift to every day of the year. (K-6) 192 pp.
3091 **$12.95**

Other Popular Poetry Books Available . . .

1006	Blue Frog, O. Cochrane	$9.95
2058	Butterscotch Dreams, S. Dunn	$13.50
1015	Crackers and Crumbs, S. Dunn	$13.50
2029	A Light in the Attic, S. Silverstein	$15.95
2036	New Kid on the Block, J. Prelutsky	$15.00
3142	Other Side of the Door, J. Moss	$15.00
3125	Rapunzel's Rap, S. Dunn	$7.95
1104	Roald Dahl's Revolting Rhymes	$3.99
3186	Sing a Song of Popcorn, collection	$18.95
3149	Something Big Has Been Here, J. Prelutsky	$14.95
2051	Where the Sidewalk Ends, S. Silverstein	$15.95

Pass the Poems Please
by Jane Baskwill

Dinosaurs and teddy bears, exploring and pretending, stargazing and camping out; all the adventures of a young child's world are gently presented in this collection of poems for pre-school and early grades. But look carefully — exciting activities are hidden away in the illustrations. Share this book with small friends and wait for them to say, "read it again."
32 pp.   1092   **$6.50**

If You're Not Here, Please Raise Your Hand: Poems About School
by Kalli Dakos

This delightful book celebrates the world of elementary school in thirty-eight poems that capture the excitement, challenge, heartbreak, and wonder of classroom life.
60 pp.   3045   **$12.95**

Let Me Be . . . THE BOSS
Poems for Kids to Perform
by Brod Bagert

Brod Bagert offers teachers an array of practical techniques to spark a child's natural love of poetry. He calls it the Performance Method, a system which recognizes that poetry is an oral art that comes alive when it is performed. The Performance Method is easy to learn, fun to do, and powerfully effective. 54 pp.
3237   **$14.95**

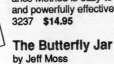

The Butterfly Jar
by Jeff Moss

Moss, one of the original creators and head writer for *Sesame Street*, will introduce the reader to wise, wacky, and memorable characters. Inside *The Butterfly Jar*, you will find Lonesome Joan, who won't let anyone teach her anything, Eugene, the boy whose socks don't match, and Johnny, who foolishly sticks jellybeans up his nose. 115 pp.
3109   **$15.00**

Alligator Pie
by Dennis Lee

Since it appeared in 1974, *Alligator Pie* has won the hearts of children throughout Canada, and the chant of "Alligator pie, alligator pie/If I don't get some I think I'm gonna die" has become a timeless children's anthem. Full of memorable verses and light-hearted illustrations. 64 pp.   2068   **$6.50**

The Ice Cream Store
by Dennis Lee

In Lee's imaginative collection, readers take a wonderful trip aboard a rocketship, meet skinny marinka dinka, dig a hole to Australia, and listen to a trombone-playing walrus. Warmly illustrated, it's a kid and crowd pleasing collection. 58 pp.   3205   **$14.95**

Street Rhymes Around the World
edited by Jane Yolen

This is a magnificent collection of games, chants and songs from around the world that children will enjoy reading and discussing. Jane Yolen has brought a wide variety of world cultures to children through the universal language of play. (ages 4-10) 40 pp.   3081   **$16.95**

Upside Down and Inside Out
by Bobbi Katz

Imagine a world where kids made all the rules and the day is upside down. Imagine a delightful collection of poems that allows us to experience the world as a bit absurd. This is one of those special books that comes along every once in a while. (ages 4-8) 32 pp.   3089   **$14.95**

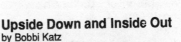

Spel . . . Is a Four-Letter Word
by J. Richard Gentry

Often spelling is taught in a way offensive to children. This creates a set of false dichotomies that prejudice children against spelling. This practical book demonstrates how children can learn to spell. *Spel . . . Is a Four-Letter Word* is devoted to helping teachers and parents teach spelling as part of the reading-writing process. 56 pp.   1113   **$7.95**

Teaching Kids to Spell
by J. Richard Gentry and Jean Wallace Gillet

This comprehensive new work offers the best treatment available for setting the foundations of spelling through the early use of invented spelling. For teachers, school administrators, and parents who want to understand the complex process of spelling, *Teaching Kids to Spell* will be a valuable resource. Heinemann. 128 pp.   3250   **$14.50**

Words I Use When I Write, Grades 1-2 *and* More Words I Use When I Write, Grades 3-4
by Alana Trisler and Patrice Howe Cardiel

Personal spelling guides that let students expand their vocabulary, practice their handwriting, and have their own dictionary of words important to them. Contains spelling for commonly used words such as colors, contractions, numbers, days, and months, etc.
Words (1-2) 64 pp.   P023
   $2.50 (30 copies $52.50)
More Words (3-4) 88 pp.   P008
   $2.75 (30 copies $60.00)

Common Ground: Whole Language and Phonics Working Together
by Priscilla L. Vail

A guide for educators who want to provide students with the phonics instruction and skills they need within the context of a whole language learning approach. *Common Ground* provides an overview of appropriate reading and instructional methods. (K-4) 86 pp.   P040   **$8.95**

Spelling for Whole Language Classrooms
by Ethel Buchanan

An experienced classroom teacher explains how increased spelling proficiency is a developmental process. Buchanan outlines the stages of spelling development and shows how to develop grade level expectations, evaluate spelling growth, and create a spelling environment.

The content is really a whole language spelling curriculum presented within the framework of a theory of spelling development. 156 pp.   3039   **$18.95**

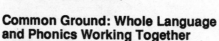

Learning Phonics and Spelling in a Whole Language Classroom

A book that assists teachers in keeping phonics and spelling in perspective and in developing strategies (word sorts, cluster analysis, homophone pairs, silent letter search, cumulative charts, word webs) for teaching these basics within the context of a language-rich classroom. (K-3) 128 pp.   3236   **$15.95**

Jim Grant Materials

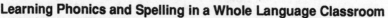

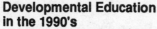

I Hate School: Some Commonsense Answers for Parents Who Wonder Why

I Hate School has helped thousands of teachers and parents become ardent supporters of developmental placement. The book focuses on the dilemma of children placed in the wrong grade. It includes signs and signals that identify the overplaced child from kindergarten through college. 124 pp.   P007   **$9.95**

Developmental Education in the 1990's

Working with thousands of educators across the country, Jim Grant understands the kinds of questions educators are facing. His book helps clarify developmental issues by answering 93 of the questions most frequently asked by teachers and parents. 144 pp.   P015   **$10.95**

Worth Repeating: Giving Children a Second Chance at School Success

Worth Repeating squarely confronts the controversial topic of grade retention for young students. Jim examines this critical issue without jargon and challenges those academic voices that study the statistics and forget the child. 205 pp. P024   **$9.95**

Jim Grant's Book of Parent Pages

Jim developed these helpful handouts so that teachers could communicate more easily with parents. Important messages are presented in an inviting format — 16 8" x 11½" pages that fold into attractively illustrated notes for individualized addressing. Topics include: childhood stress checklist, school and divorce, accepting the readiness idea, love and limits, and seven secrets to school success.   P012   **$24.95**

Every Parent's Owners' Manuals
by Jim Grant and Margot Azen

Owners' Manuals is a series of concise, humorous booklets (written as take-offs on car manuals) that outline predictable developmental behaviors of three, four, five, six, and seven-year-old models at home and in school.

Each manual presents information about the particular model's parts, language control panel, and operation and maintenance for home and school use. 16 pp. (each manual) P011 (specify model year)   **$.75**

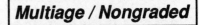

The Nongraded Elementary School
by John Goodlad & Robert Anderson

The best known work of Goodlad and Anderson, it is the single most quoted book on the topic of nongraded schools. First published in 1959, it forecasted the changes to come. 248 pp. 3303 **$20.50**

Nongradedness: Helping It To Happen
by Robert Anderson & Barbara Pavan

The most current, in-depth book by two of the nation's most knowledgeable educators on nongradedness. Along with up-to-date research, this book covers structural mechanisms, learning modes, assessment and much more. A great book for getting started. 240 pp. 3226 **$24.00**

Multiage Classrooms: The Ungrading of America's Schools
compiled by The Society For Developmental Education

Designed to help educators understand the whys and hows of setting up multiage programs. Includes research findings, articles, and the collective wisdom of many who have "been there" in addressing questions all multiage educators face. Also contains an extensive bibliography and practical, proven ideas for involving parents and assessing student progress. 190 pp. 3216 **$24.95**

The Nongraded Primary: Making Schools Fit Children

The increasing need for concise, current information on the nongraded primary was the driving force behind this booklet. Published by the American Association of School Administrators. 27 pp. 3219 **$3.50**

How to Untrack Your School
by Paul George

George will help you in achieving one of the main goals of a continuous progress program . . . untracking students. Learn how rigid ability grouping (tracking) creates inequities, erodes students' self-esteem, and produces 7 other negative consequences. 42 pp. 3214 **$9.95**

Making the Transition From Graded to Nongraded Primary Education *and* Nongraded Education: Mixed Age, Integrated and Developmentally Appropriate Education for Primary Children
both by Joan Gaustad

This pair of books will assist staff members in understanding the fundamental need to change from a graded to a nongraded primary.
Making, 41 pp. 3215 **$5.95**
Nongraded, 38 pp. 3218 **$5.95**

The Multi-Grade Classroom: Myth and Reality
by Margaret Gayfer, Ed.

This book clearly shows the advantages as well as the difficulties for children, parents and teachers in a multigraded organization. It is one of the few books that shows both sides of this topic. 57 pp. 3217 **$11.95**

Teaching Combined Graded Classes: Real Problems and Promising Practices

Down to earth presentation of the ups and downs of combined grade classes. A straight forward, easy-to-read publication that will help you avoid the pitfalls of organizing a mixed-grade classroom. 58 pp. 3220 **$7.95**

Ready to Learn: A Mandate for the Nation
by Ernest Boyer

The most up-to-date description of today's student population. This book is The Carnegie Foundation's documentation for changing to a developmental approach to education. 193 pp. 3177 **$8.95**

Developmentally Appropriate Practice in Early Childhood Programs Serving Children From Birth Through Age 8
by S. Bredekamp, Ed.

This definitive work is our profession's consensus of what are appropriate and inappropriate teaching practices for infants through eight-year-olds. 92 pp. 3284 **$6.95**

Also available:

3190	The Case for Mixed-Age Grouping in Early Education, L. Katz, D. Evangelou, & J. Hartman, 60 pp.	**$9.00**
4016	Cooperative Learning: Getting Started (see page 4)	**$9.95**
P015	Developmental Education in the 1990's (see page 10)	**$10.95**
3201	How to Change to a Nongraded School, Madeline Hunter, 82 pp.	**$9.95**

P007	I Hate School! (see page 10)	**$9.95**
3484	Whole Teaching (see back cover)	**$24.95**
P038	Positively Kindergarten (see page 5)	**$14.95**
3221	Ungraded Primary Programs: Steps Toward Developmentally Appropriate Instruction, Joint Study by KY Ed. Assoc. and AEL, 102 pp.	**$8.95**

Best Seller

Managing the Whole Language Classroom, K-6

by Beverly Eisele

This complete teaching resource guide is packed with ideas for organizing the classroom, scheduling the day, communicating with parents and integrating the curriculum. Easy-to-implement ideas, resources and forms will help you effectively manage your whole language classroom. 136 pp. 3001 **$15.00**

Top Notch Teacher Tips 1: All Across the Curriculum

Hundreds of quick activities and tips created by actual classroom teachers and compiled from the "Teacher's Express" column in INSTRUCTOR Magazine. Organized by chapters on reading, language arts, math, social studies, science. (K-6) 128 pp. 3152 **$12.95**

Top Notch Teacher Tips 2: Seasons and Holidays

A fresh, idea-packed compilation of hundreds of seasonal and holiday activities and teaching tips from the "Teacher's Express" column in INSTRUCTOR Magazine. Bulletin boards, crafts, games, and helpful management tips. (K-6) 128 pp. 3326 **$12.95**

Managing Your Child-Centered Classroom

A full range of supportive techniques and teaching aids for the child-centered classroom. This helpful guide provides an extensive compilation of photocopy masters designed to help you make learning centers, thematic units, and other whole language activities. You'll save time and will inspire your students to read and write. (1-4) 121 pp. 3131 **$18.95**

The Early Childhood Teacher's Every-Day-All-Year-Long Book

by Imogene Forte

Everything you need to make lesson plans, schedule activities, set up learning centers, develop units, prepare arts & crafts projects, create exciting bulletin boards, and teach basic skills is right here at your fingertips! (PreK-1) 304 pp. 4013 **$16.95**

Learning to Teach . . . Not Just for Beginners

A real working resource book, packed with proven, effective strategies for managing a classroom, first-day tips, classroom organization and management ideas. Also covered: the multi-ability classroom, shoring up self-esteem, and other practical strategies for mentor teachers, veterans, and beginners alike. (K-6) 304 pp. 3311 **$19.95**

The Complete Lesson Plan Book

This multi-purpose planner was designed with flexibility in mind. The oversized pages can be organized according to days of the week and/or subject areas. Also included are whole language-based ideas integrating math, science, and social studies. Plus assessment suggestions, theme-based book lists, ideas for celebrating special events, and **handy pocket pouch folders.** (K-3) 3176 **$9.95**
Quantity Discount — 25 or more **$8.45**

Whole Teaching

A Whole Language Sourcebook

Each fall, The Society For Developmental Education publishes its new sourcebook which includes up-to-date information, articles, professional bibliographies, resources, and presenter handouts.

The Sixth Edition includes sections on developmental education, education reform, learning styles/needs, multiage, integrated language arts, and assessment. (PreK-6) 352 pp. 3484 **$24.95**

"Ten Ways to Become a Better Reader" Poster

Bold, primary colors. 34" x 21".
3093 **$3.95**

Crystal Springs Books

Route 202, P.O. Box 577, Peterborough, NH 03458

To order:

Call us toll free
1-800-321-0401   OR
(603) 924-9380

Mail this form to us
at address above   OR

Fax this form to us
at (603) 924-6688

Ship to: Name _____   Grade/Title _____

Mailing Address _____
(Street address, please! UPS will not deliver to a P.O. Box)

City _____   State _____   Zip _____

Telephone   (_____) _____

IMPORTANT: Please fill in your V.I.P. # ☐ ☐ ☐ ☐   (number can be found on mailing label — back cover)

Payment By:

☐ Check Enclosed

☐ MasterCard (16 digits)

☐ Visa (13 or 16 digits)

☐ Discover (16 digits)

☐☐☐☐ ☐☐☐☐ ☐☐☐☐ ☐☐☐☐
Card Number

☐☐ — ☐☐ _____
Expiration Date   Cardholder Signature

☐ Purchase Order # _____

School Name _____

Billing Address _____

City _____ State _____ Zip _____

Billing Office Phone (_____) _____

Item No.	Description	Qty.	Price	Amount

(Prices subject to change without notice)

Subtotal	
Shipping & Handling	
TOTAL	

Shipping, Handling, and Insurance:

Up to $24.99 .... $3.50
$25.00 to $49.99 .... $5.00
$50.00 to $79.99 .... $8.00
$80.00 to $500.00 .... add 10% of order

**FREE shipping and handling
for orders over $500.**

*Thank you for
your order!*

Crystal Springs Books
Route 202, P.O. Box 577, Peterborough, NH 03458

Catalog 2SB
25794

To order:

 Call us toll free
1-800-321-0401   OR
(603) 924-9380

 Mail this form to us
at address above   OR

 Fax this form to us
at (603) 924-6688

Ship to: Name _____   Grade/Title _____

Mailing Address _____
(Street address, please! UPS will not deliver to a P.O. Box)

City _____   State _____ Zip _____

Telephone (_____) _____

IMPORTANT: Please fill in your V.I.P. # ☐ ☐ ☐ ☐   (number can be found on mailing label — back cover)

Payment By:
☐ Check Enclosed

☐ MasterCard (16 digits)   ☐ Visa (13 or 16 digits)   ☐ Discover (16 digits)

☐☐☐☐☐☐☐☐☐☐☐☐☐☐☐☐
Card Number

☐☐ — ☐☐   _____
Expiration Date   Cardholder Signature

☐ Purchase Order # _____

School Name _____

Billing Address _____

City _____ State _____ Zip _____

Billing Office Phone (_____) _____

Item No.	Description	Qty.	Price	Amount

(Prices subject to change without notice)

Subtotal _____
Shipping & Handling _____
TOTAL _____

Shipping, Handling, and Insurance:

Up to $24.99 .... $3.50
$25.00 to $49.99 .... $5.00
$50.00 to $79.99 .... $8.00
$80.00 to $500.00 .... add 10% of order

**FREE shipping and handling
for orders over $500.**

*Thank you for
your order!*

- *fold along this line* -

_____
_____
_____

Crystal Springs Books
Route 202 • PO Box 577
Peterborough, NH 03458

SB94

- -
fold along this line

Program Notes

Program Notes

Program Notes

Program Notes